Python Reinforcement Learning

Solve complex real-world problems by mastering reinforcement learning algorithms using OpenAI Gym and TensorFlow

Sudharsan Ravichandiran
Sean Saito
Rajalingappaa Shanmugamani
Yang Wenzhuo

BIRMINGHAM - MUMBAI

Python Reinforcement Learning

First published: April 2019

Production reference: 1170419

Published by Packt Publishing Ltd.
Livery Place
35 Livery Street
Birmingham
B3 2PB, UK.

ISBN 978-1-83864-977-7

www.packtpub.com

`mapt.io`

Mapt is an online digital library that gives you full access to over 5,000 books and videos, as well as industry leading tools to help you plan your personal development and advance your career. For more information, please visit our website.

Why subscribe?

- Spend less time learning and more time coding with practical eBooks and Videos from over 4,000 industry professionals

- Improve your learning with Skill Plans built especially for you

- Get a free eBook or video every month

- Mapt is fully searchable

- Copy and paste, print, and bookmark content

Packt.com

Did you know that Packt offers eBook versions of every book published, with PDF and ePub files available? You can upgrade to the eBook version at `www.packt.com` and as a print book customer, you are entitled to a discount on the eBook copy. Get in touch with us at `customercare@packtpub.com` for more details.

At `www.packt.com`, you can also read a collection of free technical articles, sign up for a range of free newsletters, and receive exclusive discounts and offers on Packt books and eBooks.

Contributors

About the authors

Sudharsan Ravichandiran is a data scientist, researcher, artificial intelligence enthusiast, and YouTuber (search for Sudharsan reinforcement learning). He completed his bachelors in information technology at Anna University. His area of research focuses on practical implementations of deep learning and reinforcement learning, which includes natural language processing and computer vision. He used to be a freelance web developer and designer and has designed award-winning websites. He is an open source contributor and loves answering questions on Stack Overflow.

Sean Saito is the youngest ever Machine Learning Developer at SAP and the first bachelor hired for the position. He currently researches and develops machine learning algorithms that automate financial processes. He graduated from Yale-NUS College in 2017 with a Bachelor of Science degree (with Honours), where he explored unsupervised feature extraction for his thesis. Having a profound interest in hackathons, Sean represented Singapore during Data Science Game 2016, the largest student data science competition. Before attending university in Singapore, Sean grew up in Tokyo, Los Angeles, and Boston.

> *Writing this book is a daunting task for any 23-year-old, and hence I would like to thank many people who made this possible. My greatest words of gratitude belong to my mother and brother for giving me as much love, understanding, and guidance as anyone can fathom. Many thanks also goes to my closest friends and mentors, all from whom I've acquired much knowledge and wisdom, for their encouragement and advice.*

Rajalingappaa Shanmugamani is currently working as an Engineering Manager for a Deep learning team at Kairos. Previously, he worked as a Senior Machine Learning Developer at SAP, Singapore and worked at various startups in developing machine learning products. He has a Masters from Indian Institute of Technology—Madras. He has published articles in peer-reviewed journals and conferences and submitted applications for several patents in the area of machine learning. In his spare time, he coaches programming and machine learning to school students and engineers.

I thank my spouse Ezhil, mom, dad, family and friends for their immense support. I thank all the teachers, colleagues and mentors from whom I have learned a lot. I thank the co-authors Wen and Sean making their contributions a pleasure to read. I thank the publishing team from Packt especially Snehal for encouraging at difficult times.

Yang Wenzhuo works as a Data Scientist at SAP, Singapore. He got a bachelor's degree in computer science from Zhejiang University in 2011 and a Ph.D. in machine learning from the National University of Singapore in 2016. His research focuses on optimization in machine learning and deep reinforcement learning. He has published papers on top machine learning/computer vision conferences including ICML and CVPR, and operations research journals including Mathematical Programming.

Packt is searching for authors like you

If you're interested in becoming an author for Packt, please visit authors.packtpub.com and apply today. We have worked with thousands of developers and tech professionals, just like you, to help them share their insight with the global tech community. You can make a general application, apply for a specific hot topic that we are recruiting an author for, or submit your own idea.

Table of Contents

Preface

Reinforcement Learning (**RL**) is the trending and most promising branch of artificial intelligence. This course will help you master not only the basic reinforcement learning algorithms but also the advanced deep reinforcement learning algorithms.

The course starts with an introduction to Reinforcement Learning followed by OpenAI Gym, and TensorFlow. You will then explore various RL algorithms and concepts, such as Markov Decision Process, Monte Carlo methods, and dynamic programming, including value and policy iteration. As you make your way through the book, you'll work on various datasets including image, text, and video. This example-rich guide will introduce you to deep reinforcement learning algorithms, such as Dueling DQN, DRQN, A3C, PPO, and TRPO. You will gain experience in several domains, including gaming, image processing, and physical simulations. You'll explore technologies such as TensorFlow and OpenAI Gym to implement deep learning reinforcement learning algorithms that also predict stock prices, generate natural language, and even build other neural networks. You will also learn about imagination-augmented agents, learning from human preference, DQfD, HER, and many more of the recent advancements in reinforcement learning.

By the end of the course, you will have all the knowledge and experience needed to implement reinforcement learning and deep reinforcement learning in your projects, and you will be all set to enter the world of artificial intelligence to solve various problems in real-life.

This Learning Path includes content from the following Packt products:

- Hands-On Reinforcement Learning with Python by Sudharsan Ravichandiran
- Python Reinforcement Learning Projects by Sean Saito, Yang Wenzhuo, and Rajalingappaa Shanmugamani

Who this book is for

If you're a machine learning developer or deep learning enthusiast interested in artificial intelligence and want to learn about reinforcement learning and deep reinforcement learning from scratch, this Learning Path is for you. You will be all ready to build a better performing, automated, and optimized self-learning agent. Some knowledge of linear algebra, calculus, basic DL approaches, and Python will help you understand the concepts.

What this book covers

Chapter 1, *Introduction to Reinforcement Learning*, helps us understand what reinforcement learning is and how it works. We will learn about various elements of reinforcement learning, such as agents, environments, policies, and models, and we will see different types of environments, platforms, and libraries used for reinforcement learning. Later in the chapter, we will see some of the applications of reinforcement learning.

Chapter 2, *Getting Started with OpenAI and TensorFlow*, helps us set up our machine for various reinforcement learning tasks. We will learn how to set up our machine by installing Anaconda, Docker, OpenAI Gym, Universe, and TensorFlow. Then we will learn how to simulate agents in OpenAI Gym, and we will see how to build a video game bot. We will also learn the fundamentals of TensorFlow and see how to use TensorBoard for visualizations.

Chapter 3, *The Markov Decision Process and Dynamic Programming*, starts by explaining what a Markov chain and a Markov process is, and then we will see how reinforcement learning problems can be modeled as Markov Decision Processes. We will also learn about several fundamental concepts, such as value functions, Q functions, and the Bellman equation. Then we will see what dynamic programming is and how to solve the frozen lake problem using value and policy iteration.

Chapter 4, *Gaming with Monte Carlo Methods*, explains Monte Carlo methods and different types of Monte Carlo prediction methods, such as first visit MC and every visit MC. We will also learn how to use Monte Carlo methods to play blackjack. Then we will explore different on-policy and off-policy Monte Carlo control methods.

Chapter 5, *Temporal Difference Learning*, covers temporal-difference (TD) learning, TD prediction, and TD off-policy and on-policy control methods such as Q learning and SARSA. We will also learn how to solve the taxi problem using Q learning and SARSA.

Chapter 6, *Multi-Armed Bandit Problem*, deals with one of the classic problems of reinforcement learning, the multi-armed bandit (MAB) or k-armed bandit problem. We will learn how to solve this problem using various exploration strategies, such as epsilon-greedy, softmax exploration, UCB, and Thompson sampling. Later in the chapter, we will see how to show the right ad banner to the user using MAB.

Chapter 7, *Playing Atari Games*, will get us creating our first deep RL algorithm to play ATARI games.

Chapter 8, *Atari Games with Deep Q Network*, covers one of the most widely used deep reinforcement learning algorithms, which is called the deep Q network (DQN). We will learn about DQN by exploring its various components, and then we will see how to build an agent to play Atari games using DQN. Then we will look at some of the upgrades to the DQN architecture, such as double DQN and dueling DQN.

Chapter 9, *Playing Doom with a Deep Recurrent Q Network*, explains the deep recurrent Q network (DRQN) and how it differs from a DQN. We will see how to build an agent to play Doom using a DRQN. Later in the chapter, we will learn about the deep attention recurrent Q network, which adds the attention mechanism to the DRQN architecture.

Chapter 10, *The Asynchronous Advantage Actor Critic Network*, explains how the Asynchronous Advantage Actor Critic (A3C) network works. We will explore the A3C architecture in detail, and then we will learn how to build an agent for driving up the mountain using A3C.

Chapter 11, *Policy Gradients and Optimization*, covers how policy gradients help us find the right policy without needing the Q function. We will also explore the deep deterministic policy gradient method. Later in the chapter, we will see state of the art policy optimization methods such as trust region policy optimization and proximal policy optimization.

Chapter 12, *Balancing CartPole*, will have us implement our first RL algorithms in Python and TensorFlow to solve the cart pole balancing problem.

Chapter 13, *Simulating Control Tasks*, provides a brief introduction to actor-critic algorithms for continuous control problems. We will learn how to simulate classic control tasks, look at how to implement basic actor-critic algorithms, and understand the state-of-the-art algorithms for control.

Chapter 14, *Building Virtual Worlds in Minecraft*, takes the advanced concepts covered in previous chapters and applies them to Minecraft, a game more complex than those found on ATARI.

Chapter 15, *Learning to Play Go*, will have us building a model that can play Go, the popular Asian board game that is considered one of the world's most complicated games.

Chapter 16, *Creating a Chatbot*, will teach us how to apply deep RL in natural language processing. Our reward function will be a future-looking function, and we will learn how to think in terms of probability when creating this function.

Chapter 17, *Generating a Deep Learning Image Classifier*, introduces one of the latest and most exciting advancements in RL: generating deep learning models using RL. We explore the cutting-edge research produced by Google Brain and implement the algorithms introduced.

Chapter 18, *Predicting Future Stock Prices*, discusses building an agent that can predict stock prices.

Chapter 19, *Capstone Project – Car Racing Using DQN*, provides a step-by-step approach for building an agent to win a car racing game using dueling DQN.

Chapter 20, *Looking Ahead*, concludes the book by discussing some of the real-world applications of reinforcement learning and introducing potential areas of future academic work.

To get the most out of this book

The examples covered in this book can be run on Windows, Ubuntu, or macOS. All the installation instructions are covered. A basic knowledge of Python and machine learning is required. It's preferred that you have GPU hardware, but it's not necessary.

You need the following software for this book:

- Anaconda
- Python
- Any web browser
- Docker

Download the example code files

You can download the example code files for this book from your account at www.packt.com. If you purchased this book elsewhere, you can visit www.packt.com/support and register to have the files emailed directly to you.

You can download the code files by following these steps:

1. Log in or register at www.packt.com.
2. Select the **SUPPORT** tab.
3. Click on **Code Downloads & Errata**.
4. Enter the name of the book in the **Search** box and follow the onscreen instructions.

Once the file is downloaded, please make sure that you unzip or extract the folder using the latest version of:

- WinRAR/7-Zip for Windows
- Zipeg/iZip/UnRarX for Mac
- 7-Zip/PeaZip for Linux

The code bundle for the book is also hosted on GitHub at `https://github.com/PacktPublishing/Python-Reinforcement-Learning`. In case there's an update to the code, it will be updated on the existing GitHub repository.

We also have other code bundles from our rich catalog of books and videos available at `https://github.com/PacktPublishing/`. Check them out!

Conventions used

There are a number of text conventions used throughout this book.

`CodeInText`: Indicates code words in text, database table names, folder names, filenames, file extensions, pathnames, dummy URLs, user input, and Twitter handles. Here is an example: "The `gym-minecraft` package has the same interface as other Gym environments."

A block of code is set as follows:

```
import logging
import minecraft_py
logging.basicConfig(level=logging.DEBUG)
```

Any command-line input or output is written as follows:

```
python3 -m pip install gym
python3 -m pip install pygame
```

Bold: Indicates a new term, an important word, or words that you see on screen. For example, words in menus or dialog boxes appear in the text like this. Here is an example: "Select **System info** from the **Administration** panel."

Warnings or important notes appear like this.

 Tips and tricks appear like this.

Get in touch

Feedback from our readers is always welcome.

General feedback: If you have questions about any aspect of this book, mention the book title in the subject of your message and email us at customercare@packtpub.com.

Errata: Although we have taken every care to ensure the accuracy of our content, mistakes do happen. If you have found a mistake in this book, we would be grateful if you would report this to us. Please visit www.packt.com/submit-errata, selecting your book, clicking on the Errata Submission Form link, and entering the details.

Piracy: If you come across any illegal copies of our works in any form on the Internet, we would be grateful if you would provide us with the location address or website name. Please contact us at copyright@packt.com with a link to the material.

If you are interested in becoming an author: If there is a topic that you have expertise in and you are interested in either writing or contributing to a book, please visit authors.packtpub.com.

Reviews

Please leave a review. Once you have read and used this book, why not leave a review on the site that you purchased it from? Potential readers can then see and use your unbiased opinion to make purchase decisions, we at Packt can understand what you think about our products, and our authors can see your feedback on their book. Thank you!

For more information about Packt, please visit packt.com.

Introduction to Reinforcement Learning

1

Reinforcement learning (**RL**) is a branch of machine learning where the learning occurs via interacting with an environment. It is goal-oriented learning where the learner is not taught what actions to take; instead, the learner learns from the consequence of its actions. It is growing rapidly with a wide variety of algorithms and it is one of the most active areas of research in **artificial intelligence** (**AI**).

In this chapter, you will learn about the following:

- Fundamental concepts of RL
- RL algorithm
- Agent environment interface
- Types of RL environments
- RL platforms
- Applications of RL

What is RL?

Consider that you are teaching the dog to catch a ball, but you cannot teach the dog explicitly to catch a ball; instead, you will just throw a ball, and every time the dog catches the ball, you will give it a cookie. If it fails to catch the ball, you will not give a cookie. The dog will figure out what actions made it receive a cookie and will repeat those actions.

Similarly, in a RL environment, you will not teach the agent what to do or how to do instead, you will give a reward to the agent for each action it does. The reward may be positive or negative. Then the agent will start performing actions which made it receive a positive reward. Thus, it is a trial and error process. In the previous analogy, the dog represents the agent. Giving a cookie to the dog upon catching the ball is a positive reward, and not giving a cookie is a negative reward.

There might be delayed rewards. You may not get a reward at each step. A reward may be given only after the completion of a task. In some cases, you get a reward at each step to find out that whether you are making any mistakes.

Imagine you want to teach a robot to walk without getting stuck by hitting a mountain, but you will not explicitly teach the robot not to go in the direction of the mountain:

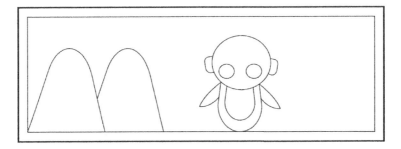

Instead, if the robot hits and get stuck on the mountain, you will take away ten points so that robot will understand that hitting the mountain will result in a negative reward and it will not go in that direction again:

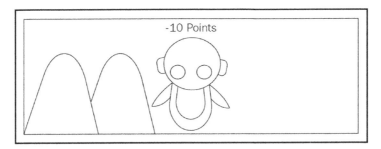

You will give 20 points to the robot when it walks in the right direction without getting stuck. So the robot will understand which is the right path and will try to maximize the rewards by going in the right direction:

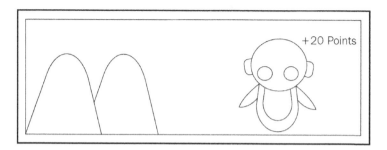

The RL agent can **explore** different actions which might provide a good reward or it can **exploit** (use) the previous action which resulted in a good reward. If the RL agent explores different actions, there is a great possibility that the agent will receive a poor reward as all actions are not going to be the best one. If the RL agent exploits only the known best action, there is also a great possibility of missing out on the best action, which might provide a better reward. There is always a trade-off between exploration and exploitation. We cannot perform both exploration and exploitation at the same time. We will discuss the exploration-exploitation dilemma in detail in the upcoming chapters.

RL algorithm

The steps involved in typical RL algorithm are as follows:

1. First, the agent interacts with the environment by performing an action
2. The agent performs an action and moves from one state to another
3. And then the agent will receive a reward based on the action it performed
4. Based on the reward, the agent will understand whether the action was good or bad
5. If the action was good, that is, if the agent received a positive reward, then the agent will prefer performing that action or else the agent will try performing another action which results in a positive reward. So it is basically a trial and error learning process

How RL differs from other ML paradigms

In supervised learning, the machine (agent) learns from training data which has a labeled set of input and output. The objective is that the model extrapolates and generalizes its learning so that it can be well applied to the unseen data. There is an external supervisor who has a complete knowledge base of the environment and supervises the agent to complete a task.

Consider the dog analogy we just discussed; in supervised learning, to teach the dog to catch a ball, we will teach it explicitly by specifying turn left, go right, move forward five steps, catch the ball, and so on. But instead in RL we just throw a ball, and every time the dog catches the ball, we give it a cookie (reward). So the dog will learn to catch the ball that meant it received a cookie.

In unsupervised learning, we provide the model with training data which only has a set of inputs; the model learns to determine the hidden pattern in the input. There is a common misunderstanding that RL is a kind of unsupervised learning but it is not. In unsupervised learning, the model learns the hidden structure whereas in RL the model learns by maximizing the rewards. Say we want to suggest new movies to the user. Unsupervised learning analyses the similar movies the person has viewed and suggests movies, whereas RL constantly receives feedback from the user, understands his movie preferences, and builds a knowledge base on top of it and suggests a new movie.

There is also another kind of learning called semi-supervised learning which is basically a combination of supervised and unsupervised learning. It involves function estimation on both the labeled and unlabeled data, whereas RL is essentially an interaction between the agent and its environment. Thus, RL is completely different from all other machine learning paradigms.

Elements of RL

The elements of RL are shown in the following sections.

Agent

Agents are the software programs that make intelligent decisions and they are basically learners in RL. Agents take action by interacting with the environment and they receive rewards based on their actions, for example, Super Mario navigating in a video game.

Policy function

A policy defines the agent's behavior in an environment. The way in which the agent decides which action to perform depends on the policy. Say you want to reach your office from home; there will be different routes to reach your office, and some routes are shortcuts, while some routes are long. These routes are called policies because they represent the way in which we choose to perform an action to reach our goal. A policy is often denoted by the symbol π. A policy can be in the form of a lookup table or a complex search process.

Value function

A value function denotes how good it is for an agent to be in a particular state. It is dependent on the policy and is often denoted by $v(s)$. It is equal to the total expected reward received by the agent starting from the initial state. There can be several value functions; the optimal value function is the one that has the highest value for all the states compared to other value functions. Similarly, an optimal policy is the one that has the optimal value function.

Model

Model is the agent's representation of an environment. The learning can be of two types—model-based learning and model-free learning. In model-based learning, the agent exploits previously learned information to accomplish a task, whereas in model-free learning, the agent simply relies on a trial-and-error experience for performing the right action. Say you want to reach your office from home faster. In model-based learning, you simply use a previously learned experience (map) to reach the office faster, whereas in model-free learning you will not use a previous experience and will try all different routes and choose the faster one.

Agent environment interface

Agents are the software agents that perform actions, A_t, at a time, t, to move from one state, S_t, to another state S_{t+1}. Based on actions, agents receive a numerical reward, R, from the environment. Ultimately, RL is all about finding the optimal actions that will increase the numerical reward:

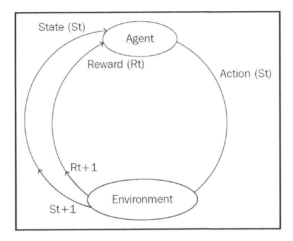

Let us understand the concept of RL with a maze game:

The objective of a maze is to reach the destination without getting stuck on the obstacles. Here's the workflow:

- The agent is the one who travels through the maze, which is our software program/ RL algorithm
- The environment is the maze

- The state is the position in a maze that the agent currently resides in
- An agent performs an action by moving from one state to another
- An agent receives a positive reward when its action doesn't get stuck on any obstacle and receives a negative reward when its action gets stuck on obstacles so it cannot reach the destination
- The goal is to clear the maze and reach the destination

Types of RL environment

Everything agents interact with is called an environment. The environment is the outside world. It comprises everything outside the agent. There are different types of environment, which are described in the next sections.

Deterministic environment

An environment is said to be deterministic when we know the outcome based on the current state. For instance, in a chess game, we know the exact outcome of moving any player.

Stochastic environment

An environment is said to be stochastic when we cannot determine the outcome based on the current state. There will be a greater level of uncertainty. For example, we never know what number will show up when throwing a dice.

Fully observable environment

When an agent can determine the state of the system at all times, it is called fully observable. For example, in a chess game, the state of the system, that is, the position of all the players on the chess board, is available the whole time so the player can make an optimal decision.

Partially observable environment

When an agent cannot determine the state of the system at all times, it is called partially observable. For example, in a poker game, we have no idea about the cards the opponent has.

Discrete environment

When there is only a finite state of actions available for moving from one state to another, it is called a discrete environment. For example, in a chess game, we have only a finite set of moves.

Continuous environment

When there is an infinite state of actions available for moving from one state to another, it is called a continuous environment. For example, we have multiple routes available for traveling from the source to the destination.

Episodic and non-episodic environment

The episodic environment is also called the **non-sequential** environment. In an episodic environment, an agent's current action will not affect a future action, whereas in a non-episodic environment, an agent's current action will affect a future action and is also called the **sequential** environment. That is, the agent performs the independent tasks in the episodic environment, whereas in the non-episodic environment all agents' actions are related.

Single and multi-agent environment

As the names suggest, a single-agent environment has only a single agent and the multi-agent environment has multiple agents. Multi-agent environments are extensively used while performing complex tasks. There will be different agents acting in completely different environments. Agents in a different environment will communicate with each other. A multi-agent environment will be mostly stochastic as it has a greater level of uncertainty.

RL platforms

RL platforms are used for simulating, building, rendering, and experimenting with our RL algorithms in an environment. There are many different RL platforms available, as described in the next sections.

OpenAI Gym and Universe

OpenAI Gym is a toolkit for building, evaluating, and comparing RL algorithms. It is compatible with algorithms written in any framework like TensorFlow, Theano, Keras, and so on. It is simple and easy to comprehend. It makes no assumption about the structure of our agent and provides an interface to all RL tasks.

OpenAI Universe is an extension to OpenAI Gym. It provides an ability to train and evaluate agents on a wide range of simple to real-time complex environments. It has unlimited access to many gaming environments. Using Universe, any program can be turned into a Gym environment without access to program internals, source code, or APIs as Universe works by launching the program automatically behind a virtual network computing remote desktop.

DeepMind Lab

DeepMind Lab is another amazing platform for AI agent-based research. It provides a rich simulated environment that acts as a lab for running several RL algorithms. It is highly customizable and extendable. The visuals are very rich, science fiction-style, and realistic.

RL-Glue

RL-Glue provides an interface for connecting agents, environments, and programs together even if they are written in different programming languages. It has the ability to share your agents and environments with others for building on top of your work. Because of this compatibility, reusability is greatly increased.

Project Malmo

Project Malmo is the another AI experimentation platform from Microsoft which builds on top of Minecraft. It provides good flexibility for customizing the environment. It is integrated with a sophisticated environment. It also allows overclocking, which enables programmers to play out scenarios faster than in standard Minecraft. However, Malmo currently only provides Minecraft gaming environments, unlike Open AI Universe.

ViZDoom

ViZDoom, as the name suggests, is a doom-based AI platform. It provides support for multi-agents and a competitive environment to test the agent. However, ViZDoom only supports the Doom game environment. It provides off-screen rendering and single and multiplayer support.

Applications of RL

With greater advancements and research, RL has rapidly evolved everyday applications in several fields ranging from playing computer games to automating a car. Some of the RL applications are listed in the following sections.

Education

Many online education platforms are using RL for providing personalized content for each and every student. Some students may learn better from video content, some may learn better by doing projects, and some may learn better from notes. RL is used to tune educational content personalized for each student according to their learning style and that can be changed dynamically according to the behavior of the user.

Medicine and healthcare

RL has endless applications in medicine and health care; some of them include personalized medical treatment, diagnosis based on a medical image, obtaining treatment strategies in clinical decision making, medical image segmentation, and so on.

Manufacturing

In manufacturing, intelligent robots are used to place objects in the right position. If it fails or succeeds in placing the object at the right position, it remembers the object and trains itself to do this with greater accuracy. The use of intelligent agents will reduce labor costs and result in better performance.

Inventory management

RL is extensively used in inventory management, which is a crucial business activity. Some of these activities include supply chain management, demand forecasting, and handling several warehouse operations (such as placing products in warehouses for managing space efficiently). Google researchers in DeepMind have developed RL algorithms for efficiently reducing the energy consumption in their own data center.

Finance

RL is widely used in financial portfolio management, which is the process of constant redistribution of a fund into different financial products and also in predicting and trading in commercial transactions markets. JP Morgan has successfully used RL to provide better trade execution results for large orders.

Natural Language Processing and Computer Vision

With the unified power of deep learning and RL, **Deep Reinforcement Learning** (DRL) has been greatly evolving in the fields of **Natural Language Processing** (NLP) and **Computer Vision** (CV). DRL has been used for text summarization, information extraction, machine translation, and image recognition, providing greater accuracy than current systems.

Summary

In this chapter, we have learned the basics of RL and also some key concepts. We learned different elements of RL and different types of RL environments. We also covered the various available RL platforms and also the applications of RL in various domains.

In Chapter 2, *Getting Started with OpenAI and TensorFlow*, we will learn the basics of and how to install OpenAI and TensorFlow, followed by simulating environments and teaching the agents to learn in the environment.

Questions

The question list is as follows:

1. What is reinforcement learning?
2. How does RL differ from other ML paradigms?
3. What are agents and how do agents learn?
4. What is the difference between a policy function and a value function?
5. What is the difference between model-based and model-free learning?
6. What are all the different types of environments in RL?
7. How does OpenAI Universe differ from other RL platforms?
8. What are some of the applications of RL?

Further reading

Overview of RL: https://www.cs.ubc.ca/~murphyk/Bayes/pomdp.html.

Getting Started with OpenAI and TensorFlow

2

OpenAI is a non-profit, open source **artificial intelligence (AI)** research company founded by Elon Musk and Sam Altman that aims to build a general AI. They are sponsored by top industry leaders and top-notch companies. OpenAI comes in two flavors, Gym and Universe, using which we can simulate realistic environments, build **reinforcement learning (RL)** algorithms, and test our agents in those environments. TensorFlow is an open source machine learning library by Google that is extensively used for numerical computation. We will use OpenAI and TensorFlow for building and evaluating powerful RL algorithms in the upcoming chapters.

In this chapter, you will learn about the following:

- Setting up your machine by installing Anaconda, Docker, OpenAI Gym, and Universe and TensorFlow
- Simulating an environment using OpenAI Gym and Universe
- Training a robot to walk
- Building a video game bot
- Fundamentals of TensorFlow
- Using TensorBoard

Setting up your machine

Installing OpenAI is not a straightforward task; there are a set of steps that have to be correctly followed for setting the system up and running it. Now, let's see how to set up our machine and install OpenAI Gym and Universe.

Installing Anaconda

All the examples in the book use the Anaconda version of Python. Anaconda is an open source distribution of Python. It is widely used for scientific computing and processing a large volume of data. It provides an excellent package management environment. It provides support for Windows, macOS, and Linux. Anaconda comes with Python installed along with popular packages used for scientific computing such as NumPy, SciPy, and so on.

To download Anaconda, visit `https://www.anaconda.com/download/`, where you will see an option for downloading Anaconda for different platforms.

If you are using Windows or Mac, you can directly download the graphical installer according to your machine architecture and install using the graphical installer.

If you are using Linux, follow these steps:

1. Open your Terminal and type the following to download Anaconda:

   ```
   wget
   https://repo.continuum.io/archive/Anaconda3-5.0.1-Linux-x86_64.sh
   ```

2. Upon completion, we can install Anaconda via the following command:

   ```
   bash Anaconda3-5.0.1-Linux-x86_64.sh
   ```

After successful installation of Anaconda, we need to create a new Anaconda environment that is basically a virtual environment. What is the need for a virtual environment? Say you are working on project A, which uses NumPy version 1.14, and project B, which uses NumPy version 1.13. So, to work on project B you either downgrade NumPy or reinstall Anaconda. In each project, we use different libraries with different versions which are not applicable to other projects. Instead of downgrading or upgrading versions or reinstalling Anaconda every time for a new project, we use a virtual environment. This creates an isolated environment for the current project so that each project can have its own dependencies and will not affect other projects. We will create such an environment using the following command and name our environment `universe`:

```
conda create --name universe python=3.6 anaconda
```

We can activate our environment using the following command:

```
source activate universe
```

Installing Docker

After installing Anaconda, we need to install Docker. Docker makes it easy to deploy applications to production. Say you built an application in your localhost that has TensorFlow and some other libraries and you want to deploy your applications into a server. You would need to install all those dependencies on the server. But with Docker, we can pack our application with its dependencies, which is called a container, and we can simply run our applications on the server without using any external dependency with our packed Docker container. OpenAI has no support for Windows, so to install OpenAI in Windows we need to use Docker. Also, the majority of OpenAI Universe's environment needs Docker to simulate the environment. Now let's see how to install Docker.

To download Docker, go to `https://docs.docker.com/` where you will see an option called **Get Docker**; if you select that, you will see options for different operating systems. If you are using either Windows or Mac, you can download Docker and install it directly using the graphical installer.

If you are using Linux, follow these steps:

Open your Terminal and type the following:

```
sudo apt-get install \
    apt-transport-https \
    ca-certificates \
    curl \
    software-properties-common
```

Then type:

```
curl -fsSL https://download.docker.com/linux/ubuntu/gpg | sudo apt-key add
-
```

And then type:

```
sudo add-apt-repository \
    "deb [arch=amd64] https://download.docker.com/linux/ubuntu \
    $(lsb_release -cs) \
    stable"
```

Finally, type:

```
sudo apt-get update
sudo apt-get install docker-ce
```

We need to be a member of the Docker user group to start using Docker. You can join the Docker user group via the following command:

```
sudo adduser $(whoami) docker
newgrp docker
groups
```

We can test the Docker installation by running the built-in `hello-world` program:

```
sudo service docker start
sudo docker run hello-world
```

In order to avoid using `sudo` to use Docker every time, we can use the following command:

```
sudo groupadd docker
sudo usermod -aG docker $USER
sudo reboot
```

Installing OpenAI Gym and Universe

Now let's see how to install OpenAI Gym and Universe. Before that, we need to install several dependencies. First, let's activate the `conda` environment we just created using the following command:

```
source activate universe
```

Then we will install the following dependencies:

```
sudo apt-get update
sudo apt-get install golang libcupti-dev libjpeg-turbo8-dev make tmux htop
chromium-browser git cmake zlib1g-dev libjpeg-dev xvfb libav-tools xorg-dev
python-opengl libboost-all-dev libsdl2-dev swig

conda install pip six libgcc swig
conda install opencv
```

Throughout this book, we will be using `gym` version `0.7.0` so you can install `gym` directly using `pip` as:

```
pip install gym==0.7.0
```

Or you can clone the `gym` repository and install the latest version by following command:

```
cd ~
git clone https://github.com/openai/gym.git
cd gym
pip install -e '.[all]'
```

The preceding commands will fetch the `gym` repository and install `gym` as a package, as shown in the following screenshot:

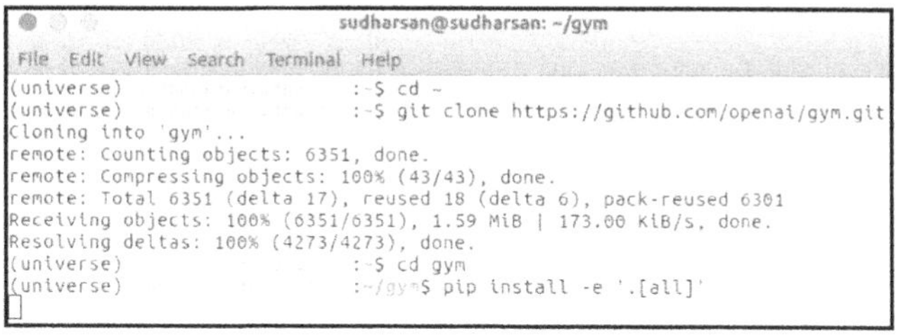

Common error fixes

There is a good chance that you will encounter any of the following errors while installing gym. If you get these errors, just run the following commands and try reinstalling:

- `Failed building wheel for pachi-py` or `Failed building wheel for pachi-py atari-py`:

  ```
  sudo apt-get update
  sudo apt-get install xvfb libav-tools xorg-dev libsdl2-dev swig
  cmake
  ```

- `Failed building wheel for mujoco-py`:

  ```
  git clone https://github.com/openai/mujoco-py.git
  cd mujoco-py
  sudo apt-get update
  sudo apt-get install libgl1-mesa-dev libgl1-mesa-glx libosmesa6-dev
  python3-pip python3-numpy python3-scipy
  pip3 install -r requirements.txt
  sudo python3 setup.py install
  ```

- `Error: command 'gcc' failed with exit status 1`:

  ```
  sudo apt-get update
  sudo apt-get install python-dev
  sudo apt-get install libevent-dev
  ```

Similarly, we can install OpenAI Universe by fetching the `universe` repository and installing the `universe` as a package:

```
cd ~
git clone https://github.com/openai/universe.git
cd universe
pip install -e .
```

The installation is shown in the following screenshot:

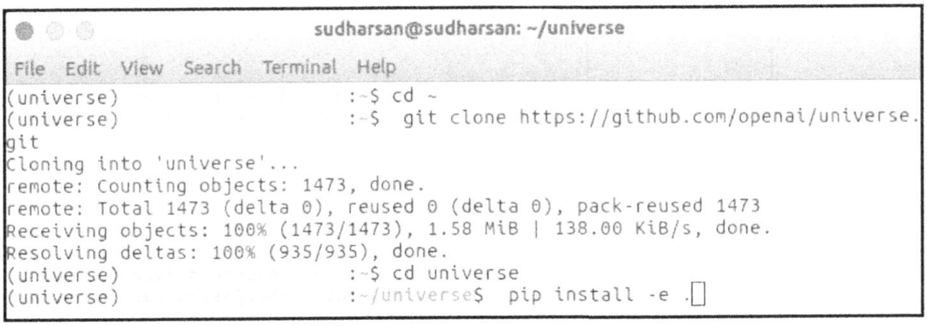

As already said, Open AI Universe needs Docker, as the majority of Universe environments run inside a Docker container.

So let's build a Docker image and name it `universe`:

```
docker build -t universe .
```

Once the Docker image is built, we run the following command, which starts a container from the Docker image:

```
docker run --privileged --rm -it -p 12345:12345 -p 5900:5900 -e
DOCKER_NET_HOST=172.17.0.1 universe /bin/bash
```

OpenAI Gym

With OpenAI Gym, we can simulate a variety of environments and develop, evaluate, and compare RL algorithms. Let's now understand how to use Gym.

Basic simulations

Let's see how to simulate a basic cart pole environment:

1. First, let's import the library:

   ```
   import gym
   ```

2. The next step is to create a simulation instance using the `make` function:

   ```
   env = gym.make('CartPole-v0')
   ```

3. Then we should initialize the environment using the `reset` method:

   ```
   env.reset()
   ```

4. Then we can loop for some time steps and render the environment at each step:

   ```
   for _ in range(1000):
       env.render()
       env.step(env.action_space.sample())
   ```

The complete code is as follows:

```
import gym
env = gym.make('CartPole-v0')
env.reset()
for _ in range(1000):
    env.render()
    env.step(env.action_space.sample())
```

If you run the preceding program, you can see the output, which shows the cart pole environment:

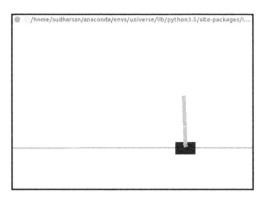

OpenAI Gym provides a lot of simulation environments for training, evaluating, and building our agents. We can check the available environments by either checking their website or simply typing the following, which will list the available environments:

```
from gym import envs
print(envs.registry.all())
```

Since Gym provides different interesting environments, let's simulate a car racing environment, shown as follows:

```
import gym
env = gym.make('CarRacing-v0')
env.reset()
for _ in range(1000):
    env.render()
    env.step(env.action_space.sample())
```

You will get the output as follows:

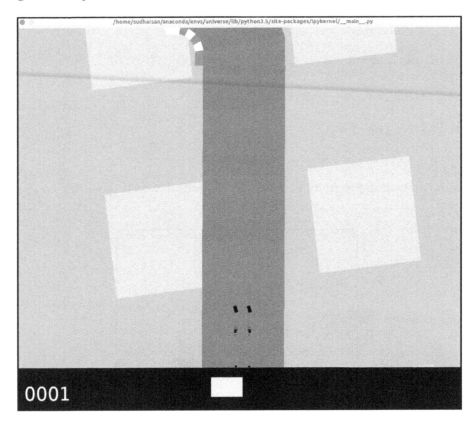

Training a robot to walk

Now let's learn how to train a robot to walk using Gym along with some fundamentals.

The strategy is that X points will be given as a reward when the robot moves forward, and if the robot fails to move then Y points will be reduced. So the robot will learn to walk in the event of maximizing the reward.

First, we will import the library, then we will create a simulation instance by the `make` function. Open AI Gym provides an environment called `BipedalWalker-v2` for training robotic agents in a simple terrain:

```
import gym
env = gym.make('BipedalWalker-v2')
```

Then, for each episode (agent-environment interaction between the initial and final state), we will initialize the environment using the `reset` method:

```
for episode in range(100):
    observation = env.reset()
```

Then we will loop and render the environment:

```
for i in range(10000):
    env.render()
```

We sample random actions from the environment's action space. Every environment has an action space which contains all possible valid actions:

```
action = env.action_space.sample()
```

For each action step, we will record `observation`, `reward`, `done`, and `info`:

```
observation, reward, done, info = env.step(action)
```

`observation` is the object representing an observation of the environment. For example, the state of the robot in the terrain.

`reward` are the rewards gained by the previous action. For example, the reward gained by a robot on successfully moving forward.

`done` is the Boolean; when it is true, it indicates that the episode has completed (that is, the robot learned to walk or failed completely). Once the episode has completed, we can initialize the environment for the next episode using `env.reset()`.

`info` is the information that is useful for debugging.

When `done` is true, we print the time steps taken for the episode and break the current episode:

```
if done:
  print("{} timesteps taken for the Episode".format(i+1))
  break
```

The complete code is as follows:

```
import gym
env = gym.make('BipedalWalker-v2')
for i_episode in range(100):
 observation = env.reset()
 for t in range(10000):
     env.render()
     print(observation)
     action = env.action_space.sample()
     observation, reward, done, info = env.step(action)
     if done:
         print("{} timesteps taken for the episode".format(t+1))
         break
```

The output is shown in the following screenshot:

OpenAI Universe

OpenAI Universe provides a wide range of realistic gaming environments. It is an extension to OpenAI Gym. It provides the ability to train and evaluate agents on a wide range of simple to real-time complex environments. It has unlimited access to many gaming environments.

Building a video game bot

Let's learn how to build a video game bot which plays a car racing game. Our objective is that the car has to move forward without getting stuck on any obstacles or hitting other cars.

First, we import the necessary libraries:

```
import gym
import universe # register universe environment
import random
```

Then we simulate our car racing environment using the `make` function:

```
env = gym.make('flashgames.NeonRace-v0')
env.configure(remotes=1) #automatically creates a local docker container
```

Let's create the variables for moving the car:

```
# Move left
left = [('KeyEvent', 'ArrowUp', True), ('KeyEvent', 'ArrowLeft', True),
        ('KeyEvent', 'ArrowRight', False)]

#Move right
right = [('KeyEvent', 'ArrowUp', True), ('KeyEvent', 'ArrowLeft', False),
        ('KeyEvent', 'ArrowRight', True)]

# Move forward
forward = [('KeyEvent', 'ArrowUp', True), ('KeyEvent', 'ArrowRight',
False),
        ('KeyEvent', 'ArrowLeft', False), ('KeyEvent', 'n', True)]
```

We will initialize some other variables:

```
# We use turn variable for deciding whether to turn or not
turn = 0

# We store all the rewards in rewards list
rewards = []

#we will use buffer as some threshold
buffer_size = 100

#we will initially set action as forward, which just move the car forward
#without any turn
action = forward
```

Now, let's allow our game agent to play in an infinite loop that continuously performs an action based on interaction with the environment:

```
while True:
    turn -= 1
# Let us say initially we take no turn and move forward.
# We will check value of turn, if it is less than 0
# then there is no necessity for turning and we just move forward.
    if turn <= 0:
        action = forward
        turn = 0
```

Then we use `env.step()` to perform an action (moving forward for now) for a one-time step:

```
action_n = [action for ob in observation_n]
observation_n, reward_n, done_n, info = env.step(action_n)
```

For each time step, we record the results in the `observation_n`, `reward_n`, `done_n`, and `info` variables:

- `observation _n`: State of the car
- `reward_n`: Reward gained by the previous action, if the car successfully moves forward without getting stuck on obstacles
- `done_n`: It is a Boolean; it will be set to `true` if the game is over
- `info_n`: Used for debugging purposes

Obviously, an agent (car) cannot move forward throughout the game; it needs to take a turn, avoid obstacles, and will also hit other vehicles. But it has to determine whether it should take a turn and, if yes, then in which direction it should turn.

First, we will calculate the mean of the rewards we obtained so far; if it is 0 then it is clear that we got stuck somewhere while moving forward and we need to take a turn. Then again, which direction do we need to turn? Do you recollect the **policy functions** we studied in Chapter 1, *Introduction to Reinforcement Learning*.

Referring to the same concept, we have two policies here: one is turning left and the other is turning right. We will take a random policy here and calculate a reward and improve upon that.

We will generate a random number and if it is less than 0.5, then we will take a right, otherwise we will take a left. Later, we will update our rewards and, based on our rewards, we will learn which direction is best:

```
if len(rewards) >= buffer_size:
        mean = sum(rewards)/len(rewards)

        if mean == 0:
            turn = 20
            if random.random() < 0.5:
                action = right
            else:
                action = left
        rewards = []
```

Then, for each episode (say the game is over), we reinitialize the environment (start the game from the beginning) using the env.render():

```
env.render()
```

The complete code is as follows:

```
import gym
import universe # register universe environment
import random

env = gym.make('flashgames.NeonRace-v0')
env.configure(remotes=1) # automatically creates a local docker container
observation_n = env.reset()

##Declare actions
#Move left
left = [('KeyEvent', 'ArrowUp', True), ('KeyEvent', 'ArrowLeft', True),
```

```
                ('KeyEvent', 'ArrowRight', False)]

    #move right
    right = [('KeyEvent', 'ArrowUp', True), ('KeyEvent', 'ArrowLeft', False),
             ('KeyEvent', 'ArrowRight', True)]

    # Move forward
    forward = [('KeyEvent', 'ArrowUp', True), ('KeyEvent', 'ArrowRight',
    False),
             ('KeyEvent', 'ArrowLeft', False), ('KeyEvent', 'n', True)]

    #Determine whether to turn or not
    turn = 0
    #store rewards in a list
    rewards = []
    #use buffer as a threshold
    buffer_size = 100
    #initial action as forward
    action = forward

    while True:
        turn -= 1
        if turn <= 0:
            action = forward
            turn = 0
        action_n = [action for ob in observation_n]
        observation_n, reward_n, done_n, info = env.step(action_n)
        rewards += [reward_n[0]]
        if len(rewards) >= buffer_size:
            mean = sum(rewards)/len(rewards)

            if mean == 0:
                turn = 20
                if random.random() < 0.5:
                    action = right
                else:
                    action = left
            rewards = []

        env.render()
```

If you run the program, you can see how the car learns to move without getting stuck or hitting other vehicles:

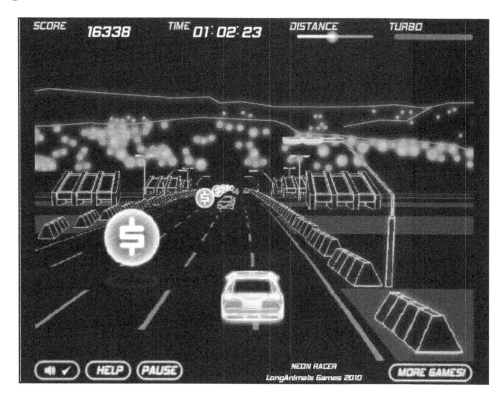

TensorFlow

TensorFlow is an open source software library from Google which is extensively used for numerical computation. It is widely used for building deep learning models and is a subset of machine learning. It uses data flow graphs that can be shared and executed on many different platforms. Tensor is nothing but a multi-dimensional array, so when we say TensorFlow, it is literally a flow of multi-dimensional arrays (tensors) in the computation graph.

With Anaconda installed, installing TensorFlow becomes very simple. Irrespective of the platform you are using, you can easily install TensorFlow by typing the following command:

```
source activate universe
conda install -c conda-forge tensorflow
```

Don't forget to activate the `universe` environment before installing TensorFlow.

We can check whether the TensorFlow installation was successful by simply running the following `Hello World` program:

```
import tensorflow as tf
hello = tf.constant("Hello World")
sess = tf.Session()
print(sess.run(hello))
```

Variables, constants, and placeholders

Variables, constants, and placeholders are the fundamental elements of TensorFlow. However, there is always confusion between these three. Let's look at each element one by one and learn the difference between them.

Variables

Variables are the containers used to store values. Variables will be used as input to several other operations in the computational graph. We can create TensorFlow variables using the `tf.Variable()` function. In the following example, we define a variable with values from a random normal distribution and name it `weights`:

```
weights = tf.Variable(tf.random_normal([3, 2], stddev=0.1), name="weights")
```

However, after defining a variable, we need to explicitly create an initialization operation using the `tf.global_variables_initializer()` method which will allocate resources for the variable.

Constants

Constants, unlike variables, cannot have their values changed. Constants are immutable; once they are assigned values they cannot be changed throughout. We can create constants using the `tf.constant()` function:

```
x = tf.constant(13)
```

Placeholders

Think of placeholders as variables where you only define the type and dimension but will not assign the value. Placeholders are defined with no values. Values for the placeholders will be fed at runtime. Placeholders have an optional argument called `shape`, which specifies the dimensions of the data. If the `shape` is set to `None` then we can feed data of any size at runtime. Placeholders can be defined using the `tf.placeholder()` function:

```
x = tf.placeholder("float", shape=None)
```

To put it in simple terms, we use `tf.Variable` to store the data and `tf.placeholder` for feeding the external data.

Computation graph

Everything in TensorFlow will be represented as a computational graph that consists of nodes and edges, where nodes are the mathematical operations, say addition, multiplication and so on, and edges are the tensors. Having a computational graph is very efficient in optimizing resources and it also promotes distributed computing.

Say we have node B, whose input is dependent on the output of node A; this type of dependency is called direct dependency.

For example:

```
A = tf.multiply(8,5)
B = tf.multiply(A,1)
```

When node B doesn't depend on node A for its input it is called indirect dependency.

For example:

```
A = tf.multiply(8,5)
B = tf.multiply(4,3)
```

So if we can understand these dependencies, we can distribute the independent computations in the available resources and reduce the computation time.

Whenever we import TensorFlow, a default graph will be created automatically and all nodes we create will get associated with the default graph.

Sessions

Computation graphs will only be defined; in order to execute the computation graph, we use TensorFlow sessions:

```
sess = tf.Session()
```

We can create the session for our computation graph using the `tf.Session()` method, which will allocate the memory for storing the current value of the variable. After creating the session, we can execute our graph with the `sess.run()` method.

In order to run anything in TensorFlow, we need to start the TensorFlow session for an instance; please refer to the code:

```
import tensorflow as tf
a = tf.multiply(2,3)
print(a)
```

It will print a TensorFlow object instead of 6. As already said, whenever we import TensorFlow a default computation graph will automatically be created and all nodes a that we created will get attached to the graph. In order to execute the graph, we need to initialize a TensorFlow session as follows:

```
#Import tensorflow
import tensorflow as tf

#Initialize variables
a = tf.multiply(2,3)

#create tensorflow session for executing the session
with tf.Session() as sess:
  #run the session
  print(sess.run(a))
```

The preceding code will print 6.

TensorBoard

TensorBoard is TensorFlow's visualization tool that can be used to visualize the computational graph. It can also be used to plot various quantitative metrics and the results of several intermediate calculations. Using TensorBoard, we can easily visualize complex models, which will be useful for debugging and also sharing.

Now, let's build a basic computation graph and visualize that in TensorBoard.

First, let's import the library:

```
import tensorflow as tf
```

Next, we initialize the variables:

```
a = tf.constant(5)
b = tf.constant(4)
c = tf.multiply(a,b)
d = tf.constant(2)
e = tf.constant(3)
f = tf.multiply(d,e)
g = tf.add(c,f)
```

Now, we will create a TensorFlow session. We will write the results of our graph to a file called event using tf.summary.FileWriter():

```
with tf.Session() as sess:
    writer = tf.summary.FileWriter("output", sess.graph)
    print(sess.run(g))
    writer.close()
```

In order to run the TensorBoard, go to your Terminal, locate the working directory, and type tensorboard --logdir=output --port=6003.

You can see the output as shown next:

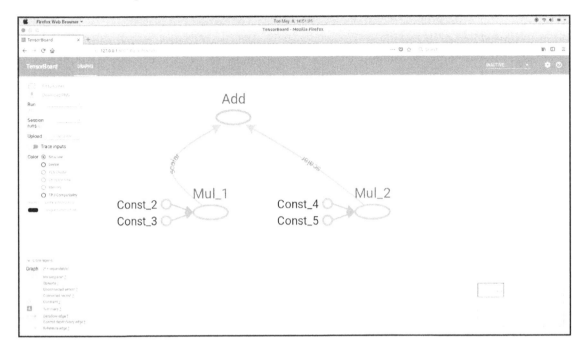

Adding scope

Scoping is used to reduce complexity and helps us to better understand the model by grouping the related nodes together. For instance, in the previous example, we can break down our graph into two different groups called computation and result. If you look at the previous example, you can see that nodes a to e perform the computation and node g calculates the result. So we can group them separately using the scope for easy understanding. Scoping can be created using the tf.name_scope() function.

Let's use the tf.name_scope() function using Computation:

```
with tf.name_scope("Computation"):
    a = tf.constant(5)
    b = tf.constant(4)
    c = tf.multiply(a,b)
    d = tf.constant(2)
    e = tf.constant(3)
    f = tf.multiply(d,e)
```

Let's use the `tf.name_scope()` function using `Result`:

```
with tf.name_scope("Result"):
    g = tf.add(c,f)
```

Look at the `Computation` scope; we can further break down into separate parts for even more understanding. We can create a scope as `Part 1`, which has nodes `a` to `c`, and a scope as `Part 2`, which has nodes `d` to `e`, as part 1 and 2 are independent of each other:

```
with tf.name_scope("Computation"):
    with tf.name_scope("Part1"):
        a = tf.constant(5)
        b = tf.constant(4)
        c = tf.multiply(a,b)
    with tf.name_scope("Part2"):
        d = tf.constant(2)
        e = tf.constant(3)
        f = tf.multiply(d,e)
```

Scoping can be better understood by visualizing them in the TensorBoard. The complete code is as follows:

```
import tensorflow as tf
with tf.name_scope("Computation"):
    with tf.name_scope("Part1"):
        a = tf.constant(5)
        b = tf.constant(4)
        c = tf.multiply(a,b)
    with tf.name_scope("Part2"):
        d = tf.constant(2)
        e = tf.constant(3)
        f = tf.multiply(d,e)

with tf.name_scope("Result"):
    g = tf.add(c,f)

with tf.Session() as sess:
    writer = tf.summary.FileWriter("output", sess.graph)
    print(sess.run(g))
    writer.close()
```

If you look at the following diagram, you can easily understand how scope helps us to reduce complexity in understanding by grouping the similar nodes together. Scoping is widely used while working on a complex project to better understand the functionality and dependencies of nodes:

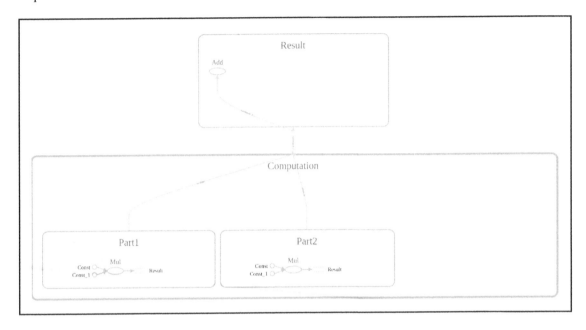

Summary

In this chapter, we learned how to set up our machine by installing Anaconda, Docker, OpenAI Gym, Universe, and TensorFlow. We also learned how to create simulations using OpenAI and how to train agents to learn in an OpenAI environment. Then we came across the fundamentals of TensorFlow followed by visualizing graphs in TensorBoard.

In the Chapter 3, *The Markov Decision Process and Dynamic Programming* we will learn about Markov Decision Process and dynamic programming and how to solve frozen lake problem using value and policy iteration.

Questions

The question list is as follows:

1. Why and how do we create a new environment in Anaconda?
2. What is the need for using Docker?
3. How do we simulate an environment in OpenAI Gym?
4. How do we check all available environments in OpenAI Gym?
5. Are OpenAI Gym and Universe the same? If not, what is the reason?
6. How are TensorFlow variables and placeholders different from each other?
7. What is a computational graph?
8. Why do we need sessions in TensorFlow?
9. What is the purpose of TensorBoard and how do we start it?

Further reading

You can further refer to these papers:

- **OpenAI blog**: https://blog.openai.com
- **OpenAI environments**: https://gym.openai.com/envs/
- **TensorFlow official website**: https://www.tensorflow.org/

3
The Markov Decision Process and Dynamic Programming

The **Markov Decision Process** (**MDP**) provides a mathematical framework for solving the **reinforcement learning** (**RL**) problem. Almost all RL problems can be modeled as MDP. MDP is widely used for solving various optimization problems. In this chapter, we will understand what MDP is and how can we use it to solve RL problems. We will also learn about dynamic programming, which is a technique for solving complex problems in an efficient way.

In this chapter, you will learn about the following topics:

- The Markov chain and Markov process
- The Markov Decision Process
- Rewards and returns
- The Bellman equation
- Solving a Bellman equation using dynamic programming
- Solving a frozen lake problem using value and policy iteration

The Markov chain and Markov process

Before going into MDP, let us understand the Markov chain and Markov process, which form the foundation of MDP.

The Markov property states that the future depends only on the present and not on the past. The Markov chain is a probabilistic model that solely depends on the current state to predict the next state and not the previous states, that is, the future is conditionally independent of the past. The Markov chain strictly follows the Markov property.

For example, if we know that the current state is cloudy, we can predict that next state could be rainy. We came to this conclusion that the next state could be rainy only by considering the current state (cloudy) and not the past states, which might be sunny, windy, and so on. However, the Markov property does not hold true for all processes. For example, throwing a dice (the next state) has no dependency on the previous number, whatever showed up on the dice (the current state).

Moving from one state to another is called **transition** and its probability is called a **transition probability**. We can formulate the transition probabilities in the form of a table, as shown next, and it is called a **Markov table**. It shows, given the current state, what the probability of moving to the next state is:

Current state	Next state	Transition probability
Cloudy	Rainy	0.6
Rainy	Rainy	0.2
Sunny	Cloudy	0.1
Rainy	Sunny	0.1

We can also represent the Markov chain in the form a state diagram that shows the transition probability:

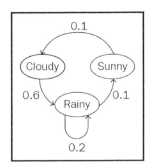

The preceding state diagram shows the probability of moving from one state to another. Still don't understand the Markov chain? Okay, let us talk.

Me: "What are you doing?"

You: "I'm reading about the Markov chain."

Me: "What is your plan after reading?"

You: "I'm going to sleep."

Me: "Are you sure you're going to sleep?"

You: "Probably. I'll watch TV if I'm not sleepy."

Me: "Cool; this is also a Markov chain."

You: "Eh?"

We can formulate our conversation into a Markov chain and draw a state diagram as follows:

The Markov chain lies in the core concept that the future depends only on the present and not on the past. A stochastic process is called a Markov process if it follows the Markov property.

Markov Decision Process

MDP is an extension of the Markov chain. It provides a mathematical framework for modeling decision-making situations. Almost all Reinforcement Learning problems can be modeled as MDP.

MDP is represented by five important elements:

- A set of states (S) the agent can actually be in.
- A set of actions (A) that can be performed by an agent, for moving from one state to another.
- A transition probability $(P_{ss'}^a)$, which is the probability of moving from one state s to another s' state by performing some action a.
- A reward probability $(R_{ss'}^a)$, which is the probability of a reward acquired by the agent for moving from one state s to another state s' by performing some action a.
- A discount factor (γ), which controls the importance of immediate and future rewards. We will discuss this in detail in the upcoming sections.

Rewards and returns

As we have learned, in an RL environment, an agent interacts with the environment by performing an action and moves from one state to another. Based on the action it performs, it receives a reward. A reward is nothing but a numerical value, say, +1 for a good action and -1 for a bad action. How do we decide if an action is good or bad? In a maze game, a good action is where the agent makes a move so that it doesn't hit a maze wall, whereas a bad action is where the agent moves and hits the maze wall.

An agent tries to maximize the total amount of rewards (cumulative rewards) it receives from the environment instead of immediate rewards. The total amount of rewards the agent receives from the environment is called returns. So, we can formulate total amount of rewards (returns) received by the agents as follows:

$$R_t = r_{t+1} + r_{t+2} + \ldots + r_T$$

r_{t+1} is the reward received by the agent at a time step t_0 while performing an action a_0 to move from one state to another. r_{t+2} is the reward received by the agent at a time step t_1 while performing an action to move from one state to another. Similarly, r_T is the reward received by the agent at a final time step T while performing an action to move from one state to another.

Episodic and continuous tasks

Episodic tasks are the tasks that have a terminal state (end). In RL, episodes are considered agent-environment interactions from initial to final states.

For example, in a car racing video game, you start the game (initial state) and play the game until it is over (final state). This is called an episode. Once the game is over, you start the next episode by restarting the game, and you will begin from the initial state irrespective of the position you were in the previous game. So, each episode is independent of the other.

In a continuous task, there is not a terminal state. Continuous tasks will never end. For example, a personal assistance robot does not have a terminal state.

Discount factor

We have seen that an agent goal is to maximize the return. For an episodic task, we can define our return as $R_t = r_{t+1} + r_{t+2} + \ldots + r_T$, where T is the final state of the episode, and we try to maximize the return R_t.

Since we don't have any final state for a continuous task, we can define our return for continuous tasks as $R_t = r_{t+1} + r_{t+2} + ...$, which sums up to infinity. But how can we maximize the return if it never stops?

That's why we introduce the notion of a discount factor. We can redefine our return with a discount factor (γ), as follows:

$$R_t = r_{t+1} + \gamma r_{t+2} + \gamma^2 r_{t+3} + \gamma^3 r_{t+4} + \cdots \quad ---(1)$$

$$= \sum_{k=0}^{\infty} \gamma^k r_{t+k+1} \quad ---(2)$$

The discount factor decides how much importance we give to the future rewards and immediate rewards. The value of the discount factor lies within *0* to *1*. A discount factor of *0* means that immediate rewards are more important, while a discount factor of *1* would mean that future rewards are more important than immediate rewards.

A discount factor of *0* will never learn considering only the immediate rewards; similarly, a discount factor of *1* will learn forever looking for the future reward, which may lead to infinity. So the optimal value of the discount factor lies between 0.2 to 0.8.

We give importance to immediate rewards and future rewards depending on the use case. In some cases, future rewards are more desirable than immediate rewards and vice versa. In a chess game, the goal is to defeat the opponent's king. If we give importance to the immediate reward, which is acquired by actions like our pawn defeating any opponent player and so on, the agent will learn to perform this sub-goal instead of learning to reach the actual goal. So, in this case, we give importance to future rewards, whereas in some cases, we prefer immediate rewards over future rewards. (Say, would you prefer chocolates if I gave you them today or 13 months later?)

The policy function

We have learned about the policy function in `Chapter 1`, *Introduction to Reinforcement Learning*, which maps the states to actions. It is denoted by π.

The policy function can be represented as $\pi(s) : S -> A$, indicating mapping from states to actions. So, basically, a policy function says what action to perform in each state. Our ultimate goal lies in finding the optimal policy which specifies the correct action to perform in each state, which maximizes the reward.

State value function

A state value function is also called simply a value function. It specifies how good it is for an agent to be in a particular state with a policy π. A value function is often denoted by *V(s)*. It denotes the value of a state following a policy.

We can define a state value function as follows:

$$V^{\pi}(s) = \mathbb{E}_{\pi}\big[R_t|s_t = s\big]$$

This specifies the expected return starting from state *s* according to policy π. We can substitute the value of R_t in the value function from (2) as follows:

$$V^{\pi}(s) = \mathbb{E}_{\pi}\Big[\sum_{k=0}^{\infty} \gamma^k r_{t+k+1}|s_t = s\Big]$$

Note that the state value function depends on the policy and it varies depending on the policy we choose.

We can view value functions in a table. Let us say we have two states and both of these states follow the policy π. Based on the value of these two states, we can tell how good it is for our agent to be in that state following a policy. The greater the value, the better the state is:

State	Value
State 1	0.3
State 2	0.9

Based on the preceding table, we can tell that it is good to be in state 2, as it has high value. We will see how to estimate these values intuitively in the upcoming sections.

State-action value function (Q function)

A state-action value function is also called the *Q* function. It specifies how good it is for an agent to perform a particular action in a state with a policy π. The *Q* function is denoted by *Q(s, a)*. It denotes the value of taking an action in a state following a policy π.

We can define *Q* function as follows:

$$Q^{\pi}(s,a) = \mathbb{E}_{\pi}\big[R_t|s_t = s, a_t = a\big]$$

This specifies the expected return starting from state *s* with the action *a* according to policy π. We can substitute the value of R_t in the Q function from (2) as follows:

$$Q^\pi(s, a) = \mathbb{E}_\pi \Big[\sum_{k=0}^{\infty} \gamma^k r_{t+k+1} | s_t = s, a_t = a \Big]$$

The difference between the value function and the Q function is that the value function specifies the goodness of a state, while a Q function specifies the goodness of an action in a state.

Like state value functions, Q functions can be viewed in a table. It is also called a Q table. Let us say we have two states and two actions; our Q table looks like the following:

State	Action	Value
State 1	Action 1	0.03
State 1	Action 2	0.02
State 2	Action 1	0.5
State 2	Action 2	0.9

Thus, the Q table shows the value of all possible state action pairs. So, by looking at this table, we can come to the conclusion that performing action 1 in state 1 and action 2 in state 2 is the better option as it has high value.

Whenever we say value function *V(S)* or Q function *Q(S, a)*, it actually means the value table and Q table, as shown previously.

The Bellman equation and optimality

The Bellman equation, named after Richard Bellman, American mathematician, helps us to solve MDP. It is omnipresent in RL. When we say solve the MDP, it actually means finding the optimal policies and value functions. There can be many different value functions according to different policies. The optimal value function $V^*(s)$ is the one which yields maximum value compared to all the other value functions:

$$V^*(s) = max_\pi V^\pi(s)$$

Similarly, the optimal policy is the one which results in an optimal value function.

Since the optimal value function $V^*(s)$ is the one that has a higher value compared to all other value functions (that is, maximum return), it will be the maximum of the Q function. So, the optimal value function can easily be computed by taking the maximum of the Q function as follows:

$$V^*(s) = max_a Q^*(s,a) \quad \text{-- (3)}$$

The Bellman equation for the value function can be represented as, (we will see how we derived this equation in the next topic):

$$V^\pi(s) = \sum_a \pi(s,a) \sum_{s'} \mathcal{P}_{ss'}^a \left[\mathcal{R}_{ss'}^a + \gamma V^\pi(s') \right]$$

It indicates the recursive relation between a value of a state and its successor state and the average over all possibilities.

Similarly, the Bellman equation for the Q function can be represented as follows:

$$Q^\pi(s,a) = \sum_{s'} \mathcal{P}_{ss'}^a \left[\mathcal{R}_{ss'}^a + \gamma \sum_{a'} Q^\pi(s',a') \right] \quad \text{--- (4)}$$

Substituting equation (4) in (3), we get:

$$V^*(s) = max_a \sum_{s'} \mathcal{P}_{ss'}^a \left[\mathcal{R}_{ss'}^a + \gamma \sum_{a'} Q^\pi(s',a') \right]$$

The preceding equation is called a Bellman optimality equation. In the upcoming sections, we will see how to find optimal policies by solving this equation.

Deriving the Bellman equation for value and Q functions

Now let us see how to derive Bellman equations for value and Q functions.

You can skip this section if you are not interested in mathematics; however, the math will be super intriguing.

First, we define, $P_{ss'}^a$ as a transition probability of moving from state s to s' while performing an action a:

$$P_{ss'}^a = pr(s_{t+1} = s' | s_t = s, a_t = a)$$

We define $R^a_{ss'}$ as a reward probability received by moving from state s to s' while performing an action a:

$$R^a_{ss'} = \mathbb{E}(R_{t+1}|s_t = s, s_{t+1} = s', a_t = a)$$

$$= \gamma \mathbb{E}_\pi \left[\sum_{k=0}^{\infty} \gamma^k r_{t+k-2}|s_{t+1} = s' \right]$$
from (2)   ---(5)

We know that the value function can be represented as:

$$V^\pi(s) = \mathbb{E}_\pi \left[R_t|s_t = s \right]$$

$$V^\pi(s) = \mathbb{E}_\pi \left[r_{t+1} + \gamma r_{t+2} + \gamma^2 r_{t+3} + \ldots |s_t = s \right]$$
from (1)

We can rewrite our value function by taking the first reward out:

$$V^\pi(s) = \mathbb{E}_\pi \left[r_{t+1} + \gamma \sum_{k=0}^{\infty} \gamma^k r_{t+k+2}|s_t = s \right]$$
---(6)

The expectations in the value function specifies the expected return if we are in the state s, performing an action a with policy π.

So, we can rewrite our expectation explicitly by summing up all possible actions and rewards as follows:

$$\mathbb{E}_\pi[r_{t+1}|s_t = s] = \sum_a \pi(s,a) \sum_{s'} \mathcal{P}^a_{ss'} \mathcal{R}^a_{ss'}$$

In the RHS, we will substitute $R^a_{ss'}$ from equation (5) as follows:

$$\sum_a \pi(s,a) \sum_{s'} \mathcal{P}^a_{ss'} \gamma \mathbb{E}_\pi \left[\sum_{k=0}^{\infty} \gamma^k r_{t+k+2}|s_{t+1} = s' \right]$$

Similarly, in the LHS, we will substitute the value of r_{t+1} from equation (2) as follows:

$$\mathbb{E}_\pi \left[\gamma \sum_{k=0}^{\infty} \gamma^k r_{t+k+2}|s_t = s \right]$$

So, our final expectation equation becomes:

$$\mathbb{E}_\pi\left[\gamma\sum_{k=0}^{\infty}\gamma^k r_{t+k+2}|s_t = s\right] = \sum_a \pi(s,a)\sum_{s'}\mathcal{P}_{ss'}^a\gamma\mathbb{E}_\pi\left[\sum_{k=0}^{\infty}\gamma^k r_{t+k+2}|s_{t+1} = s'\right]$$
---(7)

Now we will substitute our expectation (7) in value function (6) as follows:

$$V^\pi(s) = \sum_a \pi(s,a)\sum_{s'}\mathcal{P}_{ss'}^a\left[\mathcal{R}_{ss'}^a + \gamma\mathbb{E}_\pi\left[\sum_{k=0}^{\infty}\gamma^k r_{t+k+2}|s_{t+1} = s'\right]\right]$$

Instead of $\mathbb{E}_\pi\left[\sum_{k=0}^{\infty}\gamma^k r_{t+k+2}|s_{t+1} = s'\right]$, we can substitute $V^\pi(s')$ with equation (6), and our final value function looks like the following:

$$V^\pi(s) = \sum_a \pi(s,a)\sum_{s'}\mathcal{P}_{ss'}^a\left[\mathcal{R}_{ss'}^a + \gamma V^\pi(s')\right]$$

In very similar fashion, we can derive a Bellman equation for the Q function; the final equation is as follows:

$$Q^\pi(s,a) = \sum_{s'}\mathcal{P}_{ss'}^a\left[\mathcal{R}_{ss'}^a + \gamma\sum_{a'}Q^\pi(s',a')\right]$$

Now that we have a Bellman equation for both the value and Q function, we will see how to find the optimal policies.

Solving the Bellman equation

We can find the optimal policies by solving the Bellman optimality equation. To solve the Bellman optimality equation, we use a special technique called dynamic programming.

Dynamic programming

Dynamic programming (**DP**) is a technique for solving complex problems. In DP, instead of solving complex problems one at a time, we break the problem into simple sub-problems, then for each sub-problem, we compute and store the solution. If the same sub-problem occurs, we will not recompute, instead, we use the already computed solution. Thus, DP helps in drastically minimizing the computation time. It has its applications in a wide variety of fields including computer science, mathematics, bioinformatics, and so on.

We solve a Bellman equation using two powerful algorithms:

- Value iteration
- Policy iteration

Value iteration

In value iteration, we start off with a random value function. Obviously, the random value function might not be an optimal one, so we look for a new improved value function in iterative fashion until we find the optimal value function. Once we find the optimal value function, we can easily derive an optimal policy from it:

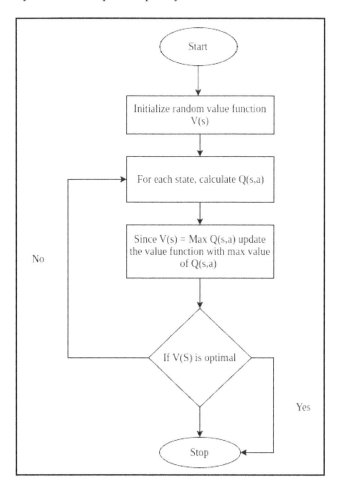

The steps involved in the value iteration are as follows:

1. First, we initialize the random value function, that is, the random value for each state.
2. Then we compute the Q function for all state action pairs of $Q(s, a)$.
3. Then we update our value function with the max value from $Q(s,a)$.
4. We repeat these steps until the change in the value function is very small.

Let us understand it intuitively by performing value iteration manually, step by step.

Consider the grid shown here. Let us say we are in state **A** and our goal is to reach state **C** without visiting state **B**, and we have two actions, 0—left/right and 1—up/down:

Can you think of what will be the optimal policy here? The optimal policy here will be the one that tells us to perform action 1 in the state **A** so that we can reach **C** without visiting **B**. How can we find this optimal policy? Let us see that now:

Initialize the random value function, that is, a random values for all the states. Let us assign **0** to all the states:

State	Value
A	0
B	0
C	0

Let's calculate the Q value for all state action pairs.

The Q value tells us the value of an action in each state. First, let us compute the Q value for state A. Recall the equation of the Q function. For calculating, we need transition and reward probabilities. Let us consider the transition and reward probability for state **A** as follows:

State (s)	Action (a)	Next State (s')	Transistion Probability ($P^a_{ss'}$)	Reward Probability ($R^a_{ss'}$)
A	0	A	0.1	0
A	0	B	0.4	-1.0
A	0	C	0.3	1.0
A	1	A	0.3	0
A	1	B	0.1	-2.0
A	1	C	0.5	1.0

The Q function for the state **A** can be calculated as follows:

$Q(s,a) =$ *Transition probability* * (*Reward probability* + *gamma* * *value_of_next_state*)

Here, *gamma* is the discount factor; we will consider it as *1*.

Q value for state *A* and action *0*:

$$Q(A,0) = (P^0_{AA} * (R^0_{AA} + \gamma * value\_of\_A)) + (P^0_{AB} * (R^0_{AB} + \gamma * value\_of\_B)) + (P^0_{AC} * (R^0_{AC} + \gamma * value\_of\_C))$$
$$Q(A,0) = (0.1 * (0+0)) + (0.4 * (-1.0+0)) + (0.3 * (1.0+0))$$

$$Q(A,0) = -0.1$$

Now we will compute the *Q* value for state *A* and action *1*:

$$Q(A,1) = (P^1_{AA} * (R^1_{AA} + \gamma * value\_of\_A)) + (P^1_{AB} * (R^1_{AB} + \gamma * value\_of\_B)) + (P^1_{AC} * (R^1_{AC} + \gamma * value\_of\_C))$$
$$Q(A,1) = (0.3 * (0+0)) + (0.1 * (-2.0 + 0)) + (0.5 * (1.0 + 0))$$

$$Q(A,1) = 0.3$$

Now we will update this in the *Q* table as follows:

State	Action	Value
A	0	-0.1
A	1	0.3
B	0	
B	1	
C	0	
C	1	

Update the value function as the max value from *Q(s,a)*.

If you look at the preceding *Q* function, *Q(A,1)* has a higher value than *Q(A,0)* so we will update the value of state *A* as *Q(A,1)*:

State	Value
A	0.3
B	
C	

Similarly, we compute the *Q* value for all state-action pairs and update the value function of each state by taking the *Q* value that has the highest state action value. Our updated value function looks like the following. This is the result of the first iteration:

State	Value
A	0.3
B	-0.2
C	0.5

We repeat this steps for several iterations. That is, we repeat step 2 to step 3 (in each iteration while calculating the Q value, we use the updated value function instead of the same randomly initialized value function).

This is the result of the second iteration:

State	Value
A	0.7
B	-0.1
C	0.5

This is the result of the third iteration:

State	Value
A	0.71
B	-0.1
C	0.53

But when do we stop this? We will stop when the change in the value between each iteration is small; if you look at iteration two and three, there is not much of a change in the value function. Given this condition, we stop iterating and consider it an optimal value function.

Okay, now that we have found the optimal value function, how can we derive the optimal policy?

It is very simple. We compute the Q function with our final optimal value function. Let us say our computed Q function looks like the following:

State	Action	Value
A	0	-0.53
A	1	0.98
B	0	-0.2
B	1	-0.3
C	0	0.2
C	1	0.01

From this Q function, we pick up actions in each state that have maximal value. At state **A**, we have a maximum value for action 1, which is our optimal policy. So if we perform action 1 in state **A** we can reach **C** without visiting **B**.

Policy iteration

Unlike value iteration, in policy iteration we start with the random policy, then we find the value function of that policy; if the value function is not optimal then we find the new improved policy. We repeat this process until we find the optimal policy.

There are two steps in policy iteration:

1. **Policy evaluation**: Evaluating the value function of a randomly estimated policy.
2. **Policy improvement**: Upon evaluating the value function, if it is not optimal, we find a new improved policy:

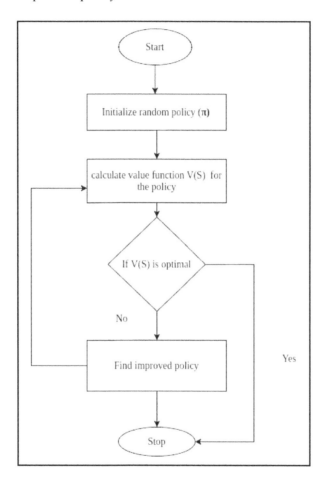

The steps involved in the policy iteration are as follows:

1. First, we initialize some random policy
2. Then we find the value function for that random policy and evaluate to check if it is optimal which is called policy evaluation
3. If it is not optimal, we find a new improved policy, which is called policy improvement
4. We repeat these steps until we find an optimal policy

Let us understand intuitively by performing policy iteration manually step by step.

Consider the same grid example we saw in the section *Value iteration*. Our goal is to find the optimal policy:

1. Initialize a random policy function.

   Let us initialize a random policy function by specifying random actions to each state:

   say *A -> 0*

       B -> 1

       C -> 0

2. Find the value function for the randomly initialized policy.

   Now we have to find the value function using our randomly initialized policy. Let us say our value function after computation looks like the following:

State	Value
A	0.3
B	-0.2
C	0.5

Now that we have a new value function according to our randomly initialized policy, let us compute a new policy using our new value function. How do we do this? It is very similar to what we did in *Value iteration*. We calculate Q value for our new value function and then take actions for each state which has a maximum value as the new policy.

Let us say the new policy results in:

A -> 0

B -> 1

C -> 1

We check our old policy, that is, the randomly initialized policy, and the new policy. If they are same, then we have attained the convergence, that is, found the optimal policy. If not, we will update our old policy (random policy) as a new policy and repeat from step 2.

Sound confusing? Look at the pseudo code:

```
policy_iteration():
    Initialize random policy
    for i in no_of_iterations:
        Q_value = value_function(random_policy)
        new_policy = Maximum state action pair from Q value
        if random_policy == new policy:
            break
        random_policy = new_policy
    return policy
```

Solving the frozen lake problem

If you haven't understood anything we have learned so far, don't worry, we will look at all the concepts along with a frozen lake problem.

Imagine there is a frozen lake stretching from your home to your office; you have to walk on the frozen lake to reach your office. But oops! There are holes in the frozen lake so you have to be careful while walking on the frozen lake to avoid getting trapped in the holes:

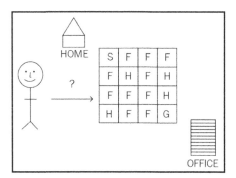

Look at the preceding diagram:

- **S** is the starting position (home)
- **F** is the frozen lake where you can walk
- **H** are the holes, which you have to be so careful about
- **G** is the goal (office)

Okay, now let us use our agent instead of you to find the correct way to reach the office. The agent's goal is to find the optimal path to go from **S** to **G** without getting trapped at **H**. How can an agent achieve this? We give +1 point as a reward to the agent if it correctly walks on the frozen lake and 0 points if it falls into a hole, so the agent can determine which is the right action. An agent will now try to find the optimal policy. Optimal policy implies taking the correct path, which maximizes the agent's reward. If the agent is maximizing the reward, apparently the agent is learning to skip the holes and reach the destination.

We can model our problem into MDP, which we studied earlier. MDP consists of the following:

- **States**: Set of states. Here we have 16 states (each little square box in the grid).
- **Actions**: Set of all possible actions (left, right, up, down; these are all the four possible actions our agent can take in our frozen lake environment).
- **Transition probabilities**: The probability of moving from one state (**F**) to another state (**H**) by performing an action *a*.
- **Rewards probabilities**: This is the probability of receiving a reward while moving from one state (**F**) to another state (**H**) by performing an action *a*.

Now our objective is to solve MDP. Solving the MDP implies finding the optimal policies. We introduce three special functions now:

- **Policy function**: Specifies what action to perform in each state
- **Value function**: Specifies how good a state is
- **Q function**: Specifies how good an action is in a particular state

When we say how good, what does that really mean? It implies how good it is to maximize the rewards.

Then, we represent the value function and *Q* function using a special equation called a Bellman Optimality equation. If we solve this equation, we can find the optimal policy. Here, solving the equation means finding the right value function and policy. If we find the right value function and policy, that will be our optimal path which yields maximum rewards.

We will use a special technique called dynamic programming to solve the Bellman optimality equation. To apply DP, the model dynamics have to be known in advance, which basically means the model environment's transition probabilities and reward probabilities have to be known in advance. Since we know the model dynamics, we can use DP here. We use two special DP algorithms to find the optimal policy:

- Value iteration
- Policy iteration

Value iteration

To put it in simple terms, in value iteration, we first initialize some random value to the value function. There is a great probability that the random value we initialize is not going to be optimal. So, we iterate over each state and find the new value function; we stop the iteration until we find the optimal value function. Once we find the optimal value function, we can easily extract the optimal policy from that.

Now we will see how to solve the frozen lake problem using value iteration.

First, we import necessary libraries:

```
import gym
import numpy as np
```

Then we make our frozen lake environment using OpenAI's Gym:

```
env = gym.make('FrozenLake-v0')
```

We will first explore the environments.

The number of states in the environment is 16 as we have a 4*4 grid:

```
print(env.observation_space.n)
```

The number of actions in the environment is four, which are up, down, left, and right:

```
print(env.observation_space.n)
```

Now we define a `value_iteration()` function which returns the optimal value function (value table). We will first see the function step by step and then look at the whole function.

First, we initialize the random value table which is 0 for all the states and numbers of iterations:

```
value_table = np.zeros(env.observation_space.n)
no_of_iterations = 100000
```

Then, upon starting each iteration, we copy the `value_table` to `updated_value_table`:

```
for i in range(no_of_iterations):
    updated_value_table = np.copy(value_table)
```

Now we calculate the Q table and pick up the maximum state-action pair which has the highest value as the value table.

We will understand the code with the example we solved previously; we computed the *Q* value for state *A* and action *1* in our previous example:

$$Q(A,1) = (0.3 * (0+0)) + (0.1 * (-1.0 + 0)) + (0.5 + (1.0 + 0))$$

$$Q(A,1) = 0.5$$

Instead of creating a *Q* table for each state, we create a list called `Q_value`, then for each action in the state, we create a list called `next_states_rewards`, which store the `Q_value` for the next transition state. Then we sum the `next_state_rewards` and append it to our `Q_value`.

Look at the preceding example, where the state is *A* and the action is *1*. *(0.3 * (0+0))* is the next state reward for the transition state *A* and *(0.1 * (-1.0 + 0))* is the next state reward for the transition state *B*. *(0.5 + (1.0 + 0))* is the next state reward for the transition state *C*. We sum all this as `next_state_reward` and append it to our `Q_value`, which would be 0.5.

As we calculate `next_state_rewards` for all actions of a state and append it to our *Q* value, we pick up the maximum *Q* value and update it as a value of our state:

```
for state in range(env.observation_space.n):
    Q_value = []
    for action in range(env.action_space.n):
        next_states_rewards = []
        for next_sr in env.P[state][action]:
            trans_prob, next_state, reward_prob, _ = next_sr
            next_states_rewards.append((trans_prob * (reward_prob + gamma *
updated_value_table[next_state])))
        Q_value.append(np.sum(next_states_rewards))
```

```
#Pick up the maximum Q value and update it as value of a state
value_table[state] = max(Q_value)
```

Then, we will check whether we have reached the convergence, that is, the difference between our value table and updated value table is very small. How do we know it is very small? We define a variable called `threshold` and then we will see if the difference is less than our `threshold`; if it is less, we break the loop and return the value function as the optimal value function:

```
threshold = 1e-20
if (np.sum(np.fabs(updated_value_table - value_table)) <= threshold):
    print ('Value-iteration converged at iteration# %d.' %(i+1))
    break
```

Look at the complete function of `value_iteration()` for a better understanding:

```
def value_iteration(env, gamma = 1.0):
    value_table = np.zeros(env.observation_space.n)
    no_of_iterations = 100000
    threshold = 1e-20

    for i in range(no_of_iterations):
        updated_value_table = np.copy(value_table)

        for state in range(env.observation_space.n):
            Q_value = []

            for action in range(env.action_space.n):
                next_states_rewards = []

                for next_sr in env.P[state][action]:
                    trans_prob, next_state, reward_prob, _ = next_sr
                    next_states_rewards.append((trans_prob * (reward_prob +
gamma * updated_value_table[next_state])))

                Q_value.append(np.sum(next_states_rewards))
            value_table[state] = max(Q_value)
        if (np.sum(np.fabs(updated_value_table - value_table)) <=
threshold):
            print ('Value-iteration converged at iteration# %d.' %(i+1))
            break
    return value_table, Q_value
```

Thus, we can derive `optimal_value_function` using the `value_iteration`:

```
optimal_value_function = value_iteration(env=env,gamma=1.0)
```

After finding `optimal_value_function`, how can we extract the optimal policy from the `optimal_value_function`? We calculate the *Q* value using our optimal value action and pick up the actions which have the highest *Q* value for each state as the optimal policy. We do this via a function called `extract_policy()`; we will look at this step by step now.

First, we define the random policy; we define it as 0 for all the states:

```
policy = np.zeros(env.observation_space.n)
```

Then, for each state, we build a `Q_table` and for each action in that state we compute the *Q* value and add it to our `Q_table`:

```
for state in range(env.observation_space.n):
        Q_table = np.zeros(env.action_space.n)
        for action in range(env.action_space.n):
            for next_sr in env.P[state][action]:
                trans_prob, next_state, reward_prob, _ = next_sr
                Q_table[action] += (trans_prob * (reward_prob + gamma *
value_table[next_state]))
```

Then we pick up the policy for the `state` as the action that has the highest *Q* value:

```
policy[state] = np.argmax(Q_table)
```

Look at the complete function:

```
def extract_policy(value_table, gamma = 1.0):

    policy = np.zeros(env.observation_space.n)
    for state in range(env.observation_space.n):
        Q_table = np.zeros(env.action_space.n)
        for action in range(env.action_space.n):
            for next_sr in env.P[state][action]:
                trans_prob, next_state, reward_prob, _ = next_sr
                Q_table[action] += (trans_prob * (reward_prob + gamma *
value_table[next_state]))
        policy[state] = np.argmax(Q_table)
    return policy
```

Thus, we can derive the `optimal_policy` as follows:

```
optimal_policy = extract_policy(optimal_value_function, gamma=1.0)
```

We will get an output as follows, which is the `optimal_policy`, the actions to be performed in each state:

```
array([0., 3., 3., 3., 0., 0., 0., 0., 3., 1., 0., 0., 0., 2., 1., 0.])
```

The complete program is given as follows:

```
import gym
import numpy as np
env = gym.make('FrozenLake-v0')

def value_iteration(env, gamma = 1.0):
    value_table = np.zeros(env.observation_space.n)
    no_of_iterations = 100000
    threshold = 1e-20
    for i in range(no_of_iterations):
        updated_value_table = np.copy(value_table)
        for state in range(env.observation_space.n):
            Q_value = []
            for action in range(env.action_space.n):
                next_states_rewards = []
                for next_sr in env.P[state][action]:
                    trans_prob, next_state, reward_prob, _ = next_sr
                    next_states_rewards.append((trans_prob * (reward_prob +
gamma * updated_value_table[next_state])))
                Q_value.append(np.sum(next_states_rewards))
            value_table[state] = max(Q_value)
        if (np.sum(np.fabs(updated_value_table - value_table)) <=
threshold):
            print ('Value-iteration converged at iteration# %d.' %(i+1))
            break
    return value_table


def extract_policy(value_table, gamma = 1.0):
    policy = np.zeros(env.observation_space.n)
    for state in range(env.observation_space.n):
        Q_table = np.zeros(env.action_space.n)
        for action in range(env.action_space.n):
            for next_sr in env.P[state][action]:
                trans_prob, next_state, reward_prob, _ = next_sr
                Q_table[action] += (trans_prob * (reward_prob + gamma *
value_table[next_state]))
        policy[state] = np.argmax(Q_table)
    return policy

optimal_value_function = value_iteration(env=env,gamma=1.0)
optimal_policy = extract_policy(optimal_value_function, gamma=1.0)

print(optimal_policy)
```

Policy iteration

In policy iteration, first we initialize a random policy. Then we will evaluate the random policies we initialized: are they good or not? But how can we evaluate the policies? We will evaluate our randomly initialized policies by computing value functions for them. If they are not good, then we find a new policy. We repeat this process until we find a good policy.

Now let us see how to solve the frozen lake problem using policy iteration.

Before looking at policy iteration, we will see how to compute a value function, given a policy.

We initialize `value_table` as zero with the number of states:

```
value_table = np.zeros(env.nS)
```

Then, for each state, we get the action from the policy, and we compute the value function according to that `action` and `state` as follows:

```
updated_value_table = np.copy(value_table)
for state in range(env.nS):
    action = policy[state]
    value_table[state] = sum([trans_prob * (reward_prob + gamma *
updated_value_table[next_state])
                    for trans_prob, next_state, reward_prob, _ in
env.P[state][action]])
```

We break this when the difference between `value_table` and `updated_value_table` is less than our `threshold`:

```
threshold = 1e-10
if (np.sum((np.fabs(updated_value_table - value_table))) <= threshold):
    break
```

Look at the following complete function:

```
def compute_value_function(policy, gamma=1.0):
    value_table = np.zeros(env.nS)
    threshold = 1e-10
    while True:
        updated_value_table = np.copy(value_table)
        for state in range(env.nS):
            action = policy[state]
            value_table[state] = sum([trans_prob * (reward_prob + gamma *
updated_value_table[next_state])
                    for trans_prob, next_state, reward_prob, _ in
env.P[state][action]])
```

```
                if (np.sum((np.fabs(updated_value_table - value_table))) <=
    threshold):
                break
        return value_table
```

Now we will see how to perform policy iteration, step by step.

First, we initialize `random_policy` as zero NumPy array with shape as number of states:

```
    random_policy = np.zeros(env.observation_space.n)
```

Then, for each iteration, we calculate the `new_value_function` according to our random policy:

```
    new_value_function = compute_value_function(random_policy, gamma)
```

We will extract the policy using the calculated `new_value_function`. The `extract_policy` function is the same as the one we used in value iteration:

```
    new_policy = extract_policy(new_value_function, gamma)
```

Then we check whether we have reached convergence, that is, whether we found the optimal policy by comparing `random_policy` and the new policy. If they are the same, we will break the iteration; otherwise we update `random_policy` with `new_policy`:

```
    if (np.all(random_policy == new_policy)):
        print ('Policy-Iteration converged at step %d.' %(i+1))
        break
    random_policy = new_policy
```

Look at the complete `policy_iteration` function:

```
def policy_iteration(env,gamma = 1.0):
    random_policy = np.zeros(env.observation_space.n)
    no_of_iterations = 200000
    gamma = 1.0
    for i in range(no_of_iterations):
        new_value_function = compute_value_function(random_policy, gamma)
        new_policy = extract_policy(new_value_function, gamma)
        if (np.all(random_policy == new_policy)):
            print ('Policy-Iteration converged at step %d.' %(i+1))
            break
        random_policy = new_policy
    return new_policy
```

Thus, we can get `optimal_policy` using `policy_iteration`:

```
optimal_policy = policy_iteration(env, gamma = 1.0)
```

We will get some output, which is the `optimal_policy`, the actions to be performed in each state:

```
array([0., 3., 3., 3., 0., 0., 0., 0., 3., 1., 0., 0., 0., 2., 1., 0.])
```

The complete program is given as follows:

```
import gym
import numpy as np

env = gym.make('FrozenLake-v0')

def compute_value_function(policy, gamma=1.0):
    value_table = np.zeros(env.nS)
    threshold = 1e-10
    while True:
        updated_value_table = np.copy(value_table)
        for state in range(env.nS):
            action = policy[state]
            value_table[state] = sum([trans_prob * (reward_prob + gamma *
updated_value_table[next_state])
                        for trans_prob, next_state, reward_prob, _ in
env.P[state][action]])
        if (np.sum((np.fabs(updated_value_table - value_table))) <=
threshold):
            break
    return value_table


def extract_policy(value_table, gamma = 1.0):
    policy = np.zeros(env.observation_space.n)
    for state in range(env.observation_space.n):
        Q_table = np.zeros(env.action_space.n)
        for action in range(env.action_space.n):
            for next_sr in env.P[state][action]:
                trans_prob, next_state, reward_prob, _ = next_sr
                Q_table[action] += (trans_prob * (reward_prob + gamma *
value_table[next_state]))
        policy[state] = np.argmax(Q_table)
    return policy

def policy_iteration(env,gamma = 1.0):
    random_policy = np.zeros(env.observation_space.n)
    no_of_iterations = 200000
```

```
gamma = 1.0
for i in range(no_of_iterations):
    new_value_function = compute_value_function(random_policy, gamma)
    new_policy = extract_policy(new_value_function, gamma)
    if (np.all(random_policy == new_policy)):
        print ('Policy-Iteration converged at step %d.' %(i+1))
        break
    random_policy = new_policy
return new_policy


print (policy_iteration(env))
```

Thus, we can derive the optimal policy, which specifies what action to perform in each state, using value and policy iteration to solve the frozen lake problem.

Summary

In this chapter, we learned what the Markov chain and Markov process are and how RL problems are represented using MDP. We have also looked at the Bellman equation, and we solved the Bellman equation to derive an optimal policy using DP. In the Chapter 4, *Gaming with Monte Carlo Methods*, we will look at the Monte Carlo tree search and how to build intelligent games using it.

Questions

The question list is as follows:

1. What is the Markov property?
2. Why do we need the Markov Decision Process?
3. When do we prefer immediate rewards?
4. What is the use of the discount factor?
5. Why do we use the Bellman function?
6. How would you derive the Bellman equation for a Q function?
7. How are the value function and Q function related?
8. What is the difference between value iteration and policy iteration?

Further reading

MDP Harvard lecture materials: `http://am121.seas.harvard.edu/site/wp-content/uploads/2011/03/MarkovDecisionProcesses-HillierLieberman.pdf`

4
Gaming with Monte Carlo Methods

Monte Carlo is one of the most popular and most commonly used algorithms in various fields ranging from physics and mechanics to computer science. The Monte Carlo algorithm is used in **reinforcement learning** (**RL**) when the model of the environment is not known. In the previous chapter, we looked at using **dynamic programming** (**DP**) to find an optimal policy where we know the model dynamics, which is transition and reward probabilities. But how can we determine the optimal policy when we don't know the model dynamics? In that case, we use the Monte Carlo algorithm; it is extremely powerful for finding optimal policies when we don't have knowledge of the environment.

In this chapter, you will learn about the following:

- Monte Carlo methods
- Monte Carlo prediction
- Playing Blackjack with Monte Carlo
- Model Carlo control
- Monte Carlo exploration starts
- On-policy Monte Carlo control
- Off-policy Monte Carlo control

Monte Carlo methods

The Monte Carlo method finds approximate solutions through random sampling, that is, it approximates the probability of an outcome by running multiple trails. It is a statistical technique to find an approximate answer through sampling. Let's better understand Monte Carlo intuitively with an example.

Fun fact: Monte Carlo is named after Stanislaw Ulam's uncle, who often borrowed money from his relatives to gamble in a Monte Carlo casino.

Estimating the value of pi using Monte Carlo

Imagine a quadrant of a circle is placed inside a square, as shown next, and we generate some random points inside the square. You can see that some of the points fall inside the circle while others are outside the circle:

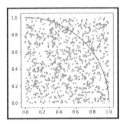

We can write:

$$\frac{Area \quad of \quad a \quad cirlce}{Area \quad of \quad a \quad square} = \frac{No \quad of \quad points \quad inside \quad the \quad circle}{No \quad of \quad points \quad inside \quad the \quad square}$$

We know that the area of a circle is πr^2 and the area of a square is a^2:

$$\frac{\pi r^2}{a^2} = \frac{No \quad of \quad points \quad inside \quad the \quad circle}{No \quad of \quad points \quad inside \quad the \quad square}$$

Let's consider that the radius of a circle is one half and the square's side is *1*, so we can substitute:

$$\frac{\pi(\frac{1}{2})^2}{1^2} = \frac{No \quad of \quad points \quad inside \quad the \quad circle}{No \quad of \quad points \quad inside \quad the \quad square}$$

Now we get the following:

$$\pi = 4 * \frac{No \quad of \quad points \quad inside \quad the \quad circle}{No \quad of \quad points \quad inside \quad the \quad square}$$

The steps to estimate π are very simple:

1. First, we generate some random points inside the square.
2. Then we can calculate the number of points that fall inside the circle by using the equation $x^2 + y^2 <= size$.
3. Then we calculate the value of π by multiplying four to the division of the number of points inside the circle to the number of points inside the square.
4. If we increase the number of samples (number of random points), the better we can approximate

Let's see how to do this in Python step by step. First, we import necessary libraries:

```
import numpy as np
import math
import random
import matplotlib.pyplot as plt
%matplotlib inline
```

Now we initialize the square size and number of points inside the circle and square. We also initialize the sample size, which denotes the number of random points to be generated. We define arc, which is basically the circle quadrant:

```
square_size = 1
points_inside_circle = 0
points_inside_square = 0
sample_size = 1000
arc = np.linspace(0, np.pi/2, 100)
```

Then we define a function called generate_points(), which generates random points inside the square:

```
def generate_points(size):
    x = random.random()*size
    y = random.random()*size
    return (x, y)
```

We define a function called is_in_circle(), which will check if the point we generated falls within the circle:

```
def is_in_circle(point, size):
    return math.sqrt(point[0]**2 + point[1]**2) <= size
```

Then we define a function for calculating the π value:

```
def compute_pi(points_inside_circle, points_inside_square):
    return 4 * (points_inside_circle / points_inside_square)
```

Then for the number of samples, we generate some random points inside the square and increment our `points_inside_square` variable, and then we will check if the points we generated lie inside the circle. If yes, then we increment the `points_inside_circle` variable:

```
plt.axes().set_aspect('equal')
plt.plot(1*np.cos(arc), 1*np.sin(arc))

for i in range(sample_size):
    point = generate_points(square_size)
    plt.plot(point[0], point[1], 'c.')
    points_inside_square += 1
    if is_in_circle(point, square_size):
        points_inside_circle += 1
```

Now we calculate the value of π using the `compute_pi()`, function which will print an approximate value of π:

```
print("Approximate value of pi is {}"
.format(calculate_pi(points_inside_circle, points_inside_square)))
```

If you run the program, you will get the output shown as follows:

```
Approximate value of pi is 3.144
```

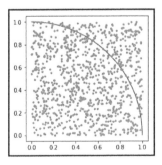

The complete program looks as follows:

```
import numpy as np
import math
import random
import matplotlib.pyplot as plt
%matplotlib inline

square_size = 1
points_inside_circle = 0
points_inside_square = 0
```

```
sample_size = 1000
arc = np.linspace(0, np.pi/2, 100)

def generate_points(size):
    x = random.random()*size
    y = random.random()*size
    return (x, y)

def is_in_circle(point, size):
    return math.sqrt(point[0]**2 + point[1]**2) <= size

def compute_pi(points_inside_circle, points_inside_square):
    return 4 * (points_inside_circle / points_inside_square)

plt.axes().set_aspect('equal')
plt.plot(1*np.cos(arc), 1*np.sin(arc))

for i in range(sample_size):
    point = generate_points(square_size)
    plt.plot(point[0], point[1], 'c.')
    points_inside_square += 1
    if is_in_circle(point, square_size):
        points_inside_circle += 1

print("Approximate value of pi is {}"
.format(calculate_pi(points_inside_circle, points_inside_square)))
```

Thus, the Monte Carlo method approximated the value of `pi` by using random sampling. We estimated the value of `pi` using the random points (samples) generated inside the square. The greater the sampling size, the better our approximation will be. Now we will see how to use Monte Carlo methods in RL.

Monte Carlo prediction

In DP, we solve the **Markov Decision Process (MDP)** by using value iteration and policy iteration. Both of these techniques require transition and reward probabilities to find the optimal policy. But how can we solve MDP when we don't know the transition and reward probabilities? In that case, we use the Monte Carlo method. The Monte Carlo method requires only sample sequences of states, actions, and rewards. the Monte Carlo methods are applied only to the episodic tasks. Since Monte Carlo doesn't require any model, it is called the model-free learning algorithm.

The basic idea of the Monte Carlo method is very simple. Do you recall how we defined the optimal value function and how we derived the optimal policy in the Chapter 3, *Markov Decision Process and Dynamic Programming*?

A value function is basically the expected return from a state S with a policy π. Here, instead of expected return, we use mean return.

 Thus, in Monte Carlo prediction, we approximate the value function by taking the mean return instead of the expected return.

Using Monte Carlo prediction, we can estimate the value function of any given policy. The steps involved in the Monte Carlo prediction are very simple and are as follows:

1. First, we initialize a random value to our value function
2. Then we initialize an empty list called a return to store our returns
3. Then for each state in the episode, we calculate the return
4. Next, we append the return to our return list
5. Finally, we take the average of return as our value function

The following flowchart makes it more simple:

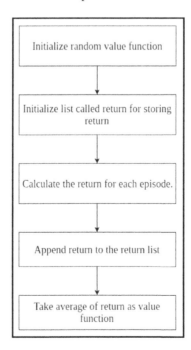

The Monte Carlo prediction algorithm is of two types:

- First visit Monte Carlo
- Every visit Monte Carlo

First visit Monte Carlo

As we have seen, in the Monte Carlo methods, we approximate the value function by taking the average return. But in the first visit MC method, we average the return only the first time the state is visited in an episode. For example, consider an agent is playing the snakes and ladder games, there is a good chance the agent will return to the state if it is bitten by a snake. When the agent revisits the state, we don't consider an average return. We consider an average return only when the agent visits the state for the first time.

Every visit Monte Carlo

In every visit Monte Carlo, we average the return every time the state is visited in an episode. Consider the same snakes and ladders game example: if the agent returns to the same state after a snake bites it, we can think of this as an average return although the agent is revisiting the state. In this case, we average return every time the agents visit the state.

Let's play Blackjack with Monte Carlo

Now let's better understand Monte Carlo with the Blackjack game. Blackjack, also called 21, is a popular card game played in casinos. The goal of the game is to have a sum of all your cards close to 21 and not exceeding 21. The value of cards J, K, and Q is 10. The value of ace can be 1 or 11; this depends on player choice. The value of the rest of the cards (1 to 10) is the same as the numbers they show.

The rules of the game are very simple:

- The game can be played with one or many players and one dealer.
- Each player competes only with the dealer and not another player.
- Initially, a player is given two cards. Both of these cards are face up, that is, visible to others.
- A dealer is also given two cards. One card is face up and the other is face down. That is, the dealer only shows one of his cards.

- If the sum of a player's cards is 21 immediately after receiving two cards (say a player has received a jack and ace which is 10+11 = 21), then it is called **natural** or **Blackjack** and the player wins.
- If the dealer's sum of cards is also 21 immediately after receiving two cards, then it is called a **draw** as both of them have 21.
- In each round, the player decides whether he needs another card or not to sum the cards close to 21.
- If a player needs a card, then it is called a **hit**.
- If a player doesn't need a card, then it is called a **stand**.
- If a player's sum of cards exceeds 21, then it is called **bust**; then the dealer will win the game.

Let's better understand Blackjack by playing. I'll let you be the player and I am the dealer:

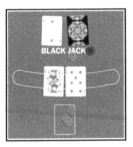

In the preceding diagram, we have one player and a dealer. Both of them are given two cards. Both of the player's two cards are face up (visible) while the dealer has one card face up (visible) and the other face down (invisible). In the first round, you have been given two cards, say a jack and a number 7, which is (10 + 7 = 17), and I as the dealer will only show you one card which is number 2. I have another card face down. Now you have to decide to either hit (need another card) or stand (don't need another card). If you choose to hit and receive number 3 you will get 10+7+3 = 20 which is close to 21 and you win:

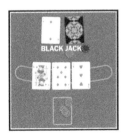

But if you received a card, say number 7, then 10+7+7 = 24, which exceeds 21. Then it is called bust and you lose the game. If you decide to stand with your initial cards, then you have only 10 + 7 = 17. Then we will check the dealer's sum of cards. If it is greater than 17 and does not exceed 21 then the dealer wins, otherwise you win:

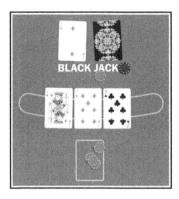

The rewards here are:

- +1 if the player won the game
- -1 if the player loses the game
- 0 if the game is a draw

The possible actions are:

- **Hit**: If the player needs a card
- **Stand**: If the player doesn't need a card

The player has to decide the value of an ace. If the player's sum of cards is 10 and the player gets an ace after a hit, he can consider it as 11, and 10 + 11 = 21. But if the player's sum of cards is 15 and the player gets an ace after a hit, if he considers it as 11 and 15+11 = 26, then it's a bust. If the player has an ace we can call it a **usable ace**; the player can consider it as 11 without being bust. If the player is bust by considering the ace as 11, then it is called a **nonusable ace**.

Now we will see how to implement Blackjack using the first visit Monte Carlo algorithm.

First, we will import our necessary libraries:

```
import gym
from matplotlib import pyplot
import matplotlib.pyplot as plt
from mpl_toolkits.mplot3d import Axes3D
from collections import defaultdict
```

```
from functools import partial
%matplotlib inline
plt.style.use('ggplot')
```

Now we will create the Blackjack environment using OpenAI's Gym:

```
env = gym.make('Blackjack-v0')
```

Then we define the policy function which takes the current state and checks if the score is greater than or equal to 2o; if it is, we return 0 or else we return 1. That is, if the score is greater than or equal to 20, we stand (0) or else we hit (1):

```
def sample_policy(observation):
    score, dealer_score, usable_ace = observation
    return 0 if score >= 20 else 1
```

Now we will see how to generate an episode. An episode is a single round of a game. We will see it step by step and then look at the complete function.

We define states, actions, and rewards as a list and initiate the environment using `env.reset` and store an observation variable:

```
states, actions, rewards = [], [], []
observation = env.reset()
```

Then, until we reach the terminal state, that is, till the end of the episode, we do the following:

1. Append the observation to the states list:

   ```
   states.append(observation)
   ```

2. Now, we create an action using our `sample_policy` function and append the actions to an `action` list:

   ```
   action = sample_policy(observation)
   actions.append(action)
   ```

3. Then, for each step in the environment, we store the `state`, `reward`, and `done` (which specifies whether we reached terminal state) and we append the rewards to the `reward` list:

   ```
   observation, reward, done, info = env.step(action)
   rewards.append(reward)
   ```

4. If we reached the terminal state, then we break:

```
if done:
    break
```

5. The complete `generate_episode` function is as follows:

```
def generate_episode(policy, env):
    states, actions, rewards = [], [], []
    observation = env.reset()
    while True:
        states.append(observation)
        action = policy(observation)
        actions.append(action)
        observation, reward, done, info = env.step(action)
        rewards.append(reward)
        if done:
            break

    return states, actions, rewards
```

This is how we generate an episode. How can we play the game? For that, we need to know the value of each state. Now we will see how to get the value of each state using the first visit Monte Carlo method.

First, we initialize the empty value table as a dictionary for storing the values of each state:

```
value_table = defaultdict(float)
```

Then, for a certain number of episodes, we do the following:

1. First, we generate an episode and store the states and rewards; we initialize returns as 0 which is the sum of rewards:

```
states, _, rewards = generate_episode(policy, env)
returns = 0
```

2. Then for each step, we store the rewards to a variable *R* and states to *S*, and we calculate returns as a sum of rewards:

```
for t in range(len(states) - 1, -1, -1):
    R = rewards[t]
    S = states[t]
    returns += R
```

3. We now perform the first visit Monte Carlo; we check if the episode is being visited for the visit time. If it is, we simply take the average of returns and assign the value of the state as an average of returns:

```
if S not in states[:t]:
    N[S] += 1
    value_table[S] += (returns - V[S]) / N[S]
```

4. Look at the complete function for better understanding:

```
def first_visit_mc_prediction(policy, env, n_episodes):
    value_table = defaultdict(float)
    N = defaultdict(int)

    for _ in range(n_episodes):
        states, _, rewards = generate_episode(policy, env)
        returns = 0
        for t in range(len(states) - 1, -1, -1):
            R = rewards[t]
            S = states[t]
            returns += R
            if S not in states[:t]:
                N[S] += 1
                value_table[S] += (returns - V[S]) / N[S]
    return value_table
```

5. We can get the value of each state:

```
value = first_visit_mc_prediction(sample_policy, env,
n_episodes=500000)
```

6. Let's see the value of a few states:

```
print(value)
defaultdict(float,
            {(4, 1, False): -1.024292170184644,
             (4, 2, False): -1.8670191351012455,
             (4, 3, False): 2.211363314854649,
             (4, 4, False): 16.903201033000823,
             (4, 5, False): -5.786238030898542,
             (4, 6, False): -16.218211752577602,
```

We can also plot the value of the state to see how it is converged, as follows:

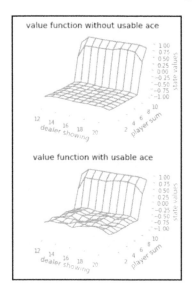

The complete code is given as follows:

```
import numpy
import gym
from matplotlib import pyplot
import matplotlib.pyplot as plt
from mpl_toolkits.mplot3d import Axes3D
from collections import defaultdict
from functools import partial
%matplotlib inline

plt.style.use('ggplot')

## Blackjack Environment

env = gym.make('Blackjack-v0')

env.action_space, env.observation_space

def sample_policy(observation):
    score, dealer_score, usable_ace = observation
    return 0 if score >= 20 else 1

def generate_episode(policy, env):
    states, actions, rewards = [], [], []
    observation = env.reset()
```

```
        while True:
            states.append(observation)
            action = sample_policy(observation)
            actions.append(action)
            observation, reward, done, info = env.step(action)
            rewards.append(reward)
            if done:
                break

        return states, actions, rewards


def first_visit_mc_prediction(policy, env, n_episodes):
    value_table = defaultdict(float)
    N = defaultdict(int)

    for _ in range(n_episodes):
        states, _, rewards = generate_episode(policy, env)
        returns = 0
        for t in range(len(states) - 1, -1, -1):
            R = rewards[t]
            S = states[t]
            returns += R
            if S not in states[:t]:
                N[S] += 1
                value_table[S] += (returns - value_table[S]) / N[S]
    return value_table

def plot_blackjack(V, ax1, ax2):
    player_sum = numpy.arange(12, 21 + 1)
    dealer_show = numpy.arange(1, 10 + 1)
    usable_ace = numpy.array([False, True])

    state_values = numpy.zeros((len(player_sum),
                                len(dealer_show),
                                len(usable_ace)))

    for i, player in enumerate(player_sum):
        for j, dealer in enumerate(dealer_show):
            for k, ace in enumerate(usable_ace):
                state_values[i, j, k] = V[player, dealer, ace]

    X, Y = numpy.meshgrid(player_sum, dealer_show)

    ax1.plot_wireframe(X, Y, state_values[:, :, 0])
    ax2.plot_wireframe(X, Y, state_values[:, :, 1])
    for ax in ax1, ax2:
        ax.set_zlim(-1, 1)
```

```
        ax.set_ylabel('player sum')
        ax.set_xlabel('dealer showing')
        ax.set_zlabel('state-value')
fig, axes = pyplot.subplots(nrows=2, figsize=(5, 8),
subplot_kw={'projection': '3d'})
axes[0].set_title('value function without usable ace')
axes[1].set_title('value function with usable ace')
plot_blackjack(value, axes[0], axes[1])
```

Monte Carlo control

In Monte Carlo prediction, we have seen how to estimate the value function. In Monte Carlo control, we will see how to optimize the value function, that is, how to make the value function more accurate than the estimation. In the control methods, we follow a new type of iteration called generalized policy iteration, where policy evaluation and policy improvement interact with each other. It basically runs as a loop between policy evaluation and improvement, that is, the policy is always improved with respect to the value function, and the value function is always improved according to the policy. It keeps on doing this. When there is no change, then we can say that the policy and value function have attained convergence, that is, we found the optimal value function and optimal policy:

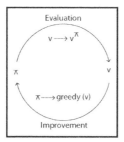

Now we will see a different Monte Carlo control algorithm as follows.

Monte Carlo exploration starts

Unlike DP methods, here we do not estimate state values. Instead, we focus on action values. State values alone are sufficient when we know the model of the environment. As we don't know about the model dynamics, it is not a good way to determine the state values alone.

Estimating an action value is more intuitive than estimating a state value because state values vary depending on the policy we choose. For example, in a Blackjack game, say we are in a state where some of the cards are 20. What is the value of this state? It solely depends on the policy. If we choose our policy as a hit, then it is not a good state to be in and the value of this state is very low. However, if we choose our policy as a stand then it is definitely a good state to be in. Thus, the value of the state depends on the policy we choose. So it is more important to estimate the value of an action instead of the value of the state.

How do we estimate the action values? Remember the Q function we learned in `Chapter 3,` *Markov Decision Process and Dynamic Programming*? The Q function denoted as $Q(s, a)$ is used for determining how good an action is in a particular state. It basically specifies the state-action pair.

But here the problem of exploration comes in. How can we know about the state-action value if we haven't been in that state? If we don't explore all the states with all possible actions, we might probably miss out the good rewards.

Say that in a Blackjack game, we are in a state where a sum of cards is 20. If we try only the action **hit** we will get a negative reward, and we learn that it is not a good state to be in. But if we try the **stand** action, we receive a positive reward and it is actually the best state to be in. So every time we come to this particular state, we stand instead of hit. For us to know which is the best action, we have to explore all possible actions in each state to find the optimal value. How can we do this?

Let me introduce a new concept called **Monte Carlo exploring starts**, which implies that for each episode we start with a random state as an initial state and perform an action. So, if we have a large number of episodes, we could possibly cover all the states with all possible actions. It is also called an **MC-ES** algorithm.

The MC-ES algorithm is very simple, as follows:

- We first initialize Q function and policy with some random values and also we initialize a return to an empty list
- Then we start the episode with our randomly initialized policy
- Then we calculate the return for all the unique state-action pairs occurring in the episode and append return to our return list
- We calculate a return only for a unique state-action pair because the same state action pair occurs in an episode multiple times and there is no point having redundant information

- Then we take an average of the returns in the return list and assign that value to our *Q* function

- Finally, we will select an optimal policy for a state, choosing an action that has the maximum *Q(s,a)* for that state
- We repeat this whole process forever or for a large number of episodes so that we can cover all different states and action pairs

Here's a flowchart of this:

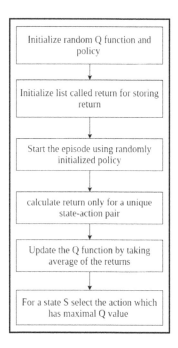

On-policy Monte Carlo control

In Monte Carlo exploration starts, we explore all state-action pairs and choose the one that gives us the maximum value. But think of a situation where we have a large number of states and actions. In that case, if we use the MC-ES algorithm, then it will take a lot of time to explore all combinations of states and actions and to choose the best one. How do we get over this? There are two different control algorithms. On policy and off policy. In on-policy Monte Carlo control, we use the ε greedy policy. Let's understand what a greedy algorithm is.

A greedy algorithm picks up the best choice available at that moment, although that choice might not be optimal when you consider the overall problem. Consider you want to find the smallest number from a list of numbers. Instead of finding the smallest number directly from the list, you will divide the list into three sublists. Then you will find the smallest number in each of the sublists (local optima). The smallest number you find in one sublist might not be the smallest number when you consider the whole list (global optima). However, if you are acting greedy then you will see the smallest number in only the current sublist (at the moment) and consider it the smallest number.

The greedy policy denotes the optimal action within the actions explored. The optimal action is the one which has the highest value.

Say we have explored some actions in the state 1, as shown in the Q table:

State	Action	Value
State 1	Action 0	0.5
State 1	Action 1	0.1
State 1	Action 2	0.8

If we are acting greedy, we would pick up the action that has maximal value out of all the actions we explored. In the preceding case, we have action 2 which has high value, so we pick up that action. But there might be other actions in the state 1 that we haven't explored and might the highest value. So we have to look for the best action or exploit the action that is best out of all explored actions. This is called an exploration-exploitation dilemma. Say you listened to Ed Sheeran and you liked him very much, so you kept on listening to Ed Sheeran only (exploiting) because you liked the music. But if you tried listening to other artists you might like someone better than Ed Sheeran (exploration). This confusion as to whether you have to listen to only Ed Sheeran (exploitation) or try listening to different artists to see if you like them (exploration) is called an exploration-exploitation dilemma.

So to avoid this dilemma, we introduce a new policy called the epsilon-greedy policy. Here, all actions are tried with a non-zero probability (epsilon). With a probability epsilon, we explore different actions randomly and with a probability 1-epsilon we choose an action that has maximum value, that is, we don't do any exploration. So instead of just exploiting the best action all the time, with probability epsilon, we explore different actions randomly. If the value of the epsilon is set to zero, then we will not do any exploration. It is simply the greedy policy, and if the value of epsilon is set to one, then it will always do only exploration. The value of the epsilon will decay over time as we don't want to explore forever. So over time our policy exploits good actions:

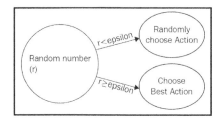

Let us say we set the value of epsilon to *0.3*. In the following code, we generate a random value from the uniform distribution and if the value is less than epsilon value, that is, 0.3, then we select a random action (in this way, we search for a different action). If the random value from the uniform distribution is greater than 0.3, then we select the action that has the best value. So, in this way, we explore actions that we haven't seen before with the probability epsilon and select the best actions out of the explored actions with the probability 1-epsilon:

```
def epsilon_greedy_policy(state, epsilon):
    if random.uniform(0,1) < epsilon:
        return env.action_space.sample()
    else:
        return max(list(range(env.action_space.n)), key = lambda x:
q[(state,x)])
```

Let us imagine that we have explored further actions in the state 1 with the epsilon-greedy policy (although not all of the actions pair) and our Q table looks as follows:

State	Action	Value
State 1	Action 0	0.5
State 1	Action 1	0.1
State 1	Action 2	0.8
State 1	Action 4	0.93

In state 1, action 4 has a higher value than the action 2 we found previously. So with the epsilon-greedy policy, we look for different actions with the probability epsilon and exploit the best action with the probability 1-epsilon.

The steps involved in the on-policy Monte Carlo method are very simple:

1. First, we initialize a random policy and a random Q function.
2. Then we initialize a list called return for storing the returns.
3. We generate an episode using the random policy π.
4. We store the return of every state action pair occurring in the episode to the return list.

5. Then we take an average of the returns in the return list and assign that value to the *Q* function.
6. Now the probability of selecting an action *a* in the state *s* will be decided by epsilon.
7. If the probability is 1-epsilon we pick up the action which has the maximal *Q* value.
8. If the probability is epsilon, we explore for different actions.

Off-policy Monte Carlo control

Off-policy Monte Carlo is another interesting Monte Carlo control method. In this method, we have two policies: one is a behavior policy and another is a target policy. In the off-policy method, agents follow one policy but in the meantime, it tries to learn and improve a different policy. The policy an agent follows is called a behavior policy and the policy an agent tries to evaluate and improve is called a target policy. The behavior and target policy are totally unrelated. The behavior policy explores all possible states and actions and that is why a behavior policy is called a soft policy, whereas a target policy is said to be a greedy policy (it selects the policy which has the maximal value).

Our goal is to estimate the *Q* function for the target policy π, but our agents behave using a completely different policy called behavior policy μ. What can we do now? We can estimate the value of π by using the common episodes that took place in μ. How can we estimate the common episodes between these two policies? We use a new technique called importance sampling. It is a technique for estimating values from one distribution given samples from another.

Importance sampling is of two types:

- Ordinary importance sampling
- Weighted importance sampling

In ordinary importance sampling, we basically take the ratio of returns obtained by the behavior policy and target policy, whereas in weighted importance sampling we take the weighted average and *C* is the cumulative sum of weights.

Let us just see this step by step:

1. First, we initialize *Q(s,a)* to random values and *C(s,a)* to *0* and weight *w* as *1*.
2. Then we choose the target policy, which is a greedy policy. This means it will pick up the policy which has a maximum value from the *Q* table.

3. We select our behavior policy. A behavior policy is not greedy and it can select any state-action pair.

4. Then we begin our episode and perform an action *a* in the state *s* according to our behavior policy and store the reward. We repeat this until the end of the episode.

5. Now, for each state in the episode, we do the following:

    1. We will calculate return *G*. We know that the return is the sum of discounted rewards: *G = discount_ factor * G + reward*.

    2. Then we update *C(s,a)* as *C(s,a) = C(s,a) + w*.

    3. We update *Q(s,a)*:
    $$Q(s, a) = Q(s, a) + \frac{w}{C(s, a)} * (G - Q(s, a))$$

    4. We update the value of *w*:
    $$w = w * \frac{1}{behaviourpolicy}$$

Summary

In this chapter, we learned about how the Monte Carlo method works and how can we use it to solve MDP when we don't know the model of the environment. We have looked at two different methods: one is Monte Carlo prediction, which is used for estimating the value function, and the other is Monte Carlo control, which is used for optimizing the value function.

We looked at two different methods in Monte Carlo prediction: first visit Monte Carlo prediction, where we average the return only the first time the state is visited in an episode, and the every visit Monte Carlo method, where we average the return every time the state is visited in an episode.

In terms of Monte Carlo control, we looked at different algorithms. We first encountered MC-ES control, which is used to cover all state-action pairs. We looked at on-policy MC control, which uses the epsilon-greedy policy, and off-policy MC control, which uses two policies at a time.

In the Chapter 5, *Temporal Difference Learning* we will look at a different model-free learning algorithm.

Questions

The question list is as follows:

1. What is the Monte Carlo Method?
2. Estimate the value of the Golden Ratio using the Monte Carlo method.
3. What is the use of Monte Carlo prediction?
4. What is the difference between first visit MC and every visit MC?
5. Why do we estimate the state-action value?
6. What is the difference between on-policy MC control and off-policy MC control?
7. Write some Python code for playing a Blackjack game with on-policy MC control.

Further reading

Please refer to the following links:

- **David Silver's model-free prediction presentation**: `http://www0.cs.ucl.ac.uk/staff/d.silver/web/Teaching_file s/MC-TD.pdf`
- **David Silver's model-free control presentation**: `http://www0.cs.ucl.ac.uk/staff/d.silver/web/Teaching_file s/control.pdf`

Temporal Difference Learning

5

In the previous chapter, we learned about the interesting Monte Carlo method, which is used for solving the **Markov Decision Process** (**MDP**) when the model dynamics of the environment are not known in advance, unlike dynamic programming. We looked at the Monte Carlo prediction method, which is used for predicting value functions and control methods for further optimizing value functions. But there are some pitfalls with the Monte Carlo method. It is applied only for episodic tasks. If an episode is very long, then we have to wait a long time for computing value functions. So, we will use another interesting algorithm called **temporal-difference** (**TD**) learning, which is a model-free learning algorithm: it doesn't require the model dynamics to be known in advance and it can be applied for non-episodic tasks as well.

In this chapter, you will learn about:

- TD learning
- Q learning
- SARSA
- Taxi scheduling using Q learning and SARSA
- The difference between Q learning and SARSA

TD learning

The TD learning algorithm was introduced by Sutton in 1988. The algorithm takes the benefits of both the Monte Carlo method and **dynamic programming** (**DP**) into account. Like the Monte Carlo method, it doesn't require model dynamics, and like DP it doesn't need to wait until the end of the episode to make an estimate of the value function. Instead, it approximates the current estimate based on the previously learned estimate, which is also called bootstrapping. If you see in Monte Carlo methods there is no bootstrapping, we made an estimate only at the end of the episode but in TD methods we can bootstrap.

TD prediction

Like we did in Monte Carlo prediction, in TD prediction we try to predict the state values. In Monte Carlo prediction, we estimate the value function by simply taking the mean return. But in TD learning, we update the value of a previous state by current state. How can we do this? TD learning using something called a TD update rule for updating the value of a state, as follows:

$$V(s) = V(s) + \alpha(r + \gamma V(s') - V(s))$$

The value of a previous state = value of previous state + learning_rate (reward + discount_factor(value of current state) - value of previous state)

What does this equation actually mean?

If you think of this equation intuitively, it is actually the difference between the actual reward ($r + \gamma V(S')$) and the expected reward ($V(s)$) multiplied by the learning rate alpha. What does the learning rate signify? The learning rate, also called step size, is useful for convergence.

Did you notice? Since we take the difference between the actual and predicted value as $(r + \gamma V(S') - V(s)$, it is actually an error. We can call it a TD error. Over several iterations, we will try to minimize this error.

Let us understand TD prediction with the frozen lake example as we have seen in the previous chapters. The frozen lake environment is shown next. First, we will initialize the value function as *0*, as in *V(S)* as *0* for all states, as shown in the following state-value diagram:

Say we are in a starting state *(s)* **(1,1)** and we take an action right and move to the next state *(s')* **(1,2)** and receive a reward *(r)* as -0.3. How can we update the value of the state using this information?

Recall the TD update equation:

$$V(s) = V(s) + \alpha[r + \gamma(V(s') - V(s)]$$

Let us consider the learning rate (α) as *0.1* and the discount factor (γ) as *0.5*; we know that the value of the state **(1,1)**, as in *v(s)*, is 0 and the value of the next state **(1,2)**, as in *V(s')*, is also **0**. The reward *(r)* we obtained is -0.3. We substitute this in the TD rule as follows:

$$V(s) = 0 + 0.1\ [\ -0.3 + 0.5\ (0)\text{-}0]$$
$$v(s) = -\ 0.03$$

So, we update the value for the state **(1,1)** as **-0.03** in the value table, as shown in the following diagram:

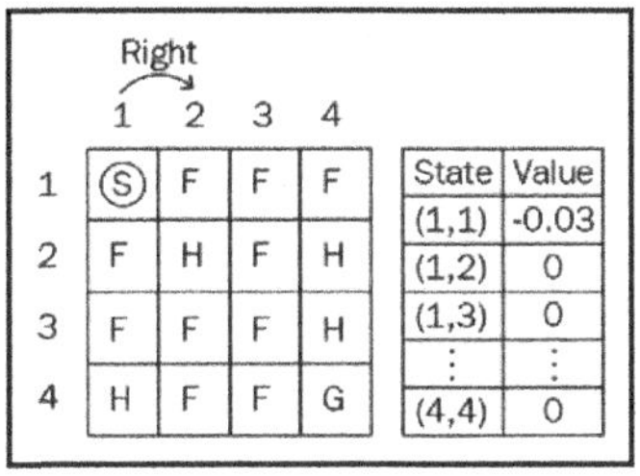

Now that we are in the state *(s)* as **(1,2)**, we take an action right and move to the next state *(s')* **(1,3)** and receive a reward *(r)* *-0.3*. How do we update the value of the state **(1, 2)** now?

Like we did previously, we will substitute the values in the TD update equation as:

$$V(s) = 0 + 0.1\ [\ -0.3 + 0.5(0)\text{-}0\ ]$$

$$V(s) = -0.03$$

So, we got the value of the state **(1,2)** as **-0.03** and we update that in the value table as shown here:

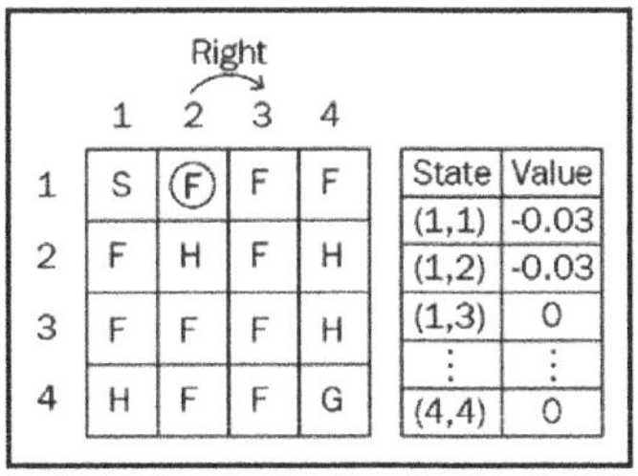

Now we are in the state *(s)* **(1,3)**; suppose we take an action left. We again go back to that state *(s')* **(1,2)** and we receive a reward *(r)* *-0.3*. Here, the value of the state **(1,3)** is **0** and the value of the next state **(1,2)** is **-0.03** in the value table.

Now we can update the value of state **(1,3)** as follows:

$$V(s) = 0 + 0.1 [-0.3 + 0.5 (-0.03)-0)]$$

$$V(s) = 0.1[-0.315]$$

$$V(s) = -0.0315$$

So, we update the value of state **(1,3)** as **-0.0315** in the value table, as shown here:

In a similar way, we update the value of all the states using the TD update rule. The steps involved in the TD-prediction algorithm are as follows:

1. First, we initialize $V(S)$ to 0 or some arbitrary values
2. Then we begin the episode and for every step in the episode, we perform an action A in the state S and receive a reward R and move to the next state (s')
3. Now, we update the value of the previous state using the TD update rule
4. We repeat steps 3 and 4 until we reach the terminal state

TD control

In TD prediction, we estimated the value function. In TD control, we optimize the value function. For TD control, we use two kinds of control algorithm:

- **Off-policy learning algorithm**: Q learning
- **On-policy learning algorithm**: SARSA

Q learning

We will now look into the very popular off-policy TD control algorithm called Q learning. Q learning is a very simple and widely used TD algorithm. In control algorithms, we don't care about state value; here, in Q learning, our concern is the state-action value pair—the effect of performing an action A in the state S.

We will update the Q value based on the following equation:

$$Q(s,a) = Q(s,a) + \alpha(r + \gamma max Q(s'a') - Q(s,a))$$

The preceding equation is similar to the TD prediction update rule with a little difference. We will see this in detail step by step. The steps involved in Q learning are as follows:

1. First, we initialize the Q function to some arbitrary values
2. We take an action from a state using epsilon-greedy policy ($\epsilon > 0$) and move it to the new state
3. We update the Q value of a previous state by following the update rule:

$$Q(s,a) = Q(s,a) + \alpha(r + \gamma max Q(s'a) - Q(s,a))$$

4. We repeat the steps 2 and 3 till we reach the terminal state

Now, we will understand the algorithm using different steps.

Consider the same frozen lake example. Let us say we are in a state (3,2) and have two actions (left and right). Now let us refer to the figure and compare it with epsilon-greedy policy:

In Q Learning, we select an action using the epsilon-greedy policy. We either explore a new action with the probability epsilon or we select the best action with a probability 1- epsilon. Let us say we select a probability epsilon and explore a new action **Down** and we select that action:

	1	2	3	4
1	S	F	F	F
2	F	H	F	H
3	F	(F)	F	H
4 Down	H	F	F	G

State	Action	Value
(3,2)	Left	0.1
(3,2)	Right	0.5
(3,2)	Down	0.8

Now that we have performed a downward action in the sate **(3,2)** and reached a new state **(4,2)** using the epsilon-greedy policy, how do we update the value of the previous state **(3,2)** using our update rule? It is very simple. Look at the *Q* table shown as following:

	1	2	3	4
1	S	F	F	F
2	F	H	F	H
3	F	(F)	F	H
4 Down	H	F	F	G

State	Action	Value
(3,2)	Left	0.1
(3,2)	Right	0.5
(3,2)	Down	0.8
(4,2)	Up	0.3
(4,2)	Down	0.5
(4,2)	Right	0.8

Let us consider alpha as *0.1* and the discount factor as *1*:

$$Q(s,a) = Q(s,a) + \alpha(r + \gamma max Q(s'a) - Q(s,a))$$

Q((3,2) down) = Q((3,2), down) + 0.1 (0.3 + 1 max [Q((4,2) action)]- Q((3,2), down)

We can say the value of a state **(3,2)** with a downward action, as in *Q((3,2), down)*, is **0.8** in the *Q* table.

What is max $Q((4,2), \text{action})$ for the state **(4,2)**? We have explored only three actions (**up**, **down**, and **right**) so we will take the maximum value only based on these actions. (Here, we will not perform epsilon greedy policy; we simply select the action that has the maximum value.)

So, based on the previous Q table, we can substitute the values as:

$$Q((3,2), down) = 0.8 + 0.1 (0.3 + 1 \max [0.3, 0.5, 0.8] - 0.8)$$

$$= 0.8 + 0.1 (0.3 + 1 (0.8) - 0.8)$$

$$= 0.83$$

So, we update the value of $Q((3,2), down)$ to *0.83*.

Remember that while choosing what action to take, we perform the epsilon-greedy policy: we either explore for new actions with a probability epsilon or take an action which has a maximum value with a probability 1-epsilon. While updating the Q value, we don't perform the epsilon-greedy policy, we simply select the action that has a maximum value.

Now that we are in a state (4,2), we have to perform an action. What action should we perform? We decide that based on the epsilon-greedy policy, we either explore a new action with a probability epsilon or select the best action with a probability *1-epsilon*. Let us say we select a probability *1-epsilon* and select the best action. So, in the **(4,2)** the action **right** has a maximum value. So we will select the **right** action:

	1	2	3	4
1	S	F	F	F
2	F	H	F	H
3	F	F	F	H
4	H	(F)	F	G

Right

State	Action	Value
(4,2)	Up	0.3
(4,2)	Down	0.5
(4,2)	Right	0.8

Now we are in a state **(4,3)** as we took a **right** action on the state **(4,2)**. How do we update the value of the previous state? Like so:

Q((4,2), right) = Q((4,2), right) + 0.1 (0.3 + 1 max [Q((4,3) action)]- Q((4,2), right)

If you look at the Q table that follows, for the state **(4,3)** we have explored only two actions (**up** and **down**) so we will take a maximum value only based on these actions. (Here, we will not perform an epsilon-greedy policy; we simply select the action which has maximum value):

Q ((4,2), right) = Q((4,2),right) + 0.1 (0.3 + 1 max [(Q (4,3), up) , (Q(4,3),down)] - Q ((4,2), right)

Q ((4,2), right) = 0.8 + 0.1 (0.3 + 1 max [0.1,0.3] - 0.8)

= 0.8 + 0.1 (0.3 + 1(0.3) - 0.8)

= 0.78

Look at the following Q table:

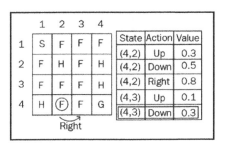

Now we update the value of the state *Q((4,2), right)* as *0.78.*

So, this is how we get the state-action values in Q learning. To decide what action to take, we use the epsilon-greedy policy and while updating the Q value we simply pick up the maximum action; here's a flowchart:

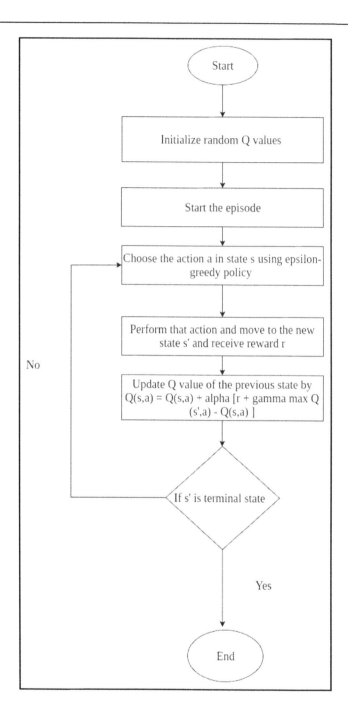

Solving the taxi problem using Q learning

To demonstrate the problem let's say our agent is the driver. There are four locations and the agent has to pick up a passenger at one location and drop them off at another. The agent will receive +20 points as a reward for successful drop off and -1 point for every time step it takes. The agent will also lose -10 points for illegal pickups and drops. So the goal of our agent is to learn to pick up and drop off passengers at the correct location in a short time without adding illegal passengers.

The environment is shown here, where the letters (**R**, **G**, **Y**, **B**) represent the different locations and a tiny rectangle is the agent driving the taxi:

Let's look at the coding part:

```
import gym
import random
```

Now we make our environment using a `gym`:

```
env = gym.make("Taxi-v1")
```

What does this taxi environment look like? Like so:

```
env.render()
```

Okay, first let us initialize our learning rate `alpha`, `epsilon` value, and `gamma`:

```
alpha = 0.4
gamma = 0.999
epsilon = 0.017
```

Then we initialize a Q table; it has a dictionary that stores the state-action value pair as (state, action):

```
q = {}
for s in range(env.observation_space.n):
    for a in range(env.action_space.n):
        q[(s,a)] = 0.0
```

We will define the function for updating the Q table via our Q learning update rule; if you look at the following function, you will see that we take the action that has a maximum value for the state-action pair and store it in a qa variable. Then we update the Q value of the previous state via our update rule, as in:

$$Q(s,a) = Q(s,a) + \alpha(r + \gamma maxQ(s'a') - Q(s,a))$$

```
def update_q_table(prev_state, action, reward, nextstate, alpha, gamma):
    qa = max([q[(nextstate, a)] for a in range(env.action_space.n)])
    q[(prev_state,action)] += alpha * (reward + gamma * qa -
q[(prev_state,action)])
```

Then, we define a function for performing the epsilon-greedy policy where we pass the state and epsilon value. We generate some random number in uniform distribution and if the number is less than the epsilon, we explore a different action in the state, or else we exploit the action that has a maximum q value:

```
def epsilon_greedy_policy(state, epsilon):
    if random.uniform(0,1) < epsilon:
        return env.action_space.sample()
    else:
        return max(list(range(env.action_space.n)), key = lambda x:
q[(state,x)])
```

We will see how to perform Q learning, putting together all these functions:

```
# For each episode
for i in range(8000):

    r = 0
    #first we initialize the environment

    prev_state = env.reset()
    while True:
        #In each state we select action by epsilon greedy policy
        action = epsilon_greedy_policy(prev_state, epsilon)
        #then we take the selected action and move to the next state
        nextstate, reward, done, _ = env.step(action)
        #and we update the q value using the update_q_table() function
        #which updates q table according to our update rule.

        update_q_table(prev_state, action, reward, nextstate, alpha, gamma)
        #then we update the previous state as next stat
        prev_state = nextstate

        #and store the rewards in r
        r += reward
```

```
        #If done i.e if we reached the terminal state of the episode
        #if break the loop and start the next episode
        if done:
            break

    print("total reward: ", r)

env.close()
```

The complete code is given here:

```
import random
import gym

env = gym.make('Taxi-v1')

alpha = 0.4
gamma = 0.999
epsilon = 0.017

q = {}
for s in range(env.observation_space.n):
 for a in range(env.action_space.n):
 q[(s,a)] = 0


def update_q_table(prev_state, action, reward, nextstate, alpha, gamma):
 qa = max([q[(nextstate, a)] for a in range(env.action_space.n)])
 q[(prev_state,action)] += alpha * (reward + gamma * qa -
 q[(prev_state,action)])

def epsilon_greedy_policy(state, epsilon):
 if random.uniform(0,1) < epsilon:
 return env.action_space.sample()
 else:
 return max(list(range(env.action_space.n)), key = lambda x: q[(state,x)])

for i in range(8000):
    r = 0
    prev_state = env.reset()
    while True:
        env.render()
        # In each state, we select the action by epsilon-greedy policy
        action = epsilon_greedy_policy(prev_state, epsilon)
        # then we perform the action and move to the next state, and
        # receive the reward
        nextstate, reward, done, _ = env.step(action)
        # Next we update the Q value using our update_q_table function
```

```
    # which updates the Q value by Q learning update rule
    update_q_table(prev_state, action, reward, nextstate, alpha, gamma)
    # Finally we update the previous state as next state
    prev_state = nextstate

    # Store all the rewards obtained
    r += reward

    #we will break the loop, if we are at the terminal
    #state of the episode
    if done:
        break

    print("total reward: ", r)

env.close()
```

SARSA

State-Action-Reward-State-Action (**SARSA**) is an on-policy TD control algorithm. Like we did in Q learning, here we also focus on state-action value instead of a state-value pair. In SARSA, we update the Q value based on the following update rule:

$$Q(s,a) = Q(s,a) + \alpha(r + \gamma Q(s'a') - Q(s,a))$$

In the preceding equation, you may notice that there is no max $Q(s',a')$, like there was in Q learning. Here it is simply $Q(s',a')$. We can understand this in detail by performing some steps. The steps involved in SARSA are as follows:

1. First, we initialize the Q values to some arbitrary values
2. We select an action by the epsilon-greedy policy ($\epsilon > 0$) and move from one state to another
3. We update the Q value previous state by following the update rule $Q(s,a) = Q(s,a) + \alpha(r + \gamma Q(s'a') - Q(s,a))$, where a' is the action selected by an epsilon-greedy policy ($\epsilon > 0$)

Now, we will understand the algorithm step by step. Let us consider the same frozen lake example. Let us say we are in state **(4,2)**. We decide the action based on the epsilon-greedy policy. Let us say we use a probability 1- epsilon and select the best action, which is **right**:

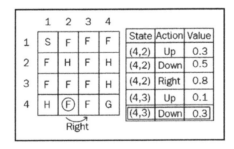

Now we are in state **(4,3)** after performing an action **right** in state **(4,2)**. How do we update a value of the previous state **(4,2)**? Let us consider the alpha as *0.1*, the reward as *0.3*, and discount factor *1*:

$$Q(s,a) = Q(s,a) + \alpha(r + \gamma Q(s'a') - Q(s,a))$$

Q((4,2), right) = Q((4,2),right) + 0.1 (0.3 + 1 Q((4,3), action)) - Q((4,2) , right)

How do we choose the value for *Q (4,3), action)*? Here, unlike in Q learning, we don't just pick up max (*Q(4,3), action)*. In SARSA, we use the epsilon-greedy policy.

Look at the Q table that follows. In state **(4,3)** we have explored two actions. Unlike Q learning, we don't select the maximum action directly as down:

	1	2	3	4		State	Action	Value
1	S	F	F	F		(4,2)	Up	0.3
2	F	H	F	H		(4,2)	Down	0.5
3	F	F	F	H		(4,2)	Right	0.8
4	H	(F)	F	G		(4,3)	Up	0.1
		Right				(4,3)	Down	0.3

We follow the epsilon-greedy policy here as well. We either explore with a probability epsilon or exploit with a probability 1-epsilon. Let us say we select probability epsilon and explore a new action. We explore a new action, **right**, and select that action:

	1	2	3	4		State	Action	Value
1	S	F	F	F		(4,2)	Up	0.3
						(4,2)	Down	0.5
2	F	H	F	H		(4,2)	Right	0.8
3	F	F	F	H		(4,3)	Up	0.1
						(4,3)	Down	0.3
4	H	(F)	F	G		(4,3)	Right	0.9

Right

$$Q\,(\,(4,2),\,right) = Q((4,2),right) + 0.1\,(0.3 + 1\,(Q\,(4,3),\,right) - Q\,((4,2),\,right\,)$$

$$Q\,(\,(4,2),\,right) = 0.8 + 0.1\,(0.3 + 1(0.9) - 0.8)$$

$$= 0.8 + 0.1\,(0.3 + 1(0.9) - 0.8)$$

$$= 0.84$$

So, this is how we get the state-action values in SARSA. We take the action using the epsilon-greedy policy and also, while updating the Q value, we pick up the action using the epsilon-greedy policy.

The following diagram explains the SARSA algorithm:

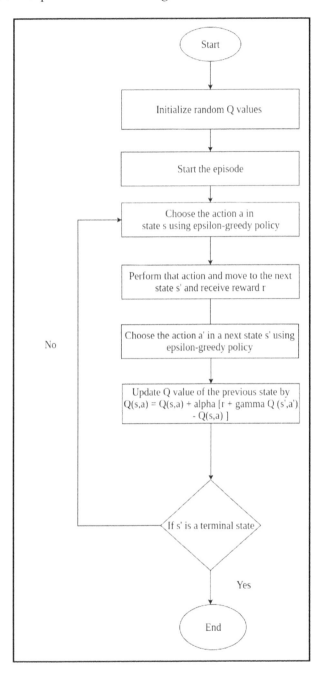

Solving the taxi problem using SARSA

Now we will solve the same taxi problem using SARSA:

```
import gym
import random
env = gym.make('Taxi-v1')
```

Also, we will initialize the learning rate, `gamma`, and `epsilon`. Q table has a dictionary:

```
alpha = 0.85
gamma = 0.90
epsilon = 0.8

Q = {}
for s in range(env.observation_space.n):
    for a in range(env.action_space.n):
        Q[(s,a)] = 0.0
```

As usual, we define an `epsilon_greedy` policy for exploration:

```
def epsilon_greedy(state, epsilon):
    if random.uniform(0,1) < epsilon:
        return env.action_space.sample()
    else:
        return max(list(range(env.action_space.n)), key = lambda x:
Q[(state,x)])
```

Now, the actual SARSA algorithm comes in:

```
for i in range(4000):
    #We store cumulative reward of each episodes in r
    r = 0
    #Then for every iterations, we initialize the state,
    state = env.reset()
    #then we pick up the action using epsilon greedy policy
    action = epsilon_greedy(state,epsilon)
    while True:
        #Then we perform the action in the state and move the next state
        nextstate, reward, done, _ = env.step(action)
        #Then we pick up the next action using epsilon greedy policy
        nextaction = epsilon_greedy(nextstate,epsilon)
        #we calculate Q value of the previous state using our update rule
        Q[(state,action)] += alpha * (reward + gamma *
Q[(nextstate,nextaction)]-Q[(state,action)])
```

```
        #finally we update our state and action with next action
        # and next state
        action = nextaction
        state = nextstate
        r += reward
        #we will break the loop, if we are at the terminal
        #state of the episode
        if done:
            break


    env.close()
```

You can run the program and see how SARSA is finding the optimal path.

The full program is given here:

```
#Like we did in Q learning, we import necessary libraries and initialize
environment

import gym
import random
env = gym.make('Taxi-v1')

alpha = 0.85
gamma = 0.90
epsilon = 0.8

#Then we initialize Q table as dictionary for storing the state-action
values
Q = {}
for s in range(env.observation_space.n):
    for a in range(env.action_space.n):
        Q[(s,a)] = 0.0

#Now, we define a function called epsilon_greedy for performing action
#according epsilon greedy policy
def epsilon_greedy(state, epsilon):
    if random.uniform(0,1) < epsilon:
        return env.action_space.sample()
    else:
        return max(list(range(env.action_space.n)), key = lambda x:
Q[(state,x)])
```

```
for i in range(4000):
    #We store cumulative reward of each episodes in
    r = 0
    #Then for every iterations, we initialize the state,
    state = env.reset()
    #then we pick up the action using epsilon greedy policy
    action = epsilon_greedy(state,epsilon)
    while True:
        #Then we perform the action in the state and move the next state
        nextstate, reward, done, _ = env.step(action)
        #Then we pick up the next action using epsilon greedy policy
        nextaction = epsilon_greedy(nextstate,epsilon)
        #we calculate Q value of the previous state using our update rule
        Q[(state,action)] += alpha * (reward + gamma *
Q[(nextstate,nextaction)]-Q[(state,action)])

        #finally we update our state and action with next action
        #and next state
        action = nextaction
        state = nextstate
        r += reward
        #we will break the loop, if we are at the terminal
        #state of the episode
        if done:
            break


env.close()
```

The difference between Q learning and SARSA

Q learning and SARSA will always be confusing for many folks. Let us break down the differences between these two. Look at the flowchart here:

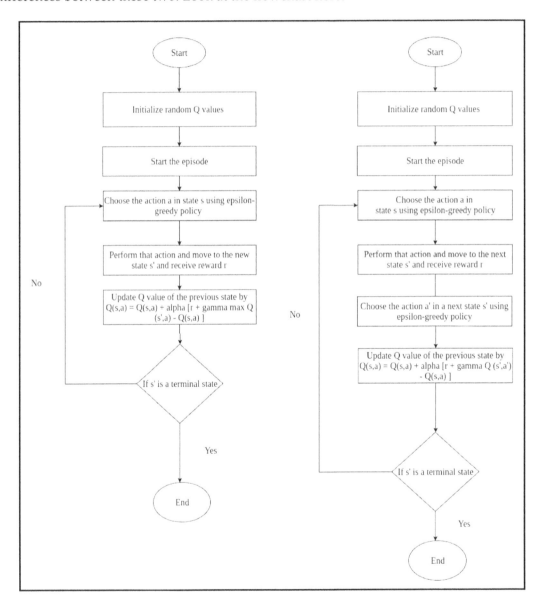

Can you spot the difference? In Q learning, we take action using an epsilon-greedy policy and, while updating the Q value, we simply pick up the maximum action. In SARSA, we take the action using the epsilon-greedy policy and also, while updating the Q value, we pick up the action using the epsilon-greedy policy.

Summary

In this chapter, we learned a different model-free learning algorithm that overcame the limitations of the Monte Carlo methods. We saw both prediction and control methods. In TD prediction, we updated the state-value of a state based on the next state. In terms of the control methods, we saw two different algorithms: Q learning and SARSA.

Questions

The question list is as follows:

1. How does TD learning differ from the Monte Carlo method?
2. What exactly is a TD error?
3. What is the difference between TD prediction and control?
4. How to build an intelligent agent using Q learning?
5. What is the difference between Q learning and SARSA?

Further reading

Sutton's original TD paper: https://pdfs.semanticscholar.org/9c06/865e912788a6a51470724e087853d72691 95.pdf

6

Multi-Armed Bandit Problem

In the previous chapters, we have learned about fundamental concepts of **reinforcement learning** (**RL**) and several RL algorithms, as well as how RL problems can be modeled as the **Markov Decision Process** (**MDP**). We have also seen different model-based and model-free algorithms that are used to solve the MDP. In this chapter, we will see one of the classical problems in RL called the **multi-armed bandit** (**MAB**) problem. We will see what the MAB problem is and how to solve the problem with different algorithms followed by how to identify the correct advertisement banner that will receive most of the clicks using MAB. We will also learn about contextual bandit that is widely used for building recommendation systems.

In the chapter, you will learn about the following:

- The MAB problem
- The epsilon-greedy algorithm
- The softmax exploration algorithm
- The upper confidence bound algorithm
- The Thompson sampling algorithm
- Applications of MAB
- Identifying the right advertisement banner using MAB
- Contextual bandits

The MAB problem

The MAB problem is one of the classical problems in RL. An MAB is actually a slot machine, a gambling game played in a casino where you pull the arm (lever) and get a payout (reward) based on a randomly generated probability distribution. A single slot machine is called a one-armed bandit and, when there are multiple slot machines it is called multi-armed bandits or k-armed bandits.

MABs are shown as follows:

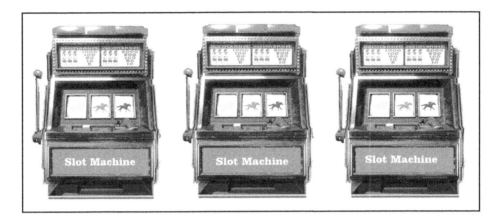

As each slot machine gives us the reward from its own probability distribution, our goal is to find out which slot machine will give us the maximum cumulative reward over a sequence of time. So, at each time step t, the agent performs an action a_t, that is, pulls an arm from the slot machine and receives a reward r_t, and the goal of our agent is to maximize the cumulative reward.

We define the value of an arm $Q(a)$ as average rewards received by pulling the arm:

$$Q(a) = \frac{Sum\,of\,rewards\,received\,from\,the\,arm}{Total\,number\,of\,times\,the\,arm\,was\,pulled}$$

So the optimal arm is the one that gives us the maximum cumulative reward, that is:

$$Q(a^*) = Max\,Q(a)$$

The goal of our agent is to find the optimal arm and also to minimize the regret, which can be defined as the cost of knowing which of the k arms is optimal. Now, how do we find the best arm? Should we explore all the arms or choose the arm that already gave us a maximum cumulative reward? Here comes the exploration-exploitation dilemma. Now we will see how to solve this dilemma using various exploration strategies as follows:

- Epsilon-greedy policy
- Softmax exploration
- Upper confidence bound algorithm
- Thomson sampling technique

Before going ahead, let us install `bandit` environments in the OpenAI Gym; you can install the `bandit` environment by typing the following command in your Terminal:

```
git clone https://github.com/JKCooper2/gym-bandits.git
cd gym-bandits
pip install -e .
```

After installing, let us import `gym` and `gym_bandits`:

```
import gym_bandits
import gym
```

Now we will initialize the environment; we use an MAB with ten arms:

```
env = gym.make("BanditTenArmedGaussian-v0")
```

Our action space will be 10, as we have 10 arms:

```
env.action_space
```

The output is as follows:

```
10
```

The epsilon-greedy policy

We have already learned a lot about the epsilon-greedy policy. In the epsilon-greedy policy, either we select the best arm with a probability 1-epsilon or we select the arms at random with a probability epsilon:

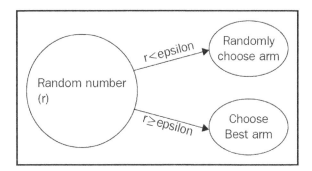

Now we will see how to select the best arm using the epsilon-greedy policy:

1. First, let us initialize all variables:

```
# number of rounds (iterations)
num_rounds = 20000

# Count of number of times an arm was pulled
count = np.zeros(10)

# Sum of rewards of each arm
sum_rewards = np.zeros(10)

# Q value which is the average reward
Q = np.zeros(10)
```

2. Now we define our `epsilon_greedy` function:

```
def epsilon_greedy(epsilon):
    rand = np.random.random()
    if rand < epsilon:
        action = env.action_space.sample()
    else:
        action = np.argmax(Q)
    return action
```

3. Start pulling the arm:

```
for i in range(num_rounds):
    # Select the arm using epsilon greedy
    arm = epsilon_greedy(0.5)
    # Get the reward
    observation, reward, done, info = env.step(arm)
    # update the count of that arm
    count[arm] += 1
    # Sum the rewards obtained from the arm
    sum_rewards[arm]+=reward
    # calculate Q value which is the average rewards of the arm
    Q[arm] = sum_rewards[arm]/count[arm]

print( 'The optimal arm is {}'.format(np.argmax(Q)))
```

The following is the output:

```
The optimal arm is 3
```

The softmax exploration algorithm

Softmax exploration, also known as Boltzmann exploration, is another strategy used for finding an optimal bandit. In the epsilon-greedy policy, we consider all of the non-best arms equivalently, but in softmax exploration, we select an arm based on a probability from the Boltzmann distribution. The probability of selecting an arm is given by:

$$P_t(a) = \frac{exp(Q_t(a)/\tau)}{\sum_{i=1}^{n} exp(Q_t(i)/\tau)}$$

τ is called a temperature factor, which specifies how many random arms we can explore. When τ is high, all arms will be explored equally, but when τ is low, high-rewarding arms will be chosen. Look at the following steps:

1. First, initialize the variables:

```
# number of rounds (iterations)
num_rounds = 20000

# Count of number of times an arm was pulled
count = np.zeros(10)

# Sum of rewards of each arm
sum_rewards = np.zeros(10)

# Q value which is the average reward
Q = np.zeros(10)
```

2. Now we define the `softmax` function:

```
def softmax(tau):
    total = sum([math.exp(val/tau) for val in Q])
    probs = [math.exp(val/tau)/total for val in Q]
    threshold = random.random()
    cumulative_prob = 0.0
    for i in range(len(probs)):
        cumulative_prob += probs[i]
        if (cumulative_prob > threshold):
            return i
    return np.argmax(probs)
```

3. Start pulling the `arm`:

```
for i in range(num_rounds):
    # Select the arm using softmax
    arm = softmax(0.5)
    # Get the reward
    observation, reward, done, info = env.step(arm)
    # update the count of that arm
    count[arm] += 1
    # Sum the rewards obtained from the arm
    sum_rewards[arm]+=reward
    # calculate Q value which is the average rewards of the arm
    Q[arm] = sum_rewards[arm]/count[arm]
print( 'The optimal arm is {}'.format(np.argmax(Q)))
```

The following is the output:

```
The optimal arm is 3
```

The upper confidence bound algorithm

With epsilon-greedy and softmax exploration, we explore random actions with a probability; the random action is useful for exploring various arms, but it might also lead us to try out actions that will not give us a good reward at all. We also don't want to miss out arms that are actually good but give poor rewards in the initial rounds. So we use a new algorithm called the **upper confidence bound** (UCB). It is based on the principle called optimism in the face of uncertainty.

The UCB algorithm helps us in selecting the best arm based on a confidence interval. Okay, what is a confidence interval? Let us say we have two arms. We pull both of these arms and find that arm one gives us 0.3 rewards and arm two gives us 0.8 rewards. But with one round of pulling the arms, we should not come to the conclusion that arm two will give us the best reward. We have to try pulling the arms several times and take the mean value of rewards obtained by each arm and select the arm whose mean is highest. But how can we find the correct mean value for each of these arms? Here is where the confidence interval comes into the picture. The confidence interval specifies the interval within which the mean reward value of arms lies. If the confidence interval of arm one is *[0.2, 0.9]*, it implies that the mean value of arm one lies within this interval, 0.2 to 0.9. 0.2 is called the lower confidence bound and 0.9 is called the UCB. The UCB selects a machine that has a high UCB to explore.

Let us say we have three slot machines and we have played each of the slot machines ten times. The confidence intervals of these three slot machines are shown in the following diagram:

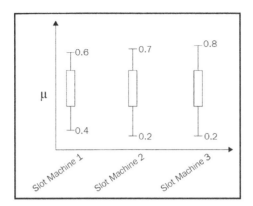

We can see that **slot machine 3** has a high UCB. But we should not come to the conclusion that **slot machine 3** will give us a good reward by just pulling ten times. Once we pull the arms several times, our confidence interval will be accurate. So, over time, the confidence interval becomes narrow and shrinks to an actual value, as shown in the next diagram. So now, we can select **slot machine 2**, which has a high UCB:

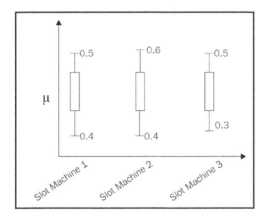

The idea behind UCB is very simple:

1. Select the action (arm) that has a high sum of average reward and upper confidence bound
2. Pull the arm and receive a reward
3. Update the arm's reward and confidence bound

But how do we calculate UCB?

We can calculate UCB using the formula $\sqrt{\frac{2log(t)}{N(a)}}$ where $N(a)$ is the number of times the arm was pulled and t is the total number of rounds.

So, in UCB, we select an arm with the following formula:

$$Arm = argmax_a [Q(a) + \sqrt{\frac{2log(t)}{N(a)}}]$$

First, initialize the variables:

```
# number of rounds (iterations)
num_rounds = 20000

# Count of number of times an arm was pulled
count = np.zeros(10)

# Sum of rewards of each arm
sum_rewards = np.zeros(10)

# Q value which is the average reward
Q = np.zeros(10)
```

Now, let us define our UCB function:

```
def UCB(iters):
    ucb = np.zeros(10)
    #explore all the arms
    if iters < 10:
        return i
    else:
        for arm in range(10):
            # calculate upper bound
            upper_bound = math.sqrt((2*math.log(sum(count))) / count[arm])
            # add upper bound to the Q value
            ucb[arm] = Q[arm] + upper_bound
        # return the arm which has maximum value
        return (np.argmax(ucb))
```

Let us start pulling the arms:

```
for i in range(num_rounds):
    # Select the arm using UCB
    arm = UCB(i)
    # Get the reward
    observation, reward, done, info = env.step(arm)
    # update the count of that arm
    count[arm] += 1
    # Sum the rewards obtained from the arm
    sum_rewards[arm]+=reward
    # calculate Q value which is the average rewards of the arm
    Q[arm] = sum_rewards[arm]/count[arm]
print( 'The optimal arm is {}'.format(np.argmax(Q)))
```

The output is as follows:

```
The optimal arm is 1
```

The Thompson sampling algorithm

Thompson sampling (TS) is another popularly used algorithm to overcome the exploration-exploitation dilemma. It is a probabilistic algorithm and is based on a prior distribution. The strategy behind TS is very simple: first, we calculate prior on the mean rewards for each of the k arms, that is, we take some n samples from each of the k arms and calculate k distributions. These initial distributions will not be the same as the true distribution, so we call it prior distribution:

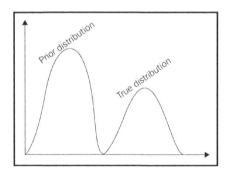

Since we have Bernoulli rewards, we use beta distribution for calculating the prior. The value of beta distribution [alpha, beta] lies within the interval [0,1]. Alpha represents the number of times we receive the positive rewards and beta represents the number of times we receive the negative rewards.

Now we will see how TS helps us in selecting the best arm. The steps involved in TS are as follows:

1. Sample a value from each of the *k* distributions and use this value as a prior mean.
2. Select the arm that has the highest prior mean and observes the reward.
3. Use the observed reward to modify the prior distribution.

So, after several rounds, a prior distribution will start resembling the true distribution:

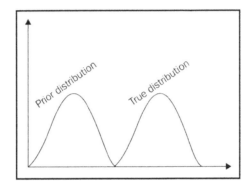

We shall better understand TS by implementing it in Python. First, let us initialize the variables:

```
# number of rounds (iterations)
num_rounds = 20000

# Count of number of times an arm was pulled
count = np.zeros(10)

# Sum of rewards of each arm
sum_rewards = np.zeros(10)

# Q value which is the average reward
Q = np.zeros(10)

# initialize alpha and beta values
alpha = np.ones(10)
beta = np.ones(10)
```

Define our `thompson_sampling` function:

```
def thompson_sampling(alpha,beta):
    samples = [np.random.beta(alpha[i]+1,beta[i]+1) for i in range(10)]

    return np.argmax(samples)
```

Start playing with the bandits using TS:

```
for i in range(num_rounds):

    # Select the arm using thompson sampling
    arm = thompson_sampling(alpha,beta)

    # Get the reward
    observation, reward, done, info = env.step(arm)

    # update the count of that arm
    count[arm] += 1

    # Sum the rewards obtained from the arm
    sum_rewards[arm]+=reward

    # calculate Q value which is the average rewards of the arm
    Q[arm] = sum_rewards[arm]/count[arm]

    # If it is a positive reward increment alpha
    if reward >0:
    alpha[arm] += 1

    # If it is a negative reward increment beta
    else:
    beta[arm] += 1

    print( 'The optimal arm is {}'.format(np.argmax(Q)))
```

The output is as follows:

```
The optimal arm is 3
```

Applications of MAB

So far, we have looked at the MAB problem and how we can solve it using various exploration strategies. But bandits are not just used for playing slot machines; they have many applications.

Bandits are used as a replacement for AB testing. AB testing is one of the commonly used classical methods of testing. Say you have two versions of the landing page of your website. How do you know which version is liked by most of the users? You conduct an AB test to understand which version is most liked by users.

In AB testing, we allocate a separate time for exploration and a separate time for exploitation. That is, it has two different dedicated periods only for exploration and exploitation alone. But the problem with this method is that this will incur a lot of regrets. So, we can minimize the regret using various exploration strategies that we use to solve MAB. Instead of performing complete exploration and exploitation separately with bandits, we perform both exploration and exploitation simultaneously in an adaptive fashion.

Bandits are widely used for website optimization, maximizing conversion rate, online advertisements, campaigning, and so on. Consider you are running a short-term campaign. If you perform AB testing here, then you will spend almost all of your time on exploring and exploitation alone, so in this case, using bandits would be very useful.

Identifying the right advertisement banner using MAB

Let us say you are running a website and you have five different banners for the same ad, and you want to know which banner attracts the user. We model this problem statement as a bandit problem. Let us say these five banners are the five arms of the bandit and we award one point if the user clicks the ad and award zero if the user does not click the ad.

In normal A/B testing, we will perform a complete exploration of all these five banners before deciding which banner is the best. But that will cost us a lot of energy and time. Instead, we will use a good exploration strategy for deciding which banner will give us the most rewards (most clicks).

First, let us import the necessary libraries:

```
import pandas as pd
import numpy as np
import matplotlib.pyplot as plt
import seaborn as sns
%matplotlib inline
```

Let us simulate a dataset with 5 x 10,000 as the shape, where the column is the `Banner_type` ad and the rows are either `0` or `1`, that is, whether the ad has been clicked (`1`) or not clicked (`0`) by the user respectively:

```
df = pd.DataFrame()
df['Banner_type_0'] = np.random.randint(0,2,100000)
df['Banner_type_1'] = np.random.randint(0,2,100000)
df['Banner_type_2'] = np.random.randint(0,2,100000)
df['Banner_type_3'] = np.random.randint(0,2,100000)
df['Banner_type_4'] = np.random.randint(0,2,100000)
```

Let us view a few rows of our data:

```
df.head()
```

	Banner_type_0	Banner_type_1	Banner_type_2	Banner_type_3	Banner_type_4
0	1	1	0	1	1
1	0	1	1	1	0
2	1	1	0	0	1
3	0	0	0	0	1
4	0	1	1	1	1
5	0	1	1	0	1
6	1	0	0	1	1
7	0	1	1	0	1
8	0	0	1	0	1
9	0	0	0	1	0

```
num_banner = 5
no_of_iterations = 100000
banner_selected = []
count = np.zeros(num_banner)
Q = np.zeros(num_banner)
sum_rewards = np.zeros(num_banner)
```

Define an epsilon-greedy policy:

```
def epsilon_greedy(epsilon):
    random_value = np.random.random()
    choose_random = random_value < epsilon
    if choose_random:
        action = np.random.choice(num_banner)
    else:
```

```
        action = np.argmax(Q)
    return action

for i in range(no_of_iterations):
    banner = epsilon_greedy(0.5)
    reward = df.values[i, banner]
    count[banner] += 1
    sum_rewards[banner]+=reward
    Q[banner] = sum_rewards[banner]/count[banner]
    banner_selected.append(banner)
```

We can plot the results and see which banner gives us the maximum number of clicks:

```
sns.distplot(banner_selected)
```

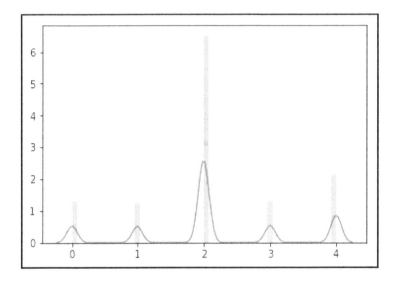

Contextual bandits

We just saw how bandits are used for recommending the correct ad banner to the user. But the banner preference varies from user to user. User A likes banner type 1, but user B might like banner type 3. So we have to personalize ad banners according to user behavior. How can we do that? We introduce a new bandit type called contextual bandits.

In a normal MABs problem, we perform the action and receive a reward. But with contextual bandits, instead of just taking the actions alone, we take the environment state as well. The state holds the context. Here, the state specifies the user behaviors, so we will take actions (show ads) according to the state (user behavior) that will result in a maximum reward (ad clicks). Thus, contextual bandits are widely used for personalizing content according to the user's preference behavior. They are used to solve cold-start problems faced in recommendation systems. Netflix uses contextual bandits for personalizing artwork for TV shows according to user behavior.

Summary

In this chapter, we have learned about the MAB problem and how it can be applied to different applications. We understood several methods to solve an explore-exploit dilemma. First, we looked at the epsilon-greedy policy, where we explored with the probability epsilon, and carried out exploration with the probability 1-epsilon. We looked at the UCB algorithm, where we picked up the best action with the maximum upper bound value, followed by the TS algorithm, where we picked up the best action via beta distribution.

In the upcoming chapters, we will learn about deep learning and how deep learning is used to solve RL problems.

Questions

The question list is as follows:

1. What is an MAB problem?
2. What is an explore-exploit dilemma?
3. What is the significance of epsilon in the epsilon-greedy policy?
4. How do we solve an explore-exploit dilemma?
5. What is a UCB algorithm?
6. How does Thompson sampling differ from the UCB algorithm?

Further reading

You can also refer to these links:

- **Contextual bandits for personalization**: https://www.microsoft.com/en-us/research/blog/contextual-bandit-breakthrough-enables-deeper-personalization/
- **How Netflix uses contextual bandits**: https://medium.com/netflix-techblog/artwork-personalization-c589f074ad76
- **Collaborative filtering using MAB**: https://arxiv.org/pdf/1708.03058.pdf

Playing Atari Games

an a machine learn how to play video games by itself and beat human players? Solving this problem is the first step toward general **artificial intelligence** (**AI**) in the field of gaming. The key technique to creating an AI player is **deep reinforcement learning**. In 2015, Google's DeepMind, one of the foremost AI/machine learning research teams (who are famous for building AlphaGo, the machine that beat Go champion Lee Sedol) proposed the deep Q-learning algorithm to build an AI player that can learn to play Atari 2600 games, and surpass a human expert on several games. This work made a great impact on AI research, showing the possibility of building general AI systems.

In this chapter, we will introduce how to use gym to play Atari 2600 games, and then explain why the deep Q-learning algorithm works and how to implement it using TensorFlow. The goal is to be able to understand deep reinforcement learning algorithms and how to apply them to solve real tasks. This chapter will be a solid foundation to understanding later chapters, where we will be introducing more complex methods.

The topics that we will cover in this chapter are as follows:

- Introduction to Atari games
- Deep Q-learning
- Implementation of DQN

Introduction to Atari games

Atari, Inc. was an American video game developer and home computer company founded in 1972 by Nolan Bushnell and Ted Dabney. In 1976, Bushnell developed the Atari video computer system, or Atari VCS (later renamed Atari 2600). Atari VCS was a flexible console that was capable of playing the existing Atari games, which included a console, two joysticks, a pair of paddles, and the combat game cartridge. The following screenshot depicts an Atari console:

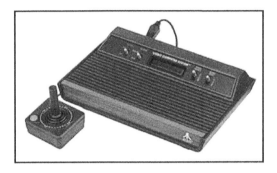

Atari 2600 has more than 500 games that were published by Atari, Sears, and some third parties. Some famous games are Breakout, Pac-Man, Pitfall!, Atlantis, Seaquest, and Space Invaders.

As a direct result of the North American video game crash of 1983, Atari, Inc. was closed and its properties were split in 1984. The home computing and game console divisions of Atari were sold to Jack Tramiel under the name Atari corporation in July 1984.

For readers who are interested in playing Atari games, here are several online Atari 2600 emulator websites where you can find many popular Atari 2600 games:

- http://www.2600online.com/

- http://www.free80sarcade.com/all2600games.php

- http://www.retrogames.cz/index.php

Because our goal is to develop an AI player for these games, it is better to play with them first and understand their difficulties. The most important thing is to: relax and have fun!

Building an Atari emulator

OpenAI gym provides an Atari 2600 game environment with a Python interface. The games are simulated by the arcade learning environment, which uses the Stella Atari emulator. For more details, read the following papers:

- MG Bellemare, Y Naddaf, J Veness, and M Bowling, *The arcade learning environment: An evaluation platform for general agents*, journal of Artificial Intelligence Research (2012)
- Stella: A Multi-Platform Atari 2600 VCS emulator, `http://stella.sourceforge.net/`

Getting started

If you don't have a full install of OpenAI `gym`, you can install the Atari environment dependencies via the following:

```
pip install gym[atari]
```

This requires the `cmake` tools. This command will automatically compile the arcade learning environment and its Python interface, `atari-py`. The compilation will take a few minutes on a common laptop, so go have a cup of coffee.

After the Atari environment is installed, try the following:

```
import gym
atari = gym.make('Breakout-v0')
atari.reset()
atari.render()
```

If it runs successfully, a small window will pop up, showing the screen of the game `Breakout`, as shown in the following screenshot:

The meaning of the v0 suffix in the `Breakout` rom name will be explained later. We will use `Breakout` to test our algorithm for training an AI game player. In `Breakout`, several layers of bricks lie on the top of the screen. A ball travels across the screen, bouncing off the top and side walls of the screen. When a brick is hitted, the ball bounces away and the brick is destroyed, giving the player several points according to the color of the brick. The player loses a turn when the ball touches the bottom of the screen. In order to prevent this from happening, the player has to move the paddle to bounce the ball back.

Atari VCS uses a joystick as the input device for controlling Atari 2600 games. The total number of inputs that a joystick and a paddle can make is 18. In the `gym` Atari environment, these actions are labeled as the integers ranged from 0 to 17. The meaning of each action is as follows:

0	1	2	3	4	5
NO OPERATION	FIRE	UP	RIGHT	LEFT	DOWN
6	7	8	9	10	11
UP+RIGHT	UP+LEFT	DOWN+RIGHT	DOWN+LEFT	UP+FIRE	RIGHT+FIRE
12	13	14	15	16	17
LEFT+FIRE	DOWN+FIRE	UP+RIGHT+FIRE	UP+LEFT+FIRE	DOWN+RIGHT+FIRE	DOWN+LEFT+FIRE

One can use the following code to get the meanings of the valid actions for a game:

```
actions = atari.env.get_action_meanings()
```

For `Breakout`, the actions include the following:

```
[0, 1, 3, 4] or ['NOOP', 'FIRE', 'RIGHT', 'LEFT']
```

To get the number of the actions, one can also use the following:

```
num_actions = atari.env.action_space.n
```

Here, the member variable, `action_space`, in `atari.env` stores all the information about the valid actions for a game. Typically, we only need to know the total number of valid actions.

We now know how to access the action information in the Atari environment. But, how do you control the game given these actions? To take an action, one can call the `step` function:

```
observation, reward, done, info = atari.step(a)
```

The input argument, `a`, is the action you want to execute, which is the index in the valid action list. For example, if one wants to take the `LEFT` action, the input should be `3` not `4`, or if one takes no action, the input should be `0`. The `step` function returns one of the following four values:

- `Observation`: An environment-specific object representing your observation of the environment. For Atari, it is the screen image of the frame after the action is executed.
- `Reward`: The amount of reward achieved by the action.
- `Done`: Whether it's time to reset the environment again. In Atari, if you lost your last life, `done` will be true, otherwise it is false.
- `Info`: Diagnostic information useful for debugging. It is not allowed to use this information in the learning algorithm, so usually we can ignore it.

Implementation of the Atari emulator

We are now ready to build a simple Atari emulator using gym. As with other computer games, the keyboard input used to control Atari games is as shown here:

w	a	s	d	space
UP	LEFT	DOWN	RIGHT	FIRE

To detect the keyboard inputs, we use the `pynput.keyboard` package, which allows us to control and monitor the keyboard (http://pythonhosted.org/pynput/). If the `pynput` package is not installed, run the following:

```
pip install pynput
```

`pynput.keyboard` provides a keyboard listener used to capture keyboard events. Before creating a keyboard listener, the `Listener` class should be imported:

```
import gym
import queue, threading, time
from pynput.keyboard import Key, Listener
```

Besides the `Listener` class, the other packages, such as `gym` and `threading`, are also necessary in this program.

The following code shows how to use `Listener` to capture keyboard inputs, that is, where one of the *w*, *a*, *s*, *d*, and *space* keys is pressed:

```
def keyboard(queue):
    def on_press(key):
        if key == Key.esc:
            queue.put(-1)
        elif key == Key.space:
            queue.put(ord(' '))
        else:
            key = str(key).replace("'", '')
            if key in ['w', 'a', 's', 'd']:
                queue.put(ord(key))

    def on_release(key):
        if key == Key.esc:
            return False

    with Listener(on_press=on_press, on_release=on_release) as listener:
        listener.join()
```

Actually, a keyboard listener is a Python `threading.Thread` object, and all callbacks will be invoked from the thread. In the `keyboard` function, the listener registers two callbacks: `on_press`, which is invoked when a key is pressed and `on_release` invoked when a key is released. This function uses a synchronized queue to share data between different threads. When *w*, *a*, *s*, *d*, or *space* is pressed, its ASCII value is sent to the queue, which can be accessed from another thread. If *esc* is pressed, a termination signal, –, is sent to the queue. Then, the listener thread stops when *esc* is released.

Starting a keyboard listener has some restrictions on macOS X; that is, one of the following should be true:

- The process must run as root
- The application must be white-listed under enable access for assistive devices

For more information, visit `https://pythonhosted.org/pynput/keyboard.html`.

Atari simulator using gym

The other part of the emulator is the `gym` Atari simulator:

```
def start_game(queue):
    atari = gym.make('Breakout-v0')
    key_to_act = atari.env.get_keys_to_action()
    key_to_act = {k[0]: a for k, a in key_to_act.items() if len(k) > 0}
    observation = atari.reset()
    import numpy
    from PIL import Image
    img = numpy.dot(observation, [0.2126, 0.7152, 0.0722])
    img = cv2_resize_image(img)
    img = Image.fromarray(img)
    img.save('save/{}.jpg'.format(0))
    while True:
        atari.render()
        action = 0 if queue.empty() else queue.get(block=False)
        if action == -1:
            break
        action = key_to_act.get(action, 0)
        observation, reward, done, _ = atari.step(action)
        if action != 0:
            print("Action {}, reward {}".format(action, reward))
        if done:
            print("Game finished")
            break
        time.sleep(0.05)
```

The first step is to create an `Atari` environment using `gym.make`. If you are interested in playing other games such as Seaquest or Pitfall, just change Breakout-v0 to Seaquest-v0 or `Pitfall-v0`. Then, `get_keys_to_action` is called to get the `key to action` mapping, which maps the ASCII values of *w*, *a*, *s*, *d*, and *space* to internal actions. Before the Atari simulator starts, the `reset` function must be called to reset the game parameters and memory, returning the first game screen image. In the main loop, `render` is called to render the Atari game at each step. The input action is pulled from the queue without blocking. If the action is the termination signal, -1, the game quits. Otherwise, this action is taken at the current step by running `atari.step`.

To start the emulator, run the following code:

```
if __name__ == "__main__":
    queue = queue.Queue(maxsize=10)
    game = threading.Thread(target=start_game, args=(queue,))
    game.start()
    keyboard(queue)
```

Press the **fire** button to start the game and enjoy it! This emulator provides a basic framework for testing AI algorithms on the `gym` Atari environment. Later, we will replace the `keyboard` function with our AI player.

Data preparation

Careful readers may notice that a suffix, v0, follows each game name, and come up with the following questions: *What is the meaning of v0? Is it allowable to replace it with v1 or v2?* Actually, this suffix has a relationship with the data preprocessing step for the screen images (observations) extracted from the Atari environment.

There are three modes for each game, for example, Breakout, BreakoutDeterministic, and BreakoutNoFrameskip, and each mode has two versions, for example, Breakout-v0 and Breakout-v4. The main difference between the three modes is the value of the frameskip parameter in the Atari environment. This parameter indicates the number of frames (steps) the one action is repeated on. This is called the **frame-skipping** technique, which allows us to play more games without significantly increasing the runtime.

For Breakout, frameskip is randomly sampled from 2 to 5. The following screenshots show the frame images returned by the `step` function when the action LEFT is submitted:

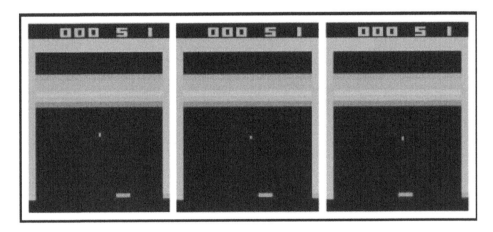

For BreakoutDeterministic, frameskip is set to 3 for the game Space Invaders, and 4 for the other games. With the same LEFT action, the `step` function returns the following:

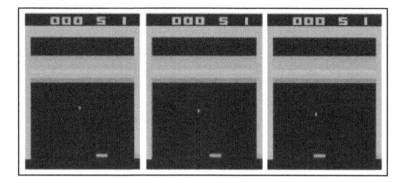

For BreakoutNoFrameskip, frameskip is always 1 for all of the games, meaning no frame-skipping. Similarly, the LEFT action is taken at each step:

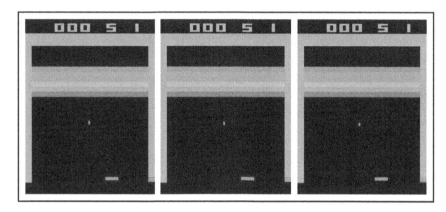

These screenshots demonstrate that although the step function is called four times with the same action, LEFT, the final positions of the paddle are quite different. Because frameskip is 4 for BreakoutDeterministic, its paddle is the closest one to the left wall. For BreakoutNoFrameskip, frameskip is set to 1 so that its paddle is farthest from the left wall. For Breakout, its paddle lies in the middle because of frameskip being sampled from [2, 5] at each step.

From this simple experiment, we can see the effect of the frameskip parameter. Its value is usually set to 4 for fast learning. Recall that there are two versions, v0 and v4, for each mode. Their main difference is the repeat_action_probability parameter. This parameter indicates the probability that a **no operation** (NOOP) action is taken, although another action is submitted. It is set to 0.25 for v0, and 0.0 for v4. Because we want a deterministic Atari environment, the v4 version is selected in this chapter.

If you have played some Atari games, you have probably noticed that the top region of the screen in a game usually contains the scoreboard, showing the current score you got and the number of lives you have. This information is not related to game playing, so that the top region can be cropped. Besides, the frame images returned by the step function are RGB images. Actually, in the Atari environment, colorful images do not provide more information than grayscale images; namely, one can play Atari games as usual with a gray screen. Therefore, it is necessary to keep only useful information by cropping frame images and converting them to grayscale.

Converting an RGB image into a grayscale image is quite easy. The value of each pixel in a grayscale image represents the light intensity, which can be calculated by this formula:

$$Y = 0.2126R + 0.7152G + 0.0722B$$

Here, R, G, and B are the red, green, and blue channels of the RGB image, respectively. Given a RGB image with shape (height, width, channel), the following Python code can be used to convert it into grayscale:

```
def rgb_to_gray(self, im):
    return numpy.dot(im, [0.2126, 0.7152, 0.0722])
```

The following image gives an example:

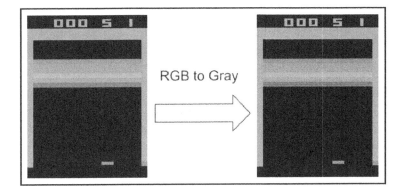

For cropping frame images, we use the opencv-python package or cv2, a Python wrapper around the original C++ OpenCV implementation. For more information, please visit the opencv-python website at http://opencv-python-tutroals.readthedocs.io/en/latest/index.html. The opencv-python package provides basic image transformation operations such as image scaling, translation, and rotation. In this chapter, we only need the image scaling function resize, which takes the input image, image size, and interpolation method as the input arguments, and returns the resized image.

The following code shows the image cropping operation, which involves two steps:

1. Reshaping the input image such that the width of the resulting image equals the resized width, 84, indicated by the resized_shape parameter.

2. Cropping the top region of the reshaped image using numpy slicing:

```
def cv2_resize_image(image, resized_shape=(84, 84),
                     method='crop', crop_offset=8):
    height, width = image.shape
    resized_height, resized_width = resized_shape
    if method == 'crop':
        h = int(round(float(height) * resized_width / width))
        resized = cv2.resize(image,
                             (resized_width, h),
                             interpolation=cv2.INTER_LINEAR)
        crop_y_cutoff = h - crop_offset - resized_height
        cropped =
resized[crop_y_cutoff:crop_y_cutoff+resized_height, :]
        return numpy.asarray(cropped, dtype=numpy.uint8)
    elif method == 'scale':
        return numpy.asarray(cv2.resize(image,
                                        (resized_width,
resized_height),
interpolation=cv2.INTER_LINEAR),
                                        dtype=numpy.uint8)
    else:
        raise ValueError('Unrecognized image resize method.')
```

For example, given a grayscale input image, the cv2_resize_image function returns a cropped image with size 84 × 84, as shown in the following screenshot:

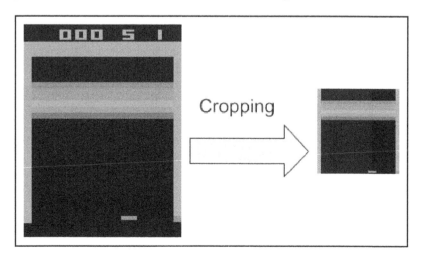

So far, we have finished the data preparation. The data is now ready to be used to train our AI player.

Deep Q-learning

Here comes the fun part—the brain design of our AI Atari player. The core algorithm is based on deep reinforcement learning or deep RL. In order to understand it better, some basic mathematical formulations are required. Deep RL is a perfect combination of deep learning and traditional reinforcement learning. Without understanding the basic concepts about reinforcement learning, it is difficult to apply deep RL correctly in real applications, for example, it is possible that someone may try to use deep RL without defining state space, reward, and transition properly.

Well, don't be afraid of the difficulty of the formulations. We only need high school-level mathematics, and will not go deep into the mathematical proofs of why traditional reinforcement learning algorithms work. The goal of this chapter is to learn the basic Q-learning algorithm, to know how to extend it into the **deep Q-learning algorithm** (**DQN**), and to understand the intuition behind these algorithms. Besides, you will also learn what the advantages and disadvantages are of DQN, what exploration and exploitation are, why a replay memory is necessary, why a target network is needed, and how to design a convolutional neural network for state feature representation.

It looks quite interesting, doesn't it? We hope this chapter not only helps you to understand how to apply deep reinforcement learning to solve practical problems, but also opens a door for deep reinforcement learning research. For the readers who are familiar with convolutional neural networks, the Markov decision process, and Q-learning, skip the first section and go directly to the implementation of DQN.

Basic elements of reinforcement learning

First, let's us recall some basic elements of reinforcement learning that we discussed in the first chapter:

- **State**: The state space defines all the possible states of the environment. In Atari games, a state is a screen image or a set of several consecutive screen images observed by the player at a given time, indicating the game status of that moment.

- **Reward function**: A reward function defines the goal of a reinforcement learning problem. It maps a state or a state-action pair of the environment to a real number, indicating the desirability of that state. The reward is the score received after taking a certain action in Atari games.
- **Policy function**: A policy function defines the behavior of the player at a given time, which maps the states of the environment to actions to be taken in those states.
- **Value function**: A value function indicates which state or state-action pair is good in the long run. The value of a state is the total (or discounted) amount of reward a player can expect to accumulate over the future, starting from that state.

Demonstrating basic Q-learning algorithm

To demonstrate the basic Q-learning algorithm, let's consider a simple problem. Imagine that our agent (player) lives in a grid world. One day, she was trapped in a weird maze, as shown in the following diagram:

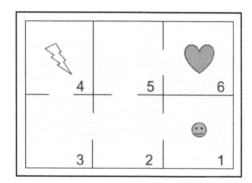

The maze contains six rooms. Our agent appears in Room 1, while she has no knowledge about the maze, that is, she doesn't know Room 6 has the sweetheart that is able to send her back home, or that Room 4 has a lightning bolt that strikes her. Therefore, she has to explore the maze carefully to escape as soon as possible. So, how do we make our lovely agent learn from experience?

Fortunately, her good friend Q-learning can help her survive. This problem can be represented as a state diagram, where each room is taken as a state and her movement from one room to another is considered as an action. The state diagram is as follows:

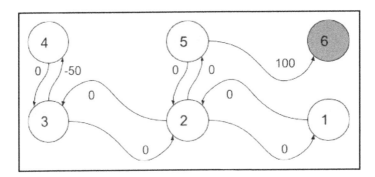

Here, an action is represented by an arrow and the number associated with an arrow is the reward of that state-action pair. For example, when our agent moves from Room 5 to Room 6, she gets 100 points because of achieving the goal. When she moves from Room 3 to Room 4, she get a negative reward because the lightning strike hurts her. This state diagram can also be represented by a matrix:

state\action	1	2	3	4	5	6
1	-	0	-	-	-	-
2	0	-	0	-	0	-
3	-	0	-	-50	-	-
4	-	-	0	-	-	-
5	-	0	-	-	-	100
6	-	-	-	-	-	-

The dash line in the matrix indicates that the action is not available in that state. For example, our agent cannot move from Room 1 to Room 6 directly because there is no door connecting them.

Let's s be a state, a be an action, $R(s, a)$ be the reward function, and $Q(s, a)$ be the value function. Recall that $Q(s, a)$ is the desirability of the state-action pair (s, a) in the long run, meaning that our agent is able to make decisions about which room she enters based on $Q(s, a)$. The Q-learning algorithm is very simple, which estimates $Q(s, a)$ for each state-action pair via the following update rule:

$$Q(s_t, a_t) = Q(s_t, a_t) + \alpha[R(s_t, a_t) + \gamma max_{a \in A(s_{t+1})} Q(s_{t+1}, a) - Q(s_t, a_t)],$$

Here, s_t is the current state, s_{t+1} is the next state after taking action a_t at s_t, $A(s_{t+1})$ is the set of the available actions at s_{t+1}, is the discount factor, and α is the learning rate. The discount factor γ lies in [0,1]. A discount factor smaller than 1 means that our agent prefers the current reward more than past rewards.

In the beginning, our agent knows nothing about the value function, so $Q(s, t)$ is initialized to 0 for all state-action pairs. She will explore from state to state until she reaches the goal. We call each exploration an episode, which consists of moving from the initial state (for example, Room 1) to the final state (for example, Room 6). The Q-learning algorithm is shown as follows:

```
Initialize Q to zero and set parameters α,γ;
Repeat for each episode:
   Randomly select an initial state s;
   While the goal state hasn't been reached:
      Select action a among all the possible actions in state s (e.g.,
using ε-greedy);
      Take action a and observe reward R(s,a), next state s';
      Update Q(s,a) = Q(s,a) + α[R(s,a) + γmax_{a∈A(s')}Q(s',a) - Q(s,a)];
      Set the current state s = s';
   End while
```

A careful reader may ask a question about how to select action a in state s, for example, is action a randomly selected among all the possible actions or chosen using the policy derived from the current estimated value function, Q? What is ϵ-greedy? These questions are related to two important concepts, namely, exploration and exploitation. Exploration means trying something new to gather more information about the environment, while exploitation means making the best decision based on all the information you have. For example, trying a new restaurant is exploration and going to your favorite restaurant is exploitation. In our maze problem, the exploration is that our agent tries to enter a new room she hasn't visited before, while the exploitation is that she chooses her favorite room based on the information she gathered from the environment.

Both exploration and exploitation are necessary in reinforcement learning. Without exploration, our agent is not able to get new knowledge about the environment, so she will make bad decisions again and again. Without exploitation, the information she got from exploration becomes meaningless since she doesn't learn from it to better make a decision. Therefore, a balance or a trade-off between exploration and exploitation is indispensable. $\epsilon-$greedy is the simplest way to make such a trade-off:

With probability	Randomly select an action among all the possible actions
With probability $1-\epsilon$	Select the best action based on Q, that is, pick so that $Q(s,a)$ is the largest among all the possible actions in state s

To further understand how Q-learning works, let's go through several steps by hand. For clarity, let's set the learning rate $\alpha = 1$ and discount factor $\gamma = 0.8$. The following code shows the implementation of Q-learning in Python:

```
import random, numpy

def Q_learning_demo():
    alpha = 1.0
    gamma = 0.8
    epsilon = 0.2
    num_episodes = 100
    R = numpy.array([
        [-1, 0, -1, -1, -1, -1],
        [ 0, -1, 0, -1, 0, -1],
        [-1, 0, -1, -50, -1, -1],
        [-1, -1, 0, -1, -1, -1],
        [-1, 0, -1, -1, -1, 100],
        [-1, -1, -1, -1, -1, -1]
        ])
    # Initialize Q
    Q = numpy.zeros((6, 6))
    # Run for each episode
    for _ in range(num_episodes):
        # Randomly choose an initial state
        s = numpy.random.choice(5)
        while s != 5:
            # Get all the possible actions
            actions = [a for a in range(6) if R[s][a] != -1]
            # Epsilon-greedy
            if numpy.random.binomial(1, epsilon) == 1:
                a = random.choice(actions)
            else:
                a = actions[numpy.argmax(Q[s][actions])]
            next_state = a
            # Update Q(s,a)
```

```
        Q[s][a] += alpha * (R[s][a] + gamma * numpy.max(Q[next_state])
- Q[s][a])
        # Go to the next state
        s = next_state
    return Q
```

After running for 100 episodes, the value function, Q, converges to the following(for the readers who are curious about why this algorithm converges, refer to *Reinforcement Learning: An Introduction* by Andrew Barto and Richard S. Sutton):

state\action	1	2	3	4	5	6
1	-	64	-	-	-	-
2	51.2	-	51.2	-	80	-
3	-	64	-	-9.04	-	-
4	-	-	51.2	-	-	-
5	-	64	-	-	-	100
6	-	-	-	-	-	-

Therefore, the resulting state diagram becomes this:

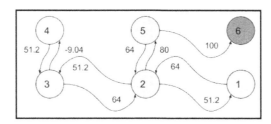

This indicates the following optimal paths to the goal state for all the other states:

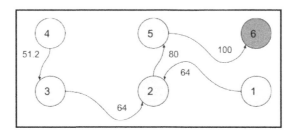

Based on this knowledge, our agent is able to go back home no matter which room she is in. More importantly, she becomes smarter and happier, achieving our goal to train a smart AI agent or player.

This simplest Q-learning algorithm can only handle discrete states and actions. For continuous states, it fails because the convergence is not guaranteed due to the existence of infinite states. How can we apply Q-learning in an infinite state space such as Atari games? The answer is replacing the tableau with neural networks to approximate the action-value function $Q(s, a)$. This is the intuition behind the *Playing Atari with deep reinforcement learning*, by Google DeepMind paper.

To extend the basic Q-learning algorithm into the deep Q-learning algorithm, there are two key questions that need to be answered:

1. What kind of neural networks can be used to extract high-level features from observed data such as screen images in the Atari environment?
2. How can we update the action-value function, $Q(s, a)$, at each training step?

For the first question, there are several possible ways of approximating the action-value function, $Q(s, a)$. One approach is that both the state and the action are used as the inputs to the neural network, which outputs the scalar estimates of their Q-value, as shown in the following diagram:

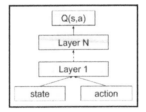

The main disadvantage of this approach is that an additional forward pass is required to compute $Q(s, a)$ as the action is taken as one of the inputs to the network, resulting in a cost that scales linearly with the number of all the possible actions. Another approach is that the state is the only input to the neural network, while there is a separate output for each possible action:

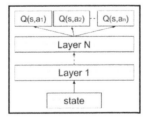

The main advantage of this approach is the ability to compute Q-values for all possible actions in a given state with only a single forward pass through the network, and the simplicity to access the Q-value for an action by picking the corresponding output head.

In the deep Q-network, the second architecture is applied. Recall that the output in the data preprocessing step is an 84×84 grayscale frame image. However, the current screen is not enough for playing Atari games because it doesn't contain the dynamic information about game status. Take Breakout as an example; if we only see one frame, we can only know the locations of the ball and the paddle, but we cannot know the direction or the velocity of the ball. Actually, the direction and the velocity are quite important for making decisions about how to move the paddle. Without them, the game is unplayable. Therefore, instead of taking only one frame image as the input, the last four frame images of a history are stacked together to produce the input to the neural network. These four frames form an $84 \times 84 \times 4$ image. Besides the input layer, the Q-network contains three convolutional layers and one fully connected layer, which is shown as follows:

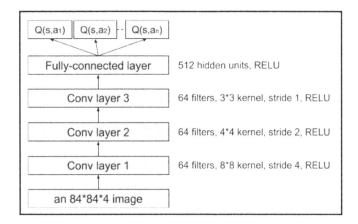

The first convolutional layer has 64 8×8 filters with stride 4, followed by a **rectifier nonlinearity (RELU)**. The second convolutional layer has 64 4×4 filters with stride 2, followed by RELU. The third convolutional layer has 64 3×3 filters with stride 2, followed by RELU. The fully connected hidden layer has 512 hidden units, again followed by RELU. The output layer is also a fully connected layer with a single output for each action.

Readers who are familiar with convolutional neural networks may ask why the first convolutional layer uses a 8×8 filter, instead of a 3×3 filter or a 5×5 filter that is widely applied in computer vision applications. The main reason of using a big filter is that Atari games usually contain very small objects such as a ball, a bullet, or a pellet. A convolutional layer with larger filters is able to zoom in on these small objects, providing benefits for learning feature representations of states. For the second and third convolutional layers, a relatively small filter is enough to capture useful features.

So far, we have discussed the architecture of the Q-network. But, how do we train this Q-network in the Atari environment with an infinite state space? Is it possible to develop an algorithm based on the basic Q-learning to train it? Fortunately, the answer is YES. Recall that the update rule for $Q(s,a)$ in basic Q-learning is as follows:

$$Q(s,a) = Q(s,a) + \alpha[R(s,a) + \gamma max_{a \in A(s')} Q(s',a) - Q(s,a)].$$

When the learning rate $\alpha = 1$, this update rule becomes as follows:

$$Q(s,a) = R(s,a) + \gamma max_{a \in A(s')} Q(s',a),$$

This is called the **Bellman equation**. Actually, the Bellman equation is the backbone of many reinforcement learning algorithms. The algorithms using the Bellman equation as an iterative update are called value iteration algorithms. In this book, we will not go into detail about value iteration or policy iteration. If you are interested in them, refer to *Reinforcement Learning: An Introduction*, by Andrew Barto and Richard S. Sutton.

The equation just shown is only suitable for a deterministic environment where the next state s' is fixed given the current state s and the action a. In a nondeterministic environment, the Bellman equation should be as follows:

$$Q(s,a) = E_{s' \sim S}[R(s,a) + \gamma max_{a \in A(s')} Q(s',a)|s,a],$$

Here, the right-hand side takes the expectation of $R(s,a) + \gamma max_{a \in A(s')} Q(s',a)$ with respect to the next state s' (for example, the distribution of s' is determined by the Atari emulator). For an infinite state space, it is common to use a function approximator such as the Q-network to estimate the action-value function $Q(s,a)$. Then, instead of iteratively updating $Q(s,a)$, the Q-network can be trained by minimizing the following loss function at the ith iteration:

$$L_i(\theta_i) = E_{s,a \sim P(s,a)}[y_i - Q(s,a;\theta_i)^2],$$

Here, $Q(s,a;)$ represents the Q-network parameterized by,
$y_i = E_{s' \sim S}[R(s,a) + \gamma max_{a \in A(s')}Q(s',a;\theta_{i-1})|s,a]$ is the target for the ith iteration, and $P(s,a)$ is a
probability distribution over sequences and actions. The parameters from the previous
iteration $i-1$ are fixed when optimizing the loss function $L_i(\theta_i)$ over θ_i. In practice, it is
impossible to exactly calculate the expectations in $L_i(\theta_i)$. Instead of optimizing $L_i(\theta_i)$
directly, we minimize the empirical loss of $L_i(\theta_i)$, which replaces the expectations by
samples $\{(s,a,s'),\cdots\}$ from the probability distribution $P(s,a)$ and the Atari emulator. As with
other deep learning algorithms, the empirical loss function can be optimized by stochastic
gradient descent.

This algorithm doesn't need to construct an estimate of the emulator, for example, it doesn't
need to know the internal game mechanism about the Atari emulator, because it only uses
samples from the emulator to solve the reinforcement learning problem. This property is
called **model-free**, namely, it can treat the underlying model as a black box. Another
property of this algorithm is off-policy. It learns about the greedy policy
$a = \arg\max_a Q(s,a;\theta)$
while following the probability distribution $P(s,a)$ that balances
exploration and exploitation of the state space. As discussed previously, $P(s,a)$ can be
selected as an $\epsilon-$greedy strategy.

The derivation of the deep Q-learning algorithm may be a little bit difficult for readers who
are not familiar with reinforcement learning or the Markov decision process. In order to
make it more understandable, let's see the following diagram:

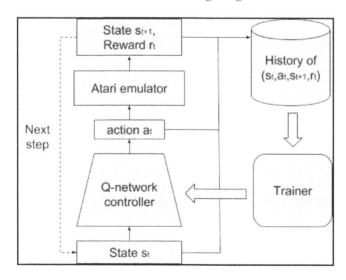

The brain of our AI player is the Q-network controller. At each time step t, she observes the screen image s_t (recall that st is an $84 \times 84 \times 4$ image that stacks the last four frames). Then, her brain analyzes this observation and comes up with an action, a_t. The Atari emulator receives this action and returns the next screen image, s_{t+1}, and the reward, r_t. The quadruplet (s_t, a_t, r_t, s_{t+1}) is stored in the memory and is taken as a sample for training the Q-network by minimizing the empirical loss function via stochastic gradient descent.

How do we draw samples from the quadruplets stored in the memory? One approach is that these samples, $\{(s_t, a_t, r_t, s_{t+1}), \cdots\}$, are drawn from our AI player's interactions with the environment, for example, samples $\{(s_t, a_t, r_t, s_{t+1}), (s_{t+1}, a_{t+1}, r_{t+1}, s_{t+2}), \cdots, (s_{t+n}, a_{t+n}, r_{t+n}, s_{t+n+1})\}$ are used to train the Q-network. The main drawback of this approach is that the samples in one batch are strongly correlated. The strong correlation breaks the assumption that the samples for constructing the empirical loss function are independent, making the training procedure unstable and leading to bad performance:

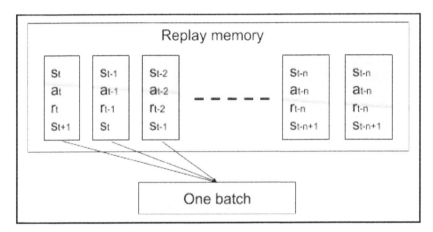

The deep Q-learning algorithm applies another approach, utilizing a technique known as experience replay. The AI player's experiences at each time step (s_t, a_t, r_t, s_{t+1}) are stored into the replay memory from which a batch of samples are randomly drawn in order to train the Q-network. Mathematically, we cannot guarantee the independence between the samples we drew. But practically, this approach can stabilize the training procedure and generate reasonable results:

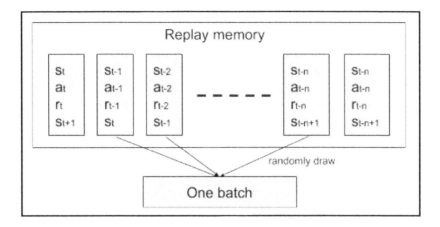

So far, we have discussed all the components in the deep Q-learning algorithm. The full algorithm is shown as follows:

```
Initialize replay memory R to capacity N;
Initialize the Q-network Q(s,a;θ) with random weights θ;
Repeat for each episode:
    Set time step t=1;
    Receive an initial screen image x₁ and do preprocessing s₁ = f(x₁);
    While the terminal state hasn't been reached:
        Select an action at via ε-greedy, i.e., select a random action with
                                    aₜ = arg max Q(sₜ,a;θ)
                                           a
probability , otherwise select                                        ;
        Execute action at in the emulator and observe reward rₜ and image
xₜ₊₁;
        Set sₜ₊₁ = f(xₜ₊₁,sₜ) and store transition (sₜ,aₜ,rₜ,sₜ₊₁) into replay
memory R;
        Randomly sample a batch of transitions (sᵢ,aᵢ,rᵢ,sᵢ₊₁) from R;
        Set yᵢ = rᵢ if sᵢ₊₁ is a terminal state or yᵢ = rᵢ + γ max Q(sᵢ₊₁,a;θ)   if sᵢ₊₁ is a
                                                              a
non-terminal state;
        Perform a gradient descent step on Σ(yᵢ - Q(sᵢ,aᵢ;θ))² ;
    End while
```

This algorithm works well for some Atari games, for example, Breakout, Seaquest, Pong, and Qbert, but it still cannot reach human-level control. One drawback is that computing the targets y_i uses the current estimate of the action-value function Q, which makes the training step unstable, that is, an update that increases $Q(s_t, a)$ usually also increases $Q(s_{t+1}, a)$ for all and hence also increases the target y_i, possibly leading to oscillations or divergence of the policy.

To address this problem, Google DeepMind introduced the target network in their paper, *Human-level control through deep reinforcement learning*, which was published in Nature. The idea behind the target network is quite simple: a separate network is used for generating the targets y_i in the Q-learning update. More precisely, for every M Q-learning updates, the network Q is cloned to obtain a target network Q, which is used for generating the targets y_i in the following M updates to Q. Therefore, the deep Q-learning algorithm becomes as follows:

```
Initialize replay memory R to capacity N;
Initialize the Q-network Q(s,a;θ) with random weights θ;
Initialize the target network Q(s,a;θ̂) with weights θ̂ = θ;
Repeat for each episode:

Set time step t = 1;
    Receive an initial screen image x₁ and do preprocessing s₁ = f(x₁);
    While the terminal state hasn't been reached:
        Select an action at via ε-greedy, i.e., select a random action with
                        aₜ = arg max Q(sₜ,a;θ)
                                a
probability , otherwise select                    ;
        Execute action at in the emulator and observe reward rₜ and image
xₜ₊₁;
        Set sₜ₊₁ = f(xₜ₊₁,sₜ) and store transition (sₜ,aₜ,rₜ,sₜ₊₁) into replay memory
R;
        Randomly sample a batch of transitions (sᵢ,aᵢ,rᵢ,sᵢ₊₁) from R;
        Set yᵢ = rᵢ if sᵢ₊₁ is a terminal state or yᵢ = rᵢ + γ max Q̂(sᵢ₊₁,a;θ̂) if sᵢ₊₁ is a
non-terminal state;
        Perform a gradient descent step on Σ(yᵢ - Q(sᵢ,aᵢ;θ))² ;
        Set Q̂=Q for every M steps;
    End while
```

With the target network, the AI player trained by the deep Q-learning algorithm is able to surpass the performance of most previous reinforcement learning algorithms and achieves a human-level performance across a set of 49 Atari 2600 games, for example, Star Gunner, Atlantis, Assault, and Space Invaders.

The deep Q-learning algorithm has made an important step toward general artificial intelligence. Although it performs well in the Atari 2600 games, it still has a lot of unsolved issues:

- **Slow convergence**: It requires a long time (7 days on one GPU) to reach human-level performance
- **Failing with sparse rewards**: It doesn't work for the game Montezuma's Revenge, which requires long-term planning
- **Need for a large amount of data**: This is a common issue among most reinforcement learning algorithms

In order to solve these issues, different variants of the deep Q-learning algorithm have been proposed recently, for example, double Q-learning, prioritized experience replay, bootstrapped DQN, and dueling network architectures. We will not discuss these algorithms in this book. For readers who want to learn more about DQN, please refer to the related papers.

Implementation of DQN

This chapter will show you how to implement all the components, for example, Q-network, replay memory, trainer, and Q-learning optimizer, of the deep Q-learning algorithm with Python and TensorFlow.

We will implement the `QNetwork` class for the Q-network that we discussed in the previous chapter, which is defined as follows:

```
class QNetwork:
    def __init__(self, input_shape=(84, 84, 4), n_outputs=4,
                 network_type='cnn', scope='q_network'):
        self.width = input_shape[0]
        self.height = input_shape[1]
        self.channel = input_shape[2]
        self.n_outputs = n_outputs
        self.network_type = network_type
        self.scope = scope
        # Frame images
        self.x = tf.placeholder(dtype=tf.float32,
                                shape=(None, self.channel,
                                       self.width, self.height))
        # Estimates of Q-value
        self.y = tf.placeholder(dtype=tf.float32, shape=(None,))
        # Selected actions
        self.a = tf.placeholder(dtype=tf.int32, shape=(None,))
```

```
with tf.variable_scope(scope):
    self.build()
    self.build_loss()
```

The constructor requires four arguments, `input_shape`, `n_outputs`, `network_type` and `scope`. `input_shape` is the size of the input image. After data preprocessing, the input is an $84 \times 84 \times 4$ image, so that the default parameter is $(84, 84, 4)$. `n_outputs` is the number of all the possible actions, for example, `n_outputs` is four in Breakout. `network_type`, indicates the type of the Q-network we want to use. Our implementation contains three different networks. Two of them are the convolutional neural networks proposed by Google DeepMind. The other one is a feed-forward neural network used for testing. `scope` is the name of the Q-network object, which can be set to `q_network` or `target_network`.

In the constructor, three input tensors are created. The x variable represents the input state (a batch of $84 \times 84 \times 4$ images). The y and a variables are the estimates of the action-value function and the selected actions corresponding to the input state, which are used for training the Q-network. After creating the input tensors, two functions, `build` and `build_loss`, are called to build the Q-network.

Constructing the Q-network using TensorFlow is quite easy, as shown here:

```
def build(self):
    self.net = {}
    self.net['input'] = tf.transpose(self.x, perm=(0, 2, 3, 1))
    init_b = tf.constant_initializer(0.01)
    if self.network_type == 'cnn':
        self.net['conv1'] = conv2d(self.net['input'], 32,
                                    kernel=(8, 8), stride=(4, 4),
                                    init_b=init_b, name='conv1')
        self.net['conv2'] = conv2d(self.net['input'], 64,
                                    kernel=(4, 4), stride=(2, 2),
                                    init_b=init_b, name='conv2')
        self.net['conv3'] = conv2d(self.net['input'], 64,
                                    kernel=(3, 3), stride=(1, 1),
                                    init_b=init_b, name='conv3')
        self.net['feature'] = dense(self.net['conv2'], 512,
                                    init_b=init_b, name='fc1')
    elif self.network_type == 'cnn_nips':
        self.net['conv1'] = conv2d(self.net['input'], 16,
                                    kernel=(8, 8), stride=(4, 4),
                                    init_b=init_b, name='conv1')
        self.net['conv2'] = conv2d(self.net['conv1'], 32,
                                    kernel=(4, 4), stride=(2, 2),
                                    init_b=init_b, name='conv2')
```

```
            self.net['feature'] = dense(self.net['conv2'], 256,
                                    init_b=init_b, name='fc1')
        elif self.network_type == 'mlp':
            self.net['fc1'] = dense(self.net['input'], 50,
                                    init_b=init_b), name='fc1')
            self.net['feature'] = dense(self.net['fc1'], 50,
                                    init_b=init_b, name='fc2')
        else:
            raise NotImplementedError('Unknown network type')
        self.net['values'] = dense(self.net['feature'],
                                    self.n_outputs, activation=None,
                                    init_b=init_b, name='values')
        self.net['q_value'] = tf.reduce_max(self.net['values'],
                                    axis=1, name='q_value')
        self.net['q_action'] = tf.argmax(self.net['values'],
                                    axis=1, name='q_action',
                                    output_type=tf.int32)
        self.vars = tf.get_collection(tf.GraphKeys.TRAINABLE_VARIABLES,
                                    tf.get_variable_scope().name)
```

As discussed in the previous chapter, the Q-network for the Atari environment contains three convolutional layers and one hidden layer, which can be constructed when the network_type is cnn. The cnn_nips type is a simplified Q-network for Atari games, which only contains two convolutional layers and one hidden layer with less filters and hidden units. The mlp type is a feed-forward neural network with two hidden layers, which is used for debugging. The vars variable is the list of all the trainable variables in the Q-network.

Recall that the loss function is $\sum_i \frac{(y_i - Q(s_i, a_i; \theta))^2}{i}$, which can be implemented as follows:

```
    def build_loss(self):
        indices = tf.transpose(tf.stack([tf.range(tf.shape(self.a)[0]),
                                    self.a], axis=0))
        value = tf.gather_nd(self.net['values'], indices)
        self.loss = 0.5 * tf.reduce_mean(tf.square((value - self.y)))
        self.gradient = tf.gradients(self.loss, self.vars)
        tf.summary.scalar("loss", self.loss, collections=['q_network'])
        self.summary_op = tf.summary.merge_all('q_network')
```

The tf.gather_nd function is used to get the action-value $Q(s_i, a_i; \theta)$ given a batch of action,s ai. The variable loss represents the loss function, and gradient is the gradient of the loss function with respect to the trainable variables. summary_op is for TensorBoard visualization.

The implementation of the replay memory doesn't involve TensorFlow:

```
class ReplayMemory:
    def __init__(self, history_len=4, capacity=1000000,
                 batch_size=32, input_scale=255.0):
        self.capacity = capacity
        self.history_length = history_len
        self.batch_size = batch_size
        self.input_scale = input_scale
        self.frames = deque([])
        self.others = deque([])
```

The `ReplayMemory` class takes four input parameters, that is, `history_len`, `capacity`, `batch_size`, and `input_scale`. `history_len` is the number of frames stacked together. Typically, `history_len` is set to 4 for Atari games, forming an $84 \times 84 \times 4$ input image. `capacity` is the capacity of the replay memory, namely, the maximum number of frames that can be stored in it. `batch_size` is the size of one batch for training. `input_scale` is the normalization factor for input images, for example, it is set to 255 for RGB images. The variable frames record all the frame images and the variable others record the corresponding actions, rewards, and termination signals.

`ReplayMemory` provides a function for adding a record (frame image, action, reward, termination signal) into the memory:

```
    def add(self, frame, action, r, termination):
        if len(self.frames) == self.capacity:
            self.frames.popleft()
            self.others.popleft()
        self.frames.append(frame)
        self.others.append((action, r, termination))
    def add_nullops(self, init_frame):
        for _ in range(self.history_length):
            self.add(init_frame, 0, 0, 0)
```

It also provides a function for constructing an $84 \times 84 \times 4$ input image by concatenating the last four frame images of a history:

```
    def phi(self, new_frame):
        assert len(self.frames) > self.history_length
        images = [new_frame] + [self.frames[-1-i] for i in
 range(self.history_length-1)]
        return numpy.concatenate(images, axis=0)
```

The following function randomly draws a transition (state, action, reward, next state, termination signal) from the replay memory:

```
def sample(self):
    while True:
        index = random.randint(a=self.history_length-1,
                                b=len(self.frames)-2)
        infos = [self.others[index-i] for i in
 range(self.history_length)]
        # Check if termination=1 before "index"
        flag = False
        for i in range(1, self.history_length):
            if infos[i][2] == 1:
                flag = True
                break
        if flag:
            continue
        state = self._phi(index)
        new_state = self._phi(index+1)
        action, r, termination = self.others[index]
        state = numpy.asarray(state / self.input_scale,
                              dtype=numpy.float32)
        new_state = numpy.asarray(new_state / self.input_scale,
                                  dtype=numpy.float32)
        return (state, action, r, new_state, termination)
```

Note that only the termination signal corresponding to the last frame in a state is allowed to be True. The _phi(index) function stacks the four frames together:

```
def _phi(self, index):
    images = [self.frames[index-i] for i in range(self.history_length)]
    return numpy.concatenate(images, axis=0)
```

The Optimizer class is used for training the Q-network:

```
class Optimizer:
    def __init__(self, config, feedback_size,
                 q_network, target_network, replay_memory):
        self.feedback_size = feedback_size
        self.q_network = q_network
        self.target_network = target_network
        self.replay_memory = replay_memory
        self.summary_writer = None
        self.gamma = config['gamma']
        self.num_frames = config['num_frames']
        optimizer = create_optimizer(config['optimizer'],
                                     config['learning_rate'],
                                     config['rho'],
```

```
                                         config['rmsprop_epsilon'])
          self.train_op = optimizer.apply_gradients(
                  zip(self.q_network.gradient,
                  self.q_network.vars))
```

It takes the Q-network, the target network, the replay memory, and the size of input images as the input arguments. In the constructor, it creates an optimizer (one of the popular optimizers such as ADAM, RMSPROP, or MOMENTUM) and then builds an operator for training.

To train the Q-network, it needs to construct a mini-batch of samples (states, actions, targets) corresponding to s_i, a_i, and y_i in the loss function $\sum_i (y_i - Q(s_i, a_i, \theta))^2$:

```
      def sample_transitions(self, sess, batch_size):
          w, h = self.feedback_size
          states = numpy.zeros((batch_size, self.num_frames, w, h),
                            dtype=numpy.float32)
          new_states = numpy.zeros((batch_size, self.num_frames, w, h),
                            dtype=numpy.float32)
          targets = numpy.zeros(batch_size, dtype=numpy.float32)
          actions = numpy.zeros(batch_size, dtype=numpy.int32)
          terminations = numpy.zeros(batch_size, dtype=numpy.int32)
          for i in range(batch_size):
              state, action, r, new_state, t = self.replay_memory.sample()
              states[i] = state
              new_states[i] = new_state
              actions[i] = action
              targets[i] = r
              terminations[i] = t

          targets += self.gamma * (1 - terminations) *
  self.target_network.get_q_value(sess, new_states)
          return states, actions, targets
```

Note that the targets y_i are computed by the target network instead of the Q-network. Given a mini-batch of states, actions, or targets, the Q-network can be easily trained by use of the following:

```
      def train_one_step(self, sess, step, batch_size):
          states, actions, targets = self.sample_transitions(sess,
  batch_size)
          feed_dict = self.q_network.get_feed_dict(states, actions, targets)
          if self.summary_writer and step % 1000 == 0:
              summary_str, _, = sess.run([self.q_network.summary_op,
                                      self.train_op],
                                    feed_dict=feed_dict)
          self.summary_writer.add_summary(summary_str, step)
```

```
            self.summary_writer.flush()
        else:
            sess.run(self.train_op, feed_dict=feed_dict)
```

Besides the training procedure, for each `1000` steps, the summary is written to the log file. This summary is for monitoring the training process, helping to tune the parameters, and debugging.

Combining these modules together, we can implement the class DQN for the main deep Q-learning algorithm:

```
class DQN:
    def __init__(self, config, game, directory,
                    callback=None, summary_writer=None):
        self.game = game
        self.actions = game.get_available_actions()
        self.feedback_size = game.get_feedback_size()
        self.callback = callback
        self.summary_writer = summary_writer
        self.config = config
        self.batch_size = config['batch_size']
        self.n_episode = config['num_episode']
        self.capacity = config['capacity']
        self.epsilon_decay = config['epsilon_decay']
        self.epsilon_min = config['epsilon_min']
        self.num_frames = config['num_frames']
        self.num_nullops = config['num_nullops']
        self.time_between_two_copies = config['time_between_two_copies']
        self.input_scale = config['input_scale']
        self.update_interval = config['update_interval']
        self.directory = directory

        self._init_modules()
```

Here, `config` includes all the parameters of DQN, for example, batch size and learning rate for training. `game` is an instance of the Atari environment. In the constructor, the replay memory, Q-network, target network, and optimizer are initialized. To begin the training process, the following function can be called:

```
    def train(self, sess, saver=None):
        num_of_trials = -1
        for episode in range(self.n_episode):
            self.game.reset()
            frame = self.game.get_current_feedback()
            for _ in range(self.num_nullops):
                r, new_frame, termination = self.play(action=0)
                self.replay_memory.add(frame, 0, r, termination)
```

```
            frame = new_frame
        for _ in range(self.config['T']):
            num_of_trials += 1
            epsilon_greedy = self.epsilon_min + \
                max(self.epsilon_decay - num_of_trials, 0) / \
                self.epsilon_decay * (1 - self.epsilon_min)

            if num_of_trials % self.update_interval == 0:
                self.optimizer.train_one_step(sess,
                                              num_of_trials,
                                              self.batch_size)
            state = self.replay_memory.phi(frame)
            action = self.choose_action(sess, state, epsilon_greedy)
            r, new_frame, termination = self.play(action)
            self.replay_memory.add(frame, action, r, termination)
            frame = new_frame
            if num_of_trials % self.time_between_two_copies == 0:
                self.update_target_network(sess)
                self.save(sess, saver)
            if self.callback:
                self.callback()
            if termination:
                score = self.game.get_total_reward()
                summary_str = sess.run(self.summary_op,
                                       feed_dict={self.t_score: score})
                self.summary_writer.add_summary(summary_str,
                                                num_of_trials)
                self.summary_writer.flush()
                break
```

This function is easy to understand. In each episode, it calls `replay_memory.phi` to get the current state and calls the `choose_action` function to select an action via the $\epsilon-$greedy policy. This action is submitted into the Atari emulator by calling the `play` function, which returns the corresponding reward, next frame image, and termination signal. Then, the transition (current frame image, action, reward, termination) is stored in the replay memory. For every `update_interval` step (`update_interval` = 1 by default), the Q-network is trained with a batch of transitions randomly sampled from the replay memory. For every `time_between_two_copies` step, the target network copies the Q-network, and the weights of the Q-network are saved to the hard disk.

After the training step, the following function can be called for evaluating the AI player's performance:

```
def evaluate(self, sess):
    for episode in range(self.n_episode):
        self.game.reset()
```

```
frame = self.game.get_current_feedback()
for _ in range(self.num_nullops):
    r, new_frame, termination = self.play(action=0)
    self.replay_memory.add(frame, 0, r, termination)
    frame = new_frame
for _ in range(self.config['T']):
    state = self.replay_memory.phi(frame)
    action = self.choose_action(sess, state, self.epsilon_min)
    r, new_frame, termination = self.play(action)
    self.replay_memory.add(frame, action, r, termination)
    frame = new_frame

    if self.callback:
        self.callback()
        if termination:
            break
```

Now, we are ready to train our first AI player for Atari games. The implementation is not hard if you understand the intuition behind the algorithm, is it? Now is the time to run the program and witness the magic!

Experiments

The full implementation of the deep Q-learning algorithm can be downloaded from GitHub (link xxx). To train our AI player for Breakout, run the following command under the `src` folder:

```
python train.py -g Breakout -d gpu
```

There are two arguments in `train.py`. One is `-g` or `--game`, indicating the name of the game one wants to test. The other one is `-d` or `--device`, which specifies the device (CPU or GPU) one wants to use to train the Q-network.

For Atari games, even with a high-end GPU, it will take 4-7 days to make our AI player achieve human-level performance. In order to test the algorithm quickly, a special game called **demo** is implemented as a lightweight benchmark. Run the demo via the following:

```
python train.py -g demo -d cpu
```

The demo game is based on the GridWorld game on the website at `https://cs.stanford.edu/people/karpathy/convnetjs/demo/rldemo.html`:

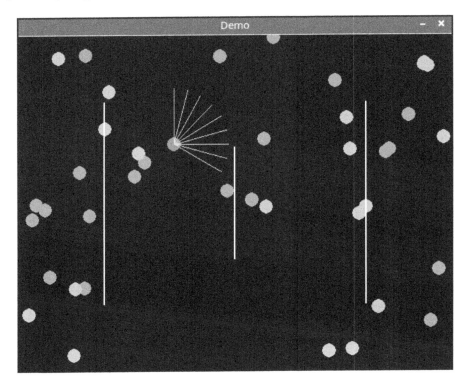

In this game, a robot in a 2D grid world has nine eyes pointing in different angles, and each eye senses three values along its direction: distance to a wall, distance to a green bean, or distance to a red bean. It navigates by using one of five actions that turn it different angles. It gets a positive reward (+1) for eating green beans while a negative reward (-1) for eating red beans. The goal is to eat green beans as much as possible in one episode.

The training will take several minutes. During the training, you can open a new terminal and type the following command to visualize the architecture of the Q-network and the training procedure:

```
tensorboard --logdir=log/demo/train
```

Here, `logdir` points to the folder where the log file of demo is stored. Once TensorBoard is running, navigate your web browser to `localhost:6006` to view the TensorBoard:

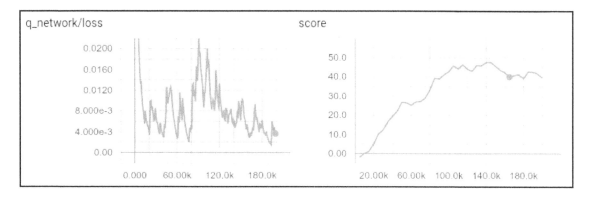

The two graphs plot the loss and the score against the training step, respectively. Clearly, after 100k training steps, the performance of the robot becomes stable, for example, the score is around 40.

You can also visualize the weights of the Q-network through TensorBoard. For more details, visit the TensorBoard guide at `https://www.tensorflow.org/programmers_guide/summaries_and_tensorboard`. This tool is quite useful for debugging and optimizing the code, especially for complicated algorithms such as DQN.

Summary

Congratulations! You just learned four important things. The first one is how to implement an Atari game emulator using gym, and how to play Atari games for relaxation and having fun. The second one is that you learned how to preprocess data in reinforcement learning tasks such as Atari games. For practical machine learning applications, you will spend a great deal of time on understanding and refining data, which affects the performance of an AI system a lot. The third one is the deep Q-learning algorithm. You learned the intuition behind it, for example, why the replay memory is necessary, why the target network is needed, where the update rule comes from, and so on. The final one is that you learned how to implement DQN using TensorFlow, and how to visualize the training process. Now, you are ready for the more advanced topics that we will discuss in the following chapters.

In the next chapter, you will learn how to simulate classic control tasks, and how to implement the state-of-the-art actor-critic algorithms for control.

Atari Games with Deep Q Network

8

Deep Q Network (DQN) is one of the very popular and widely used **deep reinforcement learning** (**DRL**) algorithms. In fact, it created a lot of buzz around the **reinforcement learning** (**RL**) community after its release. The algorithm was proposed by researchers at Google's DeepMind and achieved human-level results when playing any Atari game by just taking the game screen as input.

In this chapter, we will explore how DQN works and also learn how to build a DQN that plays any Atari game by taking only the game screen as input. We will look at some of the improvements made to DQN architecture, such as double DQN and dueling network architecture.

In this chapter, you will learn about:

- **Deep Q Networks (DQNs)**
- Architecture of DQN
- Building an agent to play Atari games
- Double DQN
- Prioritized experience replay

What is a Deep Q Network?

Before going ahead, first, let us just recap the Q function. What is a Q function? A Q function, also called a state-action value function, specifies how good an action *a* is in the state *s*. So, we store the value of all possible actions in each state in a table called a Q table and we pick the action that has the maximum value in a state as the optimal action. Remember how we learned this Q function? We used Q learning, which is an off-policy temporal difference learning algorithm for estimating the Q function. We looked at this in Chapter 5, *Temporal Difference Learning*.

So far, we have seen environments with a finite number of states with limited actions, and we did an exhaustive search through all possible state-action pairs for finding the optimal Q value. Think of an environment where we have a very large number of states and, in each state, we have a lot of actions to try. It would be time-consuming to go through all the actions in each state. A better approach would be to approximate the Q function with some parameter θ as $Q(s,a;\theta) \approx Q^*(s,a)$. We can use a neural network with weights θ to approximate the Q value for all possible actions in each state. As we are using neural networks to approximate the Q function, we can call it a Q network. Okay, but how do we train the network and what will be our objective function? Recall our Q learning update rule:

$$Q(s,a) = Q(s,a) + \alpha(r + \gamma maxQ(s'a') - Q(s,a))$$

$r + \gamma maxQ(s'a)$ is the target value and $Q(s,a)$ is the predicted value; we tried to minimize this value by learning a right policy.

Similarly, in DQN, we can define the loss function as the squared difference between the target and predicted value, and we will also try to minimize the loss by updating the weights θ:

$$Loss = (y_i - Q(s,a;\theta))^2$$

Where $y_i = r + \gamma max_{a'} Q(s',a';\theta)$.

We update the weights and minimize the loss through gradient descent. In a nutshell, in DQN, we use neural networks as function approximators for approximating a Q function, and we minimize errors through gradient descent.

Architecture of DQN

Now that we have a basic understanding of DQN, we will go into detail about how DQN works and the architecture of DQN for playing Atari games. We will look at each component and then we will view the algorithm as a whole.

Convolutional network

The first layer of DQN is the convolutional network, and the input to the network will be a raw frame of the game screen. So, we take a raw frame and pass that to the convolutional layers to understand the game state. But the raw frames will have 210 x 160 pixels with a 128 color palette and it will clearly take a lot of computation and memory if we feed the raw pixels directly. So, we downsample the pixel to 84 x 84 and convert the RGB values to grayscale values and we feed this pre-processed game screen as the input to the convolutional layers. The convolutional layer understands the game screen by identifying the spatial relationship between different objects in the image. We use two convolutional layers followed by a fully connected layer with ReLU as the activation function. Here, we don't use a pooling layer.

A pooling layer is useful when we perform tasks such as object detection or classification, where we don't consider the position of the object in the image and we just want to know whether the desired object is in the image. For example, if we want to classify whether there is a dog in an image, we only look at whether a dog is there in an image and we don't check where the dog is. In that case, a pooling layer is used to classify the image irrespective of the position of the dog. But for us to understand the game screen, the position is important as it depicts the game status. For example, in a Pong game, we don't just want to classify if there is a ball on the game screen. We want to know the position of the ball so that we can make our next move. That's why we don't use a pooling layer in our architecture.

Okay, how can we compute the Q value? If we pass one game screen and one action as an input to the DQN, it will give us the Q value. But it will require one complete forward pass, as there will be many actions in a state. Also, there will be many states in a game with one forward pass for each action, which will be computationally expensive. So, we simply pass the game screen alone as an input and get the Q values for all possible actions in the state by setting the number of units in the output layer to the number of actions in the game state.

The architecture of DQN is shown in the following diagram, where we feed a game screen and it provides the Q value for all actions in that game state:

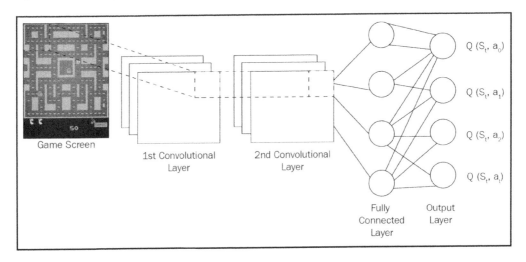

To predict the Q values of the game state, we don't use only the current game screen; we also consider the past four game screens. Why is that? Consider the Pac-Man game where the goal of the Pac-Man is to move and eat all the dots. By just looking at the current game screen, we cannot know in which direction Pac-Man is moving. But if we have past game screens, we can understand in which direction Pac-Man is moving. We use the past four game screens along with the current game screen as input.

Experience replay

We know that in RL environments, we make a transition from one state s to the next state s' by performing some action a and receive a reward r. We save this transition information as $< s, a, r, s' >$ in a buffer called a replay buffer or experience replay. These transitions are called the agent's experience.

The key idea of experience replay is that we train our deep Q network with transitions sampled from the replay buffer instead of training with the last transitions. Agent's experiences are correlated one at a time, so selecting a random batch of training samples from the replay buffer will reduce the correlation between the agent's experience and helps the agent to learn better from a wide range of experiences.

Also, neural networks will overfit with correlated experience, so by selecting a random batch of experiences from reply buffer we will reduce the overfitting. We can use uniform sampling for sampling the experience. We can think of experience replay as a queue rather than a list. A replay buffer will store only a fixed number of recent experiences, so when the new information comes in, we delete the old:

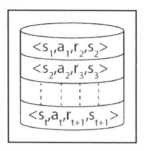

Target network

In our loss function, we calculate the squared difference between a target and predicted value:

$$Loss = (r + \gamma max_{a'} Q(s', a'; \theta) - Q(s, a; \theta))^2$$

We are using the same Q function for calculating the target value and the predicted value. In the preceding equation, you can see the same weights θ are used for both target Q and predicted Q. Since the same network is calculating the predicted value and target value, there could be a lot of divergence between these two.

To avoid this problem, we use a separate network called a target network for calculating the target value. So, our loss function becomes:

$$Loss = (r + \gamma max_{a'} Q(s', a'; \theta') - Q(s, a; \theta))^2$$

You may notice that the parameter of target Q is θ' instead of θ. Our actual Q network, which is used for predicting Q values, learns the correct weights of θ by using gradient descent. The target network is frozen for several time steps and then the target network weights are updated by copying the weights from the actual Q network. Freezing the target network for a while and then updating its weights with the actual Q network weights stabilizes the training.

Clipping rewards

How do we assign rewards? Reward assignment varies for each game. In some games, we can assign rewards such as +1 for winning, -1 for loss, and 0 for nothing, but in some other games, we have to assign rewards such as + 100 for doing an action and +50 for doing another action. To avoid this problem, we clip all the rewards to -1 and +1.

Understanding the algorithm

Now, we will see how DQN works overall. The steps involved in DQN are as follows:

1. First, we preprocess and feed the game screen (state s) to our DQN, which will return the Q values of all possible actions in the state.
2. Now we select an action using the epsilon-greedy policy: with the probability epsilon, we select a random action a and with probability 1-epsilon, we select an action that has a maximum Q value, such as $a = argmax(Q(s, a; \theta))$.
3. After selecting the action a, we perform this action in a state s and move to a new state s' and receive a reward. The next state, s', is the preprocessed image of the next game screen.
4. We store this transition in our replay buffer as `<s,a,r,s'>`.
5. Next, we sample some random batches of transitions from the replay buffer and calculate the loss.
6. We know that $Loss = (r + \gamma max_{a'} Q(s', a'; \theta') - Q(s, a; \theta))^2$, as in the squared difference between target Q and predicted Q.
7. We perform gradient descent with respect to our actual network parameters θ in order to minimize this loss.
8. After every k steps, we copy our actual network weights θ to the target network weights θ'.
9. We repeat these steps for M number of episodes.

Building an agent to play Atari games

Now we will see how to build an agent to play any Atari game. You can get the complete code as a Jupyter notebook with the explanation here (`https://github.com/sudharsan13296/Hands-On-Reinforcement-Learning-With-Python/blob/master/08.%20Atari%20Games%20with%20DQN/8.8%20Building%20an%20Agent%20to%20Play%20Atari%20Games.ipynb`).

First, we import all the necessary libraries:

```
import numpy as np
import gym
import tensorflow as tf
from tensorflow.contrib.layers import flatten, conv2d, fully_connected
from collections import deque, Counter
import random
from datetime import datetime
```

We can use any of the Atari gaming environments given here: `http://gym.openai.com/envs/#atari`.

In this example, we use the Pac-Man game environment:

```
env = gym.make("MsPacman-v0")
n_outputs = env.action_space.n
```

The Pac-Man environment is shown here:

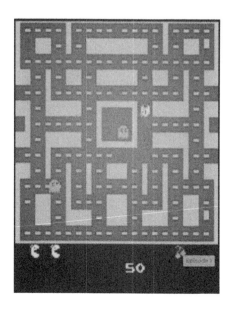

Now we define a `preprocess_observation` function for preprocessing our input game screen. We reduce the image size and convert the image to grayscale:

```
color = np.array([210, 164, 74]).mean()

def preprocess_observation(obs):

    # Crop and resize the image
    img = obs[1:176:2, ::2]

    # Convert the image to greyscale
    img = img.mean(axis=2)

    # Improve image contrast
    img[img==color] = 0

    # Next we normalize the image from -1 to +1
    img = (img - 128) / 128 - 1

    return img.reshape(88,80,1)
```

Okay, now we define a `q_network` function for building our Q network. The input to our Q network will be the game state X.

We build a Q network with three convolutional layers with the same padding, followed by a fully connected layer:

```
tf.reset_default_graph()

def q_network(X, name_scope):
    # Initialize layers
    initializer = tf.contrib.layers.variance_scaling_initializer()

    with tf.variable_scope(name_scope) as scope:

        # initialize the convolutional layers
        layer_1 = conv2d(X, num_outputs=32, kernel_size=(8,8), stride=4,
padding='SAME', weights_initializer=initializer)
        tf.summary.histogram('layer_1',layer_1)
        layer_2 = conv2d(layer_1, num_outputs=64, kernel_size=(4,4),
stride=2, padding='SAME', weights_initializer=initializer)
        tf.summary.histogram('layer_2',layer_2)
        layer_3 = conv2d(layer_2, num_outputs=64, kernel_size=(3,3),
stride=1, padding='SAME', weights_initializer=initializer)
        tf.summary.histogram('layer_3',layer_3)
        # Flatten the result of layer_3 before feeding to the
        # fully connected layer
        flat = flatten(layer_3)
```

```
        fc = fully_connected(flat, num_outputs=128,
weights_initializer=initializer)
        tf.summary.histogram('fc',fc)
        output = fully_connected(fc, num_outputs=n_outputs,
activation_fn=None, weights_initializer=initializer)
        tf.summary.histogram('output',output)

        # Vars will store the parameters of the network such as weights
        vars = {v.name[len(scope.name):]: v for v in
tf.get_collection(key=tf.GraphKeys.TRAINABLE_VARIABLES, scope=scope.name)}
        return vars, output
```

Next, we define an `epsilon_greedy` function for performing the epsilon-greedy policy. In the epsilon-greedy policy, we either select the best action with the probability 1-epsilon or a random action with the probability epsilon.

We use a decaying epsilon-greedy policy where the value of epsilon will be decaying over time as we don't want to explore forever. So, over time, our policy will be exploiting only good actions:

```
epsilon = 0.5
eps_min = 0.05
eps_max = 1.0
eps_decay_steps = 500000
def epsilon_greedy(action, step):
    p = np.random.random(1).squeeze()
    epsilon = max(eps_min, eps_max - (eps_max-eps_min) *
step/eps_decay_steps)
    if np.random.rand() < epsilon:
        return np.random.randint(n_outputs)
    else:
        return action
```

Now, we initialize our experience replay buffer of length 20000, which holds the experience.

We store all the agent's experiences (state, action, rewards) in the experience replay buffer and we sample this mini batch of experiences for training the network:

```
def sample_memories(batch_size):
    perm_batch = np.random.permutation(len(exp_buffer))[:batch_size]
    mem = np.array(exp_buffer)[perm_batch]
    return mem[:,0], mem[:,1], mem[:,2], mem[:,3], mem[:,4]
```

Next, we define all our hyperparameters:

```
num_episodes = 800
batch_size = 48
input_shape = (None, 88, 80, 1)
learning_rate = 0.001
X_shape = (None, 88, 80, 1)
discount_factor = 0.97

global_step = 0
copy_steps = 100
steps_train = 4
start_steps = 2000
logdir = 'logs'
```

Now we define the `placeholder` for our input, such as the game state:

```
X = tf.placeholder(tf.float32, shape=X_shape)
```

We define a boolean called `in_training_mode` to toggle the training:

```
in_training_mode = tf.placeholder(tf.bool)
```

We build our Q network, which takes the input X and generates Q values for all the actions in the state:

```
mainQ, mainQ_outputs = q_network(X, 'mainQ')
```

Similarly, we build our target Q network:

```
targetQ, targetQ_outputs = q_network(X, 'targetQ')
```

Define the `placeholder` for our action values:

```
X_action = tf.placeholder(tf.int32, shape=(None,))
Q_action = tf.reduce_sum(targetQ_outputs * tf.one_hot(X_action, n_outputs),
axis=-1, keep_dims=True)
```

Copy the main Q network parameters to the target Q network:

```
copy_op = [tf.assign(main_name, targetQ[var_name]) for var_name, main_name
in mainQ.items()]
copy_target_to_main = tf.group(*copy_op)
```

Define a `placeholder` for our output, such as action:

```
y = tf.placeholder(tf.float32, shape=(None,1))
```

Now we calculate the loss, which is the difference between the actual value and predicted value:

```
loss = tf.reduce_mean(tf.square(y - Q_action))
```

We use `AdamOptimizer` for minimizing the loss:

```
optimizer = tf.train.AdamOptimizer(learning_rate)
training_op = optimizer.minimize(loss)
```

Set up the log files for visualization in TensorBoard:

```
loss_summary = tf.summary.scalar('LOSS', loss)
merge_summary = tf.summary.merge_all()
file_writer = tf.summary.FileWriter(logdir, tf.get_default_graph())
```

Next, we start the TensorFlow session and run the model:

```
init = tf.global_variables_initializer()
with tf.Session() as sess:
    init.run()
    # for each episode
    for i in range(num_episodes):
        done = False
        obs = env.reset()
        epoch = 0
        episodic_reward = 0
        actions_counter = Counter()
        episodic_loss = []

        # while the state is not the terminal state
        while not done:

          #env.render()
           # get the preprocessed game screen
           obs = preprocess_observation(obs)

           # feed the game screen and get the Q values for each action
           actions = mainQ_outputs.eval(feed_dict={X:[obs],
```

```
in_training_mode:False})

            # get the action
            action = np.argmax(actions, axis=-1)
            actions_counter[str(action)] += 1

            # select the action using epsilon greedy policy
            action = epsilon_greedy(action, global_step)
            # now perform the action and move to the next state,
            # next_obs, receive reward
            next_obs, reward, done, _ = env.step(action)

            # Store this transition as an experience in the replay buffer
            exp_buffer.append([obs, action,
preprocess_observation(next_obs), reward, done])
            # After certain steps, we train our Q network with samples from
the experience replay buffer
            if global_step % steps_train == 0 and global_step >
start_steps:
                # sample experience
                o_obs, o_act, o_next_obs, o_rew, o_done =
sample_memories(batch_size)

                # states
                o_obs = [x for x in o_obs]

                # next states
                o_next_obs = [x for x in o_next_obs]

                # next actions
                next_act = mainQ_outputs.eval(feed_dict={X:o_next_obs,
in_training_mode:False})


                # reward
                y_batch = o_rew + discount_factor * np.max(next_act,
axis=-1) * (1-o_done)

                # merge all summaries and write to the file
                mrg_summary = merge_summary.eval(feed_dict={X:o_obs,
y:np.expand_dims(y_batch, axis=-1), X_action:o_act,
in_training_mode:False})
                file_writer.add_summary(mrg_summary, global_step)
```

```
                # now we train the network and calculate loss
                train_loss, _ = sess.run([loss, training_op],
feed_dict={X:o_obs, y:np.expand_dims(y_batch, axis=-1), X_action:o_act,
in_training_mode:True})
                episodic_loss.append(train_loss)
            # after some interval we copy our main Q network weights to
target Q network
            if (global_step+1) % copy_steps == 0 and global_step >
start_steps:
                copy_target_to_main.run()
            obs = next_obs
            epoch += 1
            global_step += 1
            episodic_reward += reward
        print('Epoch', epoch, 'Reward', episodic_reward,)
```

You can see the output as follows:

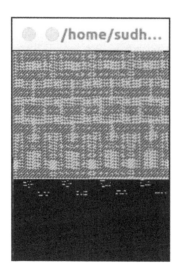

We can see the computation graph of the DQN in TensorBoard as follows:

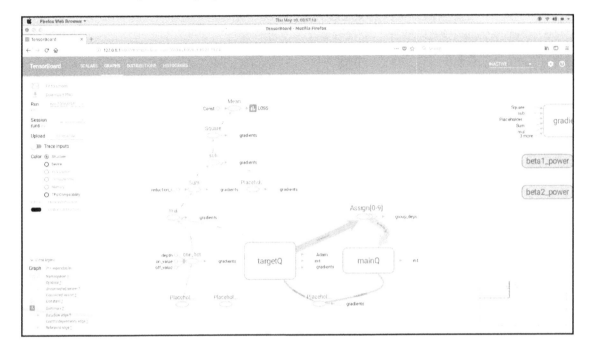

We can visualize the distribution of weights in both our main and target networks:

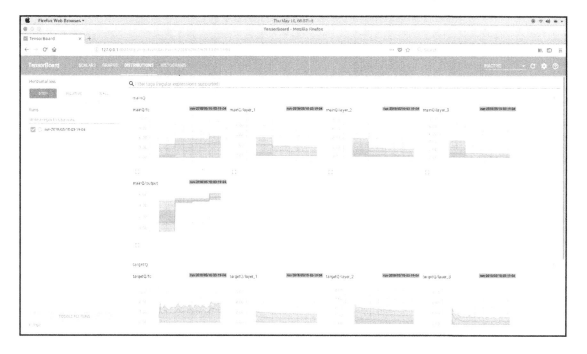

We can also see the loss:

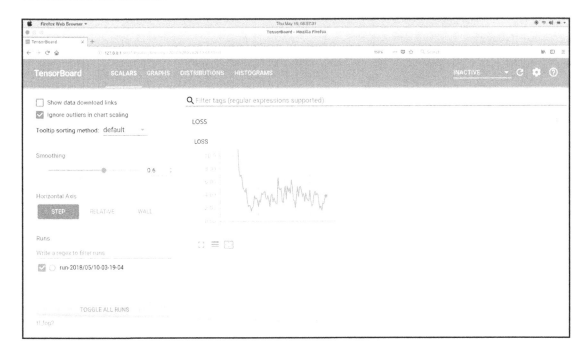

Double DQN

Deep Q learning is pretty cool, right? It has generalized its learning to play any Atari game. But the problem with DQN is that it tends to overestimate Q values. This is because of the max operator in the Q learning equation. The max operator uses the same value for both selecting and evaluating an action. What do I mean by that? Let's suppose we are in a state s and we have five actions a_1 to a_5. Let's say a_3 is the best action. When we estimate Q values for all these actions in the state s, the estimated Q values will have some noise and differ from the actual value. Due to this noise, action a_2 will get a higher value than the optimal action a_3. Now, if we select the best action as the one that has maximum value, we will end up selecting a suboptimal action a_2 instead of optimal action a_3.

We can solve this problem by having two separate Q functions, each learning independently. One Q function is used to select an action and the other Q function is used to evaluate an action. We can implement this by just tweaking the target function of DQN. Recall the target function of DQN:

$$y_i^{DQN} = r + \gamma max_{a'} Q(s', a'; \theta')$$

We can modify our target function as follows:

$$y_i^{Double DQN} = r + \gamma Q(s, argmax Q(s, a; \theta^-); \theta')$$

In the preceding equation, we have two Q functions each with different weights. So a Q function with weights θ' is used to select the action and the other Q function with weights θ^- is used to evaluate the action. We can also switch the roles of these two Q functions.

Prioritized experience replay

In DQN architecture, we use experience replay to remove correlations between the training samples. However, uniformly sampling transitions from the replay memory is not an optimal method. Instead, we can prioritize transitions and sample according to priority. Prioritizing transitions helps the network to learn swiftly and effectively. How do we prioritize the transitions? We prioritize the transitions that have a high TD error. We know that a TD error specifies the difference between the estimated Q value and the actual Q value. So, transitions with a high TD error are the transition we have to focus on and learn from because those are the transitions that deviate from our estimation. Intuitively, let us say you try to solve a set of problems, but you fail in solving two of these problems. You then give priority to those two problems alone to focus on what went wrong and try to fix that:

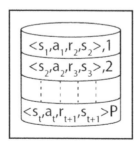

We use two types of prioritization—proportional prioritization and rank-based prioritization.

In **proportional prioritization**, we define the priority as:

$$p_i = (\delta_i + \epsilon)^\alpha$$

p_i is the priority of the transition i, δ_i is the TD error of transition i, and ϵ is simply some positive constant value that makes sure that every transition has non-zero priority. When δ is zero, adding ϵ makes the transition have a priority instead of zero priority. However, the transition will have lower priority than the transitions whose δ is not zero. The α exponent denotes the amount of prioritization being used. When α is zero, then it is simply the uniform case.

Now, we can translate this priority into a probability using the following formula:

$$P_i = \frac{p_i}{\sum_k p_k}$$

In rank-based prioritization, we define the priority as:

$$p_i = \left(\frac{1}{rank(i)}\right)^\alpha$$

rank(i) specifies the location of the transition *i* in the replay buffer where the transitions are sorted from high TD error to low TD error. After calculating the priority, we can convert the priority into a probability using the same formula, $P_i = \frac{p_i}{\sum_k p_k}$.

Dueling network architecture

We know that the *Q* function specifies how good it is for an agent to perform an action *a* in the state *s* and the value function specifies how good it is for an agent to be in a state *s*. Now we introduce a new function called an advantage function which can be defined as the difference between the value function and the advantage function. The advantage function specifies how good it is for an agent to perform an action *a* compared to other actions.

Thus, the value function specifies the goodness of a state and the advantage function specifies the goodness of an action. What would happen if we were to combine the value function and advantage function? It would tell us how good it is for an agent to perform an action a in a state s that is actually our Q function. So we can define our Q function as a sum of a value function and an advantage function, as in $Q(s, a) = V(s) + A(a)$.

Now we will see how the dueling network architecture works. The following diagram shows the architecture of dueling DQN:

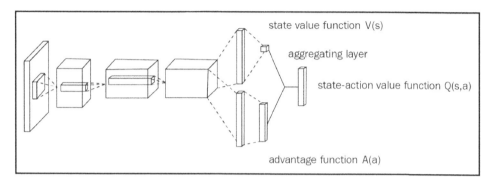

The architecture of dueling DQN is essentially the same as DQN, except that the fully connected layer at the end is divided into two streams. One stream computes the value function, and the other stream computes the advantage function. Finally, we combine these two streams using the aggregate layer and get the Q function.

Why do we have to break our Q function computation into two streams? In many states, it is not important to compute value estimates of all the actions, especially when we have a large action space in a state; then most of the actions will not have any effect on the state. Also, there could be many actions with redundant effects. In these cases, dueling DQN estimates the Q values more precisely than the existing DQN architecture:

- The first stream, as in value function stream, is useful when we have a large number of actions in the state and when estimating a value of each action is not really important
- The second stream, as in advantage function stream, is useful when the network has to decide which action is preferred over the other

The aggregator layer combines the value of these two streams and produces the Q function. Thus, a dueling network is more effective and robust than the standard DQN architecture.

Summary

In this chapter, we have learned about one of the very popular deep reinforcement learning algorithms called DQN. We saw how deep neural networks are used to approximate the Q function. We also learned how to build an agent to play Atari games. Later, we looked at several advancements to the DQN, such as double DQN, which is used to avoid overestimating Q values. We then looked at prioritized experience replay, for prioritizing the experience, and dueling network architecture, which breaks down the Q function computation into two streams, called value stream and advantage stream.

In the next chapter, Chapter 9, *Playing Doom with Deep Recurrent Q Network*, we will look at a really cool variant of DQNs called DRQN, which makes use of an RNN for approximating a Q function.

Questions

The question list is as follows:

1. What is DQN?
2. What is the need for experience replay?
3. Why do we keep a separate target network?
4. Why is DQN overestimating?
5. How does double DQN avoid overestimating the Q value?
6. How are experiences prioritized in prioritized experience replay?
7. What is the need for duel architecture?

Further reading

- **DQN paper**: https://storage.googleapis.com/deepmind-media/dqn/DQNNaturePaper.pdf
- **Double DQN paper**: https://arxiv.org/pdf/1509.06461.pdf
- **Dueling network architecture**: https://arxiv.org/pdf/1511.06581.pdf

9
Playing Doom with a Deep Recurrent Q Network

In the last chapter, we saw how to build an agent using a **Deep Q Network (DQN)** in order to play Atari games. We have taken advantage of neural networks for approximating the Q function, used the **convolutional neural network (CNN)** to understand the input game screen, and taken the past four game screens to better understand the current game state. In this chapter, we will learn how to improve the performance of our DQN by taking advantage of the **recurrent neural network (RNN)**. We will also look at what is partially observable with the **Markov Decision Process (MDP)** and how we can solve that using a **Deep Recurrent Q Network (DRQN)**. Following this, we will learn how to build an agent to play the game Doom using a DRQN. Finally, we will see a variant of DRQN called **Deep Attention Recurrent Q Network (DARQN)**, which augments the attention mechanism to the DRQN architecture.

In this chapter, you will learn the following topics:

- DRQN
- Partially observable MDP
- The architecture of DRQN
- How to build an agent to play the game Doom using a DRQN
- DARQN

DRQN

So, why do we need DRQN when our DQN performed at a human level at Atari games? To answer this question, let us understand the problem of the **partially observable Markov Decision Process (POMDP)**. An environment is called a partially observable MDP when we have a limited set of information available about the environment. So far, in the previous chapters, we have seen a fully observable MDP where we know all possible actions and states—although the agent might be unaware of transition and reward probabilities, it had complete knowledge of the environment, for example, a frozen lake environment, where we clearly know about all the states and actions of the environment; we easily modeled that environment as a fully observable MDP. But most of the real-world environments are only partially observable; we cannot see all the states. Consider the agent learning to walk in the real-world environment; obviously, the agent will not have complete knowledge of the environment, it will have no information outside its view. In POMDP, states provide only partial information, but keeping the information about past states in the memory might help the agent better understand the nature of the environment and improve the policy. Thus, in POMDP, we need to retain the information about previous states in order to take the optimal action.

To recollect what we learned in previous chapters, consider the game Pong, shown in the following. By just looking at the current game screen, we can tell the position of the ball, but we also need to know the direction in which the ball is moving and the velocity of the ball, so that we can take the optimal action. Just looking at the current game screen, however, does not give us the direction and velocity of the ball:

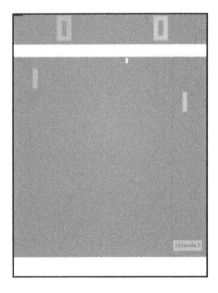

To overcome this, instead of considering only the current game screen, we will take the past four game screens to understand the direction and velocity of the ball. This is what we have seen in DQN. We feed the past four game screens as the input to the convolutional layer, along with the current game screen, and received the Q values for all possible actions in the state. But, do you think using only the past four screens will help us in understanding different environments? There will be some environments where we might even require the past 100 game screens to better understand the current game state. But, stacking the past *n* game screens will slow down our training process, and it will also increase the size of our experience replay buffer.

So, we can take the advantage of the RNN here to understand and retain information about the previous states as long as it is required. We will modify the DQN architecture by augmenting with the LSTM layer to understand the previous information. In DQN architecture, we replace the first post convolutional fully connected layer with the LSTM RNN. In this way, we can also solve the problem of partial observability, as now our agent has the ability to remember the past states and can improve the policy.

Architecture of DRQN

The architecture of DRQN is shown next. It is similar to DQN, but we replace the first post convolutional fully connected layer with the LSTM RNN, shown as follows:

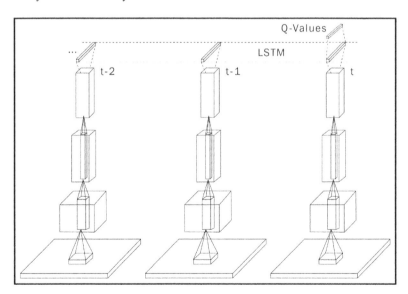

Thus, we pass the game screen as an input to the convolutional layer. The convolutional layer convolves the image and produces feature maps. The resulting feature map is then passed to the LSTM layer. The LSTM layer has the memory for holding information. The LSTM layer retains the information about important previous game states and updates its memory over time steps as required. It outputs Q values after passing through a fully connected layer. Therefore, unlike DQN, we don't estimate $Q(s_t, a_t)$ directly. Instead, we estimate $Q(h_t, a_t)$ where h_t is the input returned by the network at the previous time step. That is, $h_t = LSTM(h_{t-1}, o_t)$. As we are using RNN, we train our network by backpropagation through time.

Wait. What about the experience replay buffer? In DQN, to avoid correlated experience, we used an experience replay, which stores the game transition, and we used a random batch of experience to train the network. In the case of DRQN, we store an entire episode in an experience buffer and we randomly sample n steps from a random batch of episodes. So, in this way, we can accommodate both randomization and also an experience that actually follows another.

Training an agent to play Doom

Doom is a very popular first-person shooter game. The goal of the game is to kill monsters. Doom is another example of a partially observable MDP as the agent's (player) view is limited to 90 degrees. The agent has no idea about the rest of the environment. Now, we will see how can we use DRQN to train our agent to play Doom.

Instead of OpenAI Gym, we will use the ViZDoom package to simulate the Doom environment to train our agent. To learn more about the ViZDoom package, check out its official website at http://vizdoom.cs.put.edu.pl/. We can install ViZDoom simply by using the following command:

```
pip install vizdoom
```

ViZDoom provides a lot of Doom scenarios and those scenarios can be found in the package folder vizdoom/scenarios.

Basic Doom game

Before diving in, let us familiarize ourselves with a `vizdoom` environment by seeing a basic example:

1. Let's load the necessary libraries:

```
from vizdoom import *
import random
import time
```

2. Create an instance to the `DoomGame`:

```
game = DoomGame()
```

3. As we know ViZDoom provides a lot of Doom scenarios, let us load the basic scenario:

```
game.load_config("basic.cfg")
```

4. The `init()` method initializes the game with the scenario:

```
game.init()
```

5. Now, let's define the one with hot encoded `actions`:

```
shoot = [0, 0, 1]
left = [1, 0, 0]
right = [0, 1, 0]
actions = [shoot, left, right]
```

6. Now, let us start playing the game:

```
no_of_episodes = 10

for i in range(no_of_episodes):
    # for each episode start the game
    game.new_episode()
    # loop until the episode is over
    while not game.is_episode_finished():
        # get the game state
        state = game.get_state()
        img = state.screen_buffer
        # get the game variables
        misc = state.game_variables
```

```
                              # perform some action randomly and receive reward
                              reward = game.make_action(random.choice(actions))
                              print(reward)
                       # we will set some time before starting the next episode
                       time.sleep(2)
```

Once you run the program, you can see the output as follows:

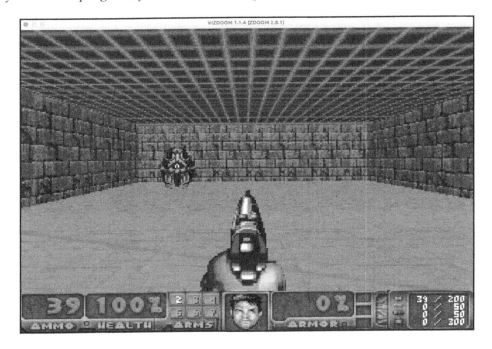

Doom with DRQN

Now, let us see how to make use of the DRQN algorithm to train our agent to play Doom. We assign positive rewards for successfully killing the monsters and negative rewards for losing life, suicide, and losing ammo (bullets). You can get the complete code as a Jupyter notebook with the explanation at `https://github.com/sudharsan13296/Hands-On-Reinforcement-Learning-With-Python/blob/master/09.%20Playing%20Doom%20Game%20using%20DRQN/9.5%20Doom%20Game%20Using%20DRQN.ipynb`. The credits for the code used in this section go to **Luthanicus** (`https://github.com/Luthanicus/losaltoshackathon-drqn`).

First, let us import all the necessary libraries:

```
import tensorflow as tf
import numpy as np
import matplotlib.pyplot as plt
from vizdoom import *
import timeit
import math
import os
import sys
```

Now, let us define the `get_input_shape` function to compute the final shape of the input image after it gets convolved after the convolutional layer:

```
def get_input_shape(Image,Filter,Stride):
    layer1 = math.ceil(((Image - Filter + 1) / Stride))
    o1 = math.ceil((layer1 / Stride))
    layer2 = math.ceil(((o1 - Filter + 1) / Stride))
    o2 = math.ceil((layer2 / Stride))
    layer3 = math.ceil(((o2 - Filter + 1) / Stride))
    o3 = math.ceil((layer3 / Stride))
    return int(o3)
```

We will now define the DRQN class, which implements the DRQN algorithm. Check the comments that precede each line of code to understand it:

```
class DRQN():
    def __init__(self, input_shape, num_actions, initial_learning_rate):
        # first, we initialize all the hyperparameters

        self.tfcast_type = tf.float32
        # shape of our input, which would be (length, width, channels)
        self.input_shape = input_shape
        # number of actions in the environment
        self.num_actions = num_actions
        # learning rate for the neural network
        self.learning_rate = initial_learning_rate
        # now we will define the hyperparameters of the convolutional
neural network

        # filter size
        self.filter_size = 5
        # number of filters
        self.num_filters = [16, 32, 64]
        # stride size
        self.stride = 2
        # pool size
        self.poolsize = 2
```

```
        # shape of our convolutional layer
        self.convolution_shape = get_input_shape(input_shape[0],
self.filter_size, self.stride) * get_input_shape(input_shape[1],
self.filter_size, self.stride) * self.num_filters[2]
        # now, we define the hyperparameters of our recurrent neural
network and the final feed forward layer
        # number of neurons
        self.cell_size = 100
        # number of hidden layers
        self.hidden_layer = 50
        # drop out probability
        self.dropout_probability = [0.3, 0.2]

        # hyperparameters for optimization
        self.loss_decay_rate = 0.96
        self.loss_decay_steps = 180

        # initialize all the variables for the CNN

        # we initialize the placeholder for input whose shape would be
(length, width, channel)
        self.input = tf.placeholder(shape = (self.input_shape[0],
self.input_shape[1], self.input_shape[2]), dtype = self.tfcast_type)
        # we will also initialize the shape of the target vector whose
shape is equal to the number of actions
        self.target_vector = tf.placeholder(shape = (self.num_actions, 1),
dtype = self.tfcast_type)

        # initialize feature maps for our corresponding 3 filters
        self.features1 = tf.Variable(initial_value =
np.random.rand(self.filter_size, self.filter_size, input_shape[2],
self.num_filters[0]),
                                     dtype = self.tfcast_type)
        self.features2 = tf.Variable(initial_value =
np.random.rand(self.filter_size, self.filter_size, self.num_filters[0],
self.num_filters[1]),
                                     dtype = self.tfcast_type)
        self.features3 = tf.Variable(initial_value =
np.random.rand(self.filter_size, self.filter_size, self.num_filters[1],
self.num_filters[2]),
                                     dtype = self.tfcast_type)

        # initialize variables for RNN
        self.h = tf.Variable(initial_value = np.zeros((1, self.cell_size)),
dtype = self.tfcast_type)
        # hidden to hidden weight matrix
        self.rW = tf.Variable(initial_value = np.random.uniform(
                                        low = -np.sqrt(6. /
```

```
(self.convolution_shape + self.cell_size)),
                                        high = np.sqrt(6. /
(self.convolution_shape + self.cell_size)),
                                        size = (self.convolution_shape,
self.cell_size)),
                             dtype = self.tfcast_type)
        # input to hidden weight matrix
        self.rU = tf.Variable(initial_value = np.random.uniform(
                                        low = -np.sqrt(6. / (2 *
self.cell_size)),
                                        high = np.sqrt(6. / (2 *
self.cell_size)),
                                        size = (self.cell_size,
self.cell_size)),
                             dtype = self.tfcast_type)
        # hidden to output weight matrix
        self.rV = tf.Variable(initial_value = np.random.uniform(
                                        low = -np.sqrt(6. / (2 *
self.cell_size)),
                                        high = np.sqrt(6. / (2 *
self.cell_size)),
                                        size = (self.cell_size,
self.cell_size)),
                             dtype = self.tfcast_type)
        # bias
        self.rb = tf.Variable(initial_value = np.zeros(self.cell_size),
dtype = self.tfcast_type)
        self.rc = tf.Variable(initial_value = np.zeros(self.cell_size),
dtype = self.tfcast_type)

        # initialize weights and bias of feed forward network
        # weights
        self.fW = tf.Variable(initial_value = np.random.uniform(
                                        low = -np.sqrt(6. /
(self.cell_size + self.num_actions)),
                                        high = np.sqrt(6. /
(self.cell_size + self.num_actions)),
                                        size = (self.cell_size,
self.num_actions)),
                             dtype = self.tfcast_type)
        # bias
        self.fb = tf.Variable(initial_value = np.zeros(self.num_actions),
dtype = self.tfcast_type)

        # learning rate
        self.step_count = tf.Variable(initial_value = 0, dtype =
self.tfcast_type)
        self.learning_rate = tf.train.exponential_decay(self.learning_rate,
```

```
                                            self.step_count,
                                            self.loss_decay_steps,
                                            self.loss_decay_steps,
                                            staircase = False)

    # now let us build the network

    # first convolutional layer
    self.conv1 = tf.nn.conv2d(input = tf.reshape(self.input, shape =
(1, self.input_shape[0], self.input_shape[1], self.input_shape[2])), filter
= self.features1, strides = [1, self.stride, self.stride, 1], padding =
"VALID")
    self.relu1 = tf.nn.relu(self.conv1)
    self.pool1 = tf.nn.max_pool(self.relu1, ksize = [1, self.poolsize,
self.poolsize, 1], strides = [1, self.stride, self.stride, 1], padding =
"SAME")

    # second convolutional layer
    self.conv2 = tf.nn.conv2d(input = self.pool1, filter =
self.features2, strides = [1, self.stride, self.stride, 1], padding =
"VALID")
    self.relu2 = tf.nn.relu(self.conv2)
    self.pool2 = tf.nn.max_pool(self.relu2, ksize = [1, self.poolsize,
self.poolsize, 1], strides = [1, self.stride, self.stride, 1], padding =
"SAME")

    # third convolutional layer
    self.conv3 = tf.nn.conv2d(input = self.pool2, filter =
self.features3, strides = [1, self.stride, self.stride, 1], padding =
"VALID")
    self.relu3 = tf.nn.relu(self.conv3)
    self.pool3 = tf.nn.max_pool(self.relu3, ksize = [1, self.poolsize,
self.poolsize, 1], strides = [1, self.stride, self.stride, 1], padding =
"SAME")

    # add dropout and reshape the input
    self.drop1 = tf.nn.dropout(self.pool3, self.dropout_probability[0])
    self.reshaped_input = tf.reshape(self.drop1, shape = [1, -1])

    # now we build the recurrent neural network, which takes the input
from the last layer of the convolutional network
    self.h = tf.tanh(tf.matmul(self.reshaped_input, self.rW) +
tf.matmul(self.h, self.rU) + self.rb)
    self.o = tf.nn.softmax(tf.matmul(self.h, self.rV) + self.rc)

    # add drop out to RNN
    self.drop2 = tf.nn.dropout(self.o, self.dropout_probability[1])
    # we feed the result of RNN to the feed forward layer
```

```
        self.output = tf.reshape(tf.matmul(self.drop2, self.fW) + self.fb,
  shape = [-1, 1])
        self.prediction = tf.argmax(self.output)

        # compute loss
        self.loss = tf.reduce_mean(tf.square(self.target_vector -
  self.output))
        # we use Adam optimizer for minimizing the error
        self.optimizer = tf.train.AdamOptimizer(self.learning_rate)
        # compute gradients of the loss and update the gradients
        self.gradients = self.optimizer.compute_gradients(self.loss)
        self.update = self.optimizer.apply_gradients(self.gradients)

        self.parameters = (self.features1, self.features2, self.features3,
                           self.rW, self.rU, self.rV, self.rb, self.rc,
                           self.fW, self.fb)
```

Now we define the `ExperienceReplay` class to implement the experience replay buffer. We store all the agent's experience, that is, state, action, and rewards in the experience replay buffer, and we sample this minibatch of experience for training the network:

```
class ExperienceReplay():
    def __init__(self, buffer_size):
        # buffer for holding the transition
        self.buffer = []
        # size of the buffer
        self.buffer_size = buffer_size
    # we remove the old transition if the buffer size has reached it's
  limit. Think off the buffer as a queue, when the new
    # one comes, the old one goes off
    def appendToBuffer(self, memory_tuplet):
        if len(self.buffer) > self.buffer_size:
            for i in range(len(self.buffer) - self.buffer_size):
                self.buffer.remove(self.buffer[0])
        self.buffer.append(memory_tuplet)
    # define a function called sample for sampling some random n number of
  transitions
    def sample(self, n):
        memories = []
        for i in range(n):
            memory_index = np.random.randint(0, len(self.buffer))
            memories.append(self.buffer[memory_index])
        return memories
```

Now, we define the `train` function for training our network:

```
def train(num_episodes, episode_length, learning_rate, scenario =
"deathmatch.cfg", map_path = 'map02', render = False):
    # discount parameter for Q-value computation
    discount_factor = .99
    # frequency for updating the experience in the buffer
    update_frequency = 5
    store_frequency = 50
    # for printing the output
    print_frequency = 1000

    # initialize variables for storing total rewards and total loss
    total_reward = 0
    total_loss = 0
    old_q_value = 0

    # initialize lists for storing the episodic rewards and losses
    rewards = []
    losses = []

    # okay, now let us get to the action!
    # first, we initialize our doomgame environment
    game = DoomGame()
    # specify the path where our scenario file is located
    game.set_doom_scenario_path(scenario)
    # specify the path of map file
    game.set_doom_map(map_path)

    # then we set screen resolution and screen format
    game.set_screen_resolution(ScreenResolution.RES_256X160)
    game.set_screen_format(ScreenFormat.RGB24)

    # we can add particles and effects we needed by simply setting them to
true or false
    game.set_render_hud(False)
    game.set_render_minimal_hud(False)
    game.set_render_crosshair(False)
    game.set_render_weapon(True)
    game.set_render_decals(False)
    game.set_render_particles(False)
    game.set_render_effects_sprites(False)
    game.set_render_messages(False)
    game.set_render_corpses(False)
    game.set_render_screen_flashes(True)

    # now we will specify buttons that should be available to the agent
    game.add_available_button(Button.MOVE_LEFT)
```

```
    game.add_available_button(Button.MOVE_RIGHT)
    game.add_available_button(Button.TURN_LEFT)
    game.add_available_button(Button.TURN_RIGHT)
    game.add_available_button(Button.MOVE_FORWARD)
    game.add_available_button(Button.MOVE_BACKWARD)
    game.add_available_button(Button.ATTACK)
    # okay, now we will add one more button called delta. The preceding
button will only
    # work like keyboard keys and will have only boolean values.

    # so we use delta button, which emulates a mouse device which will have
positive and negative values
    # and it will be useful in environment for exploring
    game.add_available_button(Button.TURN_LEFT_RIGHT_DELTA, 90)
    game.add_available_button(Button.LOOK_UP_DOWN_DELTA, 90)

    # initialize an array for actions
    actions = np.zeros((game.get_available_buttons_size(),
game.get_available_buttons_size()))
    count = 0
    for i in actions:
        i[count] = 1
        count += 1
    actions = actions.astype(int).tolist()


    # then we add the game variables, ammo, health, and killcount
    game.add_available_game_variable(GameVariable.AMMO0)
    game.add_available_game_variable(GameVariable.HEALTH)
    game.add_available_game_variable(GameVariable.KILLCOUNT)

    # we set episode_timeout to terminate the episode after some time step
    # we also set episode_start_time which is useful for skipping initial
events
    game.set_episode_timeout(6 * episode_length)
    game.set_episode_start_time(10)
    game.set_window_visible(render)
    # we can also enable sound by setting set_sound_enable to true
    game.set_sound_enabled(False)

    # we set living reward to 0, which rewards the agent for each move it
does even though the move is not useful
    game.set_living_reward(0)

    # doom has different modes such as player, spectator, asynchronous
player, and asynchronous spectator
    # in spectator mode humans will play and agent will learn from it.
    # in player mode, the agent actually plays the game, so we use player
```

```
mode.
    game.set_mode(Mode.PLAYER)

    # okay, So now we, initialize the game environment
    game.init()

    # now, let us create instance to our DRQN class and create our both
actor and target DRQN networks
    actionDRQN = DRQN((160, 256, 3), game.get_available_buttons_size() - 2,
learning_rate)
    targetDRQN = DRQN((160, 256, 3), game.get_available_buttons_size() - 2,
learning_rate)
    # we will also create an instance to the ExperienceReplay class with
the buffer size of 1000
    experiences = ExperienceReplay(1000)

    # for storing the models
    saver = tf.train.Saver({v.name: v for v in actionDRQN.parameters},
max_to_keep = 1)

    # now let us start the training process
    # we initialize variables for sampling and storing transitions from the
experience buffer
    sample = 5
    store = 50
    # start the tensorflow session
    with tf.Session() as sess:
        # initialize all tensorflow variables
        sess.run(tf.global_variables_initializer())
        for episode in range(num_episodes):
            # start the new episode
            game.new_episode()
            # play the episode till it reaches the episode length
            for frame in range(episode_length):
                # get the game state
                state = game.get_state()
                s = state.screen_buffer
                # select the action
                a = actionDRQN.prediction.eval(feed_dict =
{actionDRQN.input: s})[0]
                action = actions[a]
                # perform the action and store the reward
                reward = game.make_action(action)
                # update total reward
                total_reward += reward

                # if the episode is over then break
                if game.is_episode_finished():
```

```
                    break
                # store the transition to our experience buffer
                if (frame % store) == 0:
                    experiences.appendToBuffer((s, action, reward))

                # sample experience from the experience buffer
                if (frame % sample) == 0:
                    memory = experiences.sample(1)
                    mem_frame = memory[0][0]
                    mem_reward = memory[0][2]
                    # now, train the network
                    Q1 = actionDRQN.output.eval(feed_dict =
{actionDRQN.input: mem_frame})
                    Q2 = targetDRQN.output.eval(feed_dict =
{targetDRQN.input: mem_frame})

                    # set learning rate
                    learning_rate = actionDRQN.learning_rate.eval()

                    # calculate Q value
                    Qtarget = old_q_value + learning_rate * (mem_reward +
discount_factor * Q2 - old_q_value)
                    # update old Q value
                    old_q_value = Qtarget

                    # compute Loss
                    loss = actionDRQN.loss.eval(feed_dict =
{actionDRQN.target_vector: Qtarget, actionDRQN.input: mem_frame})
                    # update total loss
                    total_loss += loss

                    # update both networks
                    actionDRQN.update.run(feed_dict =
{actionDRQN.target_vector: Qtarget, actionDRQN.input: mem_frame})
                    targetDRQN.update.run(feed_dict =
{targetDRQN.target_vector: Qtarget, targetDRQN.input: mem_frame})

            rewards.append((episode, total_reward))
            losses.append((episode, total_loss))

            print("Episode %d - Reward = %.3f, Loss = %.3f." % (episode,
total_reward, total_loss))

            total_reward = 0
            total_loss = 0
```

Let us train for `10000` episodes, where each episode has a length of `300`:

```
train(num_episodes = 10000, episode_length = 300, learning_rate = 0.01,
render = True)
```

When you run the program, you can see the output shown as follows, and you can see how our agent is learning through episodes:

DARQN

We have improved our DQN architecture by adding a recurrent layer, which captures temporal dependency, and we called it DRQN. Do you think we can improve our DRQN architecture further? Yes. We can further improve our DRQN architecture by adding the attention layer on top of the convolutional layer. So, what is the function of the attention layer? Attention implies the literal meaning of the word. Attention mechanisms are widely used in image captioning, object detection, and so on. Consider the task of neural networks captioning the image; to understand what is in the image, the network has to give attention to the specific object in the image for generating the caption.

Similarly, when we add the attention layer to our DRQN, we can select and pay attention to small regions of the image, and ultimately this reduces the number of parameters in the network and also reduces the training and testing time. Unlike DRQN, LSTM layers in DARQN not only stored previous state information for taking the next optimal action; it also stores information for deciding which region of an image to focus on next.

Architecture of DARQN

The architecture of DARQN is shown as follows:

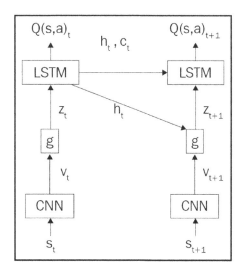

It consists of three layers; convolutional, attention, and LSTM recurrent layers. The game screen is fed as the image to the convolutional network. The convolutional network processes the image and produces the feature maps. The feature maps then feed into the attention layer. The attention layer transforms them into a vector and results in their linear combination, called context vectors. The context vectors, along with previous hidden states, are then passed to the LSTM layer. The LSTM layer gives two outputs; in one, it gives the Q value for deciding what action to perform in a state, and in the other, it helps the attention network decide what region of the image to focus on in the next time step so that better context vectors can be generated.

The attention is of two types:

- **Soft attention**: We know that feature maps produced by the convolutional layer are fed as an input to the attention layer, which then produces the context vector. With soft attention, these context vectors are simply the weighted average of all the output (feature maps) produced by the convolutional layer. Weights are chosen according to the relative importance of the features.

- **Hard attention**: With hard attention, we focus only on the particular location of an image at a time step t according to some location selection policy π. This policy is represented by a neural network whose weights are the policy parameters and the output of the network is the location selection probability. However, hard attentions are not much better than soft attentions.

Summary

In this chapter, we learned how DRQN is used to remember information about the previous states and how it overcomes the problem of partially observable MDP. We have seen how to train our agent to play the game Doom using a DRQN algorithm. We have also learned about DARQN as an improvement to DRQN, which adds an attention layer on top of the convolution layer. Following this, we saw the two types of attention mechanism; namely, soft and hard attention.

In the next chapter, Chapter 10, *Asynchronous Advantage Actor Critic Network,* we will learn about another interesting deep reinforcement learning algorithm called Asynchronous Advantage Actor Critic network.

Questions

The question list is as follows:

1. What is the difference between DQN and DRQN?
2. What are the shortcomings of DQN?
3. How do we set up an experience replay in DQN?
4. What is the difference between DRQN and DARQN?
5. Why do we need DARQN?
6. What are the different types of attention mechanism?
7. Why do we set a living reward in Doom?

Further reading

Consider the following to further your knowledge:

- **DRQN paper**: https://arxiv.org/pdf/1507.06527.pdf
- **Playing the FPS game using DRQN**: https://arxiv.org/pdf/1609.05521.pdf
- **DARQN paper**: https://arxiv.org/pdf/1512.01693.pdf

10
The Asynchronous Advantage Actor Critic Network

In the previous chapters, we have seen how cool a **Deep Q Network (DQN)** is and how it succeeded in generalizing its learning to play a series of Atari games with a human level performance. But the problem we faced is that it required a large amount of computation power and training time. So, Google's DeepMind introduced a new algorithm called the **Asynchronous Advantage Actor Critic (A3C)** algorithm, which dominates the other deep reinforcement learning algorithms, as it requires less computation power and training time. The main idea behind A3C is that it uses several agents for learning in parallel and aggregates their overall experience. In this chapter, we will see how A3C networks work. Following this, we will learn how to build an agent to drive up a mountain using A3C.

In this chapter, you will learn the following:

- The Asynchronous Advantage Actor Critic Algorithm
- The three As
- The architecture of A3C
- How A3C works
- Driving up a mountain with A3C
- Visualization in TensorBoard

The Asynchronous Advantage Actor Critic

The A3C network came as a storm and took over the DQN. Aside of the previously stated advantages, it also yields good accuracy compared to other algorithms. It works well in both continuous and discrete action spaces. It uses several agents, and each agent learns in parallel with a different exploration policy in copies of the actual environment. Then, the experience obtained from these agents is aggregated to the global agent. The global agent is also called a master network or global network and other agents are also called the workers. Now, we will see in detail how A3C works and how it differs from the DQN algorithm.

The three As

Before diving in, what does A3C mean? What do the three As signify?

In A3C, the first A, **Asynchronous**, implies how it works. Instead of having a single agent that tries to learn the optimal policy such as in DQN, here, we have multiple agents that interact with the environment. Since we have multiple agents interacting to the environment at the same time, we provide copies of the environment to every agent so that each agent can interact with its own copy of the environment. So, all these multiple agents are called worker agents and we have a separate agent called global network that all the agents report to. The global network aggregates the learning.

The second A is **Advantage**; we have seen what an advantage function is while discussing the dueling network architecture of DQN. The advantage function can be defined as the difference between the Q function and the value function. We know that the Q function specifies how good the action is in a state and the value function specifies how good the state is. Now, think intuitively; what does the difference between these two imply? It tells us how good it is for an agent to perform an action *a* in a state *s* compared to all other actions.

The third A is **Actor Critic**; the architecture has two types of network, actor and critic. The role of the actor is to learn a policy and the role of the critic is to evaluate how good the policy learned by the actor is.

The architecture of A3C

Now, let's look at the architecture of A3C. Look at the following diagram:

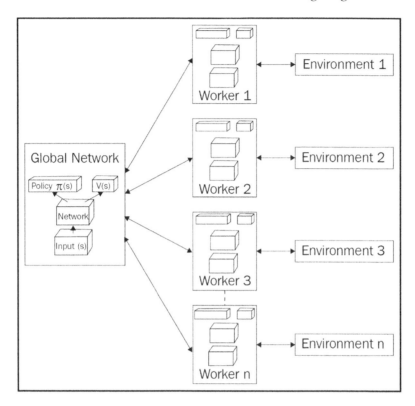

We can understand how A3C works by just looking at the preceding diagram. As we discussed, we can see there are multiple worker agents each interacting with its own copies of the environment. A worker then learns policy and calculates the gradient of the policy loss and updates the gradients to the global network. This global network is updated simultaneously by every agent. One of the advantages of A3C is that, unlike DQN, we don't use experience replay memory here. In fact, that it is one of the greatest advantages of an A3C network. Since we have multiple agents interacting with the environment and aggregating the information to the global network, there will be low to no correlation between the experience. Experience replay needs a lot of memory holding all of the experience. As A3C doesn't need that, our storage space and computation time will be reduced.

How A3C works

First, the worker agent resets the global network, and then they start interacting with the environment. Each worker follows a different exploration policy to learn an optimal policy. Following this, they compute value and policy loss and then they calculate the gradient of the loss and update the gradients to the global network. The cycle continues as the worker agent starts resetting the global network and repeats the same process. Before looking at the value and policy loss function, we will see how the advantage function is calculated. As we know, advantage is the difference between the Q function and the value function:

$$A(s,a) = Q(s,a) - V(s)$$

Since we don't actually calculate the Q value directly in A3C, we make use of discounted return as an estimate of the Q value. The discounted return R can be written as follows:

$$R = r_n + \gamma r_{n-1} + \gamma^2 r_{n-2}$$

We replace the Q function with the discounted return R as follows:

$$A(s,a) = R - V(s)$$

Now, we can write our value loss as the squared difference between the discounted return and the value of a state:

$$ValueLoss(L_v) = \sum (R - V(s))^2$$

And the policy loss can be defined as follows:

$$PolicyLoss(L_p) = Log(\pi(s)) * A(s) * \beta H(\pi)$$

Okay, what is that new term $H(\pi)$? It is the entropy term. It is used to ensure sufficient exploration of policy. Entropy tells us the spread of action probabilities. When the entropy value is high, every action's probability will be the same, so the agent will be unsure as to which action to perform, and when the entropy value is lowered, one action will have a higher probability than the others and the agent can pick up the action that has this high probability. Thus, adding entropy to the loss function encourages the agent to explore further and avoid getting stuck at the local optima.

Driving up a mountain with A3C

Let's understand A3C with a mountain car example. Our agent is the car and it is placed between two mountains. The goal of our agent is to drive up the mountain on the right. However, the car can't drive up the mountain in one pass; it has to drive up back and forth to build the momentum. A high reward will be assigned if our agent spends less energy on driving up. Credits for the code used in this section goes to Stefan Boschenriedter (`https:/ /github.com/stefanbo92/A3C-Continuous`). The environment is shown as follows:

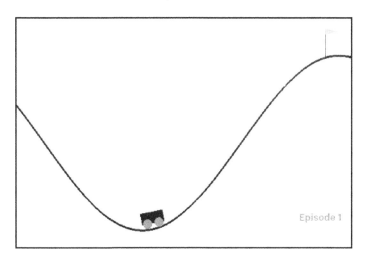

Okay, let's get to the coding! The complete code is available as the Jupyter notebook with an explanation here (`https://github.com/sudharsan13296/Hands-On-Reinforcement- Learning-With-Python/blob/master/10. %20Aysnchronous%20Advantage%20Actor%20Critic%20Network/10. 5%20Drive%20up%20the%20Mountain%20Using%20A3C.ipynb`).

First, let's import the necessary libraries:

```
import gym
import multiprocessing
import threading
import numpy as np
import os
import shutil
import matplotlib.pyplot as plt
import tensorflow as tf
```

Now, we will initialize all our parameters:

```
# number of worker agents
no_of_workers = multiprocessing.cpu_count()

# maximum number of steps per episode
no_of_ep_steps = 200

# total number of episodes
no_of_episodes = 2000

global_net_scope = 'Global_Net'

# sets how often the global network should be updated
update_global = 10

# discount factor
gamma = 0.90

# entropy factor
entropy_beta = 0.01

# learning rate for actor
lr_a = 0.0001

# learning rate for critic
lr_c = 0.001

# boolean for rendering the environment
render=False

# directory for storing logs
log_dir = 'logs'
```

Initialize our `MountainCar` environment:

```
env = gym.make('MountainCarContinuous-v0')
env.reset()
```

Get the number of `states` and `actions`, and also the `action_bound`:

```
no_of_states = env.observation_space.shape[0]
no_of_actions = env.action_space.shape[0]
action_bound = [env.action_space.low, env.action_space.high]
```

We will define our Actor Critic network in an `ActorCritic` class. As usual, we first understand the code of every function in a class and see the final code as a whole at the end. Comments are added to each line of code for better understanding. We will look into the clean uncommented whole code at the end:

```
class ActorCritic(object):
    def __init__(self, scope, sess, globalAC=None):
        # first we initialize the session and RMS prop optimizer for both
        # our actor and critic networks
        self.sess=sess
        self.actor_optimizer = tf.train.RMSPropOptimizer(lr_a,
name='RMSPropA')
        self.critic_optimizer = tf.train.RMSPropOptimizer(lr_c,
name='RMSPropC')

        # now, if our network is global then,
        if scope == global_net_scope:
            with tf.variable_scope(scope):
                # initialize states and build actor and critic network
                self.s = tf.placeholder(tf.float32, [None, no_of_states],
'S')

                # get the parameters of actor and critic networks
                self.a_params, self.c_params = self._build_net(scope)[-2:]
        # if our network is local then,
        else:
            with tf.variable_scope(scope):
                # initialize state, action, and also target value
                # as v_target
                self.s = tf.placeholder(tf.float32, [None, no_of_states],
'S')

                self.a_his = tf.placeholder(tf.float32, [None,
no_of_actions], 'A')
                self.v_target = tf.placeholder(tf.float32, [None, 1],
'Vtarget')
                # since we are in continuous actions space,
                # we will calculate
                # mean and variance for choosing action
                mean, var, self.v, self.a_params, self.c_params =
self._build_net(scope)

                # then we calculate td error as the difference
                # between v_target - v
                td = tf.subtract(self.v_target, self.v, name='TD_error')

                # minimize the TD error
                with tf.name_scope('critic_loss'):
                    self.critic_loss = tf.reduce_mean(tf.square(td))
```

```python
        # update the mean and var value by multiplying mean
        # with the action bound and adding var with 1e-4

        with tf.name_scope('wrap_action'):
            mean, var = mean * action_bound[1], var + 1e-4
        # we can generate distribution using this updated
        # mean and var
        normal_dist = tf.contrib.distributions.Normal(mean, var)
        # now we shall calculate the actor loss.
        # Recall the loss function.
        with tf.name_scope('actor_loss'):
            # calculate first term of loss which is log(pi(s))
            log_prob = normal_dist.log_prob(self.a_his)
            exp_v = log_prob * td
            # calculate entropy from our action distribution
            # for ensuring exploration
            entropy = normal_dist.entropy()
            # we can define our final loss as
            self.exp_v = exp_v + entropy_beta * entropy
            # then, we try to minimize the loss
            self.actor_loss = tf.reduce_mean(-self.exp_v)
        # now, we choose an action by drawing from the
        # distribution and clipping it between action bounds,
        with tf.name_scope('choose_action'):
            self.A =
tf.clip_by_value(tf.squeeze(normal_dist.sample(1), axis=0),
action_bound[0], action_bound[1])
        # calculate gradients for both of our actor
        # and critic networks,
        with tf.name_scope('local_grad'):

            self.a_grads = tf.gradients(self.actor_loss,
self.a_params)
            self.c_grads = tf.gradients(self.critic_loss,
self.c_params)

    # now, we update our global network weights,
    with tf.name_scope('sync'):
        # pull the global network weights to the local networks
        with tf.name_scope('pull'):
            self.pull_a_params_op = [l_p.assign(g_p) for l_p, g_p
in zip(self.a_params, globalAC.a_params)]
            self.pull_c_params_op = [l_p.assign(g_p) for l_p, g_p
in zip(self.c_params, globalAC.c_params)]
        # push the local gradients to the global network
        with tf.name_scope('push'):
            self.update_a_op =
self.actor_optimizer.apply_gradients(zip(self.a_grads, globalAC.a_params))
```

```
                    self.update_c_op =
self.critic_optimizer.apply_gradients(zip(self.c_grads, globalAC.c_params))


    # next, we define a function called _build_net for building
    # our actor and critic network
    def _build_net(self, scope):
    # initialize weights
        w_init = tf.random_normal_initializer(0., .1)
        with tf.variable_scope('actor'):
            l_a = tf.layers.dense(self.s, 200, tf.nn.relu6,
kernel_initializer=w_init, name='la')
            mean = tf.layers.dense(l_a, no_of_actions,
tf.nn.tanh,kernel_initializer=w_init, name='mean')
            var = tf.layers.dense(l_a, no_of_actions, tf.nn.softplus,
kernel_initializer=w_init, name='var')
        with tf.variable_scope('critic'):
            l_c = tf.layers.dense(self.s, 100, tf.nn.relu6,
kernel_initializer=w_init, name='lc')
            v = tf.layers.dense(l_c, 1, kernel_initializer=w_init,
name='v')
        a_params = tf.get_collection(tf.GraphKeys.TRAINABLE_VARIABLES,
scope=scope + '/actor')
        c_params = tf.get_collection(tf.GraphKeys.TRAINABLE_VARIABLES,
scope=scope + '/critic')
        return mean, var, v, a_params, c_params
    # update the local gradients to the global network
    def update_global(self, feed_dict):
        self.sess.run([self.update_a_op, self.update_c_op], feed_dict)
    # get the global parameters to the local networks
    def pull_global(self):
        self.sess.run([self.pull_a_params_op, self.pull_c_params_op])
    # select action
    def choose_action(self, s):
        s = s[np.newaxis, :]
        return self.sess.run(self.A, {self.s: s})[0]
```

Now, we will initialize the `Worker` class:

```
class Worker(object):
    def __init__(self, name, globalAC, sess):
        # initialize environment for each worker
        self.env = gym.make('MountainCarContinuous-v0').unwrapped
        self.name = name
        # create an ActorCritic agent for each worker
        self.AC = ActorCritic(name, sess, globalAC)
        self.sess=sess
    def work(self):
```

```
global global_rewards, global_episodes
total_step = 1

# store state, action, reward
buffer_s, buffer_a, buffer_r = [], [], []
# loop if the coordinator is active and the global
# episode is less than the maximum episode
while not coord.should_stop() and global_episodes < no_of_episodes:
    # initialize the environment by resetting
    s = self.env.reset()
    # store the episodic reward
    ep_r = 0
    for ep_t in range(no_of_ep_steps):
        # Render the environment for only worker 1
        if self.name == 'W_0' and render:
            self.env.render()
        # choose the action based on the policy
        a = self.AC.choose_action(s)

        # perform the action (a), receive reward (r),
        # and move to the next state (s_)
        s_, r, done, info = self.env.step(a)
        # set done as true if we reached maximum step per episode
        done = True if ep_t == no_of_ep_steps - 1 else False
        ep_r += r
        # store the state, action, and rewards in the buffer
        buffer_s.append(s)
        buffer_a.append(a)
        # normalize the reward
        buffer_r.append((r+8)/8)
        # we update the global network after a particular time step
        if total_step % update_global == 0 or done:
            if done:
                v_s_ = 0
            else:
                v_s_ = self.sess.run(self.AC.v, {self.AC.s:
s_[np.newaxis, :]})[0, 0]
                # buffer for target v
                buffer_v_target = []
                for r in buffer_r[::-1]:
                    v_s_ = r + gamma * v_s_
                    buffer_v_target.append(v_s_)
                buffer_v_target.reverse()
                buffer_s, buffer_a, buffer_v_target =
np.vstack(buffer_s), np.vstack(buffer_a), np.vstack(buffer_v_target)
                feed_dict = {
                        self.AC.s: buffer_s,
                        self.AC.a_his: buffer_a,
```

```
                            self.AC.v_target: buffer_v_target,
                        }
                # update global network
                self.AC.update_global(feed_dict)
                buffer_s, buffer_a, buffer_r = [], [], []
                # get global parameters to local ActorCritic
                self.AC.pull_global()
            s = s_
            total_step += 1
            if done:
                if len(global_rewards) < 5:
                    global_rewards.append(ep_r)
                else:
                    global_rewards.append(ep_r)
                    global_rewards[-1] =(np.mean(global_rewards[-5:]))
                global_episodes += 1
                break
```

Now, let's start the TensorFlow session and run our model:

```
# create a list for string global rewards and episodes
global_rewards = []
global_episodes = 0

# start tensorflow session
sess = tf.Session()

with tf.device("/cpu:0"):
# create an instance to our ActorCritic Class
    global_ac = ActorCritic(global_net_scope,sess)
    workers = []
    # loop for each worker
    for i in range(no_of_workers):
        i_name = 'W_%i' % i
        workers.append(Worker(i_name, global_ac,sess))

coord = tf.train.Coordinator()
sess.run(tf.global_variables_initializer())

# log everything so that we can visualize the graph in tensorboard

if os.path.exists(log_dir):
    shutil.rmtree(log_dir)

tf.summary.FileWriter(log_dir, sess.graph)

worker_threads = []
```

```
#start workers

for worker in workers:

    job = lambda: worker.work()
    t = threading.Thread(target=job)
    t.start()
    worker_threads.append(t)
coord.join(worker_threads)
```

The output is shown as follows. If you run the program, you can see how our agent is learning to climb the mountain over several episodes:

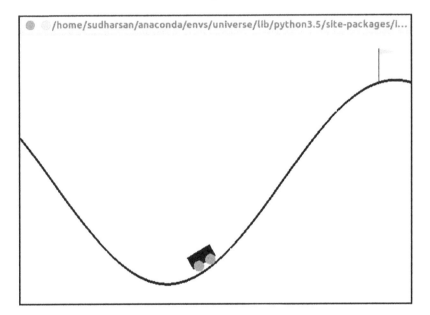

Visualization in TensorBoard

Let's visualize our network in TensorBoard. To launch TensorBoard, open your Terminal and type the following:

```
tensorboard --logdir=logs --port=6007 --host=127.0.0.1
```

This is our A3C network. We have one global network and four workers:

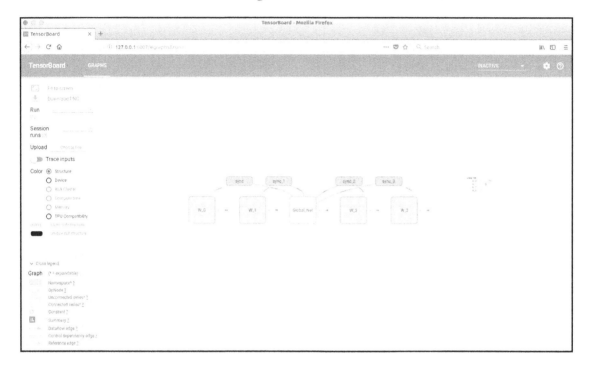

Let's expand our global network; you can see we have one actor and one critic:

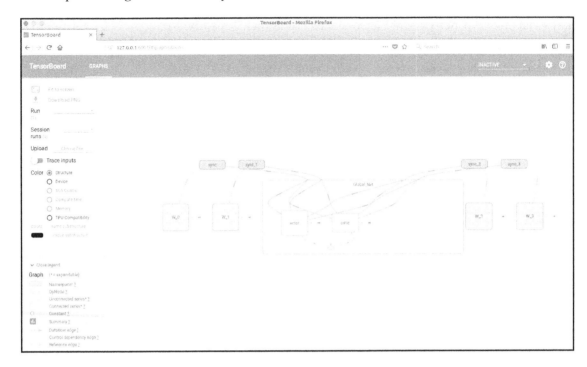

Okay, what is really going on in workers? Let's expand our worker network. You can see how the worker nodes are performing:

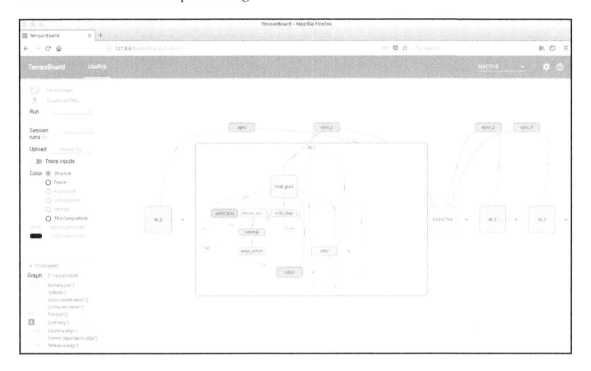

What about the sync node? What is that doing? The sync node pushes the local gradients from the local to the global network and pulls gradients from the global to the local network:

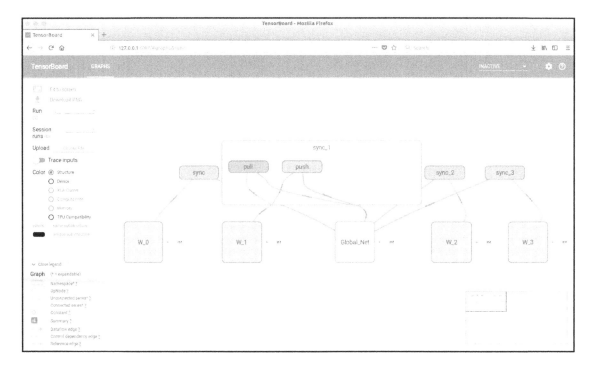

Summary

In this chapter, we learned how the A3C network works. In A3C, Asynchronous implies multiple agents working independently by interacting with multiple copies of the environment, Advantage implies the advantage function, which is the difference between the Q function and the value function, and Actor Critic refers to the Actor Critic network, where the actor network is responsible for generating a policy and the critic network evaluates the policy generated by the actor network. We have seen how A3C works, and saw how to solve a mountain car problem using the algorithm.

In the next chapter, Chapter 11, *Policy Gradients and Optimization*, we will see policy gradient methods that directly optimize the policy without requiring the Q function.

Questions

The question list is as follows:

1. What is A3C?
2. What do the three As signify?
3. Name one advantage of A3N over DQN
4. What is the difference between global and worker nodes?
5. Why do we entropy to our loss function?
6. Explain the workings of A3C.

Further reading

You can also refer to these papers:

- **A3C paper**: https://arxiv.org/pdf/1602.01783.pdf
- **Vision enhanced A3C**: http://cs231n.stanford.edu/reports/2017/pdfs/617.pdf

11
Policy Gradients and Optimization

In the last three chapters, we have learned about various deep reinforcement learning algorithms, such as **Deep Q Network (DQN)**, **Deep Recurrent Q Network (DRQN)**, and the **Asynchronous Advantage Actor Critic (A3C)** network. In all the algorithms, our goal is to find the correct policy so that we can maximize the rewards. We use the Q function to find the optimal policy as the Q function tells us which action is the best action to perform in a state. Do you think we can directly find the optimal policy without using Q function? Yes. We can. In policy gradient methods, we can find the optimal policy without using the Q function.

In this chapter, we will learn about policy gradients in detail. We will also look at different types of policy gradient methods such as deep deterministic policy gradients followed by state-of-the-art policy optimization methods such as trust region policy optimization and proximal policy optimization.

In this chapter, you will learn the following:

- Policy gradients
- Lunar lander using policy gradients
- Deep deterministic policy gradients
- Swinging a pendulum using the **deep deterministic policy gradient** (DDPG)
- Trust region policy optimization
- Proximal policy optimization

Policy gradient

The policy gradient is one of the amazing algorithms in **reinforcement learning** (**RL**) where we directly optimize the policy parameterized by some parameter θ. So far, we have used the Q function for finding the optimal policy. Now we will see how to find the optimal policy without the Q function. First, let's define the policy function as $\pi(a|s)$, that is, the probability of taking an action a given the state s. We parameterize the policy via a parameter θ as $\pi(a|s;\theta)$, which allows us to determine the best action in a state.

The policy gradient method has several advantages, and it can handle the continuous action space where we have an infinite number of actions and states. Say we are building a self-driving car. A car should be driven without hitting any other vehicles. We get a negative reward when the car hits a vehicle and a positive reward when the car does not hit any other vehicle. We update our model parameters in such a way that we receive only a positive reward so that our car will not hit any other vehicles. This is the basic idea of policy gradient: we update the model parameter in a way that maximizes the reward. Let's look at this in detail.

We use a neural network for finding the optimal policy and we call this network a policy network. The input to the policy network will be the state and the output will be the probability of each action in that state. Once we have this probability, we can sample an action from this distribution and perform that action in the state. But the action we sampled might not be the correct action to perform in the state. That's fine—we perform the action and store the reward. Similarly, we perform actions in each state by sampling an action from the distribution and we store the reward. Now, this becomes our training data. We perform gradient descent and update gradients in a such a way that actions yielding high reward in a state will have a high probability and actions yielding low reward will have a low probability. What is the loss function? Here, we use softmax cross entropy loss and then we multiply the loss by the reward value.

Lunar Lander using policy gradients

Say our agent is driving the space vehicle and the goal of our agent is to land correctly on the landing pad. If our agent (lander) lands away from the landing pad, then it loses the reward and the episode will get terminated if the agent crashes or comes to rest. Four discrete actions available in the environment are do nothing, fire left orientation engine, fire main engine, and fire right orientation engine.

Now we will see how to train our agents to correctly land on the landing pad with policy gradients. Credit for the code used in this section goes to Gabriel (`https://github.com/gabrielgarza/openai-gym-policy-gradient`):

First, we import the necessary libraries:

```
import tensorflow as tf
import numpy as np
from tensorflow.python.framework import ops
import gym
import numpy as np
import time
```

Then we define the `PolicyGradient` class, which implements the policy gradient algorithm. Let's break down the class and see each function separately. You can look at the whole program as a Jupyter notebook (`https://github.com/sudharsan13296/Hands-On-Reinforcement-Learning-With-Python/blob/master/11.%20Policy%20Gradients%20and%20Optimization/11.2%20Lunar%20Lander%20Using%20Policy%20Gradients.ipynb`):

```
class PolicyGradient:
    # first we define the __init__ method where we initialize all variables
```

```
    def __init__(self, n_x,n_y,learning_rate=0.01, reward_decay=0.95):
        # number of states in the environment
        self.n_x = n_x
        # number of actions in the environment
        self.n_y = n_y
        # learning rate of the network
        self.lr = learning_rate
        # discount factor
        self.gamma = reward_decay
        # initialize the lists for storing observations,
        # actions and rewards
        self.episode_observations, self.episode_actions,
self.episode_rewards = [], [], []
        # we define a function called build_network for
        # building the neural network
        self.build_network()
        # stores the cost i.e loss
        self.cost_history = []
        # initialize tensorflow session
        self.sess = tf.Session()
        self.sess.run(tf.global_variables_initializer())
```

Next, we define a `store_transition` function which stores the transitions, that is, `state`, `action`, and `reward`. We can use this information for training the network:

```
    def store_transition(self, s, a, r):
        self.episode_observations.append(s)
        self.episode_rewards.append(r)

        # store actions as list of arrays
        action = np.zeros(self.n_y)
        action[a] = 1
        self.episode_actions.append(action)
```

We define the `choose_action` function for choosing the `action` given the `state`:

```
    def choose_action(self, observation):

        # reshape observation to (num_features, 1)
        observation = observation[:, np.newaxis]

        # run forward propagation to get softmax probabilities
        prob_weights = self.sess.run(self.outputs_softmax, feed_dict =
{self.X: observation})
```

```
        # select action using a biased sample this will return
        # the index of the action we have sampled
        action = np.random.choice(range(len(prob_weights.ravel())),
p=prob_weights.ravel())
        return action
```

We define the `build_network` function for building the neural network:

```
    def build_network(self):
        # placeholders for input x, and output y
        self.X = tf.placeholder(tf.float32, shape=(self.n_x, None),
name="X")
        self.Y = tf.placeholder(tf.float32, shape=(self.n_y, None),
name="Y")
        # placeholder for reward
        self.discounted_episode_rewards_norm = tf.placeholder(tf.float32,
[None, ], name="actions_value")

        # we build 3 layer neural network with 2 hidden layers and
        # 1 output layer
        # number of neurons in the hidden layer
        units_layer_1 = 10
        units_layer_2 = 10
        # number of neurons in the output layer
        units_output_layer = self.n_y
        # now let us initialize weights and bias value using
        # tensorflow's tf.contrib.layers.xavier_initializer
        W1 = tf.get_variable("W1", [units_layer_1, self.n_x], initializer =
tf.contrib.layers.xavier_initializer(seed=1))
        b1 = tf.get_variable("b1", [units_layer_1, 1], initializer =
tf.contrib.layers.xavier_initializer(seed=1))
        W2 = tf.get_variable("W2", [units_layer_2, units_layer_1],
initializer = tf.contrib.layers.xavier_initializer(seed=1))
        b2 = tf.get_variable("b2", [units_layer_2, 1], initializer =
tf.contrib.layers.xavier_initializer(seed=1))
        W3 = tf.get_variable("W3", [self.n_y, units_layer_2], initializer =
tf.contrib.layers.xavier_initializer(seed=1))
        b3 = tf.get_variable("b3", [self.n_y, 1], initializer =
tf.contrib.layers.xavier_initializer(seed=1))

        # and then, we perform forward propagation

        Z1 = tf.add(tf.matmul(W1,self.X), b1)
        A1 = tf.nn.relu(Z1)
        Z2 = tf.add(tf.matmul(W2, A1), b2)
        A2 = tf.nn.relu(Z2)
        Z3 = tf.add(tf.matmul(W3, A2), b3)
        A3 = tf.nn.softmax(Z3)
```

```
        # as we require, probabilities, we apply softmax activation
        # function in the output layer,
        logits = tf.transpose(Z3)
        labels = tf.transpose(self.Y)
        self.outputs_softmax = tf.nn.softmax(logits, name='A3')

        # next we define our loss function as cross entropy loss
        neg_log_prob =
tf.nn.softmax_cross_entropy_with_logits(logits=logits, labels=labels)
        # reward guided loss
        loss = tf.reduce_mean(neg_log_prob *
self.discounted_episode_rewards_norm)

        # we use adam optimizer for minimizing the loss
        self.train_op = tf.train.AdamOptimizer(self.lr).minimize(loss)
```

Next, we define the `discount_and_norm_rewards` function which will result in the discount and normalized reward:

```
    def discount_and_norm_rewards(self):
        discounted_episode_rewards = np.zeros_like(self.episode_rewards)
        cumulative = 0
        for t in reversed(range(len(self.episode_rewards))):
            cumulative = cumulative * self.gamma + self.episode_rewards[t]
            discounted_episode_rewards[t] = cumulative

        discounted_episode_rewards -= np.mean(discounted_episode_rewards)
        discounted_episode_rewards /= np.std(discounted_episode_rewards)
        return discounted_episode_rewards
```

Now we actually perform the learning:

```
    def learn(self):
        # discount and normalize episodic reward
        discounted_episode_rewards_norm = self.discount_and_norm_rewards()

        # train the network
        self.sess.run(self.train_op, feed_dict={
            self.X: np.vstack(self.episode_observations).T,
            self.Y: np.vstack(np.array(self.episode_actions)).T,
            self.discounted_episode_rewards_norm:
discounted_episode_rewards_norm,
        })
```

```
        # reset the episodic data
        self.episode_observations, self.episode_actions,
    self.episode_rewards = [], [], []

        return discounted_episode_rewards_norm
```

You can see the output as follows:

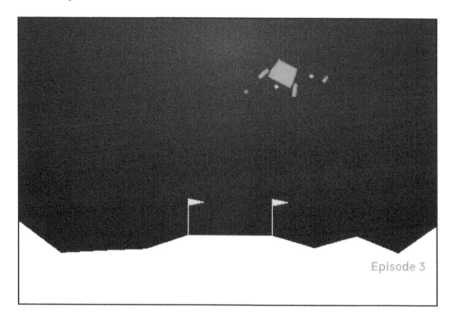

Episode 3

Deep deterministic policy gradient

In Chapter 8, *Atari Games with Deep Q Network*, we looked at how DQN works and we applied DQNs to play Atari games. However, those are discrete environments where we have a finite set of actions. Think of a continuous environment space like training a robot to walk; in those environments it is not feasible to apply Q learning because finding a greedy policy will require a lot of optimization at each and every step. Even if we make this continuous environment discrete, we might lose important features and end up with a huge set of action spaces. It is difficult to attain convergence when we have a huge action space.

So we use a new architecture called Actor Critic with two networks—Actor and Critic. The Actor Critic architecture combines the policy gradient and state action value functions. The role of the **Actor** network is to determine the best actions in the **state** by tuning the parameter θ, and the role of the **Critic** is to evaluate the action produced by the **Actor**. **Critic** evaluates the Actor's action by computing the temporal difference error. That is, we perform a policy gradient on an **Actor** network to select the actions and the **Critic** network evaluates the action produced by the **Actor** network using the TD error. The Actor Critic architecture is shown in the following diagram:

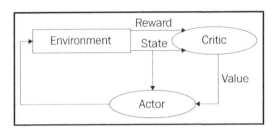

Similar to DQN, here we use an experience buffer, using which Actor and Critic networks are trained by sampling a mini batch of experiences. We also use a separate target Actor and Critic network for computing the loss.

For example, in a Pong game we will have different features of different scales such as position, velocity, and so on. So we scale the features in a way that all the features will be in the same scale. We use a method called batch normalization for scaling the features. It normalizes all the features to have unit mean and variance. How do we explore new actions? In a continuous environment, there will be n number of actions. To explore new actions we add some noise N to the action produced by the Actor network. We generate this noise using a process called the Ornstein-Uhlenbeck random process.

Now we will look at the DDPG algorithm in detail.

Let's say we have two networks: the Actor network and Critic network. We represent the Actor network with $\mu(s; \theta^\mu)$ which takes input as a state and results in the action where θ^μ is the Actor network weights. We represent the Critic network as $Q(s, a; \theta^Q)$, which takes an input as a state and action and returns the Q value where θ^Q is the Critic network weights.

Similarly, we define a target network for both the Actor network and Critic network as $\mu(s; \theta^{\mu'})$ and $Q(s, a; \theta^{Q'})$ respectively, where $\theta^{\mu'}$ and $\theta^{Q'}$ are the weights of the target Actor and Critic network.

We update Actor network weights with policy gradients and the Critic network weight with the gradients calculated from the TD error.

First, we select an action by adding the exploration noise N to the action produced by the Actor network, such as $\mu(s; \theta^\mu) + N$. We perform this action in a state, s, receive a reward, r and move to a new state, s'. We store this transition information in an experience replay buffer.

After some iterations, we sample transitions from the replay buffer and train the network, and then we calculate the target Q value $y_i = r_i + \gamma Q'(s_{i+1}, \mu'(s_{i+1}|\theta^{\mu'})|\theta^{Q'})$. We compute the TD error as:

$$L = \frac{1}{M} \sum_i (y_i - Q(s_i, a_i|\theta^Q)^2)$$

Where M is the number of samples from the replay buffer that are used for training. We update our Critic networks weights with gradients calculated from this loss L.

Similarly, we update our policy network weights using a policy gradient. Then we update the weights of Actor and Critic network in the target network. We update the weights of the target networks slowly, which promotes greater stability; it is called the soft replacement:

$$\theta' < -\tau\theta + (1 - \tau)\theta'$$

Swinging a pendulum

We have a pendulum that starts in a random position, and the goal of our agent is to swing the pendulum up so it stays upright. We will see how to use DDPG here. Credit for the code used in this section goes to wshuail (https://github.com/wangshuailong/reinforcement_learning_with_Tensorflow/tree/master/DDPG).

First, let's import the necessary libraries:

```
import tensorflow as tf
import numpy as np
import gym
```

Next, we define the hyperparameters as follows:

```
# number of steps in each episode
epsiode_steps = 500

# learning rate for actor
lr_a = 0.001

# learning rate for critic
lr_c = 0.002

# discount factor
gamma = 0.9

# soft replacement
alpha = 0.01

# replay buffer size
memory = 10000

# batch size for training
batch_size = 32
render = False
```

We will implement the DDPG algorithm in the DDPG class. We break down the class to see each function. First, we initialize everything:

```
class DDPG(object):
    def __init__(self, no_of_actions, no_of_states, a_bound,):
        # initialize the memory with shape as no of actions, no of states
and our defined memory size
        self.memory = np.zeros((memory, no_of_states * 2 + no_of_actions +
1), dtype=np.float32)
        # initialize pointer to point to our experience buffer
        self.pointer = 0
        # initialize tensorflow session
        self.sess = tf.Session()
        # initialize the variance for OU process for exploring policies
        self.noise_variance = 3.0
        self.no_of_actions, self.no_of_states, self.a_bound =
no_of_actions, no_of_states, a_bound,
        # placeholder for current state, next state and rewards
        self.state = tf.placeholder(tf.float32, [None, no_of_states], 's')
        self.next_state = tf.placeholder(tf.float32, [None, no_of_states],
's_')
        self.reward = tf.placeholder(tf.float32, [None, 1], 'r')
        # build the actor network which has separate eval(primary)
        # and target network
```

```
        with tf.variable_scope('Actor'):
            self.a = self.build_actor_network(self.state, scope='eval',
trainable=True)
            a_ = self.build_actor_network(self.next_state, scope='target',
trainable=False)
        # build the critic network which has separate eval(primary)
        # and target network
        with tf.variable_scope('Critic'):
            q = self.build_crtic_network(self.state, self.a, scope='eval',
trainable=True)
            q_ = self.build_crtic_network(self.next_state, a_,
scope='target', trainable=False)

        # initialize the network parameters
        self.ae_params = tf.get_collection(tf.GraphKeys.GLOBAL_VARIABLES,
scope='Actor/eval')
        self.at_params = tf.get_collection(tf.GraphKeys.GLOBAL_VARIABLES,
scope='Actor/target')
        self.ce_params = tf.get_collection(tf.GraphKeys.GLOBAL_VARIABLES,
scope='Critic/eval')
        self.ct_params = tf.get_collection(tf.GraphKeys.GLOBAL_VARIABLES,
scope='Critic/target')

        # update target value
        self.soft_replace = [[tf.assign(at, (1-alpha)*at+alpha*ae),
tf.assign(ct, (1-alpha)*ct+alpha*ce)]
            for at, ae, ct, ce in zip(self.at_params, self.ae_params,
self.ct_params, self.ce_params)]
        # compute target Q value, we know that Q(s,a) = reward + gamma *
          Q'(s',a')
        q_target = self.reward + gamma * q_
        # compute TD error i.e actual - predicted values
        td_error = tf.losses.mean_squared_error(labels=(self.reward + gamma
* q_), predictions=q)
        # train the critic network with adam optimizer
        self.ctrain = tf.train.AdamOptimizer(lr_c).minimize(td_error,
name="adam-ink", var_list = self.ce_params)
        # compute the loss in actor network
        a_loss = - tf.reduce_mean(q)
        # train the actor network with adam optimizer for
        # minimizing the loss
        self.atrain = tf.train.AdamOptimizer(lr_a).minimize(a_loss,
var_list=self.ae_params)
```

```
    # initialize summary writer to visualize our network in tensorboard
    tf.summary.FileWriter("logs", self.sess.graph)
    # initialize all variables
    self.sess.run(tf.global_variables_initializer())
```

How do we select an action in DDPG? We select an action by adding noise to the action space. We use the Ornstein-Uhlenbeck random process for generating noise:

```
def choose_action(self, s):
    a = self.sess.run(self.a, {self.state: s[np.newaxis, :]})[0]
    a = np.clip(np.random.normal(a, self.noise_variance), -2, 2)
    return a
```

Then we define the `learn` function where the actual training happens. Here we select a batch of `states`, `actions`, `rewards`, and the next state from the experience buffer. We train Actor and Critic networks with that:

```
def learn(self):
    # soft target replacement
    self.sess.run(self.soft_replace)

    indices = np.random.choice(memory, size=batch_size)
    batch_transition = self.memory[indices, :]
    batch_states = batch_transition[:, :self.no_of_states]
    batch_actions = batch_transition[:, self.no_of_states:
self.no_of_states + self.no_of_actions]
    batch_rewards = batch_transition[:, -self.no_of_states - 1: -
self.no_of_states]
    batch_next_state = batch_transition[:, -self.no_of_states:]

    self.sess.run(self.atrain, {self.state: batch_states})
    self.sess.run(self.ctrain, {self.state: batch_states, self.a:
batch_actions, self.reward: batch_rewards, self.next_state:
batch_next_state})
```

We define a `store_transition` function, that stores all the information in the buffer and performs the learning:

```
def store_transition(self, s, a, r, s_):
    trans = np.hstack((s,a,[r],s_))
    index = self.pointer % memory
    self.memory[index, :] = trans
    self.pointer += 1

    if self.pointer > memory:
        self.noise_variance *= 0.99995
        self.learn()
```

We define the `build_actor_network` function for building our Actor network:

```
def build_actor_network(self, s, scope, trainable):
    # Actor DPG
    with tf.variable_scope(scope):
        l1 = tf.layers.dense(s, 30, activation = tf.nn.tanh, name =
'l1', trainable = trainable)
        a = tf.layers.dense(l1, self.no_of_actions, activation =
tf.nn.tanh, name = 'a', trainable = trainable)
        return tf.multiply(a, self.a_bound, name = "scaled_a")
```

We define the `build_ crtic_network` function:

```
def build_crtic_network(self, s, a, scope, trainable):
    # Critic Q-leaning
    with tf.variable_scope(scope):
        n_l1 = 30
        w1_s = tf.get_variable('w1_s', [self.no_of_states, n_l1],
trainable = trainable)
        w1_a = tf.get_variable('w1_a', [self.no_of_actions, n_l1],
trainable = trainable)
        b1 = tf.get_variable('b1', [1, n_l1], trainable = trainable)
        net = tf.nn.tanh( tf.matmul(s, w1_s) + tf.matmul(a, w1_a) + b1
)

        q = tf.layers.dense(net, 1, trainable = trainable)
        return q
```

Now, we initialize our `gym` environment using the `make` function:

```
env = gym.make("Pendulum-v0")
env = env.unwrapped
env.seed(1)
```

We get the number of states:

```
no_of_states = env.observation_space.shape[0]
```

We get the number of actions:

```
no_of_actions = env.action_space.shape[0]
```

Also, higher bound of the action:

```
a_bound = env.action_space.high
```

Now, we create an object for our DDPG class:

```
ddpg = DDPG(no_of_actions, no_of_states, a_bound)
```

We initialize the list to store the total rewards:

```
total_reward = []
```

Set the number of episodes:

```
no_of_episodes = 300
```

Now, let's begin training:

```
# for each episodes
for i in range(no_of_episodes):
    # initialize the environment
    s = env.reset()
    # episodic reward
    ep_reward = 0
    for j in range(epsiode_steps):
        env.render()

        # select action by adding noise through OU process
        a = ddpg.choose_action(s)
        # perform the action and move to the next state s
        s_, r, done, info = env.step(a)
        # store the the transition to our experience buffer
        # sample some minibatch of experience and train the network
        ddpg.store_transition(s, a, r, s_)
        # update current state as next state
        s = s_
        # add episodic rewards
        ep_reward += r
        if j == epsiode_steps-1:
            # store the total rewards
            total_reward.append(ep_reward)
            # print rewards obtained per each episode
            print('Episode:', i, ' Reward: %i' % int(ep_reward))
            break
```

You will see the output as follows:

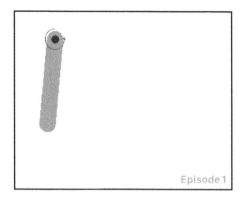

We can see the computation graph in TensorBoard:

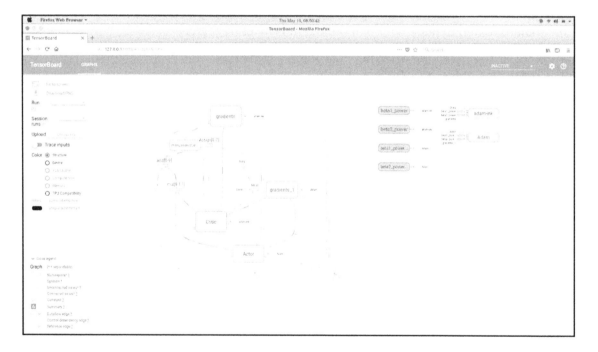

Trust Region Policy Optimization

Before understanding **Trust Region Policy Optimization** (TRPO), we need to understand constrained policy optimization. We know that in RL agents learn by trial and error to maximize the reward. To find the best policy, our agents will explore all different actions and choose the one that gives a good reward. While exploring different actions there is a very good chance that our agents will explore bad actions as well. But the biggest challenge is when we allow our agents to learn in the real world and when the reward functions are not properly designed. For example, consider an agent learning to walk without hitting any obstacles. The agent will receive a negative reward if it gets hit by any obstacle and a positive reward for not getting hit by any obstacle. To figure out the best policy, the agent explores different actions. The agent also takes action, such as hitting an obstacle to check whether it gives a good reward. But that is not safe for our agent; it is particularly unsafe when an agent is learning in a real-world environment. So we introduce constraint-based learning. We set a threshold and if the probability of hitting the obstacle is less than this threshold, then we consider our agent safe, or else we consider our agent unsafe. A constraint is added to make sure that our agent is in a safe region.

In TRPO, we iteratively improve the policy and we impose a constraint such that the **Kullback–Leibler** (**KL**) divergence between an old policy and a new policy is to be less than some constant δ. This constraint is called the trust region constraint.

So what is KL divergence? KL divergence tells us how two probability distributions are different from each other. Since our policies are probability distribution over actions, KL divergence tells us how far a new policy is from the old policy. Why do we have to keep the distance between the old policy and new policy less than some constant δ? Because we don't want our new policy to drift apart from the old policy. So we impose a constraint to keep the new policy near to the old policy. Again, why do we have to stay near the old policy? When the new policy is far away from the old policy, then it will affect our agent's learning performance and also lead to a completely different learning behavior. In a nutshell, in TRPO, we take a step toward the direction that improves our policy, that is, maximizes the reward, but we should also be sure that the trust region constraint is satisfied. It uses conjugate gradient descent (`http://www.idi.ntnu.no/~elster/tdt24/tdt24-f09/cg.pdf`) to optimize the network parameter θ while satisfying the constraint. The algorithm guarantees monotonic policy improvement and has also achieved excellent results in various continuous environments.

Now we will see how TRPO works mathematically; you can skip this section if you are not interested in math.

Get ready for some cool math.

Let 's specify the total expected discounted reward $\eta(\pi)$, as follows:

$$\eta(\pi) = \mathbf{E}_{s_0,a_0,..} \left[\sum_{t=0}^{\infty} \gamma^t r(s_t) \right]$$

Now let's consider the new policy as π'; it can be defined as the expected return of policy π' in terms of advantages over our old policy π, as follows:

$$\eta(\pi') = \eta(\pi) + \mathbf{E}_{s_0,a_0,.. \ \pi'} \left[\sum_{t=0}^{\infty} \gamma^t A_\pi(s_t, a_t) \right]$$

Okay, why are we using the advantages of the old policy? Because we are measuring how good the new policy π' is with respect to the average performance of the old policy π. We can rewrite the preceding equation with a sum over states instead of timesteps as follows:

$$\eta(\pi') = \eta(\pi) + \mathbf{E}_{s_0,a_0,.. \ \pi'} \left[\sum_{t=0}^{\infty} \gamma^t A_\pi(s_t, a_t) \right]$$

$$= \eta(\pi) + \sum_{t=0}^{\infty} \sum_{s} P(s_t = s | \pi') \sum_{a} \pi'(a|s) \gamma^t A_\pi(s, a)$$

$$= \eta(\pi) + \sum_{s} \sum_{t=0}^{\infty} P(s_t = s | \pi') \sum_{a} \pi'(a|s) \gamma^t A_{\pi_0}(s, a)$$

$$= \eta(\pi) + \sum_{s} \rho_{\pi'}(s) \sum_{a} \pi'(a|s) A_\pi(s, a)$$

ρ is the discounted visitation frequencies, that is:

$$\rho_\pi(s) = P(s_0 = s) + \gamma P(s_1 = s) + \gamma^2 P(s_2 = s) + \dots$$

If you see the preceding equation $\eta(\pi')$ there is a complex dependency of $\rho_{\pi'}(s)$ on π' and so it is difficult to optimize the equation. So we will introduce the local approximation $L_\pi(\pi')$ to $\eta(\pi')$ as follows:

$$L_\pi(\pi') = \eta(\pi) + \sum_s \rho_\pi(s) \sum_a \pi'(a|s) A_\pi(s,a)$$

L_π uses the visitation frequency ρ_π rather than $\rho_{\pi'}$, that is, we ignore the changes in state visitation frequency due to the change in policy. To put it in simple terms, we assume that the state visitation frequency is not different for both the new and old policy. When we are calculating the gradient of L_π, which will also improve η with respect to some parameter θ we can't be sure how much big of a step to take.

Kakade and Langford proposed a new policy update method called conservative policy iteration, shown as follows:

$$\pi_{new}(a|s) = (1 - \alpha)\pi_{old}(a|s) + \alpha\pi'(a|s) \quad \text{---- (1)}$$

π_{new} is the new policy. π_{old} is the old policy.

$\pi' = argmax_{\pi'} L_{\pi_{old}}(\pi')$, that is, π', is the policy which maximizes $L_{\pi_{old}}$.

Kakade and Langford derived the following equation from (1) as follows:

$$\eta(\pi') \geq L_\pi(\pi') - CD_{KL}^{max}(\pi, \pi') \quad \text{---- (2)}$$

C is the penalty coefficient and it is equal to $\dfrac{4\epsilon\gamma}{(1 - \alpha)^2}$, and $D_{KL}^{max}(\pi, \pi')$ denotes the KL divergence between the old policy and the new policy.

If we look at the preceding equation (2) closely, we notice that our expected long-term reward η increases monotonically as long as the right-hand side is maximized.

Let's define this right-hand side term as $M_i(\pi)$, as follows:

$$M_i(\pi) = L_{\pi_i}(\pi) - CD_{KL}^{max}(\pi_i, \pi) \quad \text{---- (3)}$$

Substituting equation (3) in (2), we get:

$$\eta(\pi_i + 1) \geq M_i(\pi_i + 1) \quad \text{---- (4)}$$

Since we know that the KL divergence between the two same policies will be *0*, we can write:

$$\eta(\pi) = M_i(\pi_i) \quad \text{----(5)}$$

Combining equations (4) and (5), we can write:

$$\eta(\pi_{i+1}) - \eta(\pi) \geq M_i(\pi_{i+1}) - M(\pi_i)$$

In the preceding equation, we can understand that maximizing M_i guarantees the maximization of our expected reward. So now our goal is to maximize M_i which in turn maximizes our expected reward. Since we use parameterized policies, we replace π with θ in our previous equation and we use θ_{old} to represent a policy that we want to improve, as shown next:

$$\text{maximize}_\theta \quad [L_{\theta_{old}}(\theta) - C D_{KL}^{max}(\theta_{old}, \theta)]$$

But having a penalty coefficient *C* in the preceding equation will cause the step size to be very small, which in turn slows down the updates. So, we impose a constraint on the KL divergence's old policy and new policy, which is the trust region constraint, and it will help us to find the optimal step size:

$$\begin{aligned} \text{maximize}_\theta \quad & L_{\theta_0}(\theta) \\ \text{subject to} \quad & D_{KL}^{max}(\theta_{old}, \theta) \leq \delta \end{aligned}$$

Now, the problem is KL divergence is imposed on every point in the state space and it is really not feasible to solve when we have a high dimensional state space. So we use a heuristic approximation which takes the average KL divergence as:

$$\bar{D}_{KL}^{\rho}(\theta_{old}, \theta) := \mathbf{E}_{s \sim \rho}[D_{KL}(\pi_{\theta_1}(.\,|s) \| \pi_{\theta_2}(.\,|s))]$$

So now, we can rewrite our preceding objective function with the average KL divergence constraint as:

$$\text{maximize}_\theta \qquad L_{\theta_{old}}(\theta)$$
$$\text{subject to} \qquad \bar{D}_{KL}^{\rho_{\theta_{old}}}(\theta_{old}, \theta) \leq \delta$$

Expanding the value of *L*, we get the following:

$$\text{maximize}_\theta \qquad \sum_s \rho_{\theta_{old}}(S) \sum_a \pi_\theta(a|s) A_{\theta_{old}}(s, a)$$
$$\text{subject to} \qquad \bar{D}_{KL}^{\rho_{\theta_{old}}}(\theta_{old}, \theta) \leq \delta$$

In the preceding equation, we replace sum over states $\sum_s \rho_{\theta_{old}}$ as expectation $E_{s \sim \rho_{\theta_{old}}}$ and we replace sum over actions by importance sampling estimator as:

$$\sum_a \pi_\theta(a|s_n) A_{\theta_{old}}(s_n, a) = E_{a \sim q}\left[\frac{\pi_\theta(a|s_n)}{q(a|s_n)} A_{\theta_{old}}(s_n, a)\right]$$

Then, we substitute advantage target values $A_{\theta_{old}}$ with Q values $Q_{\theta_{old}}$.

So, our final objective function will become:

$$\text{maximize}_\theta \qquad E_s \pi_{\theta_{old}}, a \pi_{\theta_{old}}\left[\frac{\pi_\theta(a|s)}{\pi_{\theta_{old}}(a|s)} A_{\theta_{old}}(s, a)\right]$$
$$\text{subject to} \qquad E_{s,\pi_{\theta_{old}}}\left[DKL(\pi_{\theta_{old}}(\cdot|s)\|\pi_{\theta_{old}}(\cdot|s))\right] \leq \delta$$

Optimizing the preceding mentioned objective function, which has a constraint, is called constrained optimization. Our constraint is to keep the average KL divergence between the old policy and new policy less than δ. We use conjugate gradient descent for optimizing the preceding function.

Proximal Policy Optimization

Now we will look at another policy optimization algorithm called **Proximal Policy Optimization (PPO)**. It acts as an improvement to TRPO and has become the default RL algorithm of choice in solving many complex RL problems due to its performance. It was proposed by researchers at OpenAI for overcoming the shortcomings of TRPO. Recall the surrogate objective function of TRPO. It is a constraint optimization problem where we impose a constraint—that average KL divergence between the old and new policy should be less than δ. But the problem with TRPO is that it requires a lot of computing power for computing conjugate gradients to perform constrained optimization.

So, PPO modifies the objective function of TRPO by changing the constraint to a penalty term so that we don't want to perform conjugate gradient. Now let's see how PPO works. We define $r_t(\theta)$ as a probability ratio between new and old policy. So, we can write our objective function as:

$$L^{CPI}(\theta) = \hat{E}_t \left[\frac{\pi_\theta(a_t|s_t)}{\pi_{\theta_{old}}(a_t|s_t)} \hat{A}_t \right]$$
$$= \hat{E}_t [r_t(\theta) \hat{A}_t]$$

L^{CPI} denotes the conservative policy iteration. But maximizing L would lead to a large policy update without constraint. So, we redefine our objective function by adding the penalty term which penalizes a large policy update. Now the objective function becomes:

$$L^{CLIP}(\theta) = \hat{E}_t [min r_t(\theta) \hat{A}_t, clip(r_t(\theta), 1 - \epsilon, 1 + \epsilon) \hat{A}_t]$$

We have just added a new term, $clip(r_t(\theta), 1 - \epsilon, 1 + \epsilon)\hat{A}_t$, to the actual equation. What does this mean? It actually clips the value of $r_t(\theta)$ between the interval $[1 - \epsilon, 1 + \epsilon]$, that is, if the value of $r_t(\theta)$ causes the objective function to increase, heavily clipping the value between an interval will reduce its effects.

We clip the probability ratio either at $1 - \epsilon$ or ϵ based on two cases:

- **Case 1:** $\hat{A}_t > 0$

  When the advantage is positive, which means that the corresponding action should be preferred over the average of all other actions. We will increase the value of $r_t(\theta)$ for that action, so it will have a greater chance of being selected. As we are performing a clipping value of $r_t(\theta)$, will not exceed greater than $1 + \epsilon$:

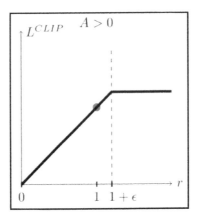

- **Case 2:** $\hat{A}_t$

  When the value of the advantage is negative, this means that the action has no significance and it should not be adopted. So, in this case, we will reduce the value of $r_t(\theta)$ for that action so that it will have a lower chance of being selected. Similarly, as we are performing clipping, a value of $r_t(\theta)$ will not decrease to less than $1 - \epsilon$:

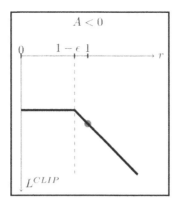

When we are using neural network architectures, we must define the loss function which includes the value function error for our objective function. We will also add entropy loss to ensure enough exploration, as we did in A3C. So our final objective function becomes:

$$L_t^{CLIP+VP+S}(\theta) = \hat{E}_t[L_t^{CLIP}(\theta) - c1 L_t^{VF}(\theta) + c_2 S[\pi_\theta](s_t)]$$

c_1 and c_2 are the coefficients, L_t^{VP} is the squared error loss between the actual and target value function, that is, $(V_\theta(s_t) - V_t^{target})^2$, and S is the entropy bonus.

Summary

We started off with policy gradient methods which directly optimized the policy without requiring the Q function. We learned about policy gradients by solving a Lunar Lander game, and we looked at DDPG, which has the benefits of both policy gradients and Q functions.

Then we looked at policy optimization algorithms such as TRPO, which ensure monotonic policy improvements by enforcing a constraint on KL divergence between the old and new policy is not greater than δ.

We also looked at proximal policy optimization, which changed the constraint to a penalty by penalizing the large policy update. In the next chapter, Chapter 19, *Capstone Project – Car Racing Using DQN*, we will see how to build an agent to win a car racing game.

Questions

The question list is as follows:

1. What are policy gradients?
2. Why are policy gradients effective?
3. What is the use of the Actor Critic network in DDPG?
4. What is the constraint optimization problem?
5. What is the trust region?
6. How does PPO overcome the drawbacks of TRPO?

Further reading

You can further refer to the following papers:

- **DDPG paper**: https://arxiv.org/pdf/1509.02971.pdf
- **TRPO paper**: https://arxiv.org/pdf/1502.05477.pdf
- **PPO paper**: https://arxiv.org/pdf/1707.06347.pdf

12
Balancing CartPole

In this chapter, you will learn about the CartPole balancing problem. The CartPole is an inverted pendulum, where the pole is balanced against gravity. Traditionally, this problem is solved by control theory, using analytical equations. However, in this chapter, we will solve the problem with machine learning.

The following topics will be covered in this chapter:

- Installing OpenAI Gym
- The different environments of Gym

OpenAI Gym

OpenAI is a non-profit organization dedicated to researching artificial intelligence. Visit `https://openai.com` for more information about the mission of OpenAI. The technologies developed by OpenAI are free for anyone to use.

Gym

Gym provides a toolkit to benchmark AI-based tasks. The interface is easy to use. The goal is to enable reproducible research. Visit `https://gym.openai.com` for more information about Gym. An agent can be taught inside of the `gym`, and learn activities such as playing games or walking. An environment is a library of problems.

The standard set of problems presented in the gym are as follows:

- CartPole
- Pendulum
- Space Invaders
- Lunar Lander

- Ant
- Mountain Car
- Acrobot
- Car Racing
- Bipedal Walker

Any algorithm can work out in the gym by training for these activities. All of the problems have the same interface. Therefore, any general reinforcement learning algorithm can be used through the interface.

Installation

The primary interface of the gym is used through Python. Once you have Python3 in an environment with the `pip` installer, the gym can be installed as follows:

```
sudo pip install gym
```

Advanced users that want to modify the source can compile from the source by using the following commands:

```
git clone https://github.com/openai/gym
cd gym
pip install -e .
```

A new environment can be added to the `gym` with the source code. There are several environments that need more dependencies. For macOS, install the dependencies by using the following command:

```
brew install cmake boost boost-python sdl2 swig wget
```

For Ubuntu, use the following commands:

```
apt-get install -y python-numpy python-dev cmake zlib1g-dev libjpeg-dev
xvfb libav-tools xorg-dev python-opengl libboost-all-dev libsdl2-dev swig
```

Once the dependencies are there, install the complete `gym` as follows:

```
pip install 'gym[all]'
```

This will install most of the environments that are required.

Running an environment

Any gym environment can be initialized and run by using a simple interface. Let's start by importing the gym library, as follows:

1. First we import the gym library:

```
import gym
```

2. Next, create an environment by passing an argument to gym.make. In the following code, CartPole is used as an example:

```
environment = gym.make('CartPole-v0')
```

3. Next, reset the environment:

```
environment.reset()
```

4. Then, start an iteration and render the environment, as follows:

```
for dummy in range(100):
    environment.render()
    environment.step(environment.action_space.sample())
```

Also, change the action space at every step, to see CartPole moving. Running the preceding program should produce a visualization. The scene should start with a visualization, as follows:

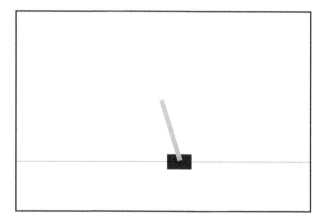

The preceding image is called a **CartPole**. The CartPole is made up of a cart that can move horizontally and a pole that can move rotationally, with respect to the center of the cart.

The pole is pivoted to the cart. After some time, you will notice that the pole is falling to one side, as shown in the following image:

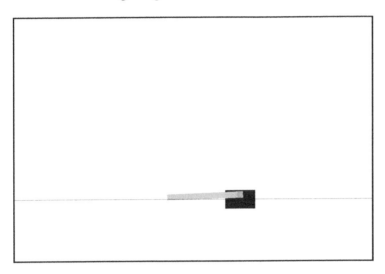

After a few more iterations, the pole will swing back, as shown in the following image. All of the movements are constrained by the laws of physics. The steps are taken randomly:

Other environments can be seen in a similar way, by replacing the argument of the gym environment, such as `MsPacman-v0` or `MountrainCar-v0`. For other environments, other licenses may be required. Next, we will go through the rest of the environments.

Atari

To play Atari games, any environment can be invoked. The following code refers to the game Space Invaders:

```
environment = gym.make('SpaceInvaders-v0')
```

Once the preceding command has executed, you will see the following screen:

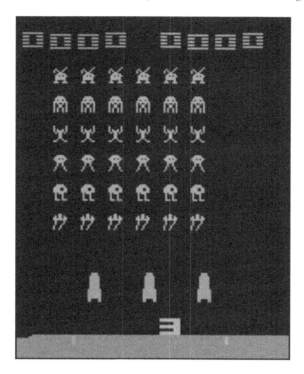

An Atari game can be played in this environment.

Algorithmic tasks

There are algorithmic tasks that can be learned through reinforcement learning. A copy environment can be invoked, as follows:

```
environment = gym.make('Copy-v0')
```

The process of copying a string is shown in the following screenshot:

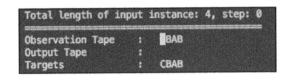

MuJoCo

MuJoCo stands for **multi-joint dynamics with contact**. It's a simulation environment for robots and multi-body dynamics:

```
environment = gym.make('Humanoid-v2')
```

The following is a visualization for the simulation of a humanoid:

Simulation of a humanoid

There are robots and other objects that can be simulated in this environment.

Robotics

A robotics environment can also be created, as follows:

```
environment = gym.make('HandManipulateBlock-v0')
```

The following is a visualization of a robot hand:

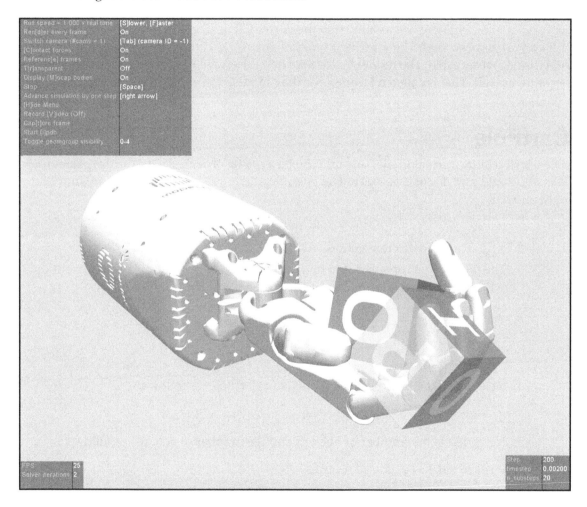

There are several environments in which OpenAI Gym can be used.

Markov models

The problem is set up as a reinforcement learning problem, with a trial and error method. The environment is described using `state_values state_values (?)`, and the `state_values` are changed by actions. The actions are determined by an algorithm, based on the current `state_value`, in order to achieve a particular `state_value` that is termed a **Markov model**. In an ideal case, the past `state_values` does have an influence on future `state_values`, but here, we assume that the current `state_value` has all of the previous `state_values` encoded. There are two types of `state_values`; one is observable, and the other is non-observable. The model has to take non-observable `state_values` into account, as well. That is called a **Hidden Markov model**.

CartPole

At each step of the cart and pole, several variables can be observed, such as the position, velocity, angle, and angular velocity. The possible `state_values` of the cart are moved right and left:

1. `state_values`: Four dimensions of continuous values.
2. `Actions`: Two discrete values.
3. The dimensions, or space, can be referred to as the `state_value` space and the action space. Let's start by importing the required libraries, as follows:

   ```
   import gym
   import numpy as np
   import random
   import math
   ```

4. Next, make the environment for playing CartPole, as follows:

   ```
   environment = gym.make('CartPole-v0')
   ```

5. Next, define the number of buckets and the number of actions, as follows:

   ```
   no_buckets = (1, 1, 6, 3)
   no_actions = environment.action_space.n
   ```

6. Next, define the `state_value_bounds`, as follows:

   ```
   state_value_bounds = list(zip(environment.observation_space.low,
   environment.observation_space.high))
   state_value_bounds[1] = [-0.5, 0.5]
   state_value_bounds[3] = [-math.radians(50), math.radians(50)]
   ```

7. Next, define the `action_index`, as follows:

```
action_index = len(no_buckets)
```

8. Next define the `q_value_table`, as follows:

```
q_value_table = np.zeros(no_buckets + (no_actions,))
```

9. Next, define the minimum exploration rate and the minimum learning rate:

```
min_explore_rate = 0.01
min_learning_rate = 0.1
```

10. Next, define the maximum episodes, the maximum time steps, the streak to the end, the solving time, the discount, and the number of streaks, as constants:

```
max_episodes = 1000
max_time_steps = 250
streak_to_end = 120
solved_time = 199
discount = 0.99
no_streaks = 0
```

11. Next, define the `select` action that can decide the action, as follows:

```
def select_action(state_value, explore_rate):
    if random.random() < explore_rate:
        action = environment.action_space.sample()
    else:
        action = np.argmax(q_value_table[state_value])
    return action
```

12. Next, select the explore state, as follows:

```
def select_explore_rate(x):
    return max(min_explore_rate, min(1, 1.0 -
math.log10((x+1)/25)))
```

13. Next, select the learning rate, as follows:

```
def select_learning_rate(x):
    return max(min_learning_rate, min(0.5, 1.0 -
math.log10((x+1)/25)))
```

14. Next, `bucketize` the `state_value`, as follows:

```
def bucketize_state_value(state_value):
    bucket_indexes = []
    for i in range(len(state_value)):
        if state_value[i] <= state_value_bounds[i][0]:
            bucket_index = 0
        elif state_value[i] >= state_value_bounds[i][1]:
            bucket_index = no_buckets[i] - 1
        else:
            bound_width = state_value_bounds[i][1] -
state_value_bounds[i][0]
            offset =
(no_buckets[i]-1)*state_value_bounds[i][0]/bound_width
            scaling = (no_buckets[i]-1)/bound_width
            bucket_index = int(round(scaling*state_value[i] -
offset))
        bucket_indexes.append(bucket_index)
    return tuple(bucket_indexes)
```

15. Next, train the episodes, as follows:

```
for episode_no in range(max_episodes):
    explore_rate = select_explore_rate(episode_no)
    learning_rate = select_learning_rate(episode_no)

    observation = environment.reset()

    start_state_value = bucketize_state_value(observation)
    previous_state_value = start_state_value

    for time_step in range(max_time_steps):
        environment.render()
        selected_action = select_action(previous_state_value,
explore_rate)
        observation, reward_gain, completed, _ =
environment.step(selected_action)
        state_value = bucketize_state_value(observation)
        best_q_value = np.amax(q_value_table[state_value])
        q_value_table[previous_state_value + (selected_action,)] +=
learning_rate * (
                reward_gain + discount * (best_q_value) -
q_value_table[previous_state_value + (selected_action,)])
```

16. Next, print all of the relevant metrics for the training process, as follows:

```
print('Episode number : %d' % episode_no)
print('Time step : %d' % time_step)
print('Selection action : %d' % selected_action)
print('Current state : %s' % str(state_value))
print('Reward obtained : %f' % reward_gain)
print('Best Q value : %f' % best_q_value)
print('Learning rate : %f' % learning_rate)
print('Explore rate : %f' % explore_rate)
print('Streak number : %d' % no_streaks)

if completed:
    print('Episode %d finished after %f time steps' %
(episode_no, time_step))
    if time_step >= solved_time:
        no_streaks += 1
    else:
        no_streaks = 0
    break

previous_state_value = state_value

if no_streaks > streak_to_end:
    break
```

17. After training for a period of time, the CartPole will be able to balance itself, as shown in the following image:

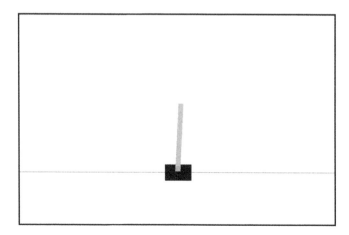

You have learned a program that will stabilize the CartPole.

Summary

In this chapter, you learned about the OpenAI Gym, used in reinforcement learning projects. You saw several examples of the training platform provided out of the box. Then, we formulated the problem of the CartPole, and made the CartPole balance by using a trial and error approach.

In the next chapter, you will learn how to play Atari games by using the Gym and a reinforcement learning approach.

13
Simulating Control Tasks

In the previous chapter, we saw the notable success of **deep Q-learning (DQN)** in training an AI agent to play Atari games. One limitation of DQN is that the action space must be discrete, namely, only a finite number of actions are available for the agent to select and the total number of actions cannot be too large. However, many practical tasks require continuous actions, which makes DQN difficult to apply. A naive remedy for DQN in this case is discretizing the continuous action space. But this remedy doesn't work due to the curse of dimensionality, meaning that DQN quickly becomes infeasible and does not generalize well.

This chapter will discuss deep reinforcement learning algorithms for control tasks with a continuous action space. Several classic control tasks, such as CartPole, Pendulum, and Acrobot, will be introduced first. You will learn how to simulate these tasks using Gym and understand the goal and the reward for each task. Then, a basic actor-critic algorithm, called the **deterministic policy gradient (DPG)**, will be represented. You will learn what the actor-critic architecture is, and why these kinds of algorithms can address continuous control tasks. Besides this, you will also learn how to implement DPG via Gym and TensorFlow. Finally, a more advanced algorithm, called the **trust region policy optimization (TRPO)**, will be introduced. You will understand why TRPO works much better than DPG and how to learn a policy by applying the conjugate gradient method.

This chapter requires some background knowledge of mathematical programming and convex/non-convex optimization. Don't be afraid-we will discuss these algorithms step by step to make sure that you fully understand the mechanism behind them. Understanding why they work, when they cannot work, and what their advantages and disadvantages are is much more important than simply knowing how to implement them with Gym and TensorFlow. After finishing this chapter, you will understand that the magic show of deep reinforcement learning is directed by mathematics and deep learning together.

The following topics will be covered in this chapter:

- Introduction to classic control tasks
- Deterministic policy gradient methods
- Trust region policy optimization for complex control tasks

Introduction to control tasks

OpenAI Gym offers classic control tasks from the classic reinforcement learning literature. These tasks include CartPole, MountainCar, Acrobot, and Pendulum. To find out more, visit the OpenAI Gym website at: `https://gym.openai.com/envs/#classic_control`. Besides this, Gym also provides more complex continuous control tasks running in the popular physics simulator MuJoCo. Here is the homepage for MuJoCo: `http://www.mujoco.org/`. MuJoCo stands for Multi-Joint Dynamics with Contact, which is a physics engine for research and development in robotics, graphics, and animation. The tasks provided by Gym are Ant, HalfCheetah, Hopper, Humanoid, InvertedPendulum, Reacher, Swimmer, and Walker2d. These names are very tricky, aren't they? For more details about these tasks, please visit the following link: `https://gym.openai.com/envs/#mujoco`.

Getting started

If you don't have a full installation of OpenAI Gym, you can install the `classic_control` and `mujoco` environment dependencies as follows:

```
pip install gym[classic_control]
pip install gym[mujoco]
```

MuJoCo is not open source, so you'll have to follow the instructions in `mujoco-py` (available at `https://github.com/openai/mujoco-py#obtaining-the-binaries-and-license-key`) to set it up. After the classic control environment is installed, try the following commands:

```
import gym
atari = gym.make('Acrobot-v1')
atari.reset()
atari.render()
```

If it runs successfully, a small window will pop up, showing the screen of the Acrobot task:

Besides Acrobot, you can replace the Acrobot-v1 task name with CartPole-v0, MountainCarContinuous-v0, and Pendulum-v0 to check out the other control tasks. You can run the following code to simulate these tasks and try to get a high-level understanding of their physical properties:

```
import gym
import time

def start(task_name):
    task = gym.make(task_name)
    observation = task.reset()
    while True:
        task.render()
        action = task.env.action_space.sample()
        observation, reward, done, _ = task.step(action)
        print("Action {}, reward {}, observation {}".format(action, reward,
observation))
        if done:
            print("Game finished")
            break
        time.sleep(0.05)
    task.close()

if __name__ == "__main__":
    task_names = ['CartPole-v0', 'MountainCarContinuous-v0',
                  'Pendulum-v0', 'Acrobot-v1']
    for task_name in task_names:
        start(task_name)
```

Gym uses the same interface for all the tasks, including Atari games, classic control tasks, and MuJoCo control tasks. At each step, an action is randomly drawn from the action space by calling `task.env.action_space.sample()` and then this action is submitted to the simulator via `task.step(action)`, which tells the simulator to execute it. The `step` function returns the observation and the reward corresponding to this action.

The classic control tasks

We will now go through the details of each control task and answer the following questions:

1. What are the control inputs and the corresponding feedbacks?
2. How is the reward function defined?
3. Is the action space continuous or discrete?

Understanding the details of these control tasks is quite important for designing proper reinforcement learning algorithms because their specifications, such as the dimension of the action space and the reward function, can affect the performance a lot.

CartPole is quite a famous control task in both the control and reinforcement learning communities. Gym implements the CartPole system described by *Barto, Sutton, and Anderson* in their paper *Neuronlike Adaptive Elements That Can Solve Difficult Learning Control Problem*, 1983. In CartPole, a pole is attached by an un-actuated joint to a cart, which moves along a frictionless track, as illustrated here:

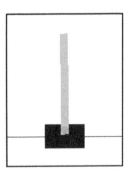

Here are the specifications of CartPole:

Goal	The goal is to prevent the pole from falling over.
Action	The action space is discrete, namely, the system is controlled by applying a force of +1 (right direction) and -1 (left direction) to the cart.
Observation	The observation is a vector with four elements, for example, [0.0316304, -0.1893631, -0.0058115, 0.27025422], which describe the positions of the pole and the cart.
Reward	A reward of +1 is provided for every timestep that the pole remains upright.
Termination	The episode ends when the pole is more than 15 degrees from vertical, or the cart moves more than 2.4 units from the center.

Because this chapter talks about solving continuous control tasks, we will later design a wrapper for CartPole to convert its discrete action space into a continuous one.

MountainCar was first described by Andrew Moore in his PhD thesis *A. Moore, Efficient Memory-Based Learning for Robot Control*, 1990, which is widely applied as the benchmark for control, **Markov decision process** (**MDP**), and reinforcement learning algorithms. In MountainCar, a small car is on a one-dimensional track, moving between two mountains and trying to reach the yellow flag, as shown here:

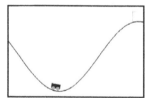

The following table provides its specifications:

Goal	The goal is to reach the top of the right mountain. However, the car's engine is not strong enough to scale the mountain in a single pass. Therefore, the only way to succeed is to drive back and forth to build up momentum.
Action	The action space is continuous. The input action is the engine force applied to the car.
Observation	The observation is a vector with two elements, for example, [-0.46786288, -0.00619457], which describe the velocity and the position of the car.
Reward	The reward is greater if you spend less energy to reach the goal.
Termination	The episode ends when the car reaches the goal flag or the maximum number of steps is reached.

The Pendulum swing-up problem is a classic problem in the control literature and is used as a benchmark for testing control algorithms. In Pendulum, a pole is attached to a pivot point, as shown here:

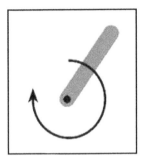

Here are the specifications of Pendulum:

Goal	The goal is to swing the pole up so it stays upright and to prevent it from falling over.
Action	The action space is continuous. The input action is the torque applied to the pole.
Observation	The observation is a vector with three elements, for example, [-0.19092327, 0.98160496, 3.36590881], which indicate the angle and angular velocity of the pole.
Reward	The reward is computed by a function with the angle, angular velocity, and the torque as the inputs.
Termination	The episode ends when the maximum number of steps is reached.

Acrobot was first described by Sutton in the paper *Generalization in Reinforcement Learning: Successful Examples Using Sparse Coarse Coding*, 1996. The Acrobot system includes two joints and two links, where the joint between the two links is actuated:

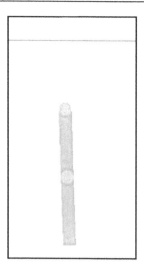

Here are the settings of Acrobot:

Goal	The goal is to swing the end of the lower link up to a given height.
Action	The action space is discrete, namely, the system is controlled by applying a torque of 0, +1 and -1 to the links.
Observation	The observation is a vector with six elements, for example, [0.9926474, 0.12104186, 0.99736744, -0.07251337, 0.47965018, -0.31494488], which describe the positions of the two links.
Reward	A reward of +1 is provided for every timestep where the lower link is at the given height or, otherwise, -1.
Termination	The episode ends when the end of the lower link is at the given height, or the maximum number of steps is reached.

Note that, in Gym, both CartPole and Acrobot have discrete action spaces, which means these two tasks can be solved by applying the deep Q-learning algorithm. Well, because this chapter considers continuous control tasks, we need to convert their action spaces into continuous ones. The following class provides a wrapper for Gym classic control tasks:

```
class Task:
    def __init__(self, name):
        assert name in ['CartPole-v0', 'MountainCar-v0',
                        'Pendulum-v0', 'Acrobot-v1']
        self.name = name
        self.task = gym.make(name)
        self.last_state = self.reset()
    def reset(self):
        state = self.task.reset()
```

```
        self.total_reward = 0
        return state
    def play_action(self, action):
        if self.name not in ['Pendulum-v0', 'MountainCarContinuous-v0']:
            action = numpy.fmax(action, 0)
            action = action / numpy.sum(action)
            action = numpy.random.choice(range(len(action)), p=action)
        else:
            low = self.task.env.action_space.low
            high = self.task.env.action_space.high
            action = numpy.fmin(numpy.fmax(action, low), high)
        state, reward, done, _ = self.task.step(action)
        self.total_reward += reward
        termination = 1 if done else 0
        return reward, state, termination
    def get_total_reward(self):
        return self.total_reward
    def get_action_dim(self):
        if self.name not in ['Pendulum-v0', 'MountainCarContinuous-v0']:
            return self.task.env.action_space.n
        else:
            return self.task.env.action_space.shape[0]
    def get_state_dim(self):
        return self.last_state.shape[0]
    def get_activation_fn(self):
        if self.name not in ['Pendulum-v0', 'MountainCarContinuous-v0']:
            return tf.nn.softmax
        else:
            return None
```

For CartPole and Acrobot, the input action should be a probability vector indicating the probability of selecting each action. In the `play_action` function, an action is randomly sampled based on this probability vector and submitted to the system.

The `get_total_reward` function returns the total reward in one episode.

The `get_action_dim` and `get_state_dim` functions return the dimension of the action space and the observation, respectively. The `get_activation_fn` function is used for the output layer in the actor network, which we will discuss later.

Deterministic policy gradient

As discussed in the previous chapter, DQN uses the Q-network to estimate the `state-action value` function, which has a separate output for each available action. Therefore, the Q-network cannot be applied, due to the continuous action space. A careful reader may remember that there is another architecture of the Q-network that takes both the state and the action as its inputs, and outputs the estimate of the corresponding Q-value. This architecture doesn't require the number of available actions to be finite, and has the capability to deal with continuous input actions:

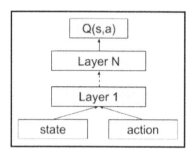

If we use this kind of network to estimate the `state-action value` function, there must be another network that defines the behavior policy of the agent, namely outputting a proper action given the observed state. In fact, this is the intuition behind actor-critic reinforcement learning algorithms. The actor-critic architecture contains two parts:

1. **Actor**: The actor defines the behavior policy of the agent. In control tasks, it outputs the control signal given the current state of the system.
2. **Critic**: The critic estimates the Q-value of the current policy. It can judge whether the policy is good or not.

Therefore, if both the actor and the critic can be trained with the feedbacks (state, reward, next state, termination signal) received from the system, as in training the Q-network in DQN, then the classic control tasks will be solved. But how do we train them?

The theory behind policy gradient

One solution is the **deep deterministic policy gradient** (DDPG) algorithm, which combines the actor-critic approach with insights from the success of DQN. This is discussed in the following papers:

- D. Silver, G. Lever, N. Heess, T. Degris, D. Wierstra and M. Riedmiller. *Deterministic policy gradient algorithms*. In ICML, 2014.
- T. P. Lillicrap, J. J. Hunt, A. Pritzel, N. Heess, T. Erez, Y. Tassa, D. Silver and D. Wierstra. *Continuous control with deep reinforcement learning*. In ICLR, 2016.

The reason why DDPG is introduced first is that it is quite similar to DQN, so you can understand the mechanism behind it much more easily after finishing the previous chapter. Recall that DQN is able to train the Q-network in a stable and robust way for the following reasons:

- The Q-network is trained with the samples randomly drawn from the replay memory to minimize the correlations between samples.
- A target network is used to estimate the target Q-value, reducing the probability that oscillation or divergence of the policy occurs. DDPG applies the same strategy, which means that DDPG is also a model-free and off-policy method.

We use the same notations as in the previous chapter for the reinforcement learning setting. At each timestep t, the agent observes state s_t, takes action a_t ,and then receives the corresponding reward r_t generated from a function $R(s_t, a_t)$. Instead of using $A(s_t)$ to represent the set of all the available actions at state s_t, here, we use $\pi(a_t|s_t)$ to denote the policy of the agent, which maps states to a probability distribution over the actions. Many approaches in reinforcement learning, such as DQN, use the Bellman equation as the backbone:

$$Q(s_t, a_t) = E_{s_{t+1} \sim S}[R(s_t, a_t) + \gamma E_{a_{t+1} \sim \pi(a_{t+1}|s_{t+1})} Q(s_{t+1}, a_{t+1})]$$

The only difference between this formulation and the one in DQN is that the policy π here is stochastic, so that the expectation of $Q(s_{t+1}, a_{t+1})$ is taken over a_{t+1}. If the target policy π is deterministic, which can be described as a function $\mu(s_t)$, then this inner expectation can be avoided:

$$Q(s_t, a_t) = E_{s_{t+1} \sim S}[R(s_t, a_t) + \gamma Q(s_{t+1}, \mu(s_{t+1}))]$$

The expectation depends only on the environment. This means that it is possible to learn the `state-action value` function Q off-policy, using transitions that are generated from other policies, as we did in DQN. The function Q, the critic, can be approximated by a neural network parameterized by θ^Q and the policy μ, the actor, can also be represented by another neural network parameterized by θ^μ (in DQN, $\mu(s_t)$ is just $^{\arg\max_a Q(s_t,a)}$). Then, the critic Q can be be trained by minimizing the following loss function:

$$L(\theta^Q) = E_{s_t \sim S, a_t \sim A}[(y_t - Q(s_t, a_t|\theta^Q))^2]$$

Here, $y_t = R(s_t, a_t) + \gamma Q(s_{t+1}, \mu(s_{t+1})|\theta^Q)$. As in DQN, y_t can be estimated via the target network and the samples for approximating $L(\theta^Q)$ can be randomly drawn from the replay memory.

To train the actor μ, we fix the critic Q, learned by minimizing the loss function L, and try to maximize $Q(s_t, \mu(s_t|\theta^\mu))$ over θ^μ, since a larger Q-value means a better policy. This can be done by following the applying the chain rule to the expected return with respect to the actor parameters:

$$\nabla_{\theta^\mu} E_{s_t \sim S}[Q(s_t, \mu(s_t|\theta^\mu)|\theta^Q)] = E_{s_t \sim S}[\nabla_a Q(s_t, a|\theta^Q)\nabla_{\theta^\mu}\mu(s_t|\theta^\mu)]$$

The following diagram shows the high-level architecture of DDPG:

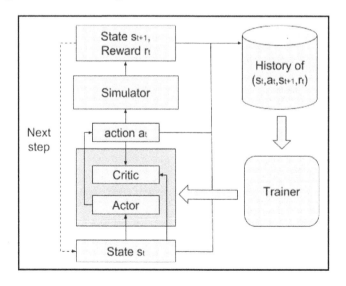

Compared to DQN, there is a small difference in updating the target network. Instead of directly copying the weights of Q to the target network after several iterations, a soft update is used:

$$\theta^{Q'} = \tau\theta^{Q} + (1 - \tau)\theta^{Q'}$$

Here, $\theta^{Q'}$ represents the weights of the target network. This update means that the target values are constrained to change slowly, greatly improving the stability of learning. This simple change moves the relatively unstable problem of learning the value function closer to the case of supervised learning.

Similar to DQN, DDPG also needs to balance exploration and exploitation during the training. Since the action generated by the policy μ is continuous, the ϵ-greedy method cannot be applied. Instead, we can construct an exploration policy μ' by adding noise sampled from a distribution P to the actor policy μ:

$$\mu'(s_t) = \mu(s_t|\theta^\mu) + \epsilon \text{ where } \epsilon \sim P$$

P can be chosen as σN, where N is the standard Gaussian distribution and σ decreases during each training step. Another choice is to apply an Ornstein-Uhlenbeck process to generate the exploration noise ϵ.

DPG algorithm

The following pseudo code shows the DDPG algorithm:

```
Initialize replay memory R to capacity N;
Initialize the critic network Q(s,a;θᵠ) and actor network μ(s;θᵘ) with random
weights θᵠ and θᵘ;
Initialize the target networks Q'(s,a;θᵠ) and μ'(s;θᵘ) with weights θᵠ = θᵠ and θᵘ = θᵘ
;
Repeat for each episode:
    Set time step t = 1;
    Initialize a random process P₁ for action exploration noise;
    Receive an initial observation state s₁;
    While the terminal state hasn't been reached:
        Select an action aₜ = μ(sₜ;θᵘ) + Pₜ according to the current policy and
exploration noise;
        Execute action aₜ in the simulator and observe reward rₜ and the next
state sₜ₊₁;
        Store transition (sₜ,aₜ,rₜ,sₜ₊₁) into replay memory R;
        Randomly sample a batch of n transitions (sᵢ,aᵢ,rᵢ,sᵢ₊₁) from R;
```

Set $y_i = r_i$ if s_{i+1} is a terminal state or $y_i = r_i + \gamma Q'(s_{i+1}, \mu'(s_{i+1}; \theta^{\mu'}); \theta^{Q'})$
if s_{i+1} is a non-terminal state;
    Update critic by minimizing the loss:

$$\frac{1}{n} \sum_i (y_i - Q(s_i, a_i; \theta^Q))^2 ;$$

    Update the actor policy using the sampled policy gradient:

$$\frac{1}{n} \sum_i \nabla_a Q(s_t, a|\theta^Q) \nabla_{\theta^\mu} \mu(s_t|\theta^\mu) ;$$

    Update the target networks:

$$\theta^{Q'} = \tau\theta^Q + (1-\tau)\theta^{Q'} ,$$
$$\theta^{\mu'} = \tau\theta^\mu + (1-\tau)\theta^{\mu'} ;$$

End while

There is a natural extension of DDPG by replacing the feedforward neural networks used for approximating the actor and the critic with recurrent neural networks. This extension is called the **recurrent deterministic policy gradient** algorithm (**RDPG**) and is discussed in the f paper N. Heess, J. J. Hunt, T. P. Lillicrap and D. Silver. *Memory-based control with recurrent neural networks*. 2015.

The recurrent critic and actor are trained using **backpropagation through time** (**BPTT**). For readers who are interested in it, the paper can be downloaded from `https://arxiv.org/abs/1512.04455`.

Implementation of DDPG

This section will show you how to implement the actor-critic architecture using TensorFlow. The code structure is almost the same as the DQN implementation that was shown in the previous chapter.

The `ActorNetwork` is a simple MLP that takes the observation state as its input:

```
class ActorNetwork:
    def __init__(self, input_state, output_dim, hidden_layers,
activation=tf.nn.relu):
        self.x = input_state
        self.output_dim = output_dim
        self.hidden_layers = hidden_layers
        self.activation = activation
        with tf.variable_scope('actor_network'):
            self.output = self._build()
            self.vars = tf.get_collection(tf.GraphKeys.TRAINABLE_VARIABLES,
                                          tf.get_variable_scope().name)
    def _build(self):
        layer = self.x
```

```
                init_b = tf.constant_initializer(0.01)
                for i, num_unit in enumerate(self.hidden_layers):
                    layer = dense(layer, num_unit, init_b=init_b,
    name='hidden_layer_{}'.format(i))
                output = dense(layer, self.output_dim, activation=self.activation,
    init_b=init_b, name='output')
                return output
```

The constructor requires four arguments: `input_state`, `output_dim`, `hidden_layers`, and `activation`. `input_state` is a tensor for the observation state. `output_dim` is the dimension of the action space. `hidden_layers` specifies the number of the hidden layers and the number of units for each layer. `activation` indicates the activation function for the output layer.

The `CriticNetwork` is also a MLP, which is enough for the classic control tasks:

```
class CriticNetwork:
    def __init__(self, input_state, input_action, hidden_layers):
        assert len(hidden_layers) >= 2
        self.input_state = input_state
        self.input_action = input_action
        self.hidden_layers = hidden_layers
        with tf.variable_scope('critic_network'):
            self.output = self._build()
            self.vars = tf.get_collection(tf.GraphKeys.TRAINABLE_VARIABLES,
                                          tf.get_variable_scope().name)
    def _build(self):
        layer = self.input_state
        init_b = tf.constant_initializer(0.01)
        for i, num_unit in enumerate(self.hidden_layers):
            if i != 1:
                layer = dense(layer, num_unit, init_b=init_b,
    name='hidden_layer_{}'.format(i))
            else:
                layer = tf.concat([layer, self.input_action], axis=1,
    name='concat_action')
                layer = dense(layer, num_unit, init_b=init_b,
    name='hidden_layer_{}'.format(i))
        output = dense(layer, 1, activation=None, init_b=init_b,
    name='output')
        return tf.reshape(output, shape=(-1,))
```

The network takes the state and the action as its inputs. It first maps the state into a hidden feature representation and then concatenates this representation with the action, followed by several hidden layers. The output layer generates the Q-value that corresponds to the inputs.

The actor-critic network combines the actor network and the critic network together:

```
class ActorCriticNet:
    def __init__(self, input_dim, action_dim,
                 critic_layers, actor_layers, actor_activation,
                 scope='ac_network'):
        self.input_dim = input_dim
        self.action_dim = action_dim
        self.scope = scope
        self.x = tf.placeholder(shape=(None, input_dim), dtype=tf.float32,
name='x')
        self.y = tf.placeholder(shape=(None,), dtype=tf.float32, name='y')
        with tf.variable_scope(scope):
            self.actor_network = ActorNetwork(self.x, action_dim,
                                              hidden_layers=actor_layers,
                                              activation=actor_activation)
            self.critic_network = CriticNetwork(self.x,
self.actor_network.get_output_layer(),
hidden_layers=critic_layers)
            self.vars = tf.get_collection(tf.GraphKeys.TRAINABLE_VARIABLES,
                                          tf.get_variable_scope().name)
            self._build()
    def _build(self):
        value = self.critic_network.get_output_layer()
        actor_loss = -tf.reduce_mean(value)
        self.actor_vars = self.actor_network.get_params()
        self.actor_grad = tf.gradients(actor_loss, self.actor_vars)
        tf.summary.scalar("actor_loss", actor_loss, collections=['actor'])
        self.actor_summary = tf.summary.merge_all('actor')
        critic_loss = 0.5 * tf.reduce_mean(tf.square((value - self.y)))
        self.critic_vars = self.critic_network.get_params()
        self.critic_grad = tf.gradients(critic_loss, self.critic_vars)
        tf.summary.scalar("critic_loss", critic_loss,
collections=['critic'])
        self.critic_summary = tf.summary.merge_all('critic')
```

The constructor requires six arguments, as follows: `input_dim` and `action_dim` are the dimensions of the state space and the action space, respectively. `critic_layers` and `actor_layers` specify the hidden layers of the critic network and the actor network. `actor_activation` indicates the activation function for the output layer of the actor network. `scope` is the scope name used for the `scope` TensorFlow variable.

The constructor first creates an instance of the `self.actor_network` actor network with an input of `self.x`, where `self.x` represents the current state. It then creates an instance of the critic network using the following as the inputs: `self.actor_network.get_output_layer()` as the output of the actor network and `self.x` as the current state. Given these two networks, the constructor calls `self._build()` to build the loss functions for the actor and critic that we discussed previously. The actor loss is `-tf.reduce_mean(value)`, where `value` is the Q-value computed by the critic network. The critic loss is `0.5 *` `tf.reduce_mean(tf.square((value - self.y)))`, where `self.y` is a tensor for the predicted target value computed by the target network.

The class `ActorCriticNet` provides the functions for calculating the action and the Q-value given the current state, that is, `get_action` and `get_value`. It also provides `get_action_value`, which computes the `state-action value` function given the current state and the action taken by the agent:

```
class ActorCriticNet:
    def get_action(self, sess, state):
        return self.actor_network.get_action(sess, state)
    def get_value(self, sess, state):
        return self.critic_network.get_value(sess, state)
    def get_action_value(self, sess, state, action):
        return self.critic_network.get_action_value(sess, state, action)
    def get_actor_feed_dict(self, state):
        return {self.x: state}
    def get_critic_feed_dict(self, state, action, target):
        return {self.x: state, self.y: target,
                self.critic_network.input_action: action}
    def get_clone_op(self, network, tau=0.9):
        update_ops = []
        new_vars = {v.name.replace(network.scope, ''): v for v in
network.vars}
        for v in self.vars:
            u = (1 - tau) * v + tau * new_vars[v.name.replace(self.scope,
'')]
            update_ops.append(tf.assign(v, u))
        return update_ops
```

Because DPG has almost the same architecture as DQN, the implementations of the replay memory and the optimizer are not shown in this chapter. For more details, you can refer to the previous chapter or visit our GitHub repository (`https://github.com/PacktPublishing/Python-Reinforcement-Learning-Projects`). By combining these modules together, we can implement the DPG class for the deterministic policy gradient algorithm:

```
class DPG:
    def __init__(self, config, task, directory, callback=None,
summary_writer=None):
        self.task = task
        self.directory = directory
        self.callback = callback
        self.summary_writer = summary_writer
        self.config = config
        self.batch_size = config['batch_size']
        self.n_episode = config['num_episode']
        self.capacity = config['capacity']
        self.history_len = config['history_len']
        self.epsilon_decay = config['epsilon_decay']
        self.epsilon_min = config['epsilon_min']
        self.time_between_two_copies = config['time_between_two_copies']
        self.update_interval = config['update_interval']
        self.tau = config['tau']
        self.action_dim = task.get_action_dim()
        self.state_dim = task.get_state_dim() * self.history_len
        self.critic_layers = [50, 50]
        self.actor_layers = [50, 50]
        self.actor_activation = task.get_activation_fn()
        self._init_modules()
```

Here, `config` includes all the parameters of DPG, for example, batch size and learning rate for training. The `task` is an instance of a certain classic control task. In the constructor, the replay memory, Q-network, target network, and optimizer are initialized by calling the `_init_modules` function:

```
    def _init_modules(self):
        # Replay memory
        self.replay_memory = ReplayMemory(history_len=self.history_len,
                                          capacity=self.capacity)
        # Actor critic network
        self.ac_network = ActorCriticNet(input_dim=self.state_dim,
                                         action_dim=self.action_dim,
                                         critic_layers=self.critic_layers,
                                         actor_layers=self.actor_layers,
                             actor_activation=self.actor_activation,
                                         scope='ac_network')
```

```
        # Target network
        self.target_network = ActorCriticNet(input_dim=self.state_dim,
                                             action_dim=self.action_dim,
critic_layers=self.critic_layers,
actor_layers=self.actor_layers,
actor_activation=self.actor_activation,
                                             scope='target_network')
        # Optimizer
        self.optimizer = Optimizer(config=self.config,
                                   ac_network=self.ac_network,
                                   target_network=self.target_network,
                                   replay_memory=self.replay_memory)
        # Ops for updating target network
        self.clone_op = self.target_network.get_clone_op(self.ac_network,
tau=self.tau)
        # For tensorboard
        self.t_score = tf.placeholder(dtype=tf.float32, shape=[],
name='new_score')
        tf.summary.scalar("score", self.t_score, collections=['dpg'])
        self.summary_op = tf.summary.merge_all('dpg')
    def choose_action(self, sess, state, epsilon=0.1):
        x = numpy.asarray(numpy.expand_dims(state, axis=0),
dtype=numpy.float32)
        action = self.ac_network.get_action(sess, x)[0]
        return action + epsilon * numpy.random.randn(len(action))
    def play(self, action):
        r, new_state, termination = self.task.play_action(action)
        return r, new_state, termination

    def update_target_network(self, sess):
        sess.run(self.clone_op)
```

The `choose_action` function selects an action based on the current estimate of the actor-critic network and the observed state.

Note that a Gaussian noise controlled by `epsilon` is added for exploration.

The `play` function submits an action into the simulator and returns the feedback from the simulator. The `update_target_network` function updates the target network from the current actor-critic network.

To begin the training process, the following function can be called:

```
def train(self, sess, saver=None):
    num_of_trials = -1
    for episode in range(self.n_episode):
        frame = self.task.reset()
        for _ in range(self.history_len+1):
            self.replay_memory.add(frame, 0, 0, 0)
        for _ in range(self.config['T']):
            num_of_trials += 1
            epsilon = self.epsilon_min + \
                    max(self.epsilon_decay - num_of_trials, 0) / \
                    self.epsilon_decay * (1 - self.epsilon_min)
            if num_of_trials % self.update_interval == 0:
                self.optimizer.train_one_step(sess, num_of_trials,
self.batch_size)
            state = self.replay_memory.phi(frame)
            action = self.choose_action(sess, state, epsilon)
            r, new_frame, termination = self.play(action)
            self.replay_memory.add(frame, action, r, termination)
            frame = new_frame
            if num_of_trials % self.time_between_two_copies == 0:
                self.update_target_network(sess)
                self.save(sess, saver)
            if self.callback:
                self.callback()
            if termination:
                score = self.task.get_total_reward()
                summary_str = sess.run(self.summary_op,
feed_dict={self.t_score: score})
                self.summary_writer.add_summary(summary_str,
num_of_trials)
                self.summary_writer.flush()
                break
```

In each episode, it calls `replay_memory.phi` to get the current state and calls the `choose_action` function to select an action based on the current state. This action is submitted into the simulator by calling the `play` function, which returns the corresponding reward, next state, and termination signal. Then, the (`current state, action, reward, termination`) transition is stored into the replay memory. For every `update_interval` step (`update_interval = 1` ,by default), the actor-critic network is trained with a batch of transitions that are randomly sampled from the replay memory. For every `time_between_two_copies` step, the target network is updated and the weights of the Q-network are saved to the hard disk.

After the training step, the following function can be called for evaluating the performance of our trained agent:

```
def evaluate(self, sess):
    for episode in range(self.n_episode):
        frame = self.task.reset()
        for _ in range(self.history_len+1):
            self.replay_memory.add(frame, 0, 0, 0)
        for _ in range(self.config['T']):
            print("episode {}, total reward {}".format(episode,
self.task.get_total_reward()))
            state = self.replay_memory.phi(frame)
            action = self.choose_action(sess, state, self.epsilon_min)
            r, new_frame, termination = self.play(action)
            self.replay_memory.add(frame, action, r, termination)
            frame = new_frame

            if self.callback:
                self.callback()
                if termination:
                    break
```

Experiments

The full implementation of DPG can be downloaded from our GitHub (`https://github.com/PacktPublishing/Python-Reinforcement-Learning-Projects`). To train an agent for CartPole, run the following command under the `src` folder:

```
python train.py -t CartPole-v0 -d cpu
```

There are two arguments in `train.py`. One is `-t`, or `--task`, indicating the name of the classic control task you want to test. The other one is `-d`, or `--device`, which specifies the device (CPU or GPU) that you want to use to train the actor-critic network. Since the dimensions of the state spaces of these classic control tasks are relatively low compared to the Atari environment, using the CPU to train the agent is fast enough. It should only take several minutes to finish.

During the training, you can open a new Terminal and type the following command to visualize both the architecture of the actor-critic network and the training procedure:

```
tensorboard --logdir=log/CartPole-v0/train
```

Here, `logdir` points to the folder where the `CartPole-v0` log file is stored. Once TensorBoard is running, navigate your web browser to `localhost:6006` to view the TensorBoard:

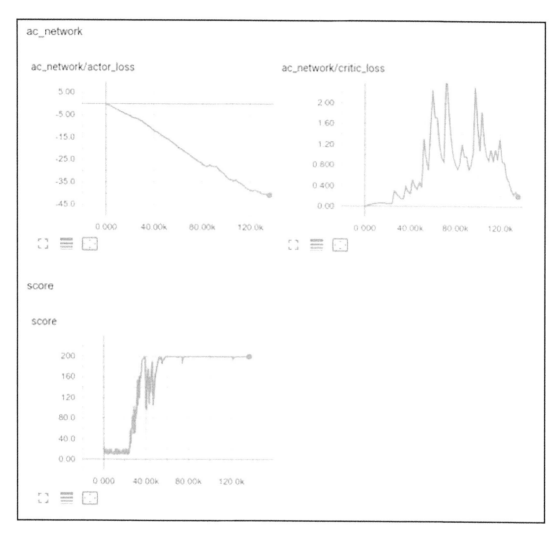

Tensorboard view

The top two graphs show the changes of the actor loss and the critic loss against the training step. For classical control tasks, the actor loss usually decreases consistently, while the critic loss has a large fluctuation. After 60,000 training steps, the score becomes stable, achieving 200, the highest score that can be reached in the CartPole simulator.

Using a similar command, you can also train an agent for the `Pendulum` task:

```
python train.py -t Pendulum-v0 -d cpu
```

Then, check the training procedure via `Tensorboard`:

```
tensorboard --logdir=log/Pendulum-v0/train
```

The following screenshot shows the changes of the score during training:

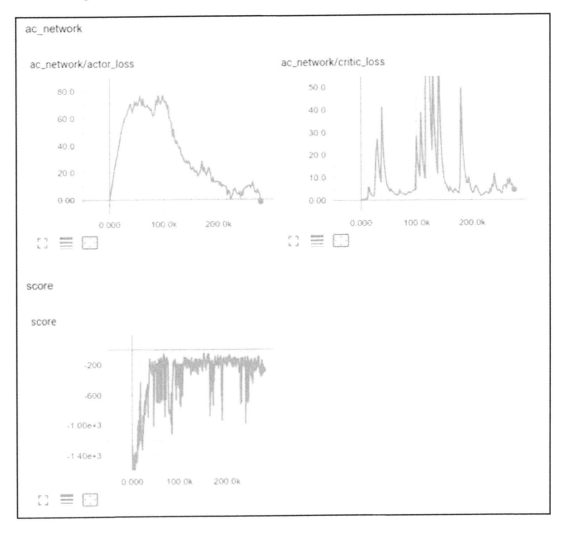

Changes in score during training

A careful reader may notice that the score of Pendulum fluctuates widely compared to the score of CartPole. There are two reasons that are causing this problem:

- In Pendulum, the starting position of the pole is not deterministic, namely, it may be different for two episodes
- The train procedure in DPG may not be always stable, especially for complicated tasks, such as MuJoCo control tasks

The MuJoCo control tasks, for example, Ant, HalfCheetah, Hopper, Humanoid, InvertedPendulum, Reacher, Swimmer, and Walker2d provided by Gym, have high-dimensional state and action space, which makes DPG fail. If you are curious about what happens when running DPG with the `Hopper-v0` task, you can try the following:

```
python train.py -t Hopper-v0 -d cpu
```

After several minutes, you will see that DPG cannot teach Hopper how to walk. The main reason why DPG fails in this case is that the simple actor and critic updates discussed here become unstable with high-dimensional inputs.

Trust region policy optimization

The **trust region policy optimization** (**TRPO**) algorithm was proposed to solve complex continuous control tasks in the following paper: Schulman, S. Levine, P. Moritz, M. Jordan and P. Abbeel. *Trust Region Policy Optimization*. In ICML, 2015.

To understand why TRPO works requires some mathematical background. The main idea is that it is better to guarantee that the new policy, π_{new}, optimized by one training step, not only monotonically decreases the optimization loss function (and thus improves the policy), but also does not deviate from the previous policy π_{old} much, which means that there should be a constraint on the difference between π_{new} and π_{old}, for example, $C(\pi_{new}, \pi_{old}) \leq \delta$ for a certain constraint function $C(\cdot)$ constant δ.

Theory behind TRPO

Let's see the mechanism behind TRPO. If you feel that this part is hard to understand, you can skip it and go directly to how to run TRPO to solve MuJoCo control tasks. Consider an infinite-horizon discounted Markov decision process denoted by $(S, a, P, c, \rho_0, \gamma)$, where S is a finite set of states, A is a finite set of actions, P is the transition probability distribution, C is the cost function, ρ_0 is the distribution of the initial state, and γ is the discount factor. Let π be a stochastic policy that we want to learn by minimizing the following expected discounted cost:

$$\eta(\pi) = E_{s_0, a_0, \cdots} \left[\sum_{t=0}^{\infty} \gamma^t c(s_t) \right]$$

Here, this is $s_0 \sim \rho_0$, $a_t \sim \pi(a_t|s_t)$ and $s_{t+1} \sim P(s|s_t, a_t)$. The definitions of the `state-action value` function Q_π, the value function V_π, and the advantage function A_π under policy π are as follows:

$$Q_\pi(s_t, a_t) = E_{s_{t+1}, a_{t+1}, \cdots} \left[\sum_{l=0}^{\infty} \gamma^l c(s_{t+l}) \right]$$

$$V_\pi(s_t) = E_{a_t, s_{t+1}, \cdots} \left[\sum_{l=0}^{\infty} \gamma^l c(s_{t+l}) \right]$$

$$A_\pi(s, a) = Q_\pi(s, a) - V_\pi(s)$$

Here, this is $a_t \sim \pi(a_t|s_t)$ and $s_{t+1} \sim P(s|s_t, a_t)$.

Our goal is to improve policy π (by reducing the expected discounted cost) during each training step. In order to design an algorithm monotonically improving π, let's consider the following equation:

$$\eta(\tilde{\pi}) = \eta(\pi) + E_{s_0, a_0, \cdots} \left[\sum_{t=0}^{\infty} \gamma^t A_\pi(s_t, a_t) \right]$$

Here, this is $s_0 \sim \rho_0$, $a_t \sim \tilde{\pi}(a_t|s_t)$ and $s_{t+1} \sim P(s|s_t, a_t)$. This equation holds for any policy $\tilde{\pi}$. For the readers who are interested in the proof of this equation, refer to the appendix in the TRPO paper or the paper *Approximately optimal approximate reinforcement learning*, written by Kakade and Langford. To simplify this equation, let ρ_π be the discounted visitation frequencies:

$$\rho_\pi(s) = P(s_0 = s) + \gamma P(s_1 = s) + \gamma^2 P(s_2 = s) + \cdots$$

By rearranging the preceding equation to sum over states instead of timesteps, it becomes the following:

$$\eta(\tilde{\pi}) = \eta(\pi) + \sum_s \rho_{\tilde{\pi}}(s) \sum_a \tilde{\pi}(a|s) A_\pi(s, a)$$

From this equation, we can see that any policy update $\pi \rightarrow \tilde{\pi}$ that has a non-positive expected advantage at every state s, that is, $\sum_a \tilde{\pi}(a|s) A_\pi(s, a) \leq 0$, is guaranteed to reduce the cost η. Therefore, for discrete action space such as the Atari environment, the deterministic policy $\tilde{\pi}(s) = \arg\min_a A_\pi(s, a)$, selected in DQN, guarantees to improves the policy if there is at least one state-action pair with a negative advantage value and nonzero state visitation probability. However, in practical problems, especially when the policy is approximated by a neural network, there will be some state for which the expected advantage is positive, due to approximation errors. Besides this, the dependency of $\rho_{\tilde{\pi}}(s)$ on $\tilde{\pi}$ makes this equation hard to optimize, so TRPO considers optimizing the following function by replacing $\rho_{\tilde{\pi}}$ with ρ_π:

$$L_\pi(\tilde{\pi}) = \eta(\pi) + \sum_s \rho_\pi(s) \sum_a \tilde{\pi}(a|s) A_\pi(s, a)$$

Kakade and Langford showed that if we have a parameterized policy, π_θ, which is a differentiable function of the parameter θ, then for any parameter θ_0:

$$L_{\pi_{\theta_0}} = \eta(\pi_{\theta_0})$$

$$\nabla_\theta L_{\pi_{\theta_0}}(\pi_\theta)|_{\theta=\theta_0} = \nabla_\theta \eta(\pi_\theta)|_{\theta=\theta_0}$$

This means that improving L will also improve η with a sufficient small update on π_θ. Based on this idea, Kakade and Langford proposed a policy updating scheme called the conservative policy iteration:

$$\pi_{new}(a|s) = (1 - \alpha)\pi_{old}(a|s) + \alpha\pi'(a|s)$$

Here, π_{old} is the current policy, π_{old} is the new policy, and π' is obtained by solving $\pi' = \arg\min_{\pi'} L_{\pi_{old}}(\pi')$. They proved the following bound for this update:

$$\eta(\pi_{new}) \leq L_{\pi_{old}}(\pi_{new}) + \frac{2\epsilon\gamma}{(1-\gamma)^2}\alpha^2, \quad \text{where} \quad \epsilon = \max_s \left|E_{a\sim\pi'(a|s)}[A_\pi(s,a)]\right|$$

Note that this bound only applies to mixture policies generated by the preceding update. In TRPO, the authors extended this bound to general stochastic policies, rather than just mixture policies. The main idea is to replace mixture weight α with a distance measure between π_{new} and π_{old}. An interesting pick of the distance measure is the total variation divergence. Taking two discrete distributions p and q as an example, the total variation divergence is defined as follows:

$$D_{TV}(p,q) = \frac{1}{2}\sum_i |p_i - q_i|$$

For policies π_{new} and π_{old}, let $D_{TV}^{\max}(\pi_{old}, \pi_{new})$ be the maximum total variation divergence over all the states:

$$D_{TV}^{\max}(\pi_{old}, \pi_{new}) = \max_s D_{TV}(\pi_{old}(\cdot|s), \pi_{new}(\cdot|s))$$

With $\alpha = D_{TV}^{\max}(\pi_{old}, \pi_{new})$ and $\epsilon = \max_s \left|E_{a\sim\pi'(a|s)}[A_\pi(s,a)]\right|$, it can be shown that:

$$\eta(\pi_{new}) \leq L_{\pi_{old}}(\pi_{new}) + CD_{TV}^{\max}(\pi_{old}, \pi_{new})^2, \quad \text{where} \quad C = \frac{2\epsilon\gamma}{(1-\gamma)^2}.$$

Actually, the total variation divergence can be upper bounded by the KL divergence, namely, $D_{TV}^{\max}(\pi_{old}, \pi_{new})^2 \leq D_{KL}^{\max}(\pi_{old}, \pi_{new})$, which means that:

$$\eta(\pi_{new}) \leq L_{\pi_{old}}(\pi_{new}) + CD_{KL}^{\max}(\pi_{old}, \pi_{new}), \quad \text{where} \quad C = \frac{2\epsilon\gamma}{(1-\gamma)^2}.$$

TRPO algorithm

Based on the preceding policy improvement bound, the following algorithm is developed:

```
Initialize policy π₀;
Repeat for each step i = 1, 2, ⋯:
    Compute all advantage values A_πᵢ(s, a);
    Solve the following optimization problem:
    π_{i+1} = arg min_π L_πᵢ(π) + CD_{KL}^{max}(πᵢ, π);
Until convergence
```

In each step, this algorithm minimizes the upper bound of $\eta(\pi)$, so that:

$$\eta(\pi_{i+1}) \leq L_{\pi_i}(\pi_{i+1}) + CD_{KL}^{max}(\pi_{i+1}, \pi_i) \leq L_{\pi_i}(\pi_i) + CD_{KL}^{max}(\pi_i, \pi_i) = \eta(\pi_i)$$

The last equation follows from that $L_\pi(\pi) = \eta(\pi)$ for any policy π. This implies that this algorithm is guaranteed to generate a sequence of monotonically improving policies.

In practice, since the exact value of ϵ in C is hard to calculate, and it is difficult to control the step size of each update using the penalty term, TRPO replaces the penalty term with the constraint that KL divergence is bounded by a constant δ:

$$\text{minimize}_\pi L_{\pi_{old}}(\pi), \text{ subject to } D_{KL}^{max}(\pi_{old}, \pi) \leq \delta$$

But this problem is still impractical to solve due to the large number of constraints. Therefore, TRPO uses a heuristic approximation that considers the average KL divergence:

$$\bar{D}_{KL}(\pi_{\theta_{old}}, \pi_\theta) = E_{s \sim \rho}[D_{KL}(\pi_{\theta_{old}}(\cdot|s), \pi_\theta(\cdot|s))]$$

This leads to the following optimization problem:

$$\text{minimize}_\pi \, L_{\pi_{old}}(\pi), \text{ subject to } \bar{D}_{KL}(\pi_{old}, \pi) \leq \delta$$

In other words, by expanding $L_{\pi_{old}}$, we need to solve the following:

$$\text{minimize}_\pi \sum_s \rho_{\pi_{old}}(s) \sum_a \pi(a|s) A_{\pi_{old}}(s, a), \text{ subject to } \bar{D}_{KL}(\pi_{old}, \pi) \leq \delta$$

Now, the question is: how do we optimize this problem? A straightforward idea is to sample several trajectories by simulating the policy π_{old} for some number of steps and then approximate the objective function of this problem using these trajectories. Since the advantage function $A_\pi(s, a) = Q_\pi(s, a) - V_\pi(s)$, we replace $A_{\pi_{old}}$ with by the Q-value $Q_{\pi_{old}}$ in the objective function, which only changes the objective by a constant. Besides, note the following:

$$\sum_a \pi(a|s) A_{\pi_{old}}(s, a) = E_{a \sim \pi_{old}(a|s)} \left[\frac{\pi(a|s)}{\pi_{old}(a|s)} A_{\pi_{old}}(s, a) \right]$$

Therefore, given a trajectory $T = \{(s_0, a_0), \cdots, (s_m, a_m)\}$ generated under policy π_{old}, we will optimize as follows:

$$\text{minimize}_\pi \frac{1}{m} \sum_{(s,a) \in T} \pi(a|s) A_{\pi_{old}}(s, a), \text{ subject to } \frac{1}{m} \sum_{(s,a) \in T} D_{KL}(\pi_{old}(\cdot|s), \pi(\cdot|s)) \leq \delta$$

For the MuJoCo control tasks, both the policy π and the `state-action value` function $Q(s, a)$ are approximated by neural networks. In order to optimize this problem, the KL divergence constraint can be approximated by the Fisher information matrix. This problem can then be solved via the conjugate gradient algorithm. For more details, you can download the source code of TRPO from GitHub and check `optimizer.py`, which implements the conjugate gradient algorithm using TensorFlow.

Experiments on MuJoCo tasks

The `Swimmer` task is a good example to test TRPO. This task involves a 3-link swimming robot in a viscous fluid, where the goal is to make it swim forward as fast as possible by actuating the two joints (`http://gym.openai.com/envs/Swimmer-v2/`). The following screenshot shows how `Swimmer` looks in the MuJoCo simulator:

To train an agent for `Swimmer`, run the following command under the `src` folder:

```
CUDA_VISIBLE_DEVICES= python train.py -t Swimmer
```

There are two arguments in `train.py`. One is `-t`, or `--task`, indicating the name of the MuJoCo or classic control task you want to test. Since the state spaces of these control tasks have relatively low dimensions compared to the Atari environment, it is enough to use CPU alone to train the agent by setting `CUDA_VISIBLE_DEVICES` to empty, which will take between 30 minutes and two hours.

During the training, you can open a new Terminal and type the following command to visualize the training procedure:

```
tensorboard --logdir=log/Swimmer
```

Here, `logdir` points to the folder where the `Swimmer` log file is stored. Once TensorBoard is running, navigate your web browser to `localhost:6006` to view the TensorBoard:

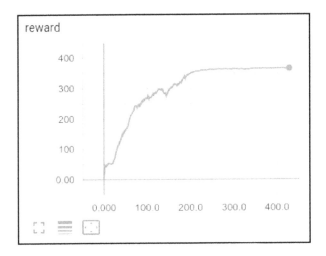

Clearly, after 200 episodes, the total reward achieved in each episode becomes stable, namely, around 366. To check how `Swimmer` moves after the training, run the following command:

```
CUDA_VISIBLE_DEVICES= python test.py -t Swimmer
```

You will see a funny-looking `Swimmer` object walking on the floor.

Summary

This chapter introduced the classical control tasks and the MuJoCo control tasks provided by Gym. You have learned the goals and specifications of these tasks and how to implement a simulator for them. The most important parts of this chapter were the deterministic DPG and the TRPO for continuous control tasks. You learned the theory behind them, which explains why they work well in these tasks. You also learned how to implement DPG and TRPO using TensorFlow, and how to visualize the training procedure.

In the next chapter, we will learn about how to apply reinforcement learning algorithms to more complex tasks, for example, playing Minecraft. We will introduce the **Asynchronous Actor-Critic (A3C)** algorithm, which is much faster than DQN at complex tasks, and has been widely applied as a framework in many deep reinforcement learning algorithms.

14
Building Virtual Worlds in Minecraft

In the two previous chapters, we discussed the **deep Q-learning (DQN)** algorithm for playing Atari games and the **Trust Region Policy Optimization (TRPO)** algorithm for continuous control tasks. We saw the big success of these algorithms in solving complex problems when compared to traditional reinforcement learning algorithms without the use of deep neural networks to approximate the value function or the policy function. Their main disadvantage, especially for DQN, is that the training step converges too slowly, for example, training an agent to play Atari games takes about one week. For more complex games, even one week's training is insufficient.

This chapter will introduce a more complicated example, Minecraft, which is a popular online video game created by Swedish game developer Markus Persson and later developed by Mojang. You will learn how to launch a Minecraft environment using OpenAI Gym and play different missions. In order to build an AI player to accomplish these missions, you will learn the **asynchronous advantage actor-critic (A3C)** algorithm, which is a lightweight framework for deep reinforcement learning that uses asynchronous gradient descent for optimization of deep neural network controllers. A3C is a widely applied deep reinforcement learning algorithm for different kinds of tasks, training for half the time on a single multi-core CPU instead of a GPU. For Atari games such as Breakout, A3C achieves human-level performance after 3 hours' training, which is much faster than DQN, which requires 3 days' training. You will learn how to implement A3C using Python and TensorFlow. This chapter does not require as much of a mathematical background as the previous chapter—just have fun!

The following topics will be covered in this chapter:

- Introduction to the Minecraft environment
- Data preparation for training an AI bot in the Minecraft environment
- The asynchronous advantage actor-critic framework
- Implementation of the A3C framework

Introduction to the Minecraft environment

The original OpenAI Gym does not contain the Minecraft environment. We need to install a Minecraft environment bundle, available at `https://github.com/tambetm/gym-minecraft`. This bundle is built based on Microsoft's Malmö, which is a platform for AI experimentation and research built on top of Minecraft.

Before installing the `gym-minecraft` package, Malmö should first be downloaded from `https://github.com/Microsoft/malmo`. We can download the latest pre-built version from `https://github.com/Microsoft/malmo/releases`. After unzipping the package, go to the `Minecraft` folder and run `launchClient.bat` on Windows, or `launchClient.sh` on Linux/MacOS, to launch a Minecraft environment. If it is successfully launched, we can now install `gym-minecraft` via the following scripts:

```
python3 -m pip install gym
python3 -m pip install pygame

git clone https://github.com/tambetm/minecraft-py.git
cd minecraft-py
python setup.py install

git clone https://github.com/tambetm/gym-minecraft.git
cd gym-minecraft
python setup.py install
```

Then, we can run the following code to test whether `gym-minecraft` has been successfully installed or not:

```
import logging
import minecraft_py
logging.basicConfig(level=logging.DEBUG)

proc, _ = minecraft_py.start()
minecraft_py.stop(proc)
```

The `gym-minecraft` package provides 15 different missions, including `MinecraftDefaultWorld1-v0` and `MinecraftBasic-v0`. For example, in `MinecraftBasic-v0`, the agent can move around in a small chamber with a box placed in the corner, and the goal is to reach the position of this box. The following screenshots show several missions available in `gym-minecraft`:

The `gym-minecraft` package has the same interface as other Gym environments, such as Atari and classic control tasks. You can run the following code to test different Minecraft missions and try to get a high-level understanding of their properties, for example, goal, reward, and observation:

```python
import gym
import gym_minecraft
import minecraft_py

def start_game():
    env = gym.make('MinecraftBasic-v0')
    env.init(start_minecraft=True)
    env.reset()
    done = False
    while not done:
        env.render(mode='human')
        action = env.action_space.sample()
        obs, reward, done, info = env.step(action)
    env.close()

if __name__ == "__main__":
    start_game()
```

At each step, an action is randomly drawn from the action space by calling `env.action_space.sample()`, and then this action is submitted to the system by calling the `env.step(action)` function, which returns the observation and the reward corresponding to this action. You can also try other missions by replacing `MinecraftBasic-v0` with other names, for example, `MinecraftMaze1-v0` and `MinecraftObstacles-v0`.

Data preparation

In the Atari environment, recall that there are three modes for each Atari game, for example, Breakout, BreakoutDeterministic, and BreakoutNoFrameskip, and each mode has two versions, for example, Breakout-v0 and Breakout-v4. The main difference between the three modes is the frameskip parameter that indicates the number of frames (steps) the one action is repeated on. This is called the **frame-skipping** technique, which allows us to play more games without significantly increasing the runtime.

However, in the Minecraft environment, there is only one mode where the frameskip parameter is equal to one. Therefore, in order to apply the frame-skipping technique, we need to explicitly repeat a certain action frameskip multiple times during one timestep. Besides this, the frame images returned by the `step` function are RGB images. Similar to the Atari environment, the observed frame images are converted to grayscale and then resized to 84x84. The following code provides the wrapper for `gym-minecraft`, which contains all the data preprocessing steps:

```
import gym
import gym_minecraft
import minecraft_py
import numpy, time
from utils import cv2_resize_image

class Game:

    def __init__(self, name='MinecraftBasic-v0', discrete_movement=False):
        self.env = gym.make(name)
        if discrete_movement:
            self.env.init(start_minecraft=True,
allowDiscreteMovement=["move", "turn"])
        else:
            self.env.init(start_minecraft=True,
allowContinuousMovement=["move", "turn"])
        self.actions = list(range(self.env.action_space.n))
        frame = self.env.reset()
        self.frame_skip = 4
        self.total_reward = 0
        self.crop_size = 84
        self.buffer_size = 8
        self.buffer_index = 0
        self.buffer = [self.crop(self.rgb_to_gray(frame)) for _ in
range(self.buffer_size)]
        self.last_frame = frame
    def rgb_to_gray(self, im):
        return numpy.dot(im, [0.2126, 0.7152, 0.0722])
    def reset(self):
```

```
        frame = self.env.reset()
        self.total_reward = 0
        self.buffer_index = 0
        self.buffer = [self.crop(self.rgb_to_gray(frame)) for _ in
range(self.buffer_size)]
        self.last_frame = frame
    def add_frame_to_buffer(self, frame):
        self.buffer_index = self.buffer_index % self.buffer_size
        self.buffer[self.buffer_index] = frame
        self.buffer_index += 1
    def get_available_actions(self):
        return list(range(len(self.actions)))
    def get_feedback_size(self):
        return (self.crop_size, self.crop_size)
    def crop(self, frame):
        feedback = cv2_resize_image(frame,
                                    resized_shape=(self.crop_size,
self.crop_size),
                                    method='scale', crop_offset=0)
        return feedback
    def get_current_feedback(self, num_frames=4):
        assert num_frames < self.buffer_size, "Frame buffer is not large
enough."
        index = self.buffer_index - 1
        frames = [numpy.expand_dims(self.buffer[index - k], axis=0) for k
in range(num_frames)]
        if num_frames > 1:
            return numpy.concatenate(frames, axis=0)
        else:
            return frames[0]
    def play_action(self, action, num_frames=4):
        reward = 0
        termination = 0
        for i in range(self.frame_skip):
            a = self.actions[action]
            frame, r, done, _ = self.env.step(a)
            reward += r
            if i == self.frame_skip - 2:
                self.last_frame = frame
            if done:
                termination = 1
self.add_frame_to_buffer(self.crop(numpy.maximum(self.rgb_to_gray(frame),
self.rgb_to_gray(self.last_frame))))
        r = numpy.clip(reward, -1, 1)
        self.total_reward += reward
        return r, self.get_current_feedback(num_frames), termination
```

In the constructor, the available actions for Minecraft are restricted to `move` and `turn` (not considering other actions, such as the camera controls). Converting an RGB image into a grayscale image is quite easy. Given an RGB image with shape (height, width, channel), the `rgb_to_gray` function is used to convert an image to grayscale. For cropping and reshaping frame images, we use the `opencv-python` or `cv2` packages, which contain a Python wrapper around the original C++ OpenCV implementation, that is, the `crop` function reshapes an image into an 84x84 matrix. Unlike the Atari environment, where `crop_offset` is set to 8 to remove the scoreboard from the screen, here, we set `crop_offset` to 0 and just reshape the frame images.

The `play_action` function submits the input action to the Minecraft environment and returns the corresponding reward, observation, and termination signal. The default frameskip parameter is set to 4, meaning that one action is repeated four times for each `play_action` call. The `get_current_feedback` function returns the observation that stacks the last four frame images together, since only considering the current frame image is not enough for playing Minecraft because it doesn't contain dynamic information about the game status.

This wrapper has the same interface as the wrappers for the Atari environment and classic control tasks. Therefore, you can try to run DQN or TRPO with the Minecraft environment without changing anything. If you have one idle GPU, it is better to run DQN first before trying the A3C algorithm that we will discuss next.

Asynchronous advantage actor-critic algorithm

In the previous chapters, we discussed the DQN for playing Atari games and the use of the DPG and TRPO algorithms for continuous control tasks. Recall that DQN has the following architecture:

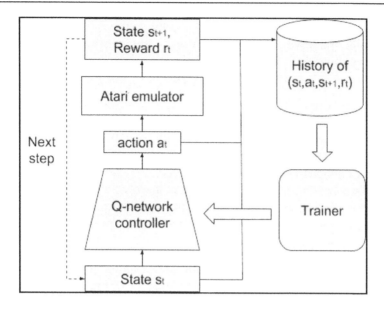

At each timestep t, the agent observes the frame image s_t and selects an action a_t based on the current learned policy. The emulator (the Minecraft environment) executes this action and returns the next frame image s_{t+1} and the corresponding reward r_t. The quadruplet $\left(s_t, a_t, r_t, s_{t+1}\right)$ is then stored in the experience memory and is taken as a sample for training the Q-network by minimizing the empirical loss function via stochastic gradient descent.

Deep reinforcement learning algorithms based on experience replay have achieved unprecedented success in playing Atari games. However, experience replay has several disadvantages:

- It uses more memory and computation per real interaction
- It requires off-policy learning algorithms that can update from data generated by an older policy

In order to reduce memory consumption and accelerate the training of an AI agent, Mnih et al. proposed an A3C framework for deep reinforcement learning that dramatically reduces the training time without performance loss. This work, *Asynchronous Methods for Deep Reinforcement Learning*, was published in ICML, 2016.

Instead of experience replay, A3C asynchronously executes multiple agents in parallel on multiple instances of the environment, such as the Atari or Minecraft environments. Since the parallel agents experience a variety of different states, this parallelism breaks the correlation between the training samples and stabilizes the training procedure, which means that the experience memory can be removed. This simple idea enables a much larger spectrum of fundamental on-policy reinforcement learning algorithms, such as Sarsa and actor-critic methods, as well as off-policy reinforcement learning algorithms, such as Q-learning, to be applied robustly and effectively using deep neural networks.

Another advantage is that A3C is able to run on a standard multi-core CPU without relying on GPUs or massively distributed architectures, and requires far less training time than GPU-based algorithms, such as DQN, when applied to Atari games. A3C is good for a beginner in deep reinforcement learning since you can apply it to Atari games on a standard PC with multiple cores. For example, for Breakout, it takes only two-three hours to achieve a score of 300 when executing eight agents in parallel.

In this chapter, we will use the same notations as before. At each timestep t, the agent observes state s_t, takes action a_t, and then receives the corresponding reward r_t generated from a function $R(s_t, a_t)$. We use $\pi(a_t|s_t)$ to denote the policy of the agent, which maps states to a probability distribution over the actions. The Bellman equation is as follows:

$$Q(s_t, a_t) = E_{s_{t+1} \sim S}[R(s_t, a_t) + \gamma E_{a_{t+1} \sim \pi(a_{t+1}|s_{t+1})} Q(s_{t+1}, a_{t+1})]$$

The state-action value function Q can be approximated by a neural network parameterized by θ^Q, and the policy π can also be represented by another neural network parameterized by θ^π. Then, Q can be be trained by minimizing the following loss function:

$$L(\theta^Q) = E_{s_t, a_t}[(y_t - Q(s_t, a_t|\theta^Q))^2]$$

y_t is the approximated state-action value function at step t. In one-step Q-learning such as DQN, $\pi(a_t|s_t)$ equals $\underset{a}{\arg\max}\, Q(s_t, a)$, so that the following is true:

$$y_t = R(s_t, a_t) + \gamma \max_a Q(s_{t+1}, a)|\theta^Q)$$

One drawback of using one-step Q-learning is that obtaining a reward $R(s_t, a_t)$ only directly affects the value of the state action pair (s_t, a_t) that led to the reward. This can make the learning process slow since many updates are required to propagate a reward to the relevant preceding states and actions. One way of propagating rewards faster is by using n-step returns. In n-step Q-learning, y_t can be set to this:

$$R(s_t, a_t) + \gamma R(s_{t+1}, a_{t+1}) + \gamma^2 R(s_{t+2}, a_{t+2}) + \cdots + \gamma^{n-1} R(s_{t+n-1}, a_{t+n-1}) + \gamma^n \max_a Q(s_{t+n}, a)|\theta^Q)$$

As opposed to value-based methods, a policy-based method, such as TRPO, directly optimizes the policy network π. Besides TRPO, a much simpler method is REINFORCE, which updates the policy parameter θ^π in the direction $\nabla_{\theta^\pi} \log \pi(a_t|s_t; \theta^\pi) A(s_t, a_t)$, where $A(a_t, s_t) = Q(s_t, a_t) - V(s_t)$ is the the advantage of action a_t in state s_t. This method is an actor-critic approach due to the fact that it is required to estimate the value function $V(s_t)$ and the policy $\pi(a_t|s_t)$.

The asynchronous reinforcement learning framework can be applied in the approaches already discussed here. The main idea is that we run multiple agents in parallel with their own instances of the environment, for example, multiple players play the same game using their own games consoles. These agents are likely to be exploring different parts of the environment. The parameters θ^Q and θ^π are shared among all agents. Each agent updates the policy and the value function asynchronously without considering read–write conflicts. Although it seems weird that there is no synchronization in updating the policy, this asynchronous method not only removes the communication costs of sending gradients and parameters, but also guarantees the convergence. For more details, please refer to the following paper: *A lock-free approach to parallelizing stochastic gradient descent*, Recht et al. This chapter focuses on A3C, namely, we apply the asynchronous reinforcement learning framework in REINFORCE. The following diagram shows the A3C architecture:

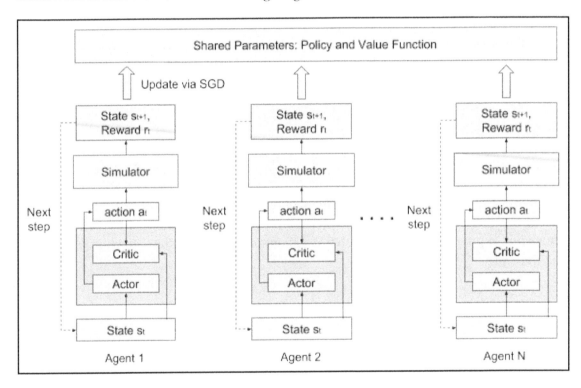

For A3C, the policy $\pi(a_t|s_t;\theta^\pi)$ and the value function $V(s_t;\theta^V)$ are approximated by two neural networks. A3C updates the policy parameter θ^π in the direction $\nabla_{\theta^\pi} \log \pi(a_t|s_t;\theta^\pi)A(s_t,a_t)$, where $A(s_t,a_t)$ is fixed, which is estimated by the following:

$$A(s_t,a_t) = \sum_{i=0}^{k-1} \gamma^i R(s_{t+1},a_{t+i}) + \gamma^k V(s_{t+k}) - V(s_t)$$

A3C updates the value function parameter θ^V by minimizing the loss:

$$(V(s_t;\theta^V) - (\sum_{i=0}^{k-1} \gamma^i R(s_{t+1},a_{t+i}) + \gamma^k V(s_{t+k})))$$

$V(s_{t+k})$ is computed via the previous estimate. To encourage exploration during training, the entropy of the policy π is also added to the policy update, acting as a regularization term. Then, the gradient for the policy update becomes the following:

$$\nabla_{\theta^\pi} \log \pi(a_t|s_t;\theta^\pi)A(s_t,a_t) + \beta\nabla_{\theta^\pi} H(\pi(s_t;\theta^\pi))$$

The following pseudo code shows the A3C algorithm for each agent (thread):

```
Initialize thread step counter t = 1;
Initialize global shared parameters θ^V and θ^π;
Repeat for each episode:
    Reset gradients dθ^π = 0 and dθ^π = 0;
    Synchronize thread-specific parameters θ_a^V = θ^V and θ_a^π = θ^π;
    Set the start time step t_start = t;
    Receive an observation state s_t;
    While s_t is not the terminal state and t - t_start < t_max:
        Select an action a_t according to π(s_t;θ_a^π);
        Execute action a_t in the simulator and observe reward r_t and the
next state s_{t+1};
        Set t = t + 1;
    End While
    Set R = 0 if s_t is the terminal state or R = V(s_t;θ_a^V) otherwise;
    For i ∈ {t - 1,···,t_start} do
        Update R = r_i + γR;
        Accumulate gradients wrt θ_a^π:
dθ^π = dθ^π + ∇_{θ_a^π} log π(a_i|s_i;θ_a^π)(R - V(s_i;θ_a^V)) + β∇_{θ_a^π} H(π(s_t;θ_a^π));
        Accumulate gradients wrt θ_a^V: dθ^V = dθ^V + ∇_{θ_a^V} (R - V(s_i;θ_a^V))²;
    End For
    Perform asynchronous update of θ^V using dθ^V and of θ^π using dθ^π.
```

A3C uses ADAM or RMSProp to perform an asynchronous update of the parameters. For different environments, it is hard to tell which method leads to better performance. We can use RMSProp for the Atari and Minecraft environments.

Implementation of A3C

We will now look at how to implement A3C using Python and TensorFlow. Here, the policy network and value network share the same feature representation. We implement two kinds of policies: one is based on the CNN architecture used in DQN, and the other is based on LSTM.

We implement the `FFPolicy` class for the policy based on CNN:

```
class FFPolicy:
    def __init__(self, input_shape=(84, 84, 4), n_outputs=4,
network_type='cnn'):
        self.width = input_shape[0]
        self.height = input_shape[1]
        self.channel = input_shape[2]
        self.n_outputs = n_outputs
        self.network_type = network_type
        self.entropy_beta = 0.01
        self.x = tf.placeholder(dtype=tf.float32,
                            shape=(None, self.channel, self.width,
self.height))
        self.build_model()
```

The constructor requires three arguments:

1. `input_shape`
2. `n_outputs`
3. `network_type`

input_shape is the size of the input image. After data preprocessing, the input is an 84x84x4 image, so the default parameter is (84, 84, 4). n_outputs is the number of all the available actions. network_type indicates the type of the feature representation we want to use. Our implementation contains two different networks. One is the CNN architecture used in DQN. The other is a feedforward neural network used for testing.

1. In the constructor, the x variable represents the input state (a batch of 84x84x4 images). After creating the input tensors, the build_model function is called to build the policy and value network. Here is the build_model:

```
def build_model(self):
    self.net = {}
    self.net['input'] = tf.transpose(self.x, perm=(0, 2, 3, 1))
    if self.network_type == 'cnn':
        self.net['conv1'] = conv2d(self.net['input'], 16, kernel=(8,
8), stride=(4, 4), name='conv1')
        self.net['conv2'] = conv2d(self.net['conv1'], 32, kernel=(4,
4), stride=(2, 2), name='conv2')
        self.net['feature'] = linear(self.net['conv2'], 256,
name='fc1')
    else:
        self.net['fc1'] = linear(self.net['input'], 50, init_b =
tf.constant_initializer(0.0), name='fc1')
        self.net['feature'] = linear(self.net['fc1'], 50, init_b =
tf.constant_initializer(0.0), name='fc2')
    self.net['value'] = tf.reshape(linear(self.net['feature'], 1,
activation=None, name='value',
                                    init_b =
tf.constant_initializer(0.0)),
                            shape=(-1,))
    self.net['logits'] = linear(self.net['feature'], self.n_outputs,
activation=None, name='logits',
                            init_b = tf.constant_initializer(0.0))
    self.net['policy'] = tf.nn.softmax(self.net['logits'],
name='policy')
    self.net['log_policy'] = tf.nn.log_softmax(self.net['logits'],
name='log_policy')
    self.vars = tf.get_collection(tf.GraphKeys.TRAINABLE_VARIABLES,
tf.get_variable_scope().name)
```

The CNN architecture contains two convolutional layers and one hidden layer, while the feedforward architecture contains two hidden layers. As discussed previously, the policy network and the value network share the same feature representation.

2. The loss function for updating the network parameters can be constructed via the following function:

```
def build_gradient_op(self, clip_grad=None):

    self.action = tf.placeholder(dtype=tf.float32, shape=(None,
self.n_outputs), name='action')
    self.reward = tf.placeholder(dtype=tf.float32, shape=(None,),
name='reward')
    self.advantage = tf.placeholder(dtype=tf.float32, shape=(None,),
name='advantage')

    value = self.net['value']
    policy = self.net['policy']
    log_policy = self.net['log_policy']
    entropy = -tf.reduce_sum(policy * log_policy, axis=1)
    p_loss = -tf.reduce_sum(tf.reduce_sum(log_policy * self.action,
axis=1) * self.advantage + self.entropy_beta * entropy)
    v_loss = 0.5 * tf.reduce_sum((value - self.reward) ** 2)
    total_loss = p_loss + v_loss
    self.gradients = tf.gradients(total_loss, self.vars)
    if clip_grad is not None:
        self.gradients, _ = tf.clip_by_global_norm(self.gradients,
clip_grad)
    tf.summary.scalar("policy_loss", p_loss,
collections=['policy_network'])
    tf.summary.scalar("value_loss", v_loss,
collections=['policy_network'])
    tf.summary.scalar("entropy", tf.reduce_mean(entropy),
collections=['policy_network'])
    self.summary_op = tf.summary.merge_all('policy_network')
    return self.gradients
```

3. This function creates three input tensors:
    1. `action`
    2. `reward`
    3. `advantage`

4. The `action` variable represents the selected actions a_t. The `reward` variable is the discounted cumulative reward R in the preceding A3C algorithm. The `advantage` variable is the advantage function computed by $R - V(s_t)$. In this implementation, the losses of the policy and the value function are combined together, since the feature representation layers are shared.

5. Therefore, instead of updating the `policy` parameter and the `value` parameter separately, our implementation updates these parameters simultaneously. This function also creates `summary_op` for TensorBoard visualization.

The implementation of the LSTM policy is quite similar to the feedforward policy. The main difference is the `build_model` function:

```
def build_model(self):
    self.net = {}
    self.net['input'] = tf.transpose(self.x, perm=(0, 2, 3, 1))
    if self.network_type == 'cnn':
        self.net['conv1'] = conv2d(self.net['input'], 16, kernel=(8,
8), stride=(4, 4), name='conv1')
        self.net['conv2'] = conv2d(self.net['conv1'], 32, kernel=(4,
4), stride=(2, 2), name='conv2')
        self.net['feature'] = linear(self.net['conv2'], 256,
name='fc1')
    else:
        self.net['fc1'] = linear(self.net['input'], 50, init_b =
tf.constant_initializer(0.0), name='fc1')
        self.net['feature'] = linear(self.net['fc1'], 50, init_b =
tf.constant_initializer(0.0), name='fc2')
    num_units = self.net['feature'].get_shape().as_list()[-1]
    self.lstm = tf.contrib.rnn.BasicLSTMCell(num_units=num_units,
forget_bias=0.0, state_is_tuple=True)
    self.init_state = self.lstm.zero_state(batch_size=1,
dtype=tf.float32)
    step_size = tf.shape(self.x)[:1]
    feature = tf.expand_dims(self.net['feature'], axis=0)
    lstm_outputs, lstm_state = tf.nn.dynamic_rnn(self.lstm, feature,
initial_state=self.init_state,
sequence_length=step_size,
                                                time_major=False)
    outputs = tf.reshape(lstm_outputs, shape=(-1, num_units))
    self.final_state = lstm_state
    self.net['value'] = tf.reshape(linear(outputs, 1, activation=None,
name='value',
                                            init_b =
tf.constant_initializer(0.0)),
                                    shape=(-1,))
    self.net['logits'] = linear(outputs, self.n_outputs,
```

```
activation=None, name='logits',
                                init_b = tf.constant_initializer(0.0))
        self.net['policy'] = tf.nn.softmax(self.net['logits'],
name='policy')
        self.net['log_policy'] = tf.nn.log_softmax(self.net['logits'],
name='log_policy')
        self.vars = tf.get_collection(tf.GraphKeys.TRAINABLE_VARIABLES,
tf.get_variable_scope().name)
```

In this function, a LSTM layer follows the feature representation layers. In TensorFlow, you can easily create a LSTM layer by constructing `BasicLSTMCell` and then calling `tf.nn.dynamic_rnn` to get the layer outputs. `tf.nn.dynamic_rnn` returns the output for each time step and the final cell state.

We now implement the main A3C algorithm—the A3C class:

```
class A3C:
    def __init__(self, system, directory, param, agent_index=0,
callback=None):
        self.system = system
        self.actions = system.get_available_actions()
        self.directory = directory
        self.callback = callback
        self.feedback_size = system.get_feedback_size()
        self.agent_index = agent_index
        self.set_params(param)
        self.init_network()
```

The `system` parameter is the emulator, either the Atari environment or Minecraft environment. `directory` indicates the folder for the saved model and logs. `param` includes all the training parameters of A3C, for example, the batch size and learning rate. `agent_index` is the label for one agent. The constructor calls `init_network` to initialize the policy network and the value network. Here is the implementation of `init_network`:

```
    def init_network(self):
        input_shape = self.feedback_size + (self.num_frames,)
        worker_device =
"/job:worker/task:{}/cpu:0".format(self.agent_index)
        with tf.device(tf.train.replica_device_setter(1,
worker_device=worker_device)):
            with tf.variable_scope("global"):
                if self.use_lstm is False:
                    self.shared_network = FFPolicy(input_shape,
len(self.actions), self.network_type)
                else:
                    self.shared_network = LSTMPolicy(input_shape,
len(self.actions), self.network_type)
```

```
                self.global_step = tf.get_variable("global_step", shape=[],
initializer=tf.constant_initializer(0, dtype=tf.int32),
                                                   trainable=False,
dtype=tf.int32)
                self.best_score = tf.get_variable("best_score", shape=[],
initializer=tf.constant_initializer(-1e2, dtype=tf.float32),
                                                   trainable=False,
dtype=tf.float32)
        with tf.device(worker_device):
            with tf.variable_scope('local'):
                if self.use_lstm is False:
                    self.network = FFPolicy(input_shape, len(self.actions),
self.network_type)
                else:
                    self.network = LSTMPolicy(input_shape,
len(self.actions), self.network_type)
                # Sync params
                self.update_local_ops =
update_target_graph(self.shared_network.vars, self.network.vars)
                # Learning rate
                self.lr = tf.get_variable(name='lr', shape=[],
initializer=tf.constant_initializer(self.learning_rate),
                                          trainable=False,
dtype=tf.float32)
                self.t_lr = tf.placeholder(dtype=tf.float32, shape=[],
name='new_lr')
                self.assign_lr_op = tf.assign(self.lr, self.t_lr)
                # Best score
                self.t_score = tf.placeholder(dtype=tf.float32, shape=[],
name='new_score')
                self.assign_best_score_op = tf.assign(self.best_score,
self.t_score)
                # Build gradient_op
                self.increase_step = self.global_step.assign_add(1)
                gradients = self.network.build_gradient_op(clip_grad=40.0)
                # Additional summaries
                tf.summary.scalar("learning_rate", self.lr,
collections=['a3c'])
                tf.summary.scalar("score", self.t_score,
collections=['a3c'])
                tf.summary.scalar("best_score", self.best_score,
collections=['a3c'])
                self.summary_op = tf.summary.merge_all('a3c')
        if self.shared_optimizer:
            with tf.device(tf.train.replica_device_setter(1,
worker_device=worker_device)):
                with tf.variable_scope("global"):
                    optimizer = create_optimizer(self.update_method,
```

```
                self.lr, self.rho, self.rmsprop_epsilon)
                        self.train_op =
        optimizer.apply_gradients(zip(gradients, self.shared_network.vars))
            else:
                with tf.device(worker_device):
                    with tf.variable_scope('local'):
                        optimizer = create_optimizer(self.update_method,
                self.lr, self.rho, self.rmsprop_epsilon)
                        self.train_op =
        optimizer.apply_gradients(zip(gradients, self.shared_network.vars))
```

The tricky part in this function is how to implement the global shared parameters. In TensorFlow, we can do this with the `tf.train.replica_device_setter` function. We first create a `global` device shared among all the agents. Within this device, the global shared network is created. Then, we create a local device and a local network for each agent. To synchronize the global and local parameters, `update_local_ops` is created by calling the `update_target_graph` function:

```
def update_target_graph(from_vars, to_vars):
    op_holder = []
    for from_var, to_var in zip(from_vars, to_vars):
        op_holder.append(to_var.assign(from_var))
    return op_holder
```

Then, the `gradients` op is constructed by calling `build_gradient_op`, which is used to compute the gradient update for each agent. With `gradients`, an optimizer is built via the `create_optimizer` function that is used for updating the global shared parameters. The `create_optimizer` function is used as follows:

```
def create_optimizer(method, learning_rate, rho, epsilon):
    if method == 'rmsprop':
        opt = tf.train.RMSPropOptimizer(learning_rate=learning_rate,
                                        decay=rho,
                                        epsilon=epsilon)
    elif method == 'adam':
        opt = tf.train.AdamOptimizer(learning_rate=learning_rate,
                                     beta1=rho)
    else:
        raise
    return opt
```

The main function in A3C is `run`, which starts and trains the agent:

```
def run(self, sess, saver=None):
    num_of_trials = -1
    for episode in range(self.num_episodes):
        self.system.reset()
```

```
            cell = self.network.run_initial_state(sess)
            state = self.system.get_current_feedback(self.num_frames)
            state = numpy.asarray(state / self.input_scale,
dtype=numpy.float32)
            replay_memory = []
            for _ in range(self.T):
                num_of_trials += 1
                global_step = sess.run(self.increase_step)
                if len(replay_memory) == 0:
                    init_cell = cell
                    sess.run(self.update_local_ops)
                action, value, cell = self.choose_action(sess, state, cell)
                r, new_state, termination = self.play(action)
                new_state = numpy.asarray(new_state / self.input_scale,
dtype=numpy.float32)
                replay = (state, action, r, new_state, value, termination)
                replay_memory.append(replay)
                state = new_state

                if len(replay_memory) == self.async_update_interval or
termination:
                    states, actions, rewards, advantages =
self.n_step_q_learning(sess, replay_memory, cell)
                    self.train(sess, states, actions, rewards, advantages,
init_cell, num_of_trials)
                    replay_memory = []

                if global_step % 40000 == 0:
                    self.save(sess, saver)
                if self.callback:
                    self.callback()
                if termination:
                    score = self.system.get_total_reward()
                    summary_str = sess.run(self.summary_op,
feed_dict={self.t_score: score})
                    self.summary_writer.add_summary(summary_str,
global_step)
                    self.summary_writer.flush()
                    break

            if global_step - self.eval_counter > self.eval_frequency:
                self.evaluate(sess, n_episode=10, saver=saver)
                self.eval_counter = global_step
```

At each timestep, it calls `choose_action` to select an action according to the current policy, and executes this action by calling `play`. Then, the received reward, the new state, and the termination signal, as well as the current state and the selected action, are stored in the `replay_memory`, which records the trajectory that the agent visited. Given this trajectory, it then calls `n_step_q_learning` to estimate the cumulative reward and the `advantage` function:

```
def n_step_q_learning(self, sess, replay_memory, cell):
        batch_size = len(replay_memory)
        w, h = self.system.get_feedback_size()
        states = numpy.zeros((batch_size, self.num_frames, w, h),
dtype=numpy.float32)
        rewards = numpy.zeros(batch_size, dtype=numpy.float32)
        advantages = numpy.zeros(batch_size, dtype=numpy.float32)
        actions = numpy.zeros((batch_size, len(self.actions)),
dtype=numpy.float32)
        for i in reversed(range(batch_size)):
            state, action, r, new_state, value, termination =
replay_memory[i]
            states[i] = state
            actions[i][action] = 1
            if termination != 0:
                rewards[i] = r
            else:
                if i == batch_size - 1:
                    rewards[i] = r + self.gamma * self.Q_value(sess,
new_state, cell)
                else:
                    rewards[i] = r + self.gamma * rewards[i+1]
            advantages[i] = rewards[i] - value
        return states, actions, rewards, advantages
```

It then updates the global shared parameters by calling `train`:

```
    def train(self, sess, states, actions, rewards, advantages, init_cell,
iter_num):
        lr = self.anneal_lr(iter_num)
        feed_dict = self.network.get_feed_dict(states, actions, rewards,
advantages, init_cell)
        sess.run(self.assign_lr_op, feed_dict={self.t_lr: lr})
        step = int((iter_num - self.async_update_interval + 1) /
self.async_update_interval)
        if self.summary_writer and step % 10 == 0:
            summary_str, _, step = sess.run([self.network.summary_op,
self.train_op, self.global_step],
                                            feed_dict=feed_dict)
            self.summary_writer.add_summary(summary_str, step)
```

```
        self.summary_writer.flush()
    else:
        sess.run(self.train_op, feed_dict=feed_dict)
```

Note that the model will be saved on the disk after 40,000 updates, and an evaluation procedure starts after `self.eval_frequency` updates.

To launch one agent, we can run the following codes written in the `worker.py` file:

```python
import numpy, time, random
import argparse, os, sys, signal
import tensorflow as tf
from a3c import A3C
from cluster import cluster_spec
from environment import new_environment

def set_random_seed(seed):
    random.seed(seed)
    numpy.random.seed(seed)

def delete_dir(path):
    if tf.gfile.Exists(path):
        tf.gfile.DeleteRecursively(path)
    tf.gfile.MakeDirs(path)
    return path

def shutdown(signal, frame):
    print('Received signal {}: exiting'.format(signal))
    sys.exit(128 + signal)

def train(args, server):
    os.environ['OMP_NUM_THREADS'] = '1'
    set_random_seed(args.task * 17)
    log_dir = os.path.join(args.log_dir, '{}/train'.format(args.env))
    if not tf.gfile.Exists(log_dir):
        tf.gfile.MakeDirs(log_dir)

    game, parameter = new_environment(args.env)
    a3c = A3C(game, log_dir, parameter.get(), agent_index=args.task,
callback=None)

    global_vars = [v for v in tf.global_variables() if not
v.name.startswith("local")]
    ready_op = tf.report_uninitialized_variables(global_vars)
    config = tf.ConfigProto(device_filters=["/job:ps",
"/job:worker/task:{}/cpu:0".format(args.task)])

    with tf.Session(target=server.target, config=config) as sess:
```

```
        saver = tf.train.Saver()
        path = os.path.join(log_dir, 'log_%d' % args.task)
        writer = tf.summary.FileWriter(delete_dir(path), sess.graph_def)
        a3c.set_summary_writer(writer)
        if args.task == 0:
            sess.run(tf.global_variables_initializer())
        else:
            while len(sess.run(ready_op)) > 0:
                print("Waiting for task 0 initializing the global
variables.")
                time.sleep(1)
        a3c.run(sess, saver)


def main():
    parser = argparse.ArgumentParser(description=None)
    parser.add_argument('-t', '--task', default=0, type=int, help='Task
index')
    parser.add_argument('-j', '--job_name', default="worker", type=str,
help='worker or ps')
    parser.add_argument('-w', '--num_workers', default=1, type=int,
help='Number of workers')
    parser.add_argument('-l', '--log_dir', default="save", type=str,
help='Log directory path')
    parser.add_argument('-e', '--env', default="demo", type=str,
help='Environment')
    args = parser.parse_args()
    spec = cluster_spec(args.num_workers, 1)
    cluster = tf.train.ClusterSpec(spec)

    signal.signal(signal.SIGHUP, shutdown)
    signal.signal(signal.SIGINT, shutdown)
    signal.signal(signal.SIGTERM, shutdown)
    if args.job_name == "worker":
        server = tf.train.Server(cluster,
                                 job_name="worker",
                                 task_index=args.task,
config=tf.ConfigProto(intra_op_parallelism_threads=0,
inter_op_parallelism_threads=0)) # Use default op_parallelism_threads
        train(args, server)
    else:
        server = tf.train.Server(cluster,
                                 job_name="ps",
                                 task_index=args.task,
config=tf.ConfigProto(device_filters=["/job:ps"]))
        # server.join()
        while True:
            time.sleep(1000)
```

```
if __name__ == "__main__":
    main()
```

The main function will create a new agent and begin the training procedure if
the `job_name` parameter is `worker`. Otherwise, it will start the TensorFlow parameter
server for the global shared parameters. Notice that before launching multiple agents, we
need to start the parameter server first. In the `train` function, an environment is created by
calling `new_environment` and then an agent is built for this environment. After the agent
is successfully created, the global shared parameters are initialized and the train procedure
starts by calling `a3c.run(sess, saver)`.

Because manually launching 8 or 16 agents is quite inconvenient, this can be
done automatically by the following script:

```
import argparse, os, sys, cluster
from six.moves import shlex_quote

parser = argparse.ArgumentParser(description="Run commands")
parser.add_argument('-w', '--num_workers', default=1, type=int,
                    help="Number of workers")
parser.add_argument('-e', '--env', type=str, default="demo",
                    help="Environment")
parser.add_argument('-l', '--log_dir', type=str, default="save",
                    help="Log directory path")

def new_cmd(session, name, cmd, logdir, shell):
    if isinstance(cmd, (list, tuple)):
        cmd = " ".join(shlex_quote(str(v)) for v in cmd)
    return name, "tmux send-keys -t {}:{} {} Enter".format(session, name,
shlex_quote(cmd))

def create_commands(session, num_workers, logdir, env, shell='bash'):

    base_cmd = ['CUDA_VISIBLE_DEVICES=',
                sys.executable,
                'worker.py',
                '--log_dir', logdir,
                '--num_workers', str(num_workers),
                '--env', env]

    cmds_map = [new_cmd(session, "ps", base_cmd + ["--job_name", "ps"],
logdir, shell)]
    for i in range(num_workers):
        cmd = base_cmd + ["--job_name", "worker", "--task", str(i)]
        cmds_map.append(new_cmd(session, "w-%d" % i, cmd, logdir, shell))
    cmds_map.append(new_cmd(session, "htop", ["htop"], logdir, shell))
    windows = [v[0] for v in cmds_map]
```

```
    notes = ["Use `tmux attach -t {}` to watch process
output".format(session),
            "Use `tmux kill-session -t {}` to kill the
job".format(session),
            "Use `ssh -L PORT:SERVER_IP:SERVER_PORT username@server_ip` to
remote Tensorboard"]

    cmds = ["kill $(lsof -i:{}-{} -t) > /dev/null
2>&1".format(cluster.PORT, num_workers+cluster.PORT),
            "tmux kill-session -t {}".format(session),
            "tmux new-session -s {} -n {} -d {}".format(session,
windows[0], shell)]
    for w in windows[1:]:
        cmds.append("tmux new-window -t {} -n {} {}".format(session, w,
shell))
    cmds.append("sleep 1")

    for _, cmd in cmds_map:
        cmds.append(cmd)
    return cmds, notes

def main():
    args = parser.parse_args()
    cmds, notes = create_commands("a3c", args.num_workers, args.log_dir,
args.env)

    print("Executing the following commands:")
    print("\n".join(cmds))
    os.environ["TMUX"] = ""
    os.system("\n".join(cmds))
    print("Notes:")
    print('\n'.join(notes))
if __name__ == "__main__":
    main()
```

This script creates the bash commands used to create the parameter server and a set of agents. To handle the consoles of all the agents, we use TMUX (more information is available at `https://github.com/tmux/tmux/wiki`). TMUX is a terminal multiplexer that allows us to switch easily between several programs in one terminal, detach them, and reattach them to a different terminal. TMUX is quite a convenient tool for checking the training status of A3C. Note that since A3C runs on CPUs, we set `CUDA_VISIBLE_DEVICES` to empty.

A3C is much more sensitive to the training parameters than DQN. Random seed, initial weights, learning rate, batch size, discount factor, and even hyperparameters for RMSProp can affect the performance a lot. After testing it on different Atari games, we select the following hyperparameters listed in the `Parameter` class:

```
class Parameter:
    def __init__(self, lr=7e-4, directory=None):
        self.directory = directory
        self.learning_rate = lr
        self.gamma = 0.99
        self.num_history_frames = 4
        self.iteration_num = 100000
        self.async_update_interval = 5
        self.rho = 0.99
        self.rmsprop_epsilon = 1e-1
        self.update_method = 'rmsprop'
        self.clip_delta = 0
        self.max_iter_num = 10 ** 8
        self.network_type = 'cnn'
        self.input_scale = 255.0
```

Here, `gamma` is the discount factor, `num_history_frames` is the parameter frameskip, `async_update_interval` is the batch size for the training update, and `rho` and `rmsprop_epsilon` are the internal hyperparameters for RMSProp. This set of hyperparameters can be used for both Atari and Minecraft.

Experiments

The full implementation of the A3C algorithm can be downloaded from our GitHub repository (`https://github.com/PacktPublishing/Python-Reinforcement-Learning-Projects`). There are three environments in our implementation we can test. The first one is the special game, `demo`, introduced in Chapter 7, *Playing Atari Games*. For this game, A3C only needs to launch two agents to achieve good performance. Run the following command in the `src` folder:

```
python3 train.py -w 2 -e demo
```

The first argument, `-w`, or `--num_workers`, indicates the number of launched agents. The second argument, `-e`, or `--env`, specifies the environment, for example, `demo`. The other two environments are Atari and Minecraft. For Atari games, A3C requires at least 8 agents running in parallel. Typically, launching 16 agents can achieve better performance:

```
python3 train.py -w 8 -e Breakout
```

For Breakout, A3C takes about 2-3 hours to achieve a score of 300. If you have a decent PC with more than 8 cores, it is better to test it with 16 agents. To test Minecraft, run the following command:

```
python3 train.py -w 8 -e MinecraftBasic-v0
```

The Gym Minecraft environment provides more than 10 missions. To try other missions, just replace `MinecraftBasic-v0` with other mission names.

After running one of the preceding commands, type the following to monitor the training procedure:

```
tmux attach -t a3c
```

To switch between console windows, press *Ctrl + b* and then press *0-9*. Window 0 is the parameter server. Windows 1-8 show the training stats of the 8 agents (if there are 8 launched agents). The last window runs htop. To detach TMUX, press *Ctrl* and then press *b*.

The `tensorboard` logs are saved in the `save/<environment_name>/train/log_<agent_index>` folder. To visualize the training procedure using TensorBoard, run the following command under this folder:

```
tensorboard --logdir=.
```

Summary

This chapter introduced the Gym Minecraft environment, available at `https://github.com/tambetm/gym-minecraft`. You have learned how to launch a Minecraft mission and how to implement an emulator for it. The most important part of this chapter was the asynchronous reinforcement learning framework. You learned what the shortcomings of DQN are, and why DQN is difficult to apply in complex tasks. Then, you learned how to apply the asynchronous reinforcement learning framework in the actor-critic method REINFORCE, which led us to the A3C algorithm. Finally, you learned how to implement A3C using Tensorflow and how to handle multiple terminals using TMUX. The tricky part in the implementation is that of the global shared parameters. This is related to creating a cluster of TensorFlow servers. For the readers who want to learn more about this, visit `https://www.tensorflow.org/deploy/distributed`.

In the following chapters, you will learn more about how to apply reinforcement learning algorithms in other tasks, for example, the board game Go, and generating deep image classifiers. This will help you to get a deep understanding about reinforcement learning and help you solve real-world problems.

15
Learning to Play Go

When considering the capabilities of AI, we often compare its performance for a particular task with what humans can achieve. AI agents are now able to surpass human-level competency in more complex tasks. In this chapter, we will build an agent that learns how to play what is considered the most complex board game of all time: Go. We will become familiar with the latest deep reinforcement learning algorithms that achieve superhuman performances, namely AlphaGo, and AlphaGo Zero, both of which were developed by Google's DeepMind. We will also learn about Monte Carlo tree search, a popular tree-searching algorithm that is an integral component of turn-based game agents.

This chapter will cover the following topics:

- Introduction to Go and relevant research in AI
- Overview of AlphaGo and AlphaGo Zero
- The Monte Carlo tree search algorithm
- Implementation of AlphaGo Zero

A brief introduction to Go

Go is a board game that was first recorded in China two millennia ago. Similar to other common board games, such as chess, shogi, and Othello, Go involves two players alternately placing black and white stones on a 19x19 board with the objective of capturing as much territory as possible by surrounding a larger total area of the board. One can capture their opponent's pieces by surrounding the opponent's pieces with their own pieces. Captured stones are removed from the board, thereby creating a void in which the opponent can no longer place stones unless the territory is captured back.

A game ends when both players refuse to place a stone or either player resigns. Upon the termination of a game, the winner is decided by counting each player's territory and the number of captured stones.

Go and other board games

Researchers have already created AI programs that outperform the best human players in board games such as chess and backgammon. In 1992, researchers from IBM developed TD-Gammon, which used classic reinforcement learning algorithms and an artificial neural network to play backgammon at the level of a top player. In 1997, Deep Blue, a chess-playing program developed by IBM and Carnegie Mellon University, defeated then world champion Garry Kasparov in a six-game face off. This was the first time that a computer program defeated the world champion in chess.

Developing Go playing agents is not a new topic, and hence one may wonder what took so long for researchers to replicate such successes in Go. The answer is simple—Go, despite its simple rules, is a far more complex game than chess. Imagine representing a board game as a tree, where each node is a snapshot of the board (which we also refer to as the **board state**) and its child nodes are possible moves the opponent can make. The height of the tree is essentially the number of moves a game lasts. A typical chess game lasts 80 moves, whereas a game in Go lasts 150; almost twice as long. Moreover, while the average number of possible moves in a chess turn is 35, a Go player has 250 possible plays per move. Based on these numbers, Go has 10^{761} total possible games, compared to 10^{120} games in chess. It is impossible to enumerate every possible state in Go in a computer, and the sheer complexity of the game has made it difficult for researchers to develop an agent that can play the game at a world-class level.

Go and AI research

In 2015, researchers from Google's DeepMind published a paper in Nature that detailed a novel reinforcement learning agent for Go called **AlphaGo**. In October of that year, AlphaGo beat Fan Hui, the European champion, 5-0. In 2016, AlphaGo challenged Lee Sedol, who, with 18 world championship titles, is considered one of the greatest players in modern history. AlphaGo won 4-1, marking a watershed moment in deep learning research and the game's history. In the following year, DeepMind published an updated version of AlphaGo, AlphaGo Zero, which defeated its predecessor 100 times in 100 games. In just a matter of days of training, AlphaGo and AlphaGo Zero were able to learn and surpass the wisdom that mankind has accumulated over the thousands of years of the game's existence.

The following sections will discuss how AlphaGo and AlphaGo Zero work, including the algorithms and techniques that they use to learn and play the game. This will be followed by an implementation of AlphaGo Zero. Our exploration begins with Monte Carlo tree search, an algorithm that is integral to both AlphaGo and AlphaGo Zero for making decisions on where to place stones.

Monte Carlo tree search

In games such as Go and chess, players have perfect information, meaning they have access to the full game state (the board and the positions of the pieces). Moreover, there lacks an element of chance that can affect the game state; only the players' decisions can affect the board. Such games are also referred to as perfect-information games. In perfect-information games, it is theoretically possible to enumerate all possible game states. As discussed earlier, this would look such as a tree, where each child node (a game state) is a possible outcome of the parent. In two-player games, alternating levels of this tree represent moves produced by the two competitors. Finding the best possible move for a given state is simply a matter of traversing the tree and finding which sequence of moves leads to a win. We can also store the value, or the expected outcome or reward (a win or a loss) of a given state, at each node.

However, constructing a perfect tree is impractical in practice for games such as Go. So how can an agent learn how to play the game without such knowledge? The **Monte Carlo tree-search** (**MCTS**) algorithm provides an efficient approximation of this complete tree. In a nutshell, MCTS involves playing a game iteratively, keeping statistics on states that were visited, and learning which moves are more favorable/likely to lead to a win. The goal of MCTS is to build a tree that approximates the aforementioned perfect tree as much as possible. Each move in a game corresponds to an iteration of the MCTS algorithm. There are four main steps in the algorithm: Selection, Expansion, Simulation, and Update (also known as **backpropagation**). We will briefly detail each procedure.

Selection

The first step of MCTS involves playing the game intelligently. That means the algorithm has enough experience to determine the next move given a state. One method for determining the next move is called **Upper Confidence Bound 1 Applied to Trees** (**UCT**). In short, this formula rates moves based on the following:

- The mean reward of games where a given move was made
- How often the move was selected

Each node's rating can be expressed as follows:

$$\bar{r}_i + c\sqrt{\frac{2\ln(n)}{n_i}}$$

Where:

- $\bar{r}_i$: Is the mean reward for choosing move i (for example, the win-rate)
- n_i: Is the number of times the algorithm selected move i
- n: Is the total number of moves made after the current state (including move i)
- c: Is an exploration parameter

The following diagram shows an example of selecting the next node. In each node, the left number represents the node's rating, and the right number represents the number of times the node was visited. The color of the node indicates which player's turn it is:

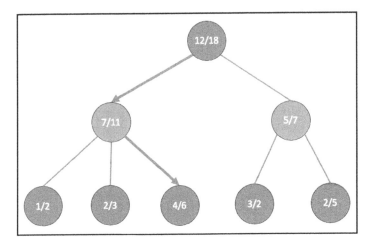

Figure 1: Selection in MCTS

In selection, the algorithm chooses the move that has the highest value for the preceding expression. The keen reader may notice that, while moves with a high mean reward, $\bar{r}_i$, are rated highly, so too are moves with fewer numbers of visits, n_i. Why is this so? In MCTS, we not only want the algorithm to choose moves that most likely result in wins but also to try less-often-selected moves. This is commonly referred to as the balance between exploitation and exploration. If the algorithm solely resorted to exploitation, the resulting tree would be very narrow and ill-experienced. Encouraging exploration allows the algorithm to learn from a broader set of experiences and simulations. In the preceding example, we simply select the node with a rating of **7** and subsequently the node with a rating of **4**.

Expansion

We apply selection to decide moves until the algorithm can no longer apply UCT to rate the next set of moves. In particular, we can no longer apply UCT when not all of the child nodes of a given state have records (number of visits, mean reward). This is when the second phase of MCTS, expansion, occurs. Here, we simply look at all possible new moves (unvisited child nodes) of a given state and randomly choose one. We then update the tree to record this new child node. The following diagram illustrates this:

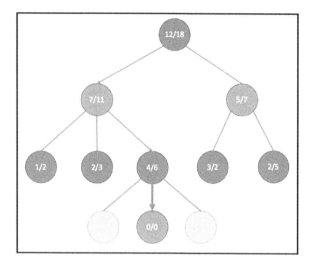

Figure 2: Expansion

You may be wondering from the preceding diagram why we initialize the visit count as zero rather than one. The visit count of this new node as well as the statistics of the nodes we have traversed so far will be incremented during the update step, which is the final step of an MCTS iteration.

Simulation

After expansion, the rest of the game is played by randomly choosing subsequent moves. This is also commonly referred to as the **playout** or **rollout**. Depending on the game, some heuristics may be applied to choose the next move. For example, in DeepBlue, simulations rely on handcrafted heuristics to select the next move intelligently rather than randomly. This is also called **heavy rollouts**. While such rollouts provide more realistic games, they are often computationally expensive, which can slow down the learning of the MCTS tree:

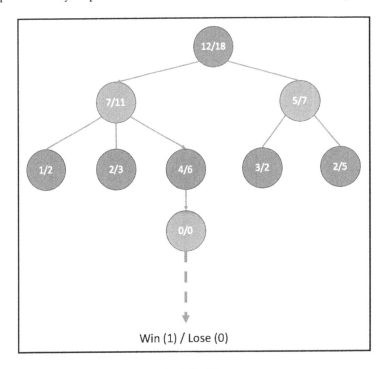

Figure 3: Simulation

In our preceding toy example, we expand a node and play until the very end of the game (represented by the dotted line), which results in either a win or loss. Simulation yields a reward, which in this case is either **1** or **0**.

Update

Finally, the update step happens when the algorithm reaches a terminal state, or when either player wins or the game culminates in a draw. For each node/state of the board that was visited during this iteration, the algorithm updates the mean reward and increments the visit count of that state. This is also called **backpropagation**:

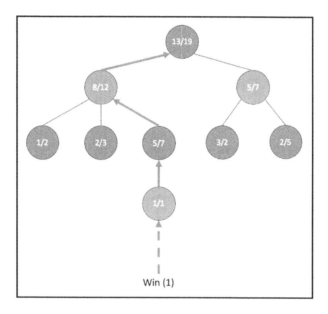

Figure 4: Update

In the preceding diagram, since we reached a terminal state that returned **1** (a win), we increment the visit count and reward accordingly for each node along the path from the root node accordingly.

That concludes the four steps that occur in one MCTS iteration. As the name Monte Carlo suggests, we conduct this search multiple times before we decide the next move to take. The number of iterations is configurable, and often depends on time/resources available. Over time, the tree learns a structure that approximates a perfect tree and can be used to guide agents to make decisions.

AlphaGo and AlphaGo Zero, DeepMind's revolutionary Go playing agents, rely on MCTS to select moves. In the next section, we will explore the two algorithms to understand how they combine neural networks and MCTS to play Go at a superhuman level of proficiency.

AlphaGo

AlphaGo's main innovation is how it combines deep learning and Monte Carlo tree search to play Go. The AlphaGo architecture consists of four neural networks: a small supervised learning policy network, a large supervised-learning policy network, a reinforcement learning policy network, and a value network. We train all four of these networks plus the MCTS tree. The following sections will cover each training step.

Supervised learning policy networks

The first step in training AlphaGo involves training policy networks on games played by two professionals (in board games such as chess and Go, it is common to keep records of historical games, the board state, and the moves made by each player at every turn). The main idea is to make AlphaGo learn and understand how human experts play Go. More formally, given a board state, s, and set of actions, a, we would like a policy network, $\pi(a|s)$, to predict the next move the human makes. The data consists of pairs (s, a) of sampled from over 30,000,000 historical games from the KGS Go server. The input to the network consists of the board state as well as metadata. AlphaGo has two supervised learning policy networks of varying sizes. The large network is a 13-layer convolutional neural network with ReLU activation functions in the hidden layers, while the smaller one is a single-layer softmax network.

Why do we train two similar networks? The larger policy network initializes the weights of the reinforcement learning policy network, which gets further refined through an RL approach called **policy gradients**. The smaller network is used during the simulation step of MCTS. Remember, while most simulations in MCTS rely on the randomized selection of moves, one can also utilize light or heavy heuristics to have more intelligent simulations. The smaller network, which lacks the accuracy of the larger supervised network yet yields much faster inference, provides light heuristics for rollout.

Reinforcement learning policy networks

Once the larger supervised learning policy network is trained, we further improve the model by having the RL policy network play against a previous version of itself. The weights of the network are updated using a method called **policy gradients**, which is a variant of gradient descent for vanilla neural networks. Formally speaking, the gradient update rule for the weights of our RL policy network can be expressed as follows:

$$\Delta w \propto \frac{\partial \log p_{rl}(a_t|s_t)}{w} z_t$$

Here, w are the weights of the RL policy network, p_{rl}, and z_t is the expected reward at timestep t. The reward is simply the outcome of the game, where a win results in +1 and a loss results in -1. Herein lies the main difference between the supervised learning policy network and the reinforcement learning policy network. For the former network, the objective is to maximize the likelihood of choosing a particular action given a state, or, in other words, to simply mimic the moves of the historical games. Since there is no reward function involved, it does not care about the eventual outcome of the game.

On the other hand, the reinforcement learning policy network incorporates the final outcome when updating the weights. More specifically, it is trying to maximize the log likelihood of the moves that contribute to higher rewards (that is, winning moves). This is because we are multiplying the gradient of the log-likelihood with the reward (either +1 or -1), which essentially determines the direction in which to move the weights. The weights of a poor move will be moved in the opposite direction, for we will likely be multiplying the gradients with -1. To summarize, the network not only tries to figure out the most likely move, but also one that helps it win. According to DeepMind's paper, the reinforcement learning policy network won the vast majority (80%~85%) of its games against its supervised counterpart and other Go playing programs, such as Pachi.

Value network

The last step of the pipeline involves training a value network to evaluate the board state, or in other words, to determine how favorable a particular board state is for winning the game. Formally speaking, given a particular policy, π, and state, s_t, we would like to predict the expected reward, z. The network is trained by minimizing the **mean-squared error** (MSE) between the predicted value, $v(s_t)$, and the final outcome:

$$\Delta w \propto \frac{\partial v(s_t)}{\partial w}(z - v(s_t))$$

Where w are the parameters of the network. In practice, the network is trained on 30,000,000 state-reward pairs, each coming from a distinct game. The dataset is constructed in this way because the board states from the same game can be highly correlated, potentially leading to overfitting.

Combining neural networks and MCTS

In AlphaGo, the policy and value networks are combined with MCTS to provide a look-ahead search when selecting actions in a game. Previously, we discussed how MCTS keeps track of the mean reward and number of visits made to each node. In AlphaGo, we have a few more values to keep track of:

- $Q(s_t, a)$: Which is the mean action value of choosing a particular action
- $P(s_t, a)$: The probability of taking an action for a given board state given by the larger supervised learning policy network
- $V(s_{leaf})$: The value evaluation of a state that is not explored yet (a leaf node)
- $N(s_t, a)$: The number of times a particular action was chosen given a state

During a single simulation of our tree search, the algorithm selects an action, a_t, for a given state, s_t, at a particular timestep, t, according to the following formula:

$$a_t = argmax_a \, Q(s_t, a) + u(s_t, a)$$

Where

$$u(s_t, a) = \frac{P(s_t, a)}{1 + N(s_t, a)}$$

Hence $u(s_t, a)$ is a value that favors moves determined to be more likely by the larger policy network, but also supports exploration by penalizing those that have been visited more frequently.

During expansion, when we don't have the preceding statistics for a given board state and move, we use the value network and the simulation to evaluate the leaf node. In particular, we take a weighted sum of the expected value given by the value network and outcome of the rollout:

$$V(s_{leaf}) = (1 - \lambda)v(s_{leaf}) + \lambda z_{leaf}$$

Where $v(s_{leaf})$ is the evaluation of the value network, z_{leaf} is the eventual reward of the
search, and λ is the weighting term that is often referred to as the mixing z_{leaf}
parameter. is obtained after rollout, where the simulations are conducted using the smaller
and faster supervised learning policy network. Having fast rollouts is important, especially
in situations where decisions are time-boxed, hence the need for the smaller policy
network.

Finally, during the update step of MCTS, visit counts for each node are updated. Moreover,
the action values are recalculated by taking the mean reward of all simulations that
included a given node:

$$Q(s_t, a) = \frac{W(s_t, a)}{N(s_t, a)}$$

Where $W(s_t, a)$ is the total reward across the $N(s_t, a)$ times MCTS took action a at node s_t.
After the MCTS search, the model chooses the most frequently-visited move when actually
playing the game.

And that concludes a rudimentary overview of AlphaGo. While an in-depth exposition of
the architecture and methodology is beyond the scope of this book, this hopefully serves as
an introductory guide to what makes AlphaGo work.

AlphaGo Zero

We will cover AlphaGo Zero, the upgraded version of its predecessor before we finally get
into some coding. The main features of AlphaGo Zero address some of the drawbacks of
AlphaGo, including its dependency on a large corpus of games played by human experts.

The main differences between AlphaGo Zero and AlphaGo are the following:

- AlphaGo Zero is trained solely with self-play reinforcement learning, meaning it
  does not rely on any human-generated data or supervision that is used to train
  AlphaGo
- Policy and value networks are represented as one network with two heads rather
  than two separate ones
- The input to the network is the board itself as an image, such as a 2D grid; the
  network does not rely on heuristics and instead uses the raw board state itself
- In addition to finding the best move, Monte Carlo tree search is also used for
  policy iteration and evaluation; moreover, AlphaGo Zero does not conduct
  rollouts during a search

Training AlphaGo Zero

Since we don't use human-generated data for training or supervision, how does AlphaGo Zero learn at all? The novel reinforcement learning algorithm developed by DeepMind involves using MCTS as a teacher for the neural network, which represents both policy and value functions.

In particular, the outputs of MCTS are 1) probabilities, π, for each selecting move during the simulation, and 2) the final outcome of the game, z. The neural network, f, takes in a board state, s, and also outputs a tuple of (p, v), where p is a vector of move probabilities and v is the value of s. Given these outputs, we want to train our network such that the network's policy, p, moves closer to the policy, π, that is produced by MCTS, and the network's value, v, moves closer to the eventual outcome, z, of the search. Note that in MCTS, the algorithm does not conduct rollouts, but instead relies on f for expansion and simulating the whole game until termination. Hence by the end of MCTS, the algorithm improves the policy from p to π and is able to act as a teacher for f. The loss function for the network consists of two parts: one is the cross-entropy between p and π, and the other is the mean-squared error between v and z. This joint loss function looks as follows:

$$L = (z - v)^2 - \pi^T \log(p) + \lambda ||\theta||^2$$

Where θ is network parameters and λ is a parameter for L2-regularization.

Comparison with AlphaGo

According to DeepMind's paper, AlphaGo Zero was able to outperform AlphaGo in 36 hours, whereas the latter took months to train. In a head-to-head competition with the version of AlphaGo that defeated Lee Sedol, AlphaGo Zero won 100 games out of 100. What's significant about these results is that, even without initial human supervision, a Go playing program can reach superhuman-level proficiency more efficiently and is able to discover much of the knowledge and wisdom that humanity spent thousands of years and millions of games cultivating.

In the following sections, we will finally implement this powerful algorithm. Additional technical details of AlphaGo Zero will be covered as we go through the code.

Implementing AlphaGo Zero

At last, we will implement AlphaGo Zero in this section. In addition to achieving better performance than AlphaGo, it is in fact relatively easier to implement. This is because, as discussed, AlphaGo Zero only relies on `selfplay` data for learning, and thus relieves us from the burden of searching for large amounts of historical data. Moreover, we only need to implement one neural network that serves as both the policy and value function. The following implementation makes some further simplifications—for example, we assume that the Go board size is 9 instead of 19. This is to allow for faster training.

The directory structure of our implementation looks such as the following:

```
alphago_zero/
|-- __init__.py
|-- config.py
|-- constants.py
|-- controller.py
|-- features.py
|-- go.py
|-- mcts.py
|-- alphagozero_agent.py
|-- network.py
|-- preprocessing.py
|-- train.py
`-- utils.py
```

We will especially pay attention to `network.py` and `mcts.py`, which contain the implementations for the dual network and the MCTS algorithm.
Moreover, `alphagozero_agent.py` contains the implementation for combining the dual network and MCTS to create a Go playing agent.

Policy and value networks

Let's get started with implementing the dual network, which we will call `PolicyValueNetwork`. First, we will create a few modules that contain configurations and constants that our `PolicyValueNetwork` will use.

preprocessing.py

The preprocessing.py module mainly deals with reading from and writing to TFRecords files, which is TensorFlow's native data-representation file format. When training AlphaGo Zero, we store MCTS self-play results and moves. As discussed, these then become the ground truths from which PolicyValueNetwork learns. TFRecords provides a convenient way to save historical moves and results from MCTS. When reading these from disk, preprocessing.py turns TFRecords into tf.train.Example, an in-memory representation of data that can be directly fed into tf.estimator.Estimator.

tf_records usually have filenames that end with *.tfrecord.zz.

The following function reads from a TFRecords file. We first turn a given list of TFRecords into tf.data.TFRecordDataset, an intermediate representation before we turn them into tf.train.Example:

```
def process_tf_records(list_tf_records, shuffle_records=True,
    buffer_size=GLOBAL_PARAMETER_STORE.SHUFFLE_BUFFER_SIZE,
                        batch_size=GLOBAL_PARAMETER_STORE.TRAIN_BATCH_SIZE):

    if shuffle_records:
        random.shuffle(list_tf_records)

    list_dataset = tf.data.Dataset.from_tensor_slices(list_tf_records)

    tensors_dataset = list_dataset.interleave(map_func=lambda x:
tf.data.TFRecordDataset(x, compression_type='ZLIB'),
cycle_length=GLOBAL_PARAMETER_STORE.CYCLE_LENGTH,
block_length=GLOBAL_PARAMETER_STORE.BLOCK_LENGTH)
    tensors_dataset =
tensors_dataset.repeat(1).shuffle(buffer_siz=buffer_size).batch(batch_size)

    return tensors_dataset
```

The next step involves parsing this dataset so that we can feed the values into PolicyValueNetwork. There are three values we care about: the input, which we call either x or board_state throughout the implementation, the policy, pi, and the outcome, z, both of which are outputted by the MCTS algorithm:

```
def parse_batch_tf_example(example_batch):
    features = {
        'x': tf.FixedLenFeature([], tf.string),
```

```
        'pi': tf.FixedLenFeature([], tf.string),
        'z': tf.FixedLenFeature([], tf.float32),
    }
    parsed_tensors = tf.parse_example(example_batch, features)

    # Get the board state
    x = tf.cast(tf.decode_raw(parsed_tensors['x'], tf.uint8), tf.float32)
    x = tf.reshape(x, [GLOBAL_PARAMETER_STORE.TRAIN_BATCH_SIZE,
GOPARAMETERS.N,
                      GOPARAMETERS.N, FEATUREPARAMETERS.NUM_CHANNELS])

    # Get the policy target, which is the distribution of possible moves
    # Each target is a vector of length of board * length of board + 1
    distribution_of_moves = tf.decode_raw(parsed_tensors['pi'], tf.float32)
    distribution_of_moves = tf.reshape(distribution_of_moves,
[GLOBAL_PARAMETER_STORE.TRAIN_BATCH_SIZE, GOPARAMETERS.N * GOPARAMETERS.N +
1])

    # Get the result of the game
    # The result is simply a scalar
    result_of_game = parsed_tensors['z']
    result_of_game.set_shape([GLOBAL_PARAMETER_STORE.TRAIN_BATCH_SIZE])

    return (x, {'pi_label': distribution_of_moves, 'z_label':
result_of_game})
```

The preceding two functions are combined in the following function to construct the input tensors to be fed into the network:

```
def get_input_tensors(list_tf_records,
buffer_size=GLOBAL_PARAMETER_STORE.SHUFFLE_BUFFER_SIZE):
    logger.info("Getting input data and tensors")
    dataset = process_tf_records(list_tf_records=list_tf_records,
                                 buffer_size=buffer_size)
    dataset = dataset.filter(lambda input_tensor:
tf.equal(tf.shape(input_tensor)[0],
GLOBAL_PARAMETER_STORE.TRAIN_BATCH_SIZE))
    dataset = dataset.map(parse_batch_tf_example)
    logger.info("Finished parsing")
    return dataset.make_one_shot_iterator().get_next()
```

Finally, the following functions are used to write self-play results to disk:

```
def create_dataset_from_selfplay(data_extracts):
    return (create_tf_train_example(extract_features(board_state), pi,
result)
            for board_state, pi, result in data_extracts)
```

```
def shuffle_tf_examples(batch_size, records_to_shuffle):
    tf_dataset = process_tf_records(records_to_shuffle,
batch_size=batch_size)
    iterator = tf_dataset.make_one_shot_iterator()
    next_dataset_batch = iterator.get_next()
    sess = tf.Session()
    while True:
        try:
            result = sess.run(next_dataset_batch)
            yield list(result)
        except tf.errors.OutOfRangeError:
            break


def create_tf_train_example(board_state, pi, result):
    board_state_as_tf_feature =
tf.train.Feature(bytes_list=tf.train.BytesList(value=[board_state.tostring(
)]))
    pi_as_tf_feature =
tf.train.Feature(bytes_list=tf.train.BytesList(value=[pi.tostring()]))
    value_as_tf_feature =
tf.train.Feature(float_list=tf.train.FloatList(value=[result]))

    tf_example = tf.train.Example(features=tf.train.Features(feature={
        'x': board_state_as_tf_feature,
        'pi': pi_as_tf_feature,
        'z': value_as_tf_feature
    }))

    return tf_example

def write_tf_examples(record_path, tf_examples, serialize=True):
    with tf.python_io.TFRecordWriter(record_path, options=TF_RECORD_CONFIG)
as tf_record_writer:
        for tf_example in tf_examples:
            if serialize:
                tf_record_writer.write(tf_example.SerializeToString())
            else:
                tf_record_writer.write(tf_example)
```

Some of these functions will be used later when we generate training data from self-play results.

features.py

This module contains helper code for turning Go board representations into proper TensorFlow tensors, which can be provided to `PolicyValueNetwork`. The main function, `extract_features`, takes `board_state`, which is our representation of a Go board, and turns it into a tensor of the `[batch_size, N, N, 17]` shape, where `N` is the shape of the board (which is by default 9), and 17 is the number of feature channels, representing the past moves as well as the color to play:

```python
import numpy as np

from config import GOPARAMETERS

def stone_features(board_state):
    # 16 planes, where every other plane represents the stones of a
particular color
    # which means we track the stones of the last 8 moves.
    features = np.zeros([16, GOPARAMETERS.N, GOPARAMETERS.N],
dtype=np.uint8)

    num_deltas_avail = board_state.board_deltas.shape[0]
    cumulative_deltas = np.cumsum(board_state.board_deltas, axis=0)
    last_eight = np.tile(board_state.board, [8, 1, 1])
    last_eight[1:num_deltas_avail + 1] -= cumulative_deltas
    last_eight[num_deltas_avail +1:] =
last_eight[num_deltas_avail].reshape(1, GOPARAMETERS.N, GOPARAMETERS.N)

    features[::2] = last_eight == board_state.to_play
    features[1::2] = last_eight == -board_state.to_play
    return np.rollaxis(features, 0, 3)

def color_to_play_feature(board_state):
    # 1 plane representing which color is to play
    # The plane is filled with 1's if the color to play is black; 0's
otherwise
    if board_state.to_play == GOPARAMETERS.BLACK:
        return np.ones([GOPARAMETERS.N, GOPARAMETERS.N, 1], dtype=np.uint8)
    else:
        return np.zeros([GOPARAMETERS.N, GOPARAMETERS.N, 1],
dtype=np.uint8)

def extract_features(board_state):
    stone_feat = stone_features(board_state=board_state)
    turn_feat = color_to_play_feature(board_state=board_state)
    all_features = np.concatenate([stone_feat, turn_feat], axis=2)
    return all_features
```

The `extract_features` function will be used by both the `preprocessing.py` and `network.py` modules to construct the feature tensors to be either written to a `TFRecord` file or fed into a neural network.

network.py

This file contains our implementation of `PolicyValueNetwork`. In short, we construct a `tf.estimator.Estimator` that is trained using board states, policies, and self-play outcomes produced by MCTS self-play. The network has two heads: one acting as a value function, and the other acting as a policy network.

First, we define some layers that will be used by `PolicyValueNetwork`:

```
import functools
import logging
import os.path

import tensorflow as tf

import features
import preprocessing
import utils
from config import GLOBAL_PARAMETER_STORE, GOPARAMETERS
from constants import *

logger = logging.getLogger(__name__)
logger.setLevel(logging.INFO)

def create_partial_bn_layer(params):
    return functools.partial(tf.layers.batch_normalization,
        momentum=params["momentum"],
        epsilon=params["epsilon"],
        fused=params["fused"],
        center=params["center"],
        scale=params["scale"],
        training=params["training"]
    )

def create_partial_res_layer(inputs, partial_bn_layer,
partial_conv2d_layer):
    output_1 = partial_bn_layer(partial_conv2d_layer(inputs))
    output_2 = tf.nn.relu(output_1)
    output_3 = partial_bn_layer(partial_conv2d_layer(output_2))
    output_4 = tf.nn.relu(tf.add(inputs, output_3))
    return output_4
```

```
def softmax_cross_entropy_loss(logits, labels):
 return
tf.reduce_mean(tf.nn.softmax_cross_entropy_with_logits(logits=logits,
labels=labels['pi_label']))

def mean_squared_loss(output_value, labels):
 return tf.reduce_mean(tf.square(output_value - labels['z_label']))

def get_losses(logits, output_value, labels):
 ce_loss = softmax_cross_entropy_loss(logits, labels)
 mse_loss = mean_squared_loss(output_value, labels)
 return ce_loss, mse_loss

def create_metric_ops(labels, output_policy, loss_policy, loss_value,
loss_l2, loss_total):
 return {'accuracy': tf.metrics.accuracy(labels=labels['pi_label'],
predictions=output_policy, name='accuracy'),
 'loss_policy': tf.metrics.mean(loss_policy),
 'loss_value': tf.metrics.mean(loss_value),
 'loss_l2': tf.metrics.mean(loss_l2),
 'loss_total': tf.metrics.mean(loss_total)}
```

Next, we have a function that is used to create `tf.estimator.Estimator`. While TensorFlow provides several prebuilt estimators, such as `tf.estimator.DNNClassifier`, our architecture is rather unique, which is why we need to build our own `Estimator`. This can be done by creating `tf.estimator.EstimatorSpec`, a skeleton class where we can define things such as the output tensors, network architecture, the loss functions, and the evaluation metrics:

```
def generate_network_specifications(features, labels, mode, params,
config=None):
 batch_norm_params = {"epsilon": 1e-5, "fused": True, "center": True,
"scale": True, "momentum": 0.997,
 "training": mode==tf.estimator.ModeKeys.TRAIN
 }
```

Our `generate_network_specifications` function takes several input:

- `features`: The tensor representation of the Go board (with the `[batch_size, 9, 9, 17]` shape)
- `labels`: Our `pi` and `z` tensors
- `mode`: Here, we can specify whether our network is being instantiated in train or test mode
- `params`: Additional parameters to specify the network structure (for example, convolutional filter size)

We then implement the shared portion of the network, the policy output head, the value output head, and then the loss functions:

```
with tf.name_scope("shared_layers"):
    partial_bn_layer = create_partial_bn_layer(batch_norm_params)
    partial_conv2d_layer = functools.partial(tf.layers.conv2d,
        filters=params[HYPERPARAMS.NUM_FILTERS], kernel_size=[3, 3],
padding="same")
    partial_res_layer = functools.partial(create_partial_res_layer,
batch_norm=partial_bn_layer,
                                          conv2d=partial_conv2d_layer)


    output_shared =
tf.nn.relu(partial_bn_layer(partial_conv2d_layer(features)))

    for i in range(params[HYPERPARAMS.NUMSHAREDLAYERS]):
        output_shared = partial_res_layer(output_shared)

# Implement the policy network
with tf.name_scope("policy_network"):
    conv_p_output =
tf.nn.relu(partial_bn_layer(partial_conv2d_layer(output_shared, filters=2,
kernel_size=[1, 1]),
center=False, scale=False))
    logits = tf.layers.dense(tf.reshape(conv_p_output, [-1, GOPARAMETERS.N
* GOPARAMETERS.N * 2]),
                             units=GOPARAMETERS.N * GOPARAMETERS.N + 1)
    output_policy = tf.nn.softmax(logits,
                                  name='policy_output')


# Implement the value network
with tf.name_scope("value_network"):
    conv_v_output =
tf.nn.relu(partial_bn_layer(partial_conv2d_layer(output_shared, filters=1,
kernel_size=[1, 1]),
        center=False, scale=False))
    fc_v_output = tf.nn.relu(tf.layers.dense(
        tf.reshape(conv_v_output, [-1, GOPARAMETERS.N * GOPARAMETERS.N]),
        params[HYPERPARAMS.FC_WIDTH]))
    fc_v_output = tf.layers.dense(fc_v_output, 1)
    fc_v_output = tf.reshape(fc_v_output, [-1])
    output_value = tf.nn.tanh(fc_v_output, name='value_output')

# Implement the loss functions
with tf.name_scope("loss_functions"):
    loss_policy, loss_value = get_losses(logits=logits,
                                         output_value=output_value,
                                         labels=labels)
```

```
loss_l2 = params[HYPERPARAMS.BETA] * tf.add_n([tf.nn.l2_loss(v)
    for v in tf.trainable_variables() if not 'bias' in v.name])
loss_total = loss_policy + loss_value + loss_l2
```

We then specify the optimization algorithm. Here, we use `tf.train.MomentumOptimizer`. We also adjust the learning rate during training; because we can't directly alter the learning rate once we create `Estimator`, we turn the learning rate update into a TensorFlow operation as well. We also log several metrics to TensorBoard:

```
# Steps and operations for training
global_step = tf.train.get_or_create_global_step()

learning_rate = tf.train.piecewise_constant(global_step,
GLOBAL_PARAMETER_STORE.BOUNDARIES,
GLOBAL_PARAMETER_STORE.LEARNING_RATE)

update_ops = tf.get_collection(tf.GraphKeys.UPDATE_OPS)

with tf.control_dependencies(update_ops):
    train_op = tf.train.MomentumOptimizer(learning_rate,
                params[HYPERPARAMS.MOMENTUM]).minimize(loss_total,
global_step=global_step)

metric_ops = create_metric_ops(labels=labels,
                               output_policy=output_policy,
                               loss_policy=loss_policy,
                               loss_value=loss_value,
                               loss_l2=loss_l2,
                               loss_total=loss_total)

for metric_name, metric_op in metric_ops.items():
    tf.summary.scalar(metric_name, metric_op[1])
```

Finally, we create a `tf.estmator.EstimatorSpec` object and return it. There are several parameters we need to specify when creating one:

- `mode`: Train or test, as specified earlier.
- `predictions`: A dictionary that maps a string (name) to the output operation of the network. Note that we can specify multiple output operations.
- `loss`: The loss function operation.
- `train_op`: The optimization operation.
- `eval_metrics_op`: Operations that are run to store several metrics, such as loss, accuracy, and variable weight values.

For the `predictions` argument, we provide outputs of both the policy and value networks:

```
return tf.estimator.EstimatorSpec(
    mode=mode,
    predictions={
        'policy_output': output_policy,
        'value_output': output_value,
    },
    loss=loss_total,
    train_op=train_op,
    eval_metric_ops=metric_ops,
)
```

In the very first step of training AlphaGo Zero, we must initialize a model with random weights. The following function implements this:

```
def initialize_random_model(estimator_dir, **kwargs):
    sess = tf.Session(graph=tf.Graph())
    params = utils.parse_parameters(**kwargs)
    initial_model_path = os.path.join(estimator_dir,
PATHS.INITIAL_CHECKPOINT_NAME)

    # Create the first model, where all we do is initialize random weights
    and immediately write them to disk
    with sess.graph.as_default():
        features, labels = get_inference_input()
        generate_network_specifications(features, labels,
tf.estimator.ModeKeys.PREDICT, params)
        sess.run(tf.global_variables_initializer())
        tf.train.Saver().save(sess, initial_model_path)
```

We use the following function to create the `tf.estimator.Estimator` object based on a given set of parameters:

```
def get_estimator(estimator_dir, **kwargs):
    params = utils.parse_parameters(**kwargs)
    return tf.estimator.Estimator(generate_network_specifications,
model_dir=estimator_dir, params=params)
```

`tf.estimator.Estimator` expects a function that provides `tf.estimator.EstimatorSpec`, which is our `generate_network_specifications` function. Here, `estimator_dir` refers to a directory in which our network stores checkpoints. By providing this parameter, our `tf.estimator.Estimator` object can load weights from a previous iteration of training.

We also implement functions for training and validating a model:

```
def train(estimator_dir, tf_records, model_version, **kwargs):
    """
    Main training function for the PolicyValueNetwork
    Args:
        estimator_dir (str): Path to the estimator directory
        tf_records (list): A list of TFRecords from which we parse the
training examples
        model_version (int): The version of the model
    """
    model = get_estimator(estimator_dir, **kwargs)
    logger.info("Training model version: {}".format(model_version))
    max_steps = model_version *
GLOBAL_PARAMETER_STORE.EXAMPLES_PER_GENERATION // \
                GLOBAL_PARAMETER_STORE.TRAIN_BATCH_SIZE
    model.train(input_fn=lambda:
preprocessing.get_input_tensors(list_tf_records=tf_records),
                max_steps=max_steps)
    logger.info("Trained model version: {}".format(model_version))


def validate(estimator_dir, tf_records, checkpoint_path=None, **kwargs):
    model = get_estimator(estimator_dir, **kwargs)
    if checkpoint_path is None:
        checkpoint_path = model.latest_checkpoint()
    model.evaluate(input_fn=lambda: preprocessing.get_input_tensors(
        list_tf_records=tf_records,
        buffer_size=GLOBAL_PARAMETER_STORE.VALIDATION_BUFFER_SIZE),
                steps=GLOBAL_PARAMETER_STORE.VALIDATION_NUMBER_OF_STEPS,
                checkpoint_path=checkpoint_path)
```

The `tf.estimator.Estimator.train` function expects a function that provides the training data in batches (`input_fn`). `input_data` uses our `get_input_tensors` function from the `preprocessing.py` module to parse `TFRecords` data and turn them into input tensors. The `tf.estimator.Estimator.evaluate` function expects the same input function.

We finally encapsulate our estimator into our `PolicyValueNetwork`. This class uses the path to a network (`model_path`) and loads its weights. It uses the network to predict the value and most probable next moves of a given board state:

```
class PolicyValueNetwork():

    def __init__(self, model_path, **kwargs):
        self.model_path = model_path
        self.params = utils.parse_parameters(**kwargs)
```

```
        self.build_network()

    def build_session(self):
        config = tf.ConfigProto()
        config.gpu_options.allow_growth = True
        return tf.Session(graph=tf.Graph(), config=config)

    def build_network(self):
        self.sess = self.build_session()

        with self.sess.graph.as_default():
            features, labels = get_inference_input()
            model_spec = generate_network_specifications(features, labels,
tf.estimator.ModeKeys.PREDICT, self.params)
            self.inference_input = features
            self.inference_output = model_spec.predictions
            if self.model_path is not None:
                self.load_network_weights(self.model_path)
            else:
                self.sess.run(tf.global_variables_initializer())

    def load_network_weights(self, save_file):
        tf.train.Saver().restore(self.sess, save_file)
```

The `model_path` argument passed to the constructor is the directory of a particular version of the model. When this is `None`, we initialize random weights. The following functions are used to predict the probabilities of the next action and the value of a given board state:

```
def predict_on_single_board_state(self, position):
    probs, values = self.predict_on_multiple_board_states([position])
    prob = probs[0]
    value = values[0]
    return prob, value

def predict_on_multiple_board_states(self, positions):
    symmetries, processed =
utils.shuffle_feature_symmetries(list(map(features.extract_features,
positions)))
    network_outputs = self.sess.run(self.inference_output,
feed_dict={self.inference_input: processed})
    action_probs, value_pred = network_outputs['policy_output'],
network_outputs['value_output']
    action_probs = utils.invert_policy_symmetries(symmetries, action_probs)
    return action_probs, value_pred
```

Do check the GitHub repository for the full implementation of the module.

Monte Carlo tree search

The second component of our AlphaGo Zero agent is the MCTS algorithm. In our `mcts.py` module, we implement an `MCTreeSearchNode` class, which represents each node in an MCTS tree during a search. This is then used by the agent implemented in `alphagozero_agent.py` to perform MCTS using `PolicyValueNetwork`, which we implemented just now.

mcts.py

`mcts.py` contains our implementation of Monte Carlo tree search. Our first class is `RootNode`, which is meant to represent the root node of the MCTS tree at the start of a simulation. By definition, the root node does not have a parent. Having a separate class for the root node is not absolutely necessary, but it does keep the code cleaner:

```
import collections
import math

import numpy as np

import utils
from config import MCTSPARAMETERS, GOPARAMETERS


class RootNode(object):

    def __init__(self):
        self.parent_node = None
        self.child_visit_counts = collections.defaultdict(float)
        self.child_cumulative_rewards = collections.defaultdict(float)
```

Next, we implement the `MCTreeSearchNode` class. This class has several attributes, the most important ones being the following:

- `parent_node`: The parent node
- `previous_move`: The previous move that led to this node's board state

- `board_state`: The current board state
- `is_visited`: Whether the leaves (child nodes) are expanded or not; this is `False` when the node is initialized
- `child_visit_counts`: A `numpy.ndarray` representing the visit counts of each child node
- `child_cumulative_rewards`: A `numpy.ndarray` representing the cumulative reward of each child node
- `children_moves`: A dictionary of children moves

We also have parameters such as `loss_counter`, `original_prior`, and `child_prior`. These are related to advanced MCTS techniques that AlphaGo Zero implements, such as paralleling the search process as well as adding noise to the search. For the sake of brevity, we won't cover these techniques, so you can ignore them for now.

Here's the __init__ function of `MCTreeSearchNode`:

```
class MCTreeSearchNode(object):

    def __init__(self, board_state, previous_move=None, parent_node=None):
        """
        A node of a MCTS tree. It is primarily responsible with keeping
track of its children's scores
        and other statistics such as visit count. It also makes decisions
about where to move next.

        board_state (go.BoardState): The Go board
        fmove (int): A number which represents the coordinate of the move
that led to this board state. None if pass
        parent (MCTreeSearchNode): The parent node
        """
        if parent_node is None:
            parent_node = RootNode()
        self.parent_node = parent_node
        self.previous_move = previous_move
        self.board_state = board_state
        self.is_visited = False
        self.loss_counter = 0
        self.illegal_moves = 1000 * (1 -
self.board_state.enumerate_possible_moves())
        self.child_visit_counts = np.zeros([GOPARAMETERS.N * GOPARAMETERS.N
+ 1], dtype=np.float32)
        self.child_cumulative_rewards = np.zeros([GOPARAMETERS.N *
GOPARAMETERS.N + 1], dtype=np.float32)
        self.original_prior = np.zeros([GOPARAMETERS.N * GOPARAMETERS.N +
1], dtype=np.float32)
```

```
            self.child_prior = np.zeros([GOPARAMETERS.N * GOPARAMETERS.N + 1],
dtype=np.float32)
            self.children_moves = {}
```

Each node keeps track of the mean reward and action value of every child node. We set these as properties:

```
@property
def child_action_score(self):
    return self.child_mean_rewards * self.board_state.to_play +
self.child_node_scores - self.illegal_moves

@property
def child_mean_rewards(self):
    return self.child_cumulative_rewards / (1 + self.child_visit_counts)

@property
def child_node_scores(self):
    # This scores each child according to the UCT scoring system
    return (MCTSPARAMETERS.c_PUCT * math.sqrt(1 + self.node_visit_count) *
self.child_prior /
            (1 + self.child_visit_counts))
```

And of course, we keep track of the action value, visit count, and cumulative reward of the node itself. Remember, child_mean_rewards is the mean reward, child_visit_counts is the number of times a child node was visited, and child_cumulative_rewards is the total reward of a node. We implement getters and setters for each attribute by adding the @property and @*.setter decorators:

```
@property
def node_mean_reward(self):
    return self.node_cumulative_reward / (1 + self.node_visit_count)

@property
def node_visit_count(self):
    return self.parent_node.child_visit_counts[self.previous_move]

@node_visit_count.setter
def node_visit_count(self, value):
    self.parent_node.child_visit_counts[self.previous_move] = value

@property
def node_cumulative_reward(self):
    return self.parent_node.child_cumulative_rewards[self.previous_move]

@node_cumulative_reward.setter
def node_cumulative_reward(self, value):
```

```
            self.parent_node.child_cumulative_rewards[self.previous_move] = value

    @property
    def mean_reward_perspective(self):
        return self.node_mean_reward * self.board_state.to_play
```

During the selection step of MCTS, the algorithm chooses the child node with the greatest action value. This can be easily done by calling `np.argmax` on the matrix of child action scores:

```
def choose_next_child_node(self):
    current = self
    pass_move = GOPARAMETERS.N * GOPARAMETERS.N
    while True:
        current.node_visit_count += 1
        # We stop searching when we reach a new leaf node
        if not current.is_visited:
            break
        if (current.board_state.recent
            and current.board_state.recent[-1].move is None
                and current.child_visit_counts[pass_move] == 0):
            current = current.record_child_node(pass_move)
            continue

        best_move = np.argmax(current.child_action_score)
        current = current.record_child_node(best_move)
    return current

def record_child_node(self, next_coordinate):
    if next_coordinate not in self.children_moves:
        new_board_state = self.board_state.play_move(
            utils.from_flat(next_coordinate))
        self.children_moves[next_coordinate] = MCTreeSearchNode(
            new_board_state, previous_move=next_coordinate,
parent_node=self)
    return self.children_moves[next_coordinate]
```

As discussed in our section about AlphaGo Zero, `PolicyValueNetwork` is used to conduct simulations in an MCTS iteration. Again, the output of the network are the probabilities and the predicted value of the node, which we then reflect in the MCTS tree itself. In particular, the predicted value is propagated throughout the tree via the `back_propagate_result` function:

```
def incorporate_results(self, move_probabilities, result, start_node):
    if self.is_visited:
        self.revert_visits(start_node=start_node)
        return
    self.is_visited = True
    self.original_prior = self.child_prior = move_probabilities
    self.child_cumulative_rewards = np.ones([GOPARAMETERS.N *
GOPARAMETERS.N + 1], dtype=np.float32) * result
    self.back_propagate_result(result, start_node=start_node)

def back_propagate_result(self, result, start_node):
    """
    This function back propagates the result of a match all the way to
where the search started from

    Args:
        result (int): the result of the search (1: black, -1: white won)
        start_node (MCTreeSearchNode): the node to back propagate until
    """
    # Keep track of the cumulative reward in this node
    self.node_cumulative_reward += result

    if self.parent_node is None or self is start_node:
        return

    self.parent_node.back_propagate_result(result, start_node)
```

Refer to the GitHub repository for a full implementation of our `MCTreeSearchNode` class and its functions.

Combining PolicyValueNetwork and MCTS

We combine our `PolicyValueNetwork` and MCTS implementations in `alphagozero_agent.py`. This module implements `AlphaGoZeroAgent`, which is the main AlphaGo Zero that conducts MCTS search and inference using `PolicyValueNetwork` to play games.

alphagozero_agent.py

Finally, we implement the agent that acts as the interface between the Go games and the algorithms. The main class we will implement is called `AlphaGoZeroAgent`. Again, this class combines `PolicyValueNetwork` with our MCTS module, as is done in AlphaGo Zero, to select moves and simulate games. Note that any missing modules (for example, `go.py`, which implements the game of Go itself) can be found in the main GitHub repository:

```python
import logging
import os
import random
import time

import numpy as np

import go
import utils
from config import GLOBAL_PARAMETER_STORE, GOPARAMETERS
from mcts import MCTreeSearchNode
from utils import make_sgf

logger = logging.getLogger(__name__)

class AlphaGoZeroAgent:

    def __init__(self, network, player_v_player=False,
workers=GLOBAL_PARAMETER_STORE.SIMULTANEOUS_LEAVES):
        self.network = network
        self.player_v_player = player_v_player
        self.workers = workers
        self.mean_reward_store = []
        self.game_description_store = []
        self.child_probability_store = []
        self.root = None
        self.result = 0
        self.logging_buffer = None
        self.conduct_exploration = True
        if self.player_v_player:
            self.conduct_exploration = True
        else:
            self.conduct_exploration = False
```

We start a Go game by initializing our agent and the game itself. This is done via the `initialize_game` method, which initializes `MCTreeSearchNode` and buffers that keep track of move probabilities and action values outputted by the network:

```
def initialize_game(self, board_state=None):
    if board_state is None:
        board_state = go.BoardState()
    self.root = MCTreeSearchNode(board_state)
    self.result = 0
    self.logging_buffer = None
    self.game_description_store = []
    self.child_probability_store = []
    self.mean_reward_store = []
```

In each turn, our agent conducts MCTS and picks a move using the `select_move` function. Notice that we allow for some exploration in the early stages of the game by selecting a random node.

The `play_move(coordinates)` method takes in a coordinate returned by `select_move` and updates the MCTS tree and board states:

```
def play_move(self, coordinates):
    if not self.player_v_player:
self.child_probability_store.append(self.root.get_children_as_probability_d
istributions())
        self.mean_reward_store.append(self.root.node_mean_reward)
        self.game_description_store.append(self.root.describe())
        self.root = self.root.record_child_node(utils.to_flat(coordinates))
        self.board_state = self.root.board_state
        del self.root.parent_node.children_moves
        return True

def select_move(self):
    # If we have conducted enough moves and this is single player mode, we
turn off exploration
    if self.root.board_state.n > GLOBAL_PARAMETER_STORE.TEMPERATURE_CUTOFF
and not self.player_v_player:
        self.conduct_exploration = False

    if self.conduct_exploration:
        child_visits_cum_sum = self.root.child_visit_counts.cumsum()
        child_visits_cum_sum /= child_visits_cum_sum[-1]
        coorindate = child_visits_cum_sum.searchsorted(random.random())
    else:
        coorindate = np.argmax(self.root.child_visit_counts)

    return utils.from_flat(coorindate)
```

These functions are encapsulated in the `search_tree` method, which conducts an iteration of MCTS using the network to select the next move:

```
def search_tree(self):
    child_node_store = []
    iteration_count = 0
    while len(child_node_store) < self.workers and iteration_count <
self.workers * 2:
        iteration_count += 1
        child_node = self.root.choose_next_child_node()
        if child_node.is_done():
            result = 1 if child_node.board_state.score() > 0 else -1
            child_node.back_propagate_result(result, start_node=self.root)
            continue
        child_node.propagate_loss(start_node=self.root)
        child_node_store.append(child_node)
    if len(child_node_store) > 0:
        move_probs, values = self.network.predict_on_multiple_board_states(
            [child_node.board_state for child_node in child_node_store])
        for child_node, move_prob, result in zip(child_node_store,
move_probs, values):
            child_node.revert_loss(start_node=self.root)
            child_node.incorporate_results(move_prob, result,
start_node=self.root)
```

Notice that once we have leaf nodes (where we can no longer select a node based on visit count), we use the `PolicyValueNetwork.predict_on_multiple_board_states(board_states)` function to output the next move probabilities and value of each leaf node.

This `AlphaGoZeroAgent` is then used for either playing against another network or against itself for self-play. We implement separate functions for each. For `play_match`, we first start by initializing an agent each for black and white pieces:

```
def play_match(black_net, white_net, games, readouts, sgf_dir):

    # Create the players for the game
    black = AlphaGoZeroAgent(black_net, player_v_player=True,
workers=GLOBAL_PARAMETER_STORE.SIMULTANEOUS_LEAVES)
    white = AlphaGoZeroAgent(white_net, player_v_player=True,
workers=GLOBAL_PARAMETER_STORE.SIMULTANEOUS_LEAVES)

    black_name = os.path.basename(black_net.model_path)
    white_name = os.path.basename(white_net.model_path)
```

During the game, we keep track of the number of moves made, which also informs us which agent's turn it is. During each agent's turn, we use MCTS and the network to choose the next move:

```
for game_num in range(games):
    # Keep track of the number of moves made in the game
    num_moves = 0

    black.initialize_game()
    white.initialize_game()

    while True:
        start = time.time()
        active = white if num_moves % 2 else black
        inactive = black if num_moves % 2 else white

        current_readouts = active.root.node_visit_count
        while active.root.node_visit_count < current_readouts + readouts:
            active.search_tree()
```

Once the tree search is done, we see whether the agent has resigned or the game has ended by other means. If so, we write the results and end the game itself:

```
    logger.info(active.root.board_state)

    # Check whether a player should resign
    if active.should_resign():
        active.set_result(-1 * active.root.board_state.to_play,
was_resign=True)
        inactive.set_result(active.root.board_state.to_play, was_resign=True)

    if active.is_done():
        sgf_file_path = "{}-{}-vs-{}-{}.sgf".format(int(time.time()),
white_name, black_name, game_num)
        with open(os.path.join(sgf_dir, sgf_file_path), 'w') as fp:
            game_as_sgf_string = make_sgf(active.board_state.recent,
active.logging_buffer,
                            black_name=black_name,
                            white_name=white_name)
            fp.write(game_as_sgf_string)
        print("Game Over", game_num, active.logging_buffer)
        break

    move = active.select_move()
    active.play_move(move)
    inactive.play_move(move)
```

The `make_sgf` method writes the outcome of the game in a format that is commonly used in other Go AIs and computer programs. In other words, the output of this module are compatible with other Go software! Although we won't delve into the technicalities, this would help you create a Go playing bot that can play other agents and even human players.

 SGF stands for **Smart Game Format**, and is a popular way of storing the results of board games such as Go. You can find more information here: `https://senseis.xmp.net/?SmartGameFormat`.

The `play_against_self()` is used during the self-play simulations of training, while `play_match()` is used to evaluate the latest model against an earlier version of the model. Again, for a full implementation of the module, please refer to the codebase.

Putting everything together

Now that we have implemented the two main components of AlphaGo Zero—the `PolicyValueNetwork` and the MCTS algorithm—we can build the controller that handles training. At the very beginning of the training procedure, we initialize a model with random weights. Next, we generate 100 self-play games. Five percent of those games and their results are held out for validation. The rest are kept for training the network. After the first initialization and self-play iteration, we essentially loop through the following steps:

1. Generate self-play data
2. Collate self-play data to create `TFRecords`
3. Train network using collated self-play data
4. Validate on `holdout` dataset

After every step 3, the resulting model is stored in a directory as the latest version. The training procedure and logic are handled by `controller.py`.

controller.py

First, we start with some import statements and helper functions that help us check directory paths and find the latest model version:

```
import argparse
import logging
import os
import random
```

```
import socket
import sys
import time

import argh
import tensorflow as tf
from tensorflow import gfile
from tqdm import tqdm

import alphagozero_agent
import network
import preprocessing
from config import GLOBAL_PARAMETER_STORE
from constants import PATHS
from alphagozero_agent import play_match
from network import PolicyValueNetwork
from utils import logged_timer as timer
from utils import print_flags, generate, detect_model_name,
detect_model_version

logging.basicConfig(
 level=logging.DEBUG,
 handlers=[logging.StreamHandler(sys.stdout)],
 format='%(asctime)s %(name)-12s %(levelname)-8s %(message)s',
)

logger = logging.getLogger(__name__)

def get_models():
 """
 Get all model versions
 """
 all_models = gfile.Glob(os.path.join(PATHS.MODELS_DIR, '*.meta'))
 model_filenames = [os.path.basename(m) for m in all_models]
 model_versionbers_names = sorted([
 (detect_model_version(m), detect_model_name(m))
 for m in model_filenames])
 return model_versionbers_names

def get_latest_model():
 """
 Get the latest model

 Returns:
 Tuple of <int, str>, or <model_version, model_name>
 """
 return get_models()[-1]
```

The first step of every training run is to initialize a random model. Note that we store model definitions and weights in the PATHS.MODELS_DIR directory, while checkpoint results outputted by the estimator object are stored in PATHS.ESTIMATOR_WORKING_DIR:

```
def initialize_random_model():
    bootstrap_name = generate(0)
    bootstrap_model_path = os.path.join(PATHS.MODELS_DIR, bootstrap_name)
    logger.info("Bootstrapping with working dir {}\n Model 0 exported to
{}".format(
        PATHS.ESTIMATOR_WORKING_DIR, bootstrap_model_path))
    maybe_create_directory(PATHS.ESTIMATOR_WORKING_DIR)
    maybe_create_directory(os.path.dirname(bootstrap_model_path))
    network.initialize_random_model(PATHS.ESTIMATOR_WORKING_DIR)
    network.export_latest_checkpoint_model(PATHS.ESTIMATOR_WORKING_DIR,
bootstrap_model_path)
```

We next implement the function for executing self-play simulations. As mentioned earlier, the output of a self-play consist of each board state and the associated moves and game outcomes produced by the MCTS algorithm. Most output are stored in PATHS.SELFPLAY_DIR, while some are stored in PATHS.HOLDOUT_DIR for validation. Self-play involves initializing one AlphaGoZeroAgent and having it play against itself. This is where we use the play_against_self function that we implemented in alphagozero_agent.py. In our implementation, we conduct self-play games according to the GLOBAL_PARAMETER_STORE.NUM_SELFPLAY_GAMES parameter specified. More self-play games allow our neural network to learn from more experience, but do bear in mind that the training time increases accordingly:

```
def selfplay():
    _, model_name = get_latest_model()
    try:
        games = gfile.Glob(os.path.join(PATHS.SELFPLAY_DIR, model_name,
'*.zz'))
        if len(games) > GLOBAL_PARAMETER_STORE.MAX_GAMES_PER_GENERATION:
            logger.info("{} has enough games ({})".format(model_name,
len(games)))
            time.sleep(600)
            sys.exit(1)
    except:
        pass

    for game_idx in range(GLOBAL_PARAMETER_STORE.NUM_SELFPLAY_GAMES):
        logger.info('=================================================')
        logger.info("Playing game {} with model {}".format(game_idx,
model_name))
        logger.info('=================================================')
        model_save_path = os.path.join(PATHS.MODELS_DIR, model_name)
```

```
game_output_dir = os.path.join(PATHS.SELFPLAY_DIR, model_name)
game_holdout_dir = os.path.join(PATHS.HOLDOUT_DIR, model_name)
sgf_dir = os.path.join(PATHS.SGF_DIR, model_name)

clean_sgf = os.path.join(sgf_dir, 'clean')
full_sgf = os.path.join(sgf_dir, 'full')
os.makedirs(clean_sgf, exist_ok=True)
os.makedirs(full_sgf, exist_ok=True)
os.makedirs(game_output_dir, exist_ok=True)
os.makedirs(game_holdout_dir, exist_ok=True)
```

During self-play, we instantiate an agent with weights of a previously-generated model and make it play against itself for a number of games defined by GLOBAL_PARAMETER_STORE.NUM_SELFPLAY_GAMES:

```
with timer("Loading weights from %s ... " % model_save_path):
    network = PolicyValueNetwork(model_save_path)

with timer("Playing game"):
    agent = alphagozero_agent.play_against_self(network,
GLOBAL_PARAMETER_STORE.SELFPLAY_READOUTS)
```

After the agent plays against itself, we store the moves it has generated as game data, which we use to train our policy and value networks:

```
output_name = '{}-{}'.format(int(time.time()), socket.gethostname())
game_play = agent.extract_data()
with gfile.GFile(os.path.join(clean_sgf, '{}.sgf'.format(output_name),
'w') as f:
    f.write(agent.to_sgf(use_comments=False))
with gfile.GFile(os.path.join(full_sgf, '{}.sgf'.format(output_name)), 'w')
as f:
    f.write(agent.to_sgf())

tf_examples = preprocessing.create_dataset_from_selfplay(game_play)

# We reserve 5% of games played for validation
holdout = random.random() < GLOBAL_PARAMETER_STORE.HOLDOUT
if holdout:
    to_save_dir = game_holdout_dir
else:
    to_save_dir = game_output_dir
tf_record_path = os.path.join(to_save_dir,
"{}.tfrecord.zz".format(output_name))

preprocessing.write_tf_examples(tf_record_path, tf_examples)
```

Notice that we reserve a percentage of the games played as the validation set.

After generating self-play data, we expect roughly five percent of the self-play games to be in the `holdout` directory, to be used in validation. The majority of self-play data is used to train the neural network. We add another step, called **aggregate**, which takes the latest model version and its self-play data to construct `TFRecords` with the format that our neural network specifies. This is where we use the functions we implemented in `preprocessing.py`:

```python
def aggregate():
    logger.info("Gathering game results")

    os.makedirs(PATHS.TRAINING_CHUNK_DIR, exist_ok=True)
    os.makedirs(PATHS.SELFPLAY_DIR, exist_ok=True)
    models = [model_dir.strip('/')
              for model_dir in
sorted(gfile.ListDirectory(PATHS.SELFPLAY_DIR))[-50:]]

    with timer("Finding existing tfrecords..."):
        model_gamedata = {
            model: gfile.Glob(
                os.path.join(PATHS.SELFPLAY_DIR, model, '*.zz'))
            for model in models
        }
    logger.info("Found %d models" % len(models))
    for model_name, record_files in sorted(model_gamedata.items()):
        logger.info("    %s: %s files" % (model_name, len(record_files)))

    meta_file = os.path.join(PATHS.TRAINING_CHUNK_DIR, 'meta.txt')
    try:
        with gfile.GFile(meta_file, 'r') as f:
            already_processed = set(f.read().split())
    except tf.errors.NotFoundError:
        already_processed = set()

    num_already_processed = len(already_processed)

    for model_name, record_files in sorted(model_gamedata.items()):
        if set(record_files) <= already_processed:
            continue
        logger.info("Gathering files for %s:" % model_name)
        for i, example_batch in enumerate(
tqdm(preprocessing.shuffle_tf_examples(GLOBAL_PARAMETER_STORE.EXAMPLES_PER_
RECORD, record_files))):
            output_record = os.path.join(PATHS.TRAINING_CHUNK_DIR,
                                         '{}-
{}.tfrecord.zz'.format(model_name, str(i)))
            preprocessing.write_tf_examples(
                output_record, example_batch, serialize=False)
```

```
            already_processed.update(record_files)

        logger.info("Processed %s new files" %
            (len(already_processed) - num_already_processed))
        with gfile.GFile(meta_file, 'w') as f:
            f.write('\n'.join(sorted(already_processed)))
```

After we generate the training data, we train a new version of the neural network. We search for the latest version of the model, load an estimator using the weights of the latest version, and execute another iteration of training:

```
def train():
    model_version, model_name = get_latest_model()
    logger.info("Training on gathered game data, initializing from
{}".format(model_name))
    new_model_name = generate(model_version + 1)
    logger.info("New model will be {}".format(new_model_name))
    save_file = os.path.join(PATHS.MODELS_DIR, new_model_name)

    try:
        logger.info("Getting tf_records")
        tf_records =
sorted(gfile.Glob(os.path.join(PATHS.TRAINING_CHUNK_DIR, '*.tfrecord.zz')))
        tf_records = tf_records[
                    -1 * (GLOBAL_PARAMETER_STORE.WINDOW_SIZE //
GLOBAL_PARAMETER_STORE.EXAMPLES_PER_RECORD):]

        print("Training from:", tf_records[0], "to", tf_records[-1])

        with timer("Training"):
            network.train(PATHS.ESTIMATOR_WORKING_DIR, tf_records,
model_version+1)
network.export_latest_checkpoint_model(PATHS.ESTIMATOR_WORKING_DIR,
save_file)

    except:
        logger.info("Got an error training")
        logging.exception("Train error")
```

Finally, after every training iteration, we would like to validate the model with the holdout dataset. When enough data is available, we take the holdout data from the last five versions:

```
def validate(model_version=None, validate_name=None):
    if model_version is None:
        model_version, model_name = get_latest_model()
    else:
        model_version = int(model_version)
```

```
        model_name = get_model(model_version)

    models = list(
        filter(lambda num_name: num_name[0] < (model_version - 1),
get_models()))

    if len(models) == 0:
        logger.info('Not enough models, including model N for validation')
        models = list(
            filter(lambda num_name: num_name[0] <= model_version,
get_models()))
    else:
        logger.info('Validating using data from following models:
{}'.format(models))

    tf_record_dirs = [os.path.join(PATHS.HOLDOUT_DIR, pair[1])
                      for pair in models[-5:]]

    working_dir = PATHS.ESTIMATOR_WORKING_DIR
    checkpoint_name = os.path.join(PATHS.MODELS_DIR, model_name)

    tf_records = []
    with timer("Building lists of holdout files"):
        for record_dir in tf_record_dirs:
            tf_records.extend(gfile.Glob(os.path.join(record_dir, '*.zz')))

    with timer("Validating from {} to
{}".format(os.path.basename(tf_records[0]),
os.path.basename(tf_records[-1]))):
        network.validate(working_dir, tf_records,
checkpoint_path=checkpoint_name, name=validate_name)
```

Lastly, we implement the `evaluate` function, which has one model play multiple games against another:

```
def evaluate(black_model, white_model):
    os.makedirs(PATHS.SGF_DIR, exist_ok=True)

    with timer("Loading weights"):
        black_net = network.PolicyValueNetwork(black_model)
        white_net = network.PolicyValueNetwork(white_model)

    with timer("Playing {}
games".format(GLOBAL_PARAMETER_STORE.EVALUATION_GAMES)):
        play_match(black_net, white_net,
GLOBAL_PARAMETER_STORE.EVALUATION_GAMES,
                   GLOBAL_PARAMETER_STORE.EVALUATION_READOUTS,
PATHS.SGF_DIR)
```

The `evaluate` method takes two parameters, `black_model` and `white_model`, where each argument refers to the path of the agent used to play a game. We use `black_model` and `white_model` to instantiate two `PolicyValueNetworks`. Typically, we want to evaluate the latest model version, which would play as either black or white.

train.py

Finally, `train.py` is where all the functions we implemented in the controller are called and coordinated. More specifically, we execute each step as `subprocess`:

```python
import subprocess
import sys
from utils import timer

import os

from constants import PATHS

import logging

logger = logging.getLogger(__name__)

def main():

    if not os.path.exists(PATHS.SELFPLAY_DIR):
        with timer("Initialize"):
            logger.info('===========================================')
            logger.info("=========== Initializing...==============")
            logger.info('===========================================')
            res = subprocess.call("python controller.py initialize-random-model", shell=True)

        with timer('Initial Selfplay'):
            logger.info('===========================================')
            logger.info('=========== Selplaying...==============')
            logger.info('===========================================')
            subprocess.call('python controller.py selfplay', shell=True)
```

Assuming that no model has been trained yet, we initialize a model with random weights and make it play against itself to generate some data for our policy and value networks. After rewards, we repeat the following:

1. Aggregate data self-play data
2. Train networks

3. Make the agent play against itself
4. Validate on validation data

This is implemented as follows:

```
while True:
    with timer("Aggregate"):
        logger.info('=======================================')
        logger.info("=========== Aggregating...=============")
        logger.info('=======================================')
        res = subprocess.call("python controller.py aggregate", shell=True)
        if res != 0:
            logger.info("Failed to gather")
            sys.exit(1)

    with timer("Train"):
        logger.info('=======================================')
        logger.info("=========== Training...==============")
        logger.info('=======================================')
        subprocess.call("python controller.py train", shell=True)

    with timer('Selfplay'):
        logger.info('=======================================')
        logger.info('=========== Selplaying...=============')
        logger.info('=======================================')
        subprocess.call('python controller.py selfplay', shell=True)

    with timer("Validate"):
        logger.info('=======================================')
        logger.info("=========== Validating...=============")
        logger.info('=======================================')
        subprocess.call("python controller.py validate", shell=True)
```

Finally, since this is the main module, we add the following at the end of the file:

```
if __name__ == '__main__':
    main()
```

And at long last, we're done!

To run the training of AlphaGo Zero, all you need to do is call this command:

```
$ python train.py
```

If everything has been implemented correctly, you should start to see the model train. However, the reader is to be warned that training will take a long, long time. To put things into perspective, DeepMind used 64 GPU workers and 19 CPU servers to train AlphaGo Zero for 40 days. If you wish to see your model attain a high level of proficiency, expect to wait a long time.

 Note that training AlphaGo Zero takes a very long time. Do not expect the model to reach professional-level proficiency any time soon!

You should be able to see output that looks such as the following:

```
2018-09-14 03:41:27,286 utils INFO Playing game: 342.685 seconds
2018-09-14 03:41:27,332 __main__ INFO
================================================
2018-09-14 03:41:27,332 __main__ INFO Playing game 9 with model 000010-
pretty-tetra
2018-09-14 03:41:27,332 __main__ INFO
================================================
INFO:tensorflow:Restoring parameters from models/000010-pretty-tetra
2018-09-14 03:41:32,352 tensorflow INFO Restoring parameters from
models/000010-pretty-tetra
2018-09-14 03:41:32,624 utils INFO Loading weights from models/000010-
pretty-tetra ... : 5.291 seconds
```

You will also be able to see the board state as the agent plays against itself or against other agents:

```
   A B C D E F G H J
9  . . . . . . . X 9
8  . . . X . . O . . 8
7  . . . . X O O . . 7
6 O . X X X<. . . . 6
5 X . O O . . O X . 5
4  . . X X . . . O . 4
3  . . X . X . O O . 3
2  . . . O . . . . X 2
1  . . . . . . . . . 1
   A B C D E F G H J
Move: 25. Captures X: 0 O: 0
 -5.5
   A B C D E F G H J
9  . . . . . . . X 9
8  . . . X . . O . . 8
7  . . . . X O O . . 7
6 O . X X X . . . . 6
```

```
5 X . O O . . O X . 5
4 . . X X . . . O . 4
3 . . X . X . O O . 3
2 . . . O . . . . X 2
1 . . . . . . . . . 1
  A B C D E F G H J
Move: 26. Captures X: 0 O: 0
```

If you want to play one model against another, you can run the following command (assuming that the models are stored in `models/`):

```
python controller.py evaluate models/{model_name_1} models/{model_name_2}
```

Summary

In this chapter, we studied reinforcement learning algorithms for one of the most complex and difficult games in the world, Go. In particular, we explored Monte Carlo tree search, a popular algorithm that learns the best moves over time. In AlphaGo, we observed how MCTS can be combined with deep neural networks to make learning more efficient and powerful. Then we investigated how AlphaGo Zero revolutionized Go agents by learning solely and entirely from self-play experience while outperforming all existing Go software and players. We then implemented this algorithm from scratch.

We also implemented AlphaGo Zero, which is the lighter version of AlphaGo since it does not depend on human game data. However, as noted, AlphaGo Zero requires enormous amounts of computational resources. Moreover, as you may have noticed, AlphaGo Zero depends on a myriad of hyperparameters, all of which require fine-tuning. In short, training AlphaGo Zero fully is a prohibitive task. We don't expect the reader to implement a state-of-the-art Go agent; rather, we hope that through this chapter, the reader has a better understanding of how Go playing deep reinforcement learning algorithms work. A firmer comprehension of these techniques and algorithms is already a valuable takeaway and outcome from this chapter. But of course, we encourage the reader to continue their exploration on this topic and build an even better version of AlphaGo Zero.

For more in-depth information and resources on the topics we covered in this chapter, please refer to the following links:

- **AlphaGo home page**: https://deepmind.com/research/alphago/
- **AlphaGo paper**: https://storage.googleapis.com/deepmind-media/alphago/AlphaGoNaturePaper.pdf
- **AlphaGo Zero paper**: https://www.nature.com/articles/nature24270
- **AlphaGo Zero blog post by DeepMind**: https://deepmind.com/blog/alphago-zero-learning-scratch/
- **A survey of MCTS methods**: http://mcts.ai/pubs/mcts-survey-master.pdf

Now that computers have surpassed human performance in board games, one may ask, What's next? What are the implications of these results? There remains much to be done; Go, which has complete information and is played turn by turn, is still considered simple compared to many real-life situations. One can imagine that the problem of self-driving cars poses a more difficult challenge given the lack of complete information and a larger number of variables. Nevertheless, AlphaGo and AlphaGo Zero have provided a crucial step toward achieving these tasks, and one can surely be excited about further developments in this field.

References

1. Silver, D., Huang, A., Maddison, C. J., Guez, A., Sifre, L., Van Den Driessche, G., ... and Dieleman, S. (2016). *Mastering the game of Go with deep neural networks and tree search*. Nature, 529(7587), 484.

2. Silver, D., Schrittwieser, J., Simonyan, K., Antonoglou, I., Huang, A., Guez, A., ... and Chen, Y. (2017). *Mastering the game of Go without human knowledge*. Nature, 550(7676), 354.

3. Browne, C. B., Powley, E., Whitehouse, D., Lucas, S. M., Cowling, P. I., Rohlfshagen, P., ... and Colton, S. (2012). *A survey of Monte Carlo tree search methods*. IEEE Transactions on Computational Intelligence and AI in games, 4(1), 1-43.

16
Creating a Chatbot

Dialogue agents and chatbots have been on the rise in recent years. Many businesses have resorted to chatbots to answer customer inquiries, and this has been largely successful. Chatbots have been growing quickly, at 5.6x in the last year (`https://chatbotsmagazine.com/chatbot-report-2018-global-trends-and-analysis-4d8bbe4d924b`). Chatbots can help organizations to communicate and interact with customers without any human intervention, at a very minimal cost. Over 51% of customers have stated that they want businesses to be available 24/7, and they expect replies in less than one hour. For businesses to achieve this kind of success in an affordable manner, especially with a large customer base, they must resort to chatbots.

The background problem

Many chatbots are created with regular machine learning natural language processing algorithms, and these focus on immediate responses. A new concept is to create chatbots with the use of deep reinforcement learning. This would mean that the future implications of our immediate responses would be considered to maintain coherence.

In this chapter, you will learn how to apply deep reinforcement learning to natural language processing. Our reward function will be a future-looking function, and you will learn how to think probabilistically through the creation of this function.

Dataset

The dataset that we will use mainly consists of conversations from selected movies. This dataset will help to stimulate and understand conversational methods in the chatbot. Also, there are movie lines, which are essentially the same as the movie conversations, albeit shorter exchanges between people. Other data sets that will be used include some containing movie titles, movie characters, and raw scripts.

Step-by-step guide

Our solution will use modeling and will focus on the future direction of a dialogue agent, so as to generate coherent and interesting dialogue. The model will simulate the dialogue between two virtual agents, with the use of policy gradient methods. These methods are designed to reward the sequences of interaction that display three important properties of conversation: informativeness (non-repeating turns), high coherence, and simplicity in answering (this is related to the forward-looking function). In our solution, an action will be defined as the dialogue or communication utterance that the chatbot generates. Also, a state will be defined as the two previous interaction turns. In order to achieve all of this, we will use the scripts in the following sections.

Data parser

The data parser script is designed to help with the cleaning and preprocessing of our datasets. There are a number of dependencies in this script, such as pickle, codecs, re, os, time, and numpy. This script contains three functions. The first function helps to filter words, by preprocessing word counts and creating vocabulary based on word count thresholds. The second function helps to parse all words into this script, and the third function helps to extract only the defined vocabulary from the data:

```
import pickle
import codecs
import re
import os
import time
import numpy as np
```

The following module cleans and preprocesses the text in the training dataset:

```
def preProBuildWordVocab(word_count_threshold=5,
all_words_path='data/all_words.txt'):
    # borrowed this function from NeuralTalk

    if not os.path.exists(all_words_path):
        parse_all_words(all_words_path)

    corpus = open(all_words_path, 'r').read().split('\n')[:-1]
    captions = np.asarray(corpus, dtype=np.object)

    captions = map(lambda x: x.replace('.', ''), captions)
    captions = map(lambda x: x.replace(',', ''), captions)
    captions = map(lambda x: x.replace('"', ''), captions)
    captions = map(lambda x: x.replace('\n', ''), captions)
```

```
captions = map(lambda x: x.replace('?', ''), captions)
captions = map(lambda x: x.replace('!', ''), captions)
captions = map(lambda x: x.replace('\\', ''), captions)
captions = map(lambda x: x.replace('/', ''), captions)
```

Next, iterate through the captions and create the vocabulary.

```
print('preprocessing word counts and creating vocab based on word count
threshold %d' % (word_count_threshold))
word_counts = {}
nsents = 0
for sent in captions:
    nsents += 1
    for w in sent.lower().split(' '):
        word_counts[w] = word_counts.get(w, 0) + 1
vocab = [w for w in word_counts if word_counts[w] >=
word_count_threshold]
print('filtered words from %d to %d' % (len(word_counts), len(vocab)))

ixtoword = {}
ixtoword[0] = '<pad>'
ixtoword[1] = '<bos>'
ixtoword[2] = '<eos>'
ixtoword[3] = '<unk>'

wordtoix = {}
wordtoix['<pad>'] = 0
wordtoix['<bos>'] = 1
wordtoix['<eos>'] = 2
wordtoix['<unk>'] = 3

for idx, w in enumerate(vocab):
    wordtoix[w] = idx+4
    ixtoword[idx+4] = w

word_counts['<pad>'] = nsents
word_counts['<bos>'] = nsents
word_counts['<eos>'] = nsents
word_counts['<unk>'] = nsents

bias_init_vector = np.array([1.0 * word_counts[ixtoword[i]] for i in
ixtoword])
bias_init_vector /= np.sum(bias_init_vector) # normalize to frequencies
bias_init_vector = np.log(bias_init_vector)
bias_init_vector -= np.max(bias_init_vector) # shift to nice numeric
range

return wordtoix, ixtoword, bias_init_vector
```

Next, parse all the words from the movie lines.

```
def parse_all_words(all_words_path):
    raw_movie_lines = open('data/movie_lines.txt', 'r', encoding='utf-8',
errors='ignore').read().split('\n')[:-1]

    with codecs.open(all_words_path, "w", encoding='utf-8',
errors='ignore') as f:
        for line in raw_movie_lines:
            line = line.split(' +++$+++ ')
            utterance = line[-1]
            f.write(utterance + '\n')
```

Extract only the vocabulary part of the data, as follows:

```
def refine(data):
    words = re.findall("[a-zA-Z'-]+", data)
    words = ["".join(word.split("'")) for word in words]
    # words = ["".join(word.split("-")) for word in words]
    data = ' '.join(words)
    return data
```

Next, the utterance dictionary is created and stored.

```
if __name__ == '__main__':
    parse_all_words('data/all_words.txt')

    raw_movie_lines = open('data/movie_lines.txt', 'r', encoding='utf-8',
errors='ignore').read().split('\n')[:-1]
    utterance_dict = {}
    with codecs.open('data/tokenized_all_words.txt', "w", encoding='utf-8',
errors='ignore') as f:
        for line in raw_movie_lines:
            line = line.split(' +++$+++ ')
            line_ID = line[0]
            utterance = line[-1]
            utterance_dict[line_ID] = utterance
            utterance = " ".join([refine(w) for w in
utterance.lower().split()])
            f.write(utterance + '\n')
        pickle.dump(utterance_dict, open('data/utterance_dict', 'wb'), True)
```

The data is parsed and can be utilized in further steps.

Data reader

The data reader script helps to generate trainable batches from the preprocessed training text from the data parser script. Let's start by importing the required methods:

```
import pickle
import random
```

This helper module helps generate trainable batches from the preprocessed training text.

```
class Data_Reader:
    def __init__(self, cur_train_index=0, load_list=False):
        self.training_data =
pickle.load(open('data/conversations_lenmax22_formersents2_with_former',
'rb'))
        self.data_size = len(self.training_data)
        if load_list:
            self.shuffle_list = pickle.load(open('data/shuffle_index_list',
'rb'))
        else:
            self.shuffle_list = self.shuffle_index()
        self.train_index = cur_train_index
```

The following code gets the batch number from the data:

```
    def get_batch_num(self, batch_size):
        return self.data_size // batch_size
```

The following code shuffles the index from the data:

```
    def shuffle_index(self):
        shuffle_index_list = random.sample(range(self.data_size),
self.data_size)
        pickle.dump(shuffle_index_list, open('data/shuffle_index_list',
'wb'), True)
        return shuffle_index_list
```

The following code generates the batch indices, based on the batch number that was obtained earlier:

```
    def generate_batch_index(self, batch_size):
        if self.train_index + batch_size > self.data_size:
            batch_index =
self.shuffle_list[self.train_index:self.data_size]
            self.shuffle_list = self.shuffle_index()
            remain_size = batch_size - (self.data_size - self.train_index)
            batch_index += self.shuffle_list[:remain_size]
            self.train_index = remain_size
```

```
        else:
            batch_index =
    self.shuffle_list[self.train_index:self.train_index+batch_size]
            self.train_index += batch_size

        return batch_index
```

The following code generates the training batch:

```
    def generate_training_batch(self, batch_size):
        batch_index = self.generate_batch_index(batch_size)
        batch_X = [self.training_data[i][0] for i in batch_index]    #
batch_size of conv_a
        batch_Y = [self.training_data[i][1] for i in batch_index]    #
batch_size of conv_b

        return batch_X, batch_Y
```

The following function generates training batch with the former.

```
    def generate_training_batch_with_former(self, batch_size):
        batch_index = self.generate_batch_index(batch_size)
        batch_X = [self.training_data[i][0] for i in batch_index]    #
batch_size of conv_a
        batch_Y = [self.training_data[i][1] for i in batch_index]    #
batch_size of conv_b
        former = [self.training_data[i][2] for i in batch_index]    #
batch_size of former utterance

        return batch_X, batch_Y, former
```

The following code generates the testing batch:

```
    def generate_testing_batch(self, batch_size):
        batch_index = self.generate_batch_index(batch_size)
        batch_X = [self.training_data[i][0] for i in batch_index]    #
batch_size of conv_a

        return batch_X
```

This concludes the data reading part.

Helper methods

This script consists of a `Seq2seq` dialogue generator model, which is used for the reverse model of the backward entropy loss. This will determine the semantic coherence reward for the policy gradients dialogue. Essentially, this script will help us to represent our future reward function. The script will achieve this via the following actions:

- Encoding
- Decoding
- Generating builds

All of the preceding actions are based on **long short-term memory** (**LSTM**) units.

The feature extractor script helps with the extraction of features and characteristics from the data, in order to help us train it better. Let us start by importing the required modules.

```
import tensorflow as tf
import numpy as np
import re
```

Next, define the model inputs. If reinforcement learning is set to True, a scalar is computed based on semantic coherence and ease of answering loss caption.

```
def model_inputs(embed_dim, reinforcement= False):
    word_vectors = tf.placeholder(tf.float32, [None, None, embed_dim], name
= "word_vectors")
    reward = tf.placeholder(tf.float32, shape = (), name = "rewards")
    caption = tf.placeholder(tf.int32, [None, None], name = "captions")
    caption_mask = tf.placeholder(tf.float32, [None, None], name =
"caption_masks")
    if reinforcement: #Normal training returns only the word_vectors,
caption and caption_mask placeholders,
        #With reinforcement learning, there is an extra placeholder for
rewards
        return word_vectors, caption, caption_mask, reward
    else:
        return word_vectors, caption, caption_mask
```

Next, define the encoding layers which perform encoding for the sequence to sequence network. The input sequence is passed into the encoder and returns the output of RNN output and the state.

```
def encoding_layer(word_vectors, lstm_size, num_layers, keep_prob,
                   vocab_size):
    cells =
tf.contrib.rnn.MultiRNNCell([tf.contrib.rnn.DropoutWrapper(tf.contrib.rnn.L
```

```
STMCell(lstm_size), keep_prob) for _ in range(num_layers)])
    outputs, state = tf.nn.dynamic_rnn(cells,
                                       word_vectors,
                                       dtype=tf.float32)
    return outputs, state
```

Next, define the training process for decoder using LSTMS cells with the encoder state together with the decoder inputs.

```
def decode_train(enc_state, dec_cell, dec_input,
                 target_sequence_length,output_sequence_length,
                 output_layer, keep_prob):
    dec_cell = tf.contrib.rnn.DropoutWrapper(dec_cell,
#Apply dropout to the LSTM cell
                                             output_keep_prob=keep_prob)
    helper = tf.contrib.seq2seq.TrainingHelper(dec_input,
#Training helper for decoder
                                               target_sequence_length)
    decoder = tf.contrib.seq2seq.BasicDecoder(dec_cell,
                                              helper,
                                              enc_state,
                                              output_layer)

    # unrolling the decoder layer
    outputs, _, _ = tf.contrib.seq2seq.dynamic_decode(decoder,
                                                      impute_finished=True,
maximum_iterations=output_sequence_length)
    return outputs
```

Next, define an inference decoder similar to the one used for the training. Makes use of a greedy helper which feeds the last output of the decoder as the next decoder input. The output returned contains the training logits and the sample id.

```
def decode_generate(encoder_state, dec_cell, dec_embeddings,
                    target_sequence_length,output_sequence_length,
                    vocab_size, output_layer, batch_size, keep_prob):
    dec_cell = tf.contrib.rnn.DropoutWrapper(dec_cell,
                                             output_keep_prob=keep_prob)
    helper = tf.contrib.seq2seq.GreedyEmbeddingHelper(dec_embeddings,
                                                      tf.fill([batch_size],
1),  #Decoder helper for inference
                                                               2)
    decoder = tf.contrib.seq2seq.BasicDecoder(dec_cell,
                                              helper,
                                              encoder_state,
                                              output_layer)
    outputs, _, _ = tf.contrib.seq2seq.dynamic_decode(decoder,
                                                      impute_finished=True,
```

```
maximum_iterations=output_sequence_length)
    return outputs
```

Next, create a decoding layer.

```
def decoding_layer(dec_input, enc_state,
                   target_sequence_length,output_sequence_length,
                   lstm_size,
                   num_layers,n_words,
                   batch_size, keep_prob,embedding_size, Train = True):
    target_vocab_size = n_words
    with tf.device("/cpu:0"):
        dec_embeddings =
tf.Variable(tf.random_uniform([target_vocab_size,embedding_size], -0.1,
0.1), name='Wemb')
    dec_embed_input = tf.nn.embedding_lookup(dec_embeddings, dec_input)
    cells = tf.contrib.rnn.MultiRNNCell([tf.contrib.rnn.LSTMCell(lstm_size)
for _ in range(num_layers)])
    with tf.variable_scope("decode"):
        output_layer = tf.layers.Dense(target_vocab_size)
    if Train:
        with tf.variable_scope("decode"):
            train_output = decode_train(enc_state,
                                              cells,
                                              dec_embed_input,
                                              target_sequence_length,
output_sequence_length,
                                              output_layer,
                                              keep_prob)

    with tf.variable_scope("decode", reuse=tf.AUTO_REUSE):
        infer_output = decode_generate(enc_state,
                                              cells,
                                              dec_embeddings,
target_sequence_length,
                                              output_sequence_length,
                                              target_vocab_size,
                                              output_layer,
                                              batch_size,
                                              keep_prob)

    if Train:
        return train_output, infer_output
    return infer_output
```

Next, create the bos inclusion which appends the index corresponding to <bos> referring to the beginning of a sentence to the first index of the caption tensor for every batch.

```
def bos_inclusion(caption,batch_size):

    sliced_target = tf.strided_slice(caption, [0,0], [batch_size, -1],
[1,1])
    concat = tf.concat([tf.fill([batch_size, 1],1), sliced_target],1)
    return concat
```

Next, define pad sequences which creates an array of size maxlen from every question by padding with zeros or truncating where necessary.

```
def pad_sequences(questions, sequence_length =22):
    lengths = [len(x) for x in questions]
    num_samples = len(questions)
    x = np.zeros((num_samples, sequence_length)).astype(int)
    for idx, sequence in enumerate(questions):
        if not len(sequence):
            continue  # empty list/array was found
        truncated  = sequence[-sequence_length:]

        truncated = np.asarray(truncated, dtype=int)

        x[idx, :len(truncated)] = truncated
    return x
```

Ignore non-vocabulary parts if the data and take only all alphabets.

```
def refine(data):
    words = re.findall("[a-zA-Z'-]+", data)
    words = ["".join(word.split("'")) for word in words]
    data = ' '.join(words)
    return data
```

Next, create batches to be fed into the network from in word vector representation.

```
def make_batch_input(batch_input, input_sequence_length, embed_dims,
word2vec):
    for i in range(len(batch_input)):
        batch_input[i] = [word2vec[w] if w in word2vec else
np.zeros(embed_dims) for w in batch_input[i]]
        if len(batch_input[i]) >input_sequence_length:
            batch_input[i] = batch_input[i][:input_sequence_length]
        else:
            for _ in range(input_sequence_length - len(batch_input[i])):
                batch_input[i].append(np.zeros(embed_dims))
```

```
        return np.array(batch_input)

def replace(target,symbols):   #Remove symbols from sequence
    for symbol in symbols:
        target = list(map(lambda x: x.replace(symbol,''),target))
    return target
def make_batch_target(batch_target, word_to_index, target_sequence_length):
    target = batch_target
    target = list(map(lambda x: '<bos> ' + x, target))
    symbols = ['.', ',', '"', '\n','?','!','\\','/']
    target = replace(target, symbols)

    for idx, each_cap in enumerate(target):
        word = each_cap.lower().split(' ')
        if len(word) < target_sequence_length:
            target[idx] = target[idx] + ' <eos>'   #Append the end of symbol
symbol
        else:
            new_word = ''
            for i in range(target_sequence_length-1):
                new_word = new_word + word[i] + ' '
            target[idx] = new_word + '<eos>'
    target_index = [[word_to_index[word] if word in word_to_index else
word_to_index['<unk>'] for word in
                        sequence.lower().split(' ')] for sequence in
target]
    #print(target_index[0])
    caption_matrix = pad_sequences(target_index,target_sequence_length)
    caption_matrix = np.hstack([caption_matrix,
np.zeros([len(caption_matrix), 1])]).astype(int)
    caption_masks = np.zeros((caption_matrix.shape[0],
caption_matrix.shape[1]))
    nonzeros = np.array(list(map(lambda x: (x != 0).sum(),
caption_matrix)))
    #print(nonzeros)
    #print(caption_matrix[1])
    for ind, row in enumerate(caption_masks): #Set the masks as an array of
ones where actual words exist and zeros otherwise
        row[:nonzeros[ind]] = 1
        #print(row)
    print(caption_masks[0])
    print(caption_matrix[0])
    return caption_matrix,caption_masks

def generic_batch(generic_responses, batch_size, word_to_index,
target_sequence_length):
    size = len(generic_responses)
    if size > batch_size:
```

```
        generic_responses = generic_responses[:batch_size]
    else:
        for j in range(batch_size - size):
            generic_responses.append('')
    return make_batch_Y(generic_responses, word_to_index,
target_sequence_length)
```

Next, generate sentences from the predicted indices. Replace <unk>, <pad> with the word with the next highest probability whenever predicted.

```
def index2sentence(generated_word_index, prob_logit, ixtoword):
    generated_word_index = list(generated_word_index)
    for i in range(len(generated_word_index)):
        if generated_word_index[i] == 3 or generated_word_index[i] == 0:
            sort_prob_logit = sorted(prob_logit[i])
            curindex = np.where(prob_logit[i] == sort_prob_logit[-2])[0][0]
            count = 1
            while curindex <= 3:
                curindex = np.where(prob_logit[i] == sort_prob_logit[(-2)-
count])[0][0]
                count += 1

            generated_word_index[i] = curindex

    generated_words = []
    for ind in generated_word_index:
        generated_words.append(ixtoword[ind])
    generated_sentence = ' '.join(generated_words)
    generated_sentence = generated_sentence.replace('<bos> ', '')   #Replace
the beginning of sentence tag
    generated_sentence = generated_sentence.replace('<eos>', '')    #Replace
the end of sentence tag
    generated_sentence = generated_sentence.replace('--', '')       #Replace
the other symbols predicted
    generated_sentence = generated_sentence.split('  ')
    for i in range(len(generated_sentence)):        #Begin sentences with
Upper case
        generated_sentence[i] = generated_sentence[i].strip()
        if len(generated_sentence[i]) > 1:
            generated_sentence[i] = generated_sentence[i][0].upper() +
generated_sentence[i][1:] + '.'
        else:
            generated_sentence[i] = generated_sentence[i].upper()
    generated_sentence = ' '.join(generated_sentence)
    generated_sentence = generated_sentence.replace(' i ', ' I ')
    generated_sentence = generated_sentence.replace("i'm", "I'm")
    generated_sentence = generated_sentence.replace("i'd", "I'd")
```

```
    return generated_sentence
```

This concludes all the helper functions.

Chatbot model

The following script contains the policy gradient model, which will be used where it combines reinforcement learning rewards with the cross-entropy loss. The dependencies include `numpy` and `tensorflow`. Our policy gradient is based on an LSTM encoder-decoder. We will use a stochastic demonstration of our policy gradient, which will be a probability distribution of actions over specified states. The script represents all of these, and specifies the policy gradient loss to be minimized.

Run the output of the first cell through the second cell; the input is concatenated with zeros. The final state for the responses mostly consists of two components—the latent representation of the input by the encoder, and the state of the decoder, based on the selected words. The return includes placeholder tensors and other tensors, such as losses and training optimization operation. Let's start by importing the required libraries.

```
import tensorflow as tf
import numpy as np
import helper as h
```

We will create a chatbot class to create the model.

```
class Chatbot():
    def __init__(self, embed_dim, vocab_size, lstm_size, batch_size,
input_sequence_length, target_sequence_length, learning_rate =0.0001,
keep_prob = 0.5, num_layers = 1, policy_gradients = False, Training =
True):
        self.embed_dim = embed_dim
        self.lstm_size = lstm_size
        self.batch_size = batch_size
        self.vocab_size = vocab_size
        self.input_sequence_length =
tf.fill([self.batch_size],input_sequence_length+1)
        self.target_sequence_length =
tf.fill([self.batch_size],target_sequence_length+1)
        self.output_sequence_length = target_sequence_length +1
        self.learning_rate = learning_rate
        self.keep_prob = keep_prob
        self.num_layers = num_layers
        self.policy_gradients = policy_gradients
        self.Training = Training
```

Next, create a method that builds the model. If policy gradients are requested, then get the input accordingly.

```
def build_model(self):
    if self.policy_gradients:
        word_vectors, caption, caption_mask, rewards =
h.model_inputs(self.embed_dim, True)
        place_holders = {'word_vectors': word_vectors,
            'caption': caption,
            'caption_mask': caption_mask, "rewards": rewards
                }
    else:
        word_vectors, caption, caption_mask =
h.model_inputs(self.embed_dim)
        place_holders = {'word_vectors': word_vectors,
            'caption': caption,
            'caption_mask': caption_mask}
    enc_output, enc_state = h.encoding_layer(word_vectors,
self.lstm_size, self.num_layers,
                                self.keep_prob, self.vocab_size)
    #dec_inp = h.bos_inclusion(caption, self.batch_size)
    dec_inp = caption
```

Next, get the inference layer.

```
    if not self.Training:
        print("Test mode")
        inference_out = h.decoding_layer(dec_inp,
enc_state,self.target_sequence_length,
self.output_sequence_length,
                                    self.lstm_size,
self.num_layers,
                                    self.vocab_size,
self.batch_size,
                                    self.keep_prob,
self.embed_dim, False)
        logits = tf.identity(inference_out.rnn_output, name =
"train_logits")
        predictions = tf.identity(inference_out.sample_id, name =
"predictions")
        return place_holders, predictions, logits
```

Next, get the loss layers.

```
    train_out, inference_out = h.decoding_layer(dec_inp,
enc_state,self.target_sequence_length,
self.output_sequence_length,
                                    self.lstm_size,
```

```
        self.num_layers,
                                                  self.vocab_size,
        self.batch_size,
                                                  self.keep_prob,
        self.embed_dim)
        training_logits = tf.identity(train_out.rnn_output, name =
"train_logits")
        prediction_logits = tf.identity(inference_out.sample_id, name =
"predictions")
        cross_entropy = tf.contrib.seq2seq.sequence_loss(training_logits,
caption, caption_mask)
        losses = {"entropy": cross_entropy}
```

Depending on the state of the policy gradient, either minimize cross entropy loss or policy gradient loss.

```
        if self.policy_gradients:
            pg_loss = tf.contrib.seq2seq.sequence_loss(training_logits,
caption, caption_mask*rewards)
            with tf.variable_scope(tf.get_variable_scope(), reuse=False):
                optimizer =
tf.train.AdamOptimizer(self.learning_rate).minimize(pg_loss)
            losses.update({"pg":pg_loss})
        else:
            with tf.variable_scope(tf.get_variable_scope(), reuse=False):
                optimizer =
tf.train.AdamOptimizer(self.learning_rate).minimize(cross_entropy)
        return optimizer, place_holders,prediction_logits,training_logits,
losses
```

Now we have all the methods that are required for training.

Training the data

The scripts that were written previously were combined with training the dataset. Let's start the training by importing all the modules that are developed in the previous sections as shown here:

```
from data_reader import Data_Reader
import data_parser
from gensim.models import KeyedVectors
import helper as h
from seq_model import Chatbot
import tensorflow as tf
import numpy as np
```

Next, let's create a set of generic responses observed in the original `seq2seq` model which the policy gradients are trained to avoid:

```
generic_responses = [
    "I don't know what you're talking about.",
    "I don't know.",
    "You don't know.",
    "You know what I mean.",
    "I know what you mean.",
    "You know what I'm saying.",
    "You don't know anything."
]
```

Next, we will define all the constants that are required for the training. Tha

```
checkpoint = True
forward_model_path = 'model/forward'
reversed_model_path = 'model/reversed'
rl_model_path = "model/rl"
model_name = 'seq2seq'
word_count_threshold = 20
reversed_word_count_threshold = 6
dim_wordvec = 300
dim_hidden = 1000
input_sequence_length = 22
output_sequence_length = 22
learning_rate = 0.0001
epochs = 1
batch_size = 200
forward_ = "forward"
reverse_ = "reverse"
forward_epochs = 50
reverse_epochs = 50
display_interval = 100
```

Next, define the training function. Based on the type, either the forward or reverse sequence to sequence model is loaded. The data is also read in reverse model based on the model as shown here:

```
def train(type_, epochs=epochs, checkpoint=False):
    tf.reset_default_graph()
    if type_ == "forward":
        path = "model/forward/seq2seq"
        dr = Data_Reader(reverse=False)
    else:
        dr = Data_Reader(reverse=True)
        path = "model/reverse/seq2seq"
```

Next, create the vocabulary as shown here:

```
    word_to_index, index_to_word, _ =
data_parser.preProBuildWordVocab(word_count_threshold=word_count_threshold)
```

The above command print should print the following indicated the vocabulary size that is filtered.

```
preprocessing word counts and creating vocab based on word count threshold
20
filtered words from 76029 to 6847
```

The `word_to_index` variable is filled with the map of filtered words to an integer as shown here:

```
{'': 4,
'deposition': 1769,
'next': 3397,
'dates': 1768,
'chance': 2597,
'slipped': 4340,...
```

The `index_to_word` variable is filled with the map of integer to the filtered works which will work as a reverse lookup.

```
5: 'tastes',
6: 'shower',
7: 'agent',
8: 'lack',
```

Next, load the word to vector model from `gensim` library.

```
    word_vector =
KeyedVectors.load_word2vec_format('model/word_vector.bin', binary=True)
```

Next, instantiate and build the model the Chatbot model with all the constants that were defined. Restore a checkpoint, if present from the previous run or initialize the graph.

```
    model = Chatbot(dim_wordvec, len(word_to_index), dim_hidden,
batch_size,
                    input_sequence_length, output_sequence_length,
learning_rate)
    optimizer, place_holders, predictions, logits, losses =
model.build_model()
    saver = tf.train.Saver()
    sess = tf.InteractiveSession()
    if checkpoint:
        saver.restore(sess, path)
```

```
        print("checkpoint restored at path: {}".format(path))
    else:
        tf.global_variables_initializer().run()
```

Next, start the training by iterating through the epochs and start the batches.

```
    for epoch in range(epochs):
        n_batch = dr.get_batch_num(batch_size=batch_size)
        for batch in range(n_batch):

            batch_input, batch_target =
    dr.generate_training_batch(batch_size)
```

The `batch_input` has the list of words from the training set. The `batch_target` has the list of sentences for the input which will be the target. The list of words is converted to vector form using the helper functions. Make the feed dictionary for the graph using the transformed inputs, masks and targets.

```
            inputs_ = h.make_batch_input(batch_input,
    input_sequence_length, dim_wordvec, word_vector)

            targets, masks = h.make_batch_target(batch_target,
    word_to_index, output_sequence_length)
            feed_dict = {
                place_holders['word_vectors']: inputs_,
                place_holders['caption']: targets,
                place_holders['caption_mask']: masks
            }
```

Next, train the model by calling the optimizer by feeding the training data. Log the loss value at certain intervals to see the progress of the training. Save the model at the end.

```
            _, loss_val, preds = sess.run([optimizer, losses["entropy"],
    predictions],
                                            feed_dict=feed_dict)

            if batch % display_interval == 0:
                print(preds.shape)
                print("Epoch: {}, batch: {}, loss: {}".format(epoch, batch,
    loss_val))
    print("========================================================")

        saver.save(sess, path)

        print("Model saved at {}".format(path))
    print("Training done")

    sess.close()
```

The output should appear as shown here.

```
(200, 23)
Epoch: 0, batch: 0, loss: 8.831538200378418
=============================================================
```

The model is trained for both forward and reverse and the corresponding models are stored. In the next function, the models are restored and trained again to create the chatbot.

```
def pg_train(epochs=epochs, checkpoint=False):
    tf.reset_default_graph()
    path = "model/reinforcement/seq2seq"
    word_to_index, index_to_word, _ =
data_parser.preProBuildWordVocab(word_count_threshold=word_count_threshold)
    word_vector =
KeyedVectors.load_word2vec_format('model/word_vector.bin', binary=True)
    generic_caption, generic_mask = h.generic_batch(generic_responses,
batch_size, word_to_index,
                                        output_sequence_length)

    dr = Data_Reader()
    forward_graph = tf.Graph()
    reverse_graph = tf.Graph()
    default_graph = tf.get_default_graph()
```

Two graphs are created to load the trained models.

```
    with forward_graph.as_default():
        pg_model = Chatbot(dim_wordvec, len(word_to_index), dim_hidden,
batch_size,
                            input_sequence_length, output_sequence_length,
learning_rate, policy_gradients=True)
        optimizer, place_holders, predictions, logits, losses =
pg_model.build_model()

        sess = tf.InteractiveSession()
        saver = tf.train.Saver()
        if checkpoint:
            saver.restore(sess, path)
            print("checkpoint restored at path: {}".format(path))
        else:
            tf.global_variables_initializer().run()
            saver.restore(sess, 'model/forward/seq2seq')
    # tf.global_variables_initializer().run()
    with reverse_graph.as_default():
        model = Chatbot(dim_wordvec, len(word_to_index), dim_hidden,
batch_size,
                            input_sequence_length, output_sequence_length,
```

```
learning_rate)
        _, rev_place_holders, _, _, reverse_loss = model.build_model()
        sess2 = tf.InteractiveSession()
        saver2 = tf.train.Saver()

        saver2.restore(sess2, "model/reverse/seq2seq")
        print("reverse model restored")

    dr = Data_Reader(load_list=True)
```

Next, the data is loaded to train the data in batches.

```
    for epoch in range(epochs):
        n_batch = dr.get_batch_num(batch_size=batch_size)
        for batch in range(n_batch):

            batch_input, batch_caption, prev_utterance =
dr.generate_training_batch_with_former(batch_size)
            targets, masks = h.make_batch_target(batch_caption,
word_to_index, output_sequence_length)
            inputs_ = h.make_batch_input(batch_input,
input_sequence_length, dim_wordvec, word_vector)

            word_indices, probabilities = sess.run([predictions, logits],
feed_dict={place_holders['word_vectors']: inputs_

                                                    ,
place_holders["caption"]: targets})

            sentence = [h.index2sentence(generated_word, probability,
index_to_word) for
                        generated_word, probability in zip(word_indices,
probabilities)]

            word_list = [word.split() for word in sentence]

            generic_test_input = h.make_batch_input(word_list,
input_sequence_length, dim_wordvec, word_vector)

            forward_coherence_target, forward_coherence_masks =
h.make_batch_target(sentence,
word_to_index,
output_sequence_length)

            generic_loss = 0.0
```

Also, learn when to say generic texts as shown here:

```
for response in generic_test_input:
    sentence_input = np.array([response] * batch_size)
    feed_dict = {place_holders['word_vectors']: sentence_input,
                 place_holders['caption']: generic_caption,
                 place_holders['caption_mask']: generic_mask,
                }
    generic_loss_i = sess.run(losses["entropy"],
feed_dict=feed_dict)
    generic_loss -= generic_loss_i / batch_size

# print("generic loss work: {}".format(generic_loss))

feed_dict = {place_holders['word_vectors']: inputs_,
             place_holders['caption']:
forward_coherence_target,
             place_holders['caption_mask']:
forward_coherence_masks,
            }

forward_entropy = sess.run(losses["entropy"],
feed_dict=feed_dict)

previous_utterance, previous_mask =
h.make_batch_target(prev_utterance,
word_to_index, output_sequence_length)

feed_dict = {rev_place_holders['word_vectors']:
generic_test_input,
             rev_place_holders['caption']: previous_utterance,
             rev_place_holders['caption_mask']: previous_mask,
            }
reverse_entropy = sess2.run(reverse_loss["entropy"],
feed_dict=feed_dict)

rewards = 1 / (1 + np.exp(-reverse_entropy - forward_entropy -
generic_loss))

feed_dict = {place_holders['word_vectors']: inputs_,
             place_holders['caption']: targets,
             place_holders['caption_mask']: masks,
             place_holders['rewards']: rewards
            }

_, loss_pg, loss_ent = sess.run([optimizer, losses["pg"],
losses["entropy"]], feed_dict=feed_dict)
```

```
                  if batch % display_interval == 0:
                      print("Epoch: {}, batch: {}, Entropy loss: {}, Policy
      gradient loss: {}".format(epoch, batch, loss_ent,
      loss_pg))

                      print("rewards: {}".format(rewards))
      print("===========================================================")
              saver.save(sess, path)
              print("Model saved at {}".format(path))
          print("Training done")
```

Next, call the functions defined in sequence. First train a forward model, followed by reverse model and policy gradient at the end.

```
      train(forward_, forward_epochs, False)
      train(reverse_, reverse_epochs, False)
      pg_train(100, False)
```

This concludes the training of the chatbot. The model is trained in forward and reverse manner to

Testing and results

After training the model, we tested it against our test dataset and obtained reasonably coherent dialogue. There is one very important issue: the context of the communication. Hence, depending on the dataset that is used, the result will be in its context. For our context, the results that were obtained were very reasonable, and they satisfied our three measures of performance—informativeness (non-repeating turns), high coherence, and simplicity in answering (this is related to the forward-looking function).

```
      import data_parser
      from gensim.models import KeyedVectors
      from seq_model import Chatbot
      import tensorflow as tf
      import numpy as np
      import helper as h
```

Next, declare the paths to the various model that are already trained.

```
      reinforcement_model_path = "model/reinforcement/seq2seq"
      forward_model_path = "model/forward/seq2seq"
      reverse_model_path = "model/reverse/seq2seq"
```

Next, declare the path of the files consisting of questions and responses.

```
path_to_questions = 'results/sample_input.txt'
responses_path = 'results/sample_output_RL.txt'
```

Next, declare the constants required for the model.

```
word_count_threshold = 20
dim_wordvec = 300
dim_hidden = 1000

input_sequence_length = 25
target_sequence_length = 22

batch_size = 2
```

Next, load the data and the model as shown here:

```
def test(model_path=forward_model_path):
    testing_data = open(path_to_questions, 'r').read().split('\n')
    word_vector =
KeyedVectors.load_word2vec_format('model/word_vector.bin', binary=True)

    _, index_to_word, _ =
data_parser.preProBuildWordVocab(word_count_threshold=word_count_threshold)

    model = Chatbot(dim_wordvec, len(index_to_word), dim_hidden,
batch_size,
                            input_sequence_length, target_sequence_length,
Training=False)

    place_holders, predictions, logits = model.build_model()

    sess = tf.InteractiveSession()

    saver = tf.train.Saver()

    saver.restore(sess, model_path)
```

Next, open the responses file and prepare the list of questions as shown here:

```
    with open(responses_path, 'w') as out:

        for idx, question in enumerate(testing_data):
            print('question =>', question)

            question = [h.refine(w) for w in question.lower().split()]
            question = [word_vector[w] if w in word_vector else
np.zeros(dim_wordvec) for w in question]
```

```
            question.insert(0, np.random.normal(size=(dim_wordvec,)))   #
insert random normal at the first step

            if len(question) > input_sequence_length:
                question = question[:input_sequence_length]
            else:
                for _ in range(input_sequence_length - len(question)):
                    question.append(np.zeros(dim_wordvec))

            question = np.array([question])

            feed_dict = {place_holders["word_vectors"]:
np.concatenate([question] * 2, 0),
                        }

            word_indices, prob_logit = sess.run([predictions, logits],
feed_dict=feed_dict)

            # print(word_indices[0].shape)
            generated_sentence = h.index2sentence(word_indices[0],
prob_logit[0], index_to_word)

            print('generated_sentence =>', generated_sentence)
            out.write(generated_sentence + '\n')


test(reinforcement_model_path)
```

By passing the path to the model, we can test the chatbot for various responses.

Summary

Chatbots are taking the world by storm, and are predicted to become more prevalent in the coming years. The coherence of the results obtained from dialogues with these chatbots has to constantly improve if they are to gain widespread acceptance. One way to achieve this would be via the use of reinforcement learning.

In this chapter, we implemented reinforcement learning in the creation of a chatbot. The learning was based on a policy gradient method that focused on the future direction of a dialogue agent, in order to generate coherent and interesting interactions. The datasets that we used were from movie conversations. We proceeded to clean and preprocess the datasets, obtaining the vocabulary from them. We then formulated our policy gradient method. Our reward functions were represented by a sequence to sequence model. We then trained and tested our data and obtained very reasonable results, proving the viability of using reinforcement learning for dialogue agents.

17

Generating a Deep Learning Image Classifier

Over the past decade, deep learning has made a name for itself by producing state-of-the-heart results across computer vision, natural language processing, speech recognition, and many more such applications. Some of the models that human researchers have designed and engineered have also gained popularity, including AlexNet, Inception, VGGNet, ResNet, and DenseNet; some of them are now the go-to standard for their respective tasks. However, it seems that the better the model gets, the more complex the architecture becomes, especially with the introduction of residual connections between convolutional layers. The task of designing a high-performance neural network has thus become a very arduous one. Hence the question arises: is it possible for an algorithm to learn how to generate neural network architectures?

As the title of this chapter suggests, it is indeed possible to train a neural network to generate neural networks that perform well on a given task. In this chapter, we will examine **Neural Architecture Search** (referred to as **NAS** henceforth), a novel framework developed by Barret Zoph and Quoc V. Le from the Google Brain team that uses deep reinforcement learning to train a Controller to produce child networks that learn to accomplish tasks. We will learn how policy gradient methods (REINFORCE in particular) can train such a Controller. We will then implement a Controller that uses NAS to generate child networks that train on CIFAR-10 data.

In this chapter, we will cover the following:

- Understanding NAS and how it learns to generate other neural networks
- Implementing a simple NAS framework that generates neural networks for training on CIFAR-10 data

You can find the original sources of the ensuing topics from the following sources:

1. Zoph, B., and Le, Q. V. (2016). *Neural Architecture Search with reinforcement learning.* arXiv preprint arXiv:1611.01578.
2. Pham, H., Guan, M. Y., Zoph, B., Le, Q. V., and Dean, J. (2018). *Efficient Neural Architecture Search via Parameter Sharing.* arXiv preprint arXiv:1802.03268.

Neural Architecture Search

The next few sections will describe the NAS framework. You will learn about how the framework learns to generate other neural networks to complete tasks using a popular reinforcement learning scheme called **REINFORCE**, which is a type of policy gradient algorithm.

Generating and training child networks

Research on algorithms that generate neural architectures has been around since the 1970's. What sets NAS apart from previous works is its ability to cater to large-scale deep learning algorithms and its formulation of the task as a reinforcement learning problem. More specifically, the agent, which we will refer to as the Controller, is a recurrent neural network that generates a sequence of values. You can think of these values as a sort of genetic code of the child network that defines its architecture; it sets the sizes of each convolutional kernel, the length of each kernel, the number of filters in each layer, and so on. In more advanced frameworks, the values also determine the connections between layers to generate residual layers:

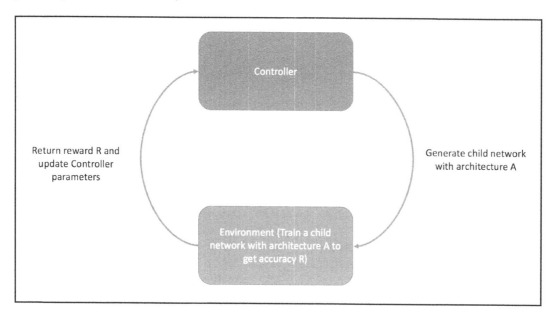

Figure 1: Overview of the NAS framework

Moreover, each value of the genetic code that the Controller outputs counts as an action, a, that is sampled with probability, p. Because the Controller is a recurrent neural network, we can represent the tth action as $p(a_t | a_{t-1})$. Once we have a list of $\quad A = a_1, a_2, \ldots, a_T$ actions, —where T is some predefined parameter that sets the maximum size of the genetic code—we can generate the child network with the specified architecture, A:

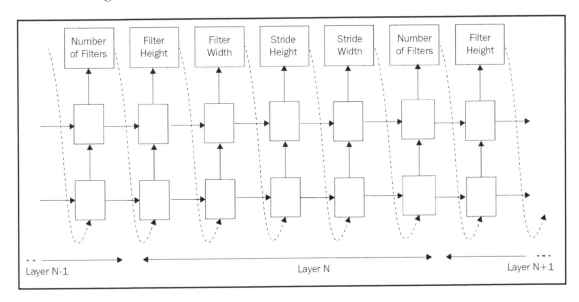

Figure 2: The architecture of the Controller

Once the Controller generates a child network, we train it on a given task until either some termination criteria is met (for example, after a specified number of epochs). We then evaluate the child network on the validation set to produce some validation accuracy, R. The validation accuracy acts as the reward signal for the Controller. So, the objective of the Controller is to maximize the expected reward:

$$J(\theta_c) = E_A[R]$$

Here, J is the reward function (also referred to as the fit function), θ_c is the parameters of the Controller, and the right-hand side of the equation is the expectation of the reward given a child network architecture, A. In practice, this expectation is calculated by averaging the rewards over m child network models that the Controller produces in one batch:

$$J(\theta_c) = \frac{1}{m} \sum_{k=1}^{m} R_k$$

Training the Controller

How do we use this reward signal to update the Controller? Remember, this reward signal is not differentiable like a loss function in supervised learning; we may not backpropagate this through the Controller on its own. Instead, we employ a policy gradient method called **REINFORCE** to iteratively update the Controller parameters, θ_c. In REINFORCE, the gradient of the reward function, J, with respect to the parameters of the Controller, θ_c, is defined as follows:

$$\nabla_{\theta_c} J(\theta_c) = \frac{1}{m} \sum_{k=1}^{m} \sum_{t=1}^{T} \nabla_{\theta_c} \log P(a_t | a_{(t-1):1}; \theta_c) R_k$$

You may recall seeing a similar expression in `Chapter 15`, *Learning to Play Go*. Indeed, this is the policy gradient method that AlphaGo and AlphaGo Zero use to update the weights of their reinforcement learning policy networks. We briefly introduced the method then, but we will go a bit more in-depth here.

Let's break the preceding equation down. On the right-hand side, we would like to represent the probability of choosing some architecture, A. In particular, $P(a_t | a_{(t-1):1}; \theta_c)$ represents the probability that the Controller takes action a_t given all the previous actions, $a_{(t-1):1}$, and the parameters of the Controller, θ_c. Again, action a_t corresponds to the tth value in the genetic sequence that represents the child network's architecture. The joint probability of choosing all actions, $a_1, a_2, \cdots, a_T$, can be formulated as follows:

$$P(A) = P(a_1; \theta_c) \prod_{t=2}^{T} P(a_t | a_{(t-1):1}; \theta_c)$$

By transforming this joint probability to the log space, we can turn the product into a sum of probabilities:

$$\log P(A) = \sum_{t=1}^{T} \log P(a_t | a_{(t-1):1}; \theta_c)$$

In general, we want to maximize this log conditional probability for taking some action. In other words, we want to increase the likelihood of the Controller generating a particular sequence of genetic codes. Hence we perform gradient ascent on this objective with respect to the Controller's parameters by taking the derivative of the log probability of sampling architecture A:

$$\nabla_{\theta_c} \log P(A) = \sum_{t=1}^{T} \nabla_{\theta_c} \log P(a_t | a_{(t-1):1}; \theta_c)$$

But how do we update the Controller parameters so that better architectures are generated? This is where we make use of the reward signal, R. By multiplying the preceding with the reward signal, we can control the size of the policy gradient. In other words, if a particular architecture achieved high validation accuracy (with the highest possible being 1.0), the gradients for that policy will be relatively strong and the Controller will learn to produce similar architectures. On the other hand, smaller validation accuracies will mean smaller gradients, which helps the Controller ignore those architectures.

One problem with the REINFORCE algorithm is that the reward signal R can have high variance, which can lead to unstable training curves. To reduce the variance, it is common to subtract the reward with some value, b, which we refer to as the baseline function. In Zoph et al., the baseline function is defined as the exponential moving average of the past rewards. Hence our REINFORCE policy gradient is now defined as follows:

$$\nabla_{\theta_c} J(\theta_c) = \frac{1}{m} \sum_{k=1}^{m} \sum_{t=1}^{T} \nabla_{\theta_c} \log P(a_t | a_{(t-1):1}; \theta_c)(R_k - b)$$

Once we have this gradient, we apply the usual backpropagation algorithm to update the Controller parameters, θ_c.

Training algorithm

The training steps for the Controller is as follows:

- For each episode, do the following:
  1. Generate m child network architectures
  2. Train child networks on given task and obtain m validation accuracies
  3. Calculate $\nabla_{\theta_c} J(\theta_c)$
  4. Update θ_c

In Zoph et al., the training procedure is done with several copies of the Controller. Each Controller is parameterized by θ_c, which itself is stored in a distributed manner among multiple servers, which we call parameter servers.

In each episode of training, the Controller creates several child architectures and trains them independently. The policy gradient calculated as a result is then sent to the parameter servers to update the Controller's parameters:

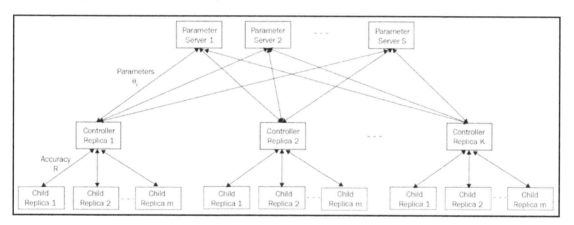

Figure 3: The training architecture

The Controller's parameters are shared among a number of parameter servers. Moreover, multiple copies of the Controller are trained in parallel, each one calculating rewards and gradients for its respective batches of child network architectures.

This architecture allows the Controller to be trained quickly given enough resources. For our purposes, however, we will stick to one Controller that generates m child network architectures. Once we have trained the Controller for a specified number of episodes, we calculate the test accuracy by choosing the child network architecture that had the best validation accuracy and measuring its performance on the test set.

Implementing NAS

In this section, we will implement NAS. In particular, our Controller is tasked with generating child network architectures that learn to classify images from the CIFAR-10 dataset. The architecture of the child network will be represented by a list of numbers. Every four values in this list represent a convolutional layer in the child network, each describing the kernel size, stride length, number of filters, and the pooling window size in the subsequent pooling layer. Moreover, we specify the number of layers in a child network as a hyper-parameters. For example, if our child network has three layers, its architecture is represented as a vector of length 12. If we have an architecture represented as [3, 1, 12, 2, 5, 1, 24, 2], then the child network is a two-layer network where the first layer has kernel size of 3, stride length of 1, 12 filters, and a max-pooling window size of 2, and the second layer has kernel size of 5, stride length of 1, 24 filters, and max-pooling window size of 2. We set the activation function between each layer as ReLU. The final layer involves flattening the last convolutional layer output and applying a linear layer with the number of classes as its width, followed by a Softmax activation. The following sections will walk you through the implementation.

child_network.py

We will first implement our child network module. This module contains a class called ChildCNN, which constructs a child network given some architecture configuration, which we call cnn_dna. As mentioned previously, cnn_dna is simply a list of numbers, with each value representing a parameter of its respective convolutional layer. In our config.py, we specify the max number of layers a child network can have. For our implementation, each convolutional layer is represented by four parameters, where each corresponds to the kernel size, stride length, number of filters, and subsequent max-pooling window size.

Our ChildCNN is a class that takes the following parameters in its constructor:

- cnn_dna: The network architecture
- child_id: A string that simply identifies the child network architecture
- beta: Weight parameter for L2 regularization
- drop_rate: Dropout rate

```
import logging

import tensorflow as tf
```

```
logger = logging.getLogger(__name__)

class ChildCNN(object):

    def __init__(self, cnn_dna, child_id, beta=1e-4, drop_rate=0.2,
**kwargs):
        self.cnn_dna = self.process_raw_controller_output(cnn_dna)
        self.child_id = child_id
        self.beta = beta
        self.drop_rate = drop_rate
        self.is_training = tf.placeholder_with_default(True, shape=None,
name="is_training_{}".format(self.child_id))
        self.num_classes = 10
```

We also implement a helper function called `proces_raw_controller_output()`, which
parses `cnn_dna` that the Controller outputs:

```
def process_raw_controller_output(self, output):
    """
    A helper function for preprocessing the output of the NASCell
    Args:
        output (numpy.ndarray) The output of the NASCell

    Returns:
        (list) The child network's architecture
    """
    output = output.ravel()
    cnn_dna = [list(output[x:x+4]) for x in range(0, len(output), 4)]
    return cnn_dna
```

Finally, we include the `build` method, which builds our child network using the
given `cnn_dna`. You will notice that, although we are letting the Controller decide the
architecture of our child network, we are still hardcoding several things, such as the
activation function, `tf.nn.relu`, and the way we initialize the kernels. The fact that we are
adding a max-pooling layer after each convolutional layer is also hardcoded. A more
sophisticated NAS framework would also let the Controller decide these components of the
architecture as well, with the trade off being longer training time:

```
def build(self, input_tensor):
    """
    Method for creating the child neural network
    Args:
        input_tensor: The tensor which represents the input

    Returns:
        The tensor which represents the output logit (pre-softmax
activation)
```

```
    """
    logger.info("DNA is: {}".format(self.cnn_dna))
    output = input_tensor
    for idx in range(len(self.cnn_dna)):
        # Get the configuration for the layer
        kernel_size, stride, num_filters, max_pool_size = self.cnn_dna[idx]
        with tf.name_scope("child_{}_conv_layer_{}".format(self.child_id,
idx)):
            output = tf.layers.conv2d(output,
                    # Specify the number of filters the convolutional layer
will output
                    filters=num_filters,
                    # This specifies the size (height, width) of the
convolutional kernel
                    kernel_size=(kernel_size, kernel_size),
                    # The size of the stride of the kernel
                    strides=(stride, stride),
                    # We add padding to the image
                    padding="SAME",
                    # It is good practice to name your layers
                    name="conv_layer_{}".format(idx),
                    activation=tf.nn.relu,
kernel_initializer=tf.contrib.layers.xavier_initializer(),
                    bias_initializer=tf.zeros_initializer(),
kernel_regularizer=tf.contrib.layers.l2_regularizer(scale=self.beta))
```

Each convolutional layer is followed by a max-pooling layer and a dropout layer:

```
            # We apply 2D max pooling on the output of the conv layer
            output = tf.layers.max_pooling2d(
                output, pool_size=(max_pool_size, max_pool_size),
strides=1,
                padding="SAME", name="pool_out_{}".format(idx)
            )
            # Dropout to regularize the network further
            output = tf.layers.dropout(output, rate=self.drop_rate,
training=self.is_training)
```

Finally, after several blocks of convolutional, pooling, and dropout layers, we flatten the output volume and a fully connected layer:

```
    # Lastly, we flatten the outputs and add a fully-connected layer
    with tf.name_scope("child_{}_fully_connected".format(self.child_id)):
        output = tf.layers.flatten(output, name="flatten")
        logits = tf.layers.dense(output, self.num_classes)

    return logits
```

The argument to our `build` method is an input tensor, which has by default a shape of (32, 32, 3), which is the `CIFAR-10` data shape. The reader is free to tweak the architecture of this network, including adding a few more fully connected layers or inserting batch normalization layers in between convolutions.

cifar10_processor.py

This module contains code for processing `CIFAR-10` data, which we use to train our child networks. In particular, we construct an input data pipeline using TensorFlow's native `tf.data.Dataset` API. Those who have used TensorFlow for some time may be more familiar with creating `tf.placeholder` tensors and feeding data via `sess.run(..., feed_dict={...})`. However, this is no longer the preferred way of feeding data into the network; in fact, it is the slowest way to train a network, for the repetitive conversions from data in `numpy` format to a native TensorFlow format cause significant computational overhead. `tf.data.Dataset` alleviates this problem by turning the input pipeline into TensorFlow operations that are part of the symbolic graph. In other words, the data is converted into tensors right from the get-go. This allows for a much smoother input pipeline that can speed up training.

Refer to this official tutorial (`https://www.tensorflow.org/guide/datasets_for_estimators`) for more information on the `tf.data.Dataset` API.

The `cifar10_processor.py` contains a single method to create `CIFAR-10` data into tensors. We first implement a helper function for creating a `tf.data.Dataset` object:

```
import logging

import numpy as np
import tensorflow as tf
from keras.datasets import cifar10
from keras.utils import np_utils

logger = logging.getLogger(__name__)

def _create_tf_dataset(x, y, batch_size):
    return tf.data.Dataset.zip((tf.data.Dataset.from_tensor_slices(x),
tf.data.Dataset.from_tensor_slices(y))).shuffle(500).repeat().batch(batch_s
ize)
```

In the main data processor function, we first load `CIFAR-10` data. We use the `keras.datasets` API to do this (run `pip install keras` in your Terminal if you don't have Keras):

```
def get_tf_datasets_from_numpy(batch_size, validation_split=0.1):
    """
    Main function getting tf.Data.datasets for training, validation, and
testing

    Args:
        batch_size (int): Batch size
        validation_split (float): Split for partitioning training and
validation sets. Between 0.0 and 1.0.
    """
    # Load data from keras datasets api
    (X, y), (X_test, y_test) = cifar10.load_data()

    logger.info("Dividing pixels by 255")
    X = X / 255.
    X_test = X_test / 255.

    X = X.astype(np.float32)
    X_test = X_test.astype(np.float32)
    y = y.astype(np.float32)
    y_test = y_test.astype(np.float32)

    # Turn labels into onehot encodings
    if y.shape[1] != 10:
        y = np_utils.to_categorical(y, num_classes=10)
        y_test = np_utils.to_categorical(y_test, num_classes=10)

    logger.info("Loaded data from keras")

    split_idx = int((1.0 - validation_split) * len(X))
    X_train, y_train = X[:split_idx], y[:split_idx]
    X_valid, y_valid = X[split_idx:], y[split_idx:]
```

We then turn these NumPy arrays into TensorFlow tensors, which we can feed directly to our network. What actually happens in our `_create_tf_dataset` helper function? We use the `tf.dataset.Dataset.from_tensor_slices()` function to turn the data and the labels, both of which are NumPy arrays, into TensorFlow tensors. We then create the native dataset by zipping these tensors. The `shuffle`, `repeat`, and `batch` functions after zipping the data and labels define how we want the input pipeline to work. In our case, we are shuffling the input data, repeating the dataset once we reach the end, and batching the data with a given batch size. We also calculate the number of batches that each dataset has and return them:

```
train_dataset = _create_tf_dataset(X_train, y_train, batch_size)
valid_dataset = _create_tf_dataset(X_valid, y_valid, batch_size)
test_dataset = _create_tf_dataset(X_test, y_test, batch_size)

# Get the batch sizes for the train, valid, and test datasets
num_train_batches = int(X_train.shape[0] // batch_size)
num_valid_batches = int(X_valid.shape[0] // batch_size)
num_test_batches = int(X_test.shape[0] // batch_size)

return train_dataset, valid_dataset, test_dataset, num_train_batches,
num_valid_batches, num_test_batches
```

And with that, we have an optimized input data pipeline that is much faster than using `feed_dict`.

controller.py

The `controller.py` module is where everything comes together. We will implement the Controller, which handles training each child network as well as its own parameter updates. We first implement a helper function that calculates an exponential moving average of a list of numbers. We use this as the baseline function for our REINFORCE gradient calculation, as mentioned previously, to calculate the exponential moving average of the past rewards:

```
import logging

import numpy as np
import tensorflow as tf

from child_network import ChildCNN
from cifar10_processor import get_tf_datasets_from_numpy
from config import child_network_params, controller_params

logger = logging.getLogger(__name__)
```

```
def ema(values):
    """
    Helper function for keeping track of an exponential moving average of a
list of values.
    For this module, we use it to maintain an exponential moving average of
rewards
    Args:
        values (list): A list of rewards

    Returns:
        (float) The last value of the exponential moving average
    """
    weights = np.exp(np.linspace(-1., 0., len(values)))
    weights /= weights.sum()
    a = np.convolve(values, weights, mode="full")[:len(values)]
    return a[-1]
```

Next, we define our `Controller` class:

```
class Controller(object):

    def __init__(self):
        self.graph = tf.Graph()
        self.sess = tf.Session(graph=self.graph)
        self.num_cell_outputs = controller_params['components_per_layer'] *
controller_params['max_layers']
        self.reward_history = []
        self.architecture_history = []
        self.divison_rate = 100
        with self.graph.as_default():
            self.build_controller()
```

There are several attributes to note: `self.num_cell_outputs` refers to the number of values that our **recurrent neural network (RNN)** should output and corresponds to the length of the child network architecture configuration. `self.reward_history` and `self.ar chitecture_history` are simply buffers that allow us to keep track of rewards and child network architectures that the RNN generated.

Method for generating the Controller

We next implement a method for generating the Controller, which we
call `build_controller`. The first step in constructing our Controller is defining the input
placeholders. We create two of these—one is for the child network DNA, which is fed as
input to the RNN for generating a new child network DNA, and the second is a list for
storing discounted rewards when calculating the gradients for REINFORCE:

```
def build_controller(self):
    logger.info('Building controller network')
    # Build inputs and placeholders
    with tf.name_scope('controller_inputs'):
        # Input to the NASCell
        self.child_network_architectures = tf.placeholder(tf.float32,
[None, self.num_cell_outputs],
name='controller_input')
        # Discounted rewards
        self.discounted_rewards = tf.placeholder(tf.float32, (None, ),
name='discounted_rewards')
```

We then define the output tensors of our RNN (to be implemented here). Note that the
outputs of the RNN are small, in the range of (-1, 1). So, we multiply the output by 10 in
order to create the child network DNA:

```
# Build controller
with tf.name_scope('network_generation'):
    with tf.variable_scope('controller'):
        self.controller_output =
tf.identity(self.network_generator(self.child_network_architectures),
                                        name='policy_scores')
        self.cnn_dna_output = tf.cast(tf.scalar_mul(self.divison_rate,
self.controller_output), tf.int32,
                                name='controller_prediction')
```

We then define the loss function and optimizer. We use `RMSPropOptimizer` as our
backpropagation algorithm, where the learning rate decays exponentially. Rather than
calling `optimizer.minimize(loss)` as is usually done with other neural network
models, we call the `compute_gradients` method to obtain gradients for calculating
REINFORCE gradients:

```
# Set up optimizer
self.global_step = tf.Variable(0, trainable=False)
self.learning_rate = tf.train.exponential_decay(0.99, self.global_step,
500, 0.96, staircase=True)
self.optimizer =
tf.train.RMSPropOptimizer(learning_rate=self.learning_rate)
```

```
# Gradient and loss computation
with tf.name_scope('gradient_and_loss'):
    # Define policy gradient loss for the controller
    self.policy_gradient_loss =
tf.reduce_mean(tf.nn.softmax_cross_entropy_with_logits(
        logits=self.controller_output[:, -1, :],
        labels=self.child_network_architectures))
    # L2 weight decay for Controller weights
    self.l2_loss = tf.reduce_sum(tf.add_n([tf.nn.l2_loss(v) for v in
tf.trainable_variables(scope="controller")]))
    # Add the above two losses to define total loss
    self.total_loss = self.policy_gradient_loss + self.l2_loss *
controller_params["beta"]
    # Compute the gradients
    self.gradients = self.optimizer.compute_gradients(self.total_loss)

    # Gradients calculated using REINFORCE
    for i, (grad, var) in enumerate(self.gradients):
        if grad is not None:
            self.gradients[i] = (grad * self.discounted_rewards, var)
```

Finally, we apply the REINFORCE gradients on the Controller parameters:

```
with tf.name_scope('train_controller'):
    # The main training operation. This applies REINFORCE on the weights of
the Controller
    self.train_op = self.optimizer.apply_gradients(self.gradients,
global_step=self.global_step)

logger.info('Successfully built controller')
```

The actual Controller network is created via the `network_generator` function. As mentioned, the Controller is a recurrent neural network with a special kind of cell. However, we don't have to implement this from scratch, as the developers behind TensorFlow have already implemented a custom `tf.contrib.rnn.NASCell`. We simply need to use this to construct our recurrent neural network and obtain the outputs:

```
def network_generator(self, nas_cell_hidden_state):
    # number of output units we expect from a NAS cell
    with tf.name_scope('network_generator'):
        nas = tf.contrib.rnn.NASCell(self.num_cell_outputs)
        network_architecture, nas_cell_hidden_state =
tf.nn.dynamic_rnn(nas, tf.expand_dims(
            nas_cell_hidden_state, -1), dtype=tf.float32)
        bias_variable = tf.Variable([0.01] * self.num_cell_outputs)
        network_architecture = tf.nn.bias_add(network_architecture,
bias_variable)
        return network_architecture[:, -1:, :]
```

Generating a child network using the Controller

Now, we implement a method that generates a child network using the Controller:

```
def generate_child_network(self, child_network_architecture):
    with self.graph.as_default():
        return self.sess.run(self.cnn_dna_output,
{self.child_network_architectures: child_network_architecture})
```

Once we generate our child network, we call the `train_child_network` function to train it. This function takes `child_dna` and `child_id` and returns the validation accuracy that the child network achieves. First, we instantiate a new `tf.Graph()` and a new `tf.Session()` so that the child network is separated from the Controller's graph:

```
def train_child_network(self, cnn_dna, child_id):
    """
    Trains a child network and returns reward, or the validation accuracy
    Args:
        cnn_dna (list): List of tuples representing the child network's DNA
        child_id (str): Name of child network

    Returns:
        (float) validation accuracy
    """
    logger.info("Training with dna: {}".format(cnn_dna))
    child_graph = tf.Graph()
    with child_graph.as_default():
        sess = tf.Session()

        child_network = ChildCNN(cnn_dna=cnn_dna, child_id=child_id,
**child_network_params)
```

We then define the input data pipeline, which uses the `tf.data.Dataset` creator we implemented here. In particular, we use `tf.data.Iterator` to create a generator that yields a batch of input tensors every time we call `iterator.get_next()`. We initialize an iterator for the training and validation datasets respectively. The batch of input tensors contains the `CIFAR-10` images and the corresponding labels, which we unpack at the end:

```
# Create input pipeline
train_dataset, valid_dataset, test_dataset, num_train_batches,
num_valid_batches, num_test_batches = \
get_tf_datasets_from_numpy(batch_size=child_network_params["batch_size"])

# Generic iterator
iterator = tf.data.Iterator.from_structure(train_dataset.output_types,
train_dataset.output_shapes)
next_tensor_batch = iterator.get_next()
```

```
# Separate train and validation set init ops
train_init_ops = iterator.make_initializer(train_dataset)
valid_init_ops = iterator.make_initializer(valid_dataset)

# Build the graph
input_tensor, labels = next_tensor_batch
```

The `input_tensor` becomes the argument to the child network's `build` method. We then define all the TensorFlow operations needed for training, including the prediction, loss, optimizer, and accuracy operations:

```
# Build the child network, which returns the pre-softmax logits of the
child network
logits = child_network.build(input_tensor)

# Define the loss function for the child network
loss_ops = tf.nn.softmax_cross_entropy_with_logits_v2(labels=labels,
logits=logits, name="loss")

# Define the training operation for the child network
train_ops =
tf.train.AdamOptimizer(learning_rate=child_network_params["learning_rate"])
.minimize(loss_ops)

# The following operations are for calculating the accuracy of the child
network
pred_ops = tf.nn.softmax(logits, name="preds")
correct = tf.equal(tf.argmax(pred_ops, 1), tf.argmax(labels, 1),
name="correct")
accuracy_ops = tf.reduce_mean(tf.cast(correct, tf.float32),
name="accuracy")

initializer = tf.global_variables_initializer()
```

We then train the child network. Notice that when calling `sess.run(...)`, we are no longer passing an argument for the `feed_dict` parameter. Instead, we are simply calling the operations we want to run (`loss_ops`, `train_ops`, and `accuracy_ops`). This is because the inputs are already represented as tensors in the child network's graph:

```
# Training
sess.run(initializer)
sess.run(train_init_ops)

logger.info("Training child CNN {} for {} epochs".format(child_id,
child_network_params["max_epochs"]))
for epoch_idx in range(child_network_params["max_epochs"]):
    avg_loss, avg_acc = [], []
```

```
for batch_idx in range(num_train_batches):
    loss, _, accuracy = sess.run([loss_ops, train_ops, accuracy_ops])
    avg_loss.append(loss)
    avg_acc.append(accuracy)

logger.info("\tEpoch {}:\tloss - {:.6f}\taccuracy -
{:.3f}".format(epoch_idx,
np.mean(avg_loss), np.mean(avg_acc)))
```

Once training finishes, we calculate the validation accuracy and return it:

```
# Validate and return reward
logger.info("Finished training, now calculating validation accuracy")
sess.run(valid_init_ops)
avg_val_loss, avg_val_acc = [], []
for batch_idx in range(num_valid_batches):
    valid_loss, valid_accuracy = sess.run([loss_ops, accuracy_ops])
    avg_val_loss.append(valid_loss)
    avg_val_acc.append(valid_accuracy)
logger.info("Valid loss - {:.6f}\tValid accuracy -
{:.3f}".format(np.mean(avg_val_loss),
np.mean(avg_val_acc)))

return np.mean(avg_val_acc)
```

Finally, we implement a method for training the Controller. Due to computational resource constraints, we will not parallelize the training procedure (that is, *m* child networks trained in parallel per Controller epoch). Instead, we will sequentially generate these child networks and keep track of the mean validation accuracy among them.

train_controller method

The `train_controller` method is called after we build the Controller. The first step is thus to initialize all the variables and the first state:

```
def train_controller(self):
    with self.graph.as_default():
        self.sess.run(tf.global_variables_initializer())

    step = 0
    total_rewards = 0
    child_network_architecture = np.array([[10.0, 128.0, 1.0, 1.0] *
controller_params['max_layers']], dtype=np.float32)
```

The first `child_network_architecture` is a list that resembles an architecture configuration and will be the argument to `NASCell`, which would output the first child DNA.

The training procedure consists of two `for` loops: one for the number of epochs for the Controller, and another for each child network the Controller generates per epoch. In the inner `for` loop, we generate a new `child_network_architecture` using `NASCell` and train a child network based on it to obtain a validation accuracy:

```
for episode in range(controller_params['max_episodes']):
    logger.info('=============> Episode {} for Controller'.format(episode))
    step += 1
    episode_reward_buffer = []

    for sub_child in range(controller_params["num_children_per_episode"]):
        # Generate a child network architecture
        child_network_architecture =
self.generate_child_network(child_network_architecture)[0]

        if np.any(np.less_equal(child_network_architecture, 0.0)):
            reward = -1.0
        else:
            reward =
self.train_child_network(cnn_dna=child_network_architecture,
child_id='child/{}'.format("{}_{}".format(episode, sub_child)))
        episode_reward_buffer.append(reward)
```

After we obtain *m* validation accuracies, we update our Controller using the mean reward and the gradients computed with respect to the last child network's DNA. We also keep track of past mean rewards. Using the `ema` method implemented previously, we calculate the baseline, which we then subtract from the latest mean reward. We then call `self.sess.run([self.train_op, self.total_loss]...)` to update the Controller and calculate the Controller's loss:

```
mean_reward = np.mean(episode_reward_buffer)

self.reward_history.append(mean_reward)
self.architecture_history.append(child_network_architecture)
total_rewards += mean_reward

child_network_architecture = np.array(self.architecture_history[-
step:]).ravel() / self.divison_rate
child_network_architecture = child_network_architecture.reshape((-1,
self.num_cell_outputs))
baseline = ema(self.reward_history)
last_reward = self.reward_history[-1]
```

```
rewards = [last_reward - baseline]
logger.info("Buffers before loss calculation")
logger.info("States: {}".format(child_network_architecture))
logger.info("Rewards: {}".format(rewards))

with self.graph.as_default():
    _, loss = self.sess.run([self.train_op, self.total_loss],
                            {self.child_network_architectures:
child_network_architecture,
                             self.discounted_rewards: rewards})

logger.info('Episode: {} | Loss: {} | DNA: {} | Reward : {}'.format(
    episode, loss, child_network_architecture.ravel(), mean_reward))
```

And that's it! You can find the full implementation of `controller.py` in the main GitHub repository.

Testing ChildCNN

Now that we have implemented both `child_network` and `controller`, it would be great to test the training of `ChildCNN` via our `Controller` with custom child network configurations. We would like to make sure that, with a sensible architecture, `ChildCNN` can learn sufficiently.

To do this, first open up your favorite Terminal and start a Jupyter console:

```
$ ipython
Python 3.6.4 (default, Jan 6 2018, 11:49:38)
Type 'copyright', 'credits' or 'license' for more information
IPython 6.4.0 -- An enhanced Interactive Python. Type '?' for help.
```

We first configure our logger so we can see the outputs on the Terminal:

```
In [1]: import sys

In [2]: import logging

In [3]: logging.basicConfig(stream=sys.stdout,
   ...: level=logging.DEBUG,
   ...: format='%(asctime)s %(name)-12s %(levelname)-8s %(message)s')
   ...:

In [4]:
```

Next, we import the `Controller` class from `controller.py`:

```
In [4]: import numpy as np

In [5]: from controller import Controller

In [6]:
```

We then handcraft some child network architecture to be passed to the
Controller's `train_child_network` function:

```
In [7]: dna = np.array([[3, 1, 30, 2], [3, 1, 30, 2], [3, 1, 40, 2]])
```

Finally, we instantiate our `Controller` and call the `train_child_network` method:

```
In [8]: controller = Controller()

...

2018-09-16 01:58:54,978 controller INFO Successfully built controller

In [9]: controller.train_child_network(dna, "test")

2018-09-16 01:58:59,208 controller INFO Training with dna: [[ 3 1 30 2]
 [ 3 1 30 2]
 [ 3 1 40 2]]
2018-09-16 01:58:59,605 cifar10_processor INFO Dividing pixels by 255
2018-09-16 01:59:01,289 cifar10_processor INFO Loaded data from keras
2018-09-16 01:59:03,150 child_network INFO DNA is: [[3, 1, 30, 2], [3, 1,
30, 2], [3, 1, 40, 2]]
2018-09-16 01:59:14,270 controller INFO Training child CNN first for 1000
epochs
```

If successful, you should be seeing decent accuracy scores after several epochs of training:

```
2018-09-16 06:25:01,927 controller INFO Epoch 436: loss - 1.119608 accuracy
- 0.663
2018-09-16 06:25:19,310 controller INFO Epoch 437: loss - 0.634937 accuracy
- 0.724
2018-09-16 06:25:36,438 controller INFO Epoch 438: loss - 0.769766 accuracy
- 0.702
2018-09-16 06:25:53,413 controller INFO Epoch 439: loss - 0.760520 accuracy
- 0.711
2018-09-16 06:26:10,530 controller INFO Epoch 440: loss - 0.606741 accuracy
- 0.812
```

config.py

The `config.py` module includes configurations used by the Controller and the child networks. Here, you can adjust several training parameters, such as the number of episodes, the learning rate, and the number of child networks generated by the Controller per epoch. You can also experiment with child network sizes, but do note that the larger the child network, the longer training takes for both the Controller and the child network:

```
child_network_params = {
    "learning_rate": 3e-5,
    "max_epochs": 100,
    "beta": 1e-3,
    "batch_size": 20
}

controller_params = {
    "max_layers": 3,
    "components_per_layer": 4,
    'beta': 1e-4,
    'max_episodes': 2000,
    "num_children_per_episode": 10
}
```

Some of these numbers (such as `max_episodes`) are arbitrarily chosen. We encourage the reader to tweak these numbers to understand how they affect the training of both the Controller and the child networks.

train.py

This `train.py` module acts as our top-level entry to training the Controller:

```
import logging
import sys

from .controller import Controller

if __name__ == '__main__':
    # Configure the logger
    logging.basicConfig(stream=sys.stdout,
                        level=logging.DEBUG,
                        format='%(asctime)s %(name)-12s %(levelname)-8s
%(message)s')
    controller = Controller()
    controller.train_controller()
```

And there we have it; a neural network that generates other neural networks! Make sure your implementation has the following directory structure:

```
src
|-- __init__.py
|-- child_network.py
|-- cifar10_processor.py
|-- config.py
|-- constants.py
|-- controller.py
`-- train.py
```

To execute training, simply run the following command:

```
$ python train.py
```

If all works well, you should be seeing output like the following:

```
2018-09-16 04:13:45,484 src.controller INFO Successfully built controller
2018-09-16 04:13:45,542 src.controller INFO ==============> Episode 0 for
Controller
2018-09-16 04:13:45,952 src.controller INFO Training with dna: [[ 2 10 2 4
1 1 12 14 7 1 1 1]] 2018-09-16 04:13:45.953482: I
tensorflow/core/common_runtime/gpu/gpu_device.cc:1484] Adding visible gpu
devices: 0
2018-09-16 04:13:45.953530: I
tensorflow/core/common_runtime/gpu/gpu_device.cc:965] Device interconnect
StreamExecutor with strength 1 edge matrix:
2018-09-16 04:13:45.953543: I
tensorflow/core/common_runtime/gpu/gpu_device.cc:971] 0
2018-09-16 04:13:45.953558: I
tensorflow/core/common_runtime/gpu/gpu_device.cc:984] 0: N
2018-09-16 04:13:45.953840: I
tensorflow/core/common_runtime/gpu/gpu_device.cc:1097] Created TensorFlow
device (/job:localhost/replica:0/task:0/device:GPU:0 wi th 21618 MB memory)
-> physical GPU (device: 0, name: Tesla M40 24GB, pci bus id: 0000:03:00.0,
compute capability: 5.2)
2018-09-16 04:13:47,143 src.cifar10_processor INFO Dividing pixels by 255
2018-09-16 04:13:55,119 src.cifar10_processor INFO Loaded data from keras
2018-09-16 04:14:09,050 src.child_network INFO DNA is: [[2, 10, 2, 4], [1,
1, 12, 14], [7, 1, 1, 1]]
2018-09-16 04:14:21,326 src.controller INFO Training child CNN child/0_0
for 100 epochs
2018-09-16 04:14:32,830 src.controller INFO Epoch 0: loss - 2.351300
accuracy - 0.100
2018-09-16 04:14:43,976 src.controller INFO Epoch 1: loss - 2.202928
accuracy - 0.180
2018-09-16 04:14:53,412 src.controller INFO Epoch 2: loss - 2.102713
```

```
accuracy - 0.220
2018-09-16 04:15:03,704 src.controller INFO Epoch 3: loss - 2.092676
accuracy - 0.232
2018-09-16 04:15:14,349 src.controller INFO Epoch 4: loss - 2.092633
accuracy - 0.240
```

You should see logging statements for each child network architecture its CIFAR-10 training logs. During CIFAR-10 training, we print the loss and accuracy for each epoch as well as the validation accuracy which we return to the Controller.

Additional exercises

In this section, we have implemented the NAS framework for `CIFAR-10` data. While this is a great start, there are additional features one can implement, which we will leave to the reader as exercises:

- How can we make the Controller create child networks that solve problems in other domains, such as text and speech recognition?
- How can we make the Controller train multiple child networks in parallel in order to speed up the training process?
- How can we visualize the training process using TensorBoard?
- How can we make the Controller design child networks that include residual connections?

Some of these exercises may require significant changes in the code base but are beneficial for deepening your understanding of NAS. We definitely recommend giving these a try!

Advantages of NAS

The biggest advantage of NAS is that one does not need to spend copious amounts of time designing a neural network for a particular problem. This also means that those who are not data scientists can also create machine learning agents as long as they can prepare data. In fact, Google has already productized this framework as Cloud AutoML, which allows anyone to train customized machine learning models with minimum effort. According to Google, Cloud AutoML provides the following benefits:

- Users only need to interact with a simple GUI to create machine learning models.
- Users can have Cloud AutoML annotate their own datasets if they are not labeled already. This is similar to Amazon's Mechanical Turk service.

- Models generated by Cloud AutoML are guaranteed to have high accuracy and fast performance.
- Easy end-to-end pipeline for uploading data, training and validating the model, deploying the model, and creating a REST endpoint for fetching predictions.

Currently, Cloud AutoML can be used for image classification/detection, natural language processing (text classification), and translation.

 For more information on Cloud AutoML, check out their official page here: https://cloud.google.com/automl/

Another advantage that NAS provides is the ability to generate more compact models than those designed by humans. According to *Efficient Neural Architecture Search via Parameter Sharing* by Hieu Pham et. al., whereas the most recent state-of-the-art neural network for CIFAR-10 classification had 26.2 million parameters, a NAS-generated neural network that achieved comparable test accuracy (97.44% for human-designed network versus 97.35% for the NAS-generated network) only had 3.3 million parameters. Note that older, less-accurate models such as VGG16, ResNet50, and InceptionV3 have 138 million, 25 million, and 23 million parameters respectively. The vast reduction in parameter size allows for more efficient inference time and model storage, both of which are important aspects when deploying models into production.

Summary

In this chapter, we have implemented NAS, a framework where a reinforcement learning agent (the Controller) generates child neural networks to complete a certain task. We studied the theory behind how the Controller learns to generate better child network architectures via policy gradient methods. We then implemented a simplified version of NAS that generates child networks that learn to classify `CIFAR-10` images.

For more information on related topics, refer to the following list of links:

- NAS with reinforcement learning: `https://arxiv.org/abs/1611.01578`
- Efficient NAS via parameter sharing: `https://arxiv.org/pdf/1802.03268`
- Google Cloud AutoML: `https://cloud.google.com/automl/`
- Awesome Architecture Search—a curated list of papers related to generating neural networks: `https://github.com/markdtw/awesome-architecture-search`

The NAS framework marks an exciting development in the deep learning field, for we have figured out how to automatically design neural network architectures, a decision previously made by humans. There are now improved versions of NAS and other kinds of algorithms that generate neural networks automatically, which we encourage the reader to look into as well.

18
Predicting Future Stock Prices

The financial market is a very important part of any economy. For an economy to thrive, its financial market must be solid. Since the advent of machine learning, companies have begun to adopt algorithmic trading in the purchase of stocks and other financial assets. There has been proven successful with this method, and it has risen in prominence over time. Given its rise, several machine models have been developed and adopted for algorithmic trading. One popular machine learning model for trading is the time series analysis. You have already learned about reinforcement learning and Keras, and in this chapter, they will be used to develop a model that can predict stock prices.

Background problem

Automation is taking over in almost every sector, and the financial market is no exception. Creating automated algorithmic trading models will provide for a faster and more accurate analysis of stocks before purchase. Multiple indicators can be analyzed at a speed that humans are incapable of. Also, in trading, it is dangerous to operate with emotions. Machine learning models can solve that problem. There is also a reduction in transaction costs, as there is no need for continuous supervision.

In this tutorial, you will learn how to combine reinforcement learning with time series modeling, in order to predict the prices of stocks, based on real-life data.

Data used

The data that we will use will be the standard and poor's 500. According to Wikipedia, it is *An American stock market index based on the market capitalizations of 500 large companies having common stock listed on the NYSE or NASDAQ*. Here is a link to the data (`https://ca.finance.yahoo.com/quote/%255EGSPC/history?p=%255EGSPC`).

The data has the following columns:

1. **Date**: This indicates the date under consideration
2. **Open**: This indicates the price at which the market opens on the date
3. **High**: This indicates the highest market price on the date
4. **Low**: This indicates the lowest market price on the date
5. **Close**: This indicates the price at which the market closes on the date, adjusted for the split
6. **Adj Close**: This indicates the adjusted closing price for both the split and dividends
7. **Volume**: This indicates the total volume of shares available

The date under consideration for training the data is as follows:

```
Start: 14 August 2006
End: 13th August 2015
```

On the website, filter the date as follows, and download the dataset:

For testing, we will use the following date range:

```
Start: 14 August 2015
End: 14 August 2018
```

Change the dates on the website accordingly, and download the dataset for testing, as follows:

In the next section, we will define some possible actions that the agent can carry out.

Step-by-step guide

Our solution uses an actor-critic reinforcement learning model, along with an infused time series, to help us predict the best action, based on the stock prices. The possible actions are as follows:

1. **Hold**: This means that based on the price and projected profit, the trader should hold a stock
2. **Sell**: This means that based on the price and projected profit, the trader should sell a stock
3. **Buy**: This means that based on the price and projected profit, the trader should buy a stock

The actor-critic network is a family of reinforcement learning methods premised on two interacting network models. These models have two components: the actor and the critic. In our case, the network models that we will use will be neural networks. We will use the Keras package, which you have already learned about, to create the neural networks. The reward function that we are looking to improve is the profit.

The actor takes in the state of the environment, then returns the best action, or a policy that refers to a probability distribution over actions. This seems like a natural way to perform reinforcement learning, as policies are directly returned as a function of the state.

The critic evaluates the actions returned by the actor-network. This is similar to the traditional deep Q network; in the environment state and an action to return a score representing the value of taking that action given the state. The job of the critic is to compute an approximation, which is then used to update the actor in the direction of its gradient. The critic is trained itself temporal difference algorithm.

These two networks are trained simultaneously. With time, the critic network is able to improve its `Q_value` prediction, and the actor also learns how to make better decisions, given the state.

There are five scripts that make up this solution, and they will be described in the next sections.

Actor script

The actor script is where the policy model is defined. We begin by importing certain modules from Keras: layers, optimizers, models, and the backend. These modules will help us to construct our neural network: Let's start by importing the required functions from Keras.

```
from keras import layers, models, optimizers
from keras import backend as K
```

1. We create a class called `Actor`, whose object takes in the parameters of the `state` and `action` size:

```
class Actor:
    # """Actor (policy) Model. """

    def __init__(self, state_size, action_size):
        self.state_size = state_size
        self.action_size = action_size
```

2. The preceding code shows the state size, which represents the dimension of each state, and the action size, which represents the dimensions of the actions. Next, call a function to build the model, as follows:

```
self.build_model()
```

3. Build a policy model that maps the states to actions, and start by defining the input layer, as follows:

```
def build_model(self):
    states = layers.Input(shape=(self.state_size,), name='states')
```

4. Add hidden layers to the model. There are two dense layers, each one followed by a batch normalization and an activation layer. The dense layers are regularized. The two layers have 16 and 32 hidden units, respectively:

```
    net =
layers.Dense(units=16,kernel_regularizer=layers.regularizers.l2(1e-
6))(states)
        net = layers.BatchNormalization()(net)
        net = layers.Activation("relu")(net)
        net =
layers.Dense(units=32,kernel_regularizer=layers.regularizers.l2(1e-
6))(net)
        net = layers.BatchNormalization()(net)
        net = layers.Activation("relu")(net)
```

5. The final output layer will predict the action probabilities that have an activation of `softmax`:

```
        actions = layers.Dense(units=self.action_size,
activation='softmax', name = 'actions')(net)
        self.model = models.Model(inputs=states, outputs=actions)
```

6. Define the loss function by using the action value (`Q_value`) gradients, as follows:

```
    action_gradients = layers.Input(shape=(self.action_size,))
    loss = K.mean(-action_gradients * actions)
```

7. Define the `optimizer` and training function, as follows:

```
        optimizer = optimizers.Adam(lr=.00001)
        updates_op =
optimizer.get_updates(params=self.model.trainable_weights,
loss=loss)
        self.train_fn = K.function(
            inputs=[self.model.input, action_gradients,
K.learning_phase()],
            outputs=[],
            updates=updates_op)
```

The custom training function for the actor-network that makes use of the Q gradients with respect to the action probabilities. With this custom function, the training aims to maximize the profits (in other words, minimize the negatives of the `Q_values`).

Critic script

We begin by importing certain modules from Keras: layers, optimizers, models, and the backend. These modules will help us to construct our neural network:

```
from keras import layers, models, optimizers
from keras import backend as K
```

1. We create a class called `Critic`, whose object takes in the following parameters:

```
    class Critic:
        """Critic (Value) Model."""

        def __init__(self, state_size, action_size):
            """Initialize parameters and build model.
            Params
            ======
```

```
        state_size (int): Dimension of each state
        action_size (int): Dimension of each action
    """
    self.state_size = state_size
    self.action_size = action_size

    self.build_model()
```

2. Build a critic (value) network that maps `state` and `action` pairs (`Q_values`), and define input layers, as follows:

```
def build_model(self):
    states = layers.Input(shape=(self.state_size,),
name='states')
    actions = layers.Input(shape=(self.action_size,),
name='actions')
```

3. Add the hidden layers for the state pathway, as follows:

```
    net_states =
layers.Dense(units=16,kernel_regularizer=layers.regularizers.l2(1e-
6))(states)
    net_states = layers.BatchNormalization()(net_states)
    net_states = layers.Activation("relu")(net_states)

    net_states = layers.Dense(units=32,
kernel_regularizer=layers.regularizers.l2(1e-6))(net_states)
```

4. Add the hidden layers for the action pathway, as follows:

```
    net_actions =
layers.Dense(units=32,kernel_regularizer=layers.regularizers.l2(1e-
6))(actions)
```

5. Combine the state and action pathways, as follows:

```
net = layers.Add()([net_states, net_actions])
net = layers.Activation('relu')(net)
```

6. Add the final output layer to produce the action values (`Q_values`):

```
    Q_values = layers.Dense(units=1,
name='q_values',kernel_initializer=layers.initializers.RandomUnifor
m(minval=-0.003, maxval=0.003))(net)
```

7. Create the Keras model, as follows:

```
        self.model = models.Model(inputs=[states, actions],
    outputs=Q_values)
```

8. Define the `optimizer` and compile a model for training with the built-in loss function:

```
optimizer = optimizers.Adam(lr=0.001)
self.model.compile(optimizer=optimizer, loss='mse')
```

9. Compute the action gradients (the derivative of `Q_values`, with respect to `actions`):

```
action_gradients = K.gradients(Q_values, actions)
```

10. Define an additional function to fetch the action gradients (to be used by the actor model), as follows:

```
self.get_action_gradients = K.function(
    inputs=[*self.model.input, K.learning_phase()],
    outputs=action_gradients)
```

This concludes the critic script.

Agent script

In this section, we will train an agent that will perform reinforcement learning based on the actor and critic networks. We will perform the following steps to achieve this:

1. Create an agent class whose initial function takes in the batch size, state size, and an evaluation Boolean function, to check whether the training is ongoing.
2. In the agent class, create the following methods:
3. Import the `actor` and `critic` scripts:

```
from actor import Actor
from critic import Critic
```

4. Import numpy, random, namedtuple, and deque from the collections package:

```
import numpy as np
from numpy.random import choice
import random

from collections import namedtuple, deque
```

5. Create a ReplayBuffer class that adds, samples, and evaluates a buffer:

```
class ReplayBuffer:
    #Fixed sized buffer to stay experience tuples
    def __init__(self, buffer_size, batch_size):
    #Initialize a replay buffer object.
    #parameters
    #buffer_size: maximum size of buffer. Batch size: size of each
batch
        self.memory = deque(maxlen = buffer_size)  #memory size of
replay buffer
        self.batch_size = batch_size                #Training batch
size for Neural nets
        self.experience = namedtuple("Experience", field_names =
["state", "action", "reward", "next_state", "done"])
    #Tuple containing experienced replay
```

6. Add a new experience to the replay buffer memory:

```
    def add(self, state, action, reward, next_state, done):
        e = self.experience(state, action, reward, next_state,
done)
        self.memory.append(e)
```

7. Randomly sample a batch of experienced tuples from the memory. In the following function, we randomly sample states from a memory buffer. We do this so that the states that we feed to the model are not temporally correlated. This will reduce overfitting:

```
    def sample(self, batch_size = 32):
        return random.sample(self.memory, k=self.batch_size)
```

8. Return the current size of the buffer memory, as follows:

```
    def __len__(self):
        return len(self.memory)
```

9. The reinforcement learning agent that learns using the actor-critic network is as follows:

```
class Agent:
    def __init__(self, state_size, batch_size, is_eval = False):
        self.state_size = state_size #
```

10. The number of actions are defined as 3: sit, buy, sell

```
self.action_size = 3
```

11. Define the replay memory size

```
self.buffer_size = 1000000
self.batch_size = batch_size
self.memory = ReplayBuffer(self.buffer_size, self.batch_size)
self.inventory = []
```

12. Define whether or not training is ongoing. This variable will be changed during the training and evaluation phase:

```
self.is_eval = is_eval
```

13. Discount factor in Bellman equation:

```
self.gamma = 0.99
```

14. A soft update of the actor and critic networks can be done as follows:

```
self.tau = 0.001
```

15. The actor policy model maps states to actions and instantiates the actor networks (local and target models, for soft updates of parameters):

```
self.actor_local = Actor(self.state_size, self.action_size)
self.actor_target = Actor(self.state_size, self.action_size)
```

16. The critic (value) model that maps the state-action pairs to Q_values is as follows:

```
self.critic_local = Critic(self.state_size, self.action_size)
```

17. Instantiate the critic model (the local and target models are utilized to allow for soft updates), as follows:

```
self.critic_target = Critic(self.state_size,
self.action_size)
self.critic_target.model.set_weights(self.critic_local.model.get_we
ights())
```

18. The following code sets the target model parameters to local model parameters:

```
self.actor_target.model.set_weights(self.actor_local.model.get_weig
hts()
```

19. Returns an action, given a state, using the actor (policy network) and the output of the `softmax` layer of the actor-network, returning the probability for each action. An action method that returns an action, given a state, using the actor (policy network) is as follows:

```
def act(self, state):
        options = self.actor_local.model.predict(state)
        self.last_state = state
        if not self.is_eval:
            return choice(range(3), p = options[0])
        return np.argmax(options[0])
```

20. Returns a stochastic policy, based on the action probabilities in the training model and a deterministic action corresponding to the maximum probability during testing. There is a set of actions to be carried out by the agent at every step of the episode. A method (step) that returns the set of actions to be carried out by the agent at every step of the episode is as follows:

```
def step(self, action, reward, next_state, done):
```

21. The following code adds a new experience to the memory:

```
self.memory.add(self.last_state, action, reward, next_state,
    done)
```

22. The following code asserts that enough experiences are present in the memory to train:

```
if len(self.memory) > self.batch_size:
```

23. The following code samples a random batch from the memory to train:

```
experiences = self.memory.sample(self.batch_size)
```

24. Learn from the sampled experiences, as follows:

```
self.learn(experiences)
```

25. The following code updates the state to the next state:

```
self.last_state = next_state
```

26. Learning from the sampled experiences through the actor and the critic. Create a method to learn from the sampled experiences through the actor and the critic, as follows:

```
def learn(self, experiences):
    states = np.vstack([e.state for e in experiences if e is
not None]).astype(np.float32).reshape(-1,self.state_size)
    actions = np.vstack([e.action for e in experiences if e is
not None]).astype(np.float32).reshape(-1,self.action_size)
    rewards = np.array([e.reward for e in experiences if e is
not None]).astype(np.float32).reshape(-1,1)
    dones = np.array([e.done for e in experiences if e is not
None]).astype(np.float32).reshape(-1,1)
    next_states = np.vstack([e.next_state for e in experiences
if e is not None]).astype(np.float32).reshape(-1,self.state_size)
```

27. Return a separate array for each experience in the replay component and predict actions based on the next states, as follows:

```
actions_next =
self.actor_target.model.predict_on_batch(next_states)
```

28. Predict the Q_value of the actor output for the next state, as follows:

```
Q_targets_next =
self.critic_target.model.predict_on_batch([next_states,
actions_next])
```

29. Target the Q_value to serve as a label for the critic network, based on the temporal difference, as follows:

```
Q_targets = rewards + self.gamma * Q_targets_next * (1 - dones)
```

30. Fit the critic model to the time difference of the target, as follows:

```
self.critic_local.model.train_on_batch(x = [states,
actions], y = Q_targets)
```

31. Train the actor model (local) using the gradient of the critic network output with respect to the action probabilities fed from the actor-network:

```
action_gradients =
np.reshape(self.critic_local.get_action_gradients([states, actions,
0]),(-1, self.action_size))
```

32. Next, define a custom training function, as follows:

```
self.actor_local.train_fn([states, action_gradients, 1])
```

33. Next, initiate a soft update of the parameters of both networks, as follows:

```
self.soft_update(self.actor_local.model,
self.actor_target.model)
```

34. This performs soft updates on the model parameters, based on the parameter tau to avoid drastic model changes. A method that updates the model by performing soft updates on the model parameters, based on the parameter tau (to avoid drastic model changes), is as follows:

```
def soft_update(self, local_model, target_model):
    local_weights = np.array(local_model.get_weights())
    target_weights = np.array(target_model.get_weights())
    assert len(local_weights) == len(target_weights)
    new_weights = self.tau * local_weights + (1 - self.tau) *
target_weights
    target_model.set_weights(new_weights)
```

This concludes the agent script.

Helper script

In this script, we will create functions that will be helpful for training, via the following steps:

1. Import the numpy and math modules, as follows:

```
import numpy as np
import math
```

2. Next, define a function to format the price to two decimal places, to reduce the ambiguity of the data:

```
def formatPrice(n):
    if n>=0:
        curr = "$"
    else:
        curr = "-$"
    return (curr +"{0:.2f}".format(abs(n)))
```

3. Return a vector of stock data from the CSV file. Convert the closing stock prices from the data to vectors, and return a vector of all stock prices, as follows:

```
def getStockData(key):
    datavec = []
    lines = open("data/" + key + ".csv", "r").read().splitlines()
    for line in lines[1:]:
        datavec.append(float(line.split(",")[4]))
    return datavec
```

4. Next, define a function to generate states from the input vector. Create the time series by generating the states from the vectors created in the previous step. The function for this takes three parameters: the data; a time, *t* (the day that you want to predict); and a window (how many days to go back in time). The rate of change between these vectors will then be measured and based on the sigmoid function:

```
def getState(data, t, window):
    if t - window >= -1:
        vec = data[t - window+ 1:t+ 1]
    else:
        vec = -(t-window+1)*[data[0]]+data[0: t + 1]
    scaled_state = []
    for i in range(window - 1):
```

5. Next, scale the state vector from 0 to 1 with a sigmoid function. The sigmoid function can map any input value, from 0 to 1. This helps to normalize the values to probabilities:

```
        scaled_state.append(1/(1 + math.exp(vec[i] - vec[i+1])))
    return np.array([scaled_state])
```

All of the necessary functions and classes are now defined, so we can start the training process.

Training the data

We will proceed to train the data, based on our agent and helper methods. This will provide us with one of three actions, based on the states of the stock prices at the end of the day. These states can be to buy, sell, or hold. During training, the prescribed action for each day is predicted, and the price (profit, loss, or unchanged) of the action is calculated. The cumulative sum will be calculated at the end of the training period, and we will see whether there has been a profit or a loss. The aim is to maximize the total profit.

Let's start with the imports, as follows:

```
from agent import Agent
from helper import getStockData, getState
import sys
```

1. Next, define the number of market days to consider as the window size, and define the batch size with which the neural network will be trained, as follows:

```
window_size = 100
batch_size = 32
```

2. Instantiate the stock agent with the window size and batch size, as follows:

```
agent = Agent(window_size, batch_size)
```

3. Next, read the training data from the CSV file, using the helper function:

```
data = getStockData("^GSPC")
l = len(data) - 1
```

4. Next, the episode count is defined as 300. The agent will look at the data for so many numbers of times. An episode represents a complete pass over the data:

```
episode_count = 300
```

5. Next, we can start to iterate through the episodes, as follows:

```
for e in range(episode_count):
    print("Episode " + str(e) + "/" + str(episode_count))
```

6. Each episode has to be started with a state based on the data and window size. The inventory of stocks is initialized before going through the data:

```
state = getState(data, 0, window_size + 1)
agent.inventory = []
total_profit = 0
done = False
```

7. Next, start to iterate over every day of the stock data. The action probability is predicted by the agent, based on the `state`:

```
for t in range(l):
    action = agent.act(state)
    action_prob = agent.actor_local.model.predict(state)

    next_state = getState(data, t + 1, window_size + 1)
    reward = 0
```

8. The `action` can be held, if the agent decides not to do anything with the stock. Another possible action is to buy (hence, the stock will be added to the inventory), as follows:

```
if action == 1:
    agent.inventory.append(data[t])
    print("Buy:" + formatPrice(data[t]))
```

9. If the `action` is 2, the agent sells the stocks and removes it from the inventory. Based on the sale, the profit (or loss) is calculated:

```
elif action == 2 and len(agent.inventory) > 0:  # sell
    bought_price = agent.inventory.pop(0)
    reward = max(data[t] - bought_price, 0)
    total_profit += data[t] - bought_price
    print("sell: " + formatPrice(data[t]) + "| profit: " +
        formatPrice(data[t] - bought_price))

if t == l - 1:
    done = True
agent.step(action_prob, reward, next_state, done)
state = next_state

if done:
    print("--------------------------------------------")
    print("Total Profit: " + formatPrice(total_profit))
    print("--------------------------------------------")
```

10. You can see logs similar to those that follow during the training process. The stocks are bought and sold at certain prices:

```
sell: $2102.15| profit: $119.30
sell: $2079.65| profit: $107.36
Buy:$2067.64
sell: $2108.57| profit: $143.75
Buy:$2108.63
Buy:$2093.32
```

```
Buy:$2099.84
Buy:$2083.56
Buy:$2077.57
Buy:$2104.18
sell: $2084.07| profit: $115.18
sell: $2086.05| profit: $179.92
------------------------------------------
Total Profit: $57473.53
```

11. Next, the test data is read from the CSV file. The initial state is inferred from the data. The steps are very similar to a single episode of the training process:

```
test_data = getStockData("^GSPC Test")
l_test = len(test_data) - 1
state = getState(test_data, 0, window_size + 1)
```

12. The profit starts at 0. The agent is initialized with a zero inventory and in test mode:

```
total_profit = 0
agent.inventory = []
agent.is_eval = False
done = False
```

13. Next, every day of trading is iterated, and the agent can act upon the data. Every day, the agent decides an action. Based on the action, the stock is held, sold, or bought:

```
for t in range(l_test):
    action = agent.act(state)
```

14. If the action is 0, then there is no trade. The state can be called **holding** during that period:

```
next_state = getState(test_data, t + 1, window_size + 1)
reward = 0
```

15. If the action is 1, buy the stock by adding it to the inventory, as follows:

```
if action == 1:

    agent.inventory.append(test_data[t])
    print("Buy: " + formatPrice(test_data[t]))
```

16. If the action is 2, the agent sells the stock by removing it from the inventory. The difference in price is recorded as a profit or a loss:

```
elif action == 2 and len(agent.inventory) > 0:
    bought_price = agent.inventory.pop(0)
    reward = max(test_data[t] - bought_price, 0)
    total_profit += test_data[t] - bought_price
    print("Sell: " + formatPrice(test_data[t]) + " | profit: "
+ formatPrice(test_data[t] - bought_price))

    if t == l_test - 1:
        done = True
    agent.step(action_prob, reward, next_state, done)
    state = next_state

    if done:
        print("----------------------------------------")
        print("Total Profit: " + formatPrice(total_profit))
        print("----------------------------------------")
```

17. Once the script starts to run, the model will get better over time through training. You can see the logs, as follows:

```
Sell: $2818.82 | profit: $44.80
Sell: $2802.60 | profit: $4.31
Buy: $2816.29
Sell: $2827.22 | profit: $28.79
Buy: $2850.40
Sell: $2857.70 | profit: $53.21
Buy: $2853.58
Buy: $2833.28
----------------------------------------
Total Profit: $10427.24
```

The model has traded and made a total profit of $10,427. Please note that this style of trading is not suitable for the real world, as trading involves more costs and uncertainty; hence, this trading style could have adverse effects.

Final result

After training the data, we tested it against the `test` dataset. Our model resulted in a total profit of `$10427.24`. The best thing about the model was that the profits kept improving over time, indicating that it was learning well and taking better actions.

Summary

In conclusion, machine learning can be applied to several industries and can be applied very efficiently in financial markets, as you saw in this chapter. We can combine different models, as we did with reinforcement learning and time series, to produce stronger models that suit our use cases. We discussed the use of reinforcement learning and time series to predict the stock market. We worked with an actor-critic model that determined the best action, based on the state of the stock prices, with the aim of maximizing profits. In the end, we obtained a result that boasted an overall profit and included increasing profits over time, indicating that the agent learned more with each state.

In the next chapter, you will learn about the future areas of work.

19
Capstone Project - Car Racing Using DQN

In the last few chapters, we have learned how Deep Q learning works by approximating the q function with a neural network. Following this, we have seen various improvements to **Deep Q Network (DQN)** such as Double Q learning, dueling network architectures, and the Deep Recurrent Q Network. We have seen how DQN makes use of a replay buffer to store the agent's experience and trains the network with the mini-batch of samples from the buffer. We have also implemented DQNs for playing Atari games and a **Deep Recurrent Q Network (DRQN)** for playing the Doom game. In this chapter, let's get into the detailed implementation of a dueling DQN, which is essentially the same as a regular DQN, except the final fully connected layer will be broken down into two streams, namely a value stream and an advantage stream, and these two streams will be clubbed together to compute the Q function. We will see how to train an agent for winning the car racing game with a dueling DQN.

In this chapter, you will learn how to implement the following:

- Environment wrapper functions
- A dueling network
- Replay buffer
- Training the network
- Car racing

Environment wrapper functions

The credit for the code used in this chapter goes to Giacomo Spigler's GitHub repository (`https://github.com/spiglerg/DQN_DDQN_Dueling_and_DDPG_ Tensorflow`). Throughout this chapter, the code is explained at each and every line. For a complete structured code, check the above GitHub repository.

First, we import all the necessary libraries:

```
import numpy as np
import tensorflow as tf
import gym
from gym.spaces import Box
from scipy.misc import imresize
import random
import cv2
import time
import logging
import os
import sys
```

We define the `EnvWrapper` class and define some of the environment wrapper functions:

```
class EnvWrapper:
```

We define the `__init__` method and initialize variables:

```
def __init__(self, env_name, debug=False):
```

Initialize the `gym` environment:

```
self.env = gym.make(env_name)
```

Get the `action_space`:

```
self.action_space = self.env.action_space
```

Get the `observation_space`:

```
self.observation_space = Box(low=0, high=255, shape=(84, 84, 4))
```

Initialize `frame_num` for storing the frame count:

```
self.frame_num = 0
```

Initialize `monitor` for recording the game screen:

```
self.monitor = self.env.monitor
```

Initialize `frames`:

```
self.frames = np.zeros((84, 84, 4), dtype=np.uint8)
```

Initialize a Boolean called `debug`, which, when set to `true` displays the last few frames:

```
self.debug = debug

if self.debug:
    cv2.startWindowThread()
    cv2.namedWindow("Game")
```

Next, we define a function called `step`, which takes the current state as input and returns the preprocessed next state's frame:

```
def step(self, a):
    ob, reward, done, xx = self.env.step(a)
   return self.process_frame(ob), reward, done, xx
```

We define a function called `reset` for resetting the environment; after resetting, it will return the preprocessed game screen:

```
def reset(self):
    self.frame_num = 0
    return self.process_frame(self.env.reset())
```

Next, we define another function for rendering the environment:

```
def render(self):
    return self.env.render()
```

Now, we define the `process_frame` function for preprocessing the frame:

```
def process_frame(self, frame):

    # convert the image to gray
    state_gray = cv2.cvtColor(frame, cv2.COLOR_BGR2GRAY)

    # change the size
```

```
state_resized = cv2.resize(state_gray,(84,110))
#resize
gray_final = state_resized[16:100,:]


if self.frame_num == 0:
    self.frames[:, :, 0] = gray_final
    self.frames[:, :, 1] = gray_final
    self.frames[:, :, 2] = gray_final
    self.frames[:, :, 3] = gray_final

else:
    self.frames[:, :, 3] = self.frames[:, :, 2]
    self.frames[:, :, 2] = self.frames[:, :, 1]
    self.frames[:, :, 1] = self.frames[:, :, 0]
    self.frames[:, :, 0] = gray_final

# Next we increment the frame_num counter

self.frame_num += 1

if self.debug:
    cv2.imshow('Game', gray_final)

return self.frames.copy()
```

After preprocessing, our game screen looks like the following screenshot:

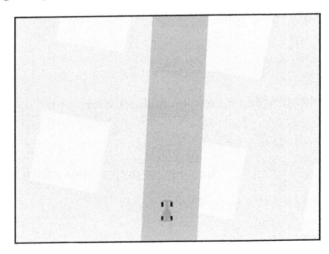

Dueling network

Now, we build our dueling DQN; we build three convolutional layers followed by two fully connected layers, and the final fully connected layer will be split into two separate layers for value stream and advantage stream. We will use the aggregate layer, which combines both the value stream and the advantage stream, to compute the q value. The dimensions of these layers are given as follows:

- **Layer 1**: 32 8x8 filters with stride 4 + RELU
- **Layer 2**: 64 4x4 filters with stride 2 + RELU
- **Layer 3**: 64 3x3 filters with stride 1 + RELU
- **Layer 4a**: 512 unit fully-connected layer + RELU
- **Layer 4b**: 512 unit fully-connected layer + RELU
- **Layer 5a**: 1 unit FC + RELU (state value)
- **Layer 5b**: Actions FC + RELU (advantage value)
- **Layer6**: Aggregate $V(s)+A(s,a)$

```
class QNetworkDueling(QNetwork):
```

We define the __init__ method to initialize all layers:

```
def __init__(self, input_size, output_size, name):
    self.name = name
    self.input_size = input_size
    self.output_size = output_size
    with tf.variable_scope(self.name):

        # Three convolutional Layers
        self.W_conv1 = self.weight_variable([8, 8, 4, 32])
        self.B_conv1 = self.bias_variable([32])
        self.stride1 = 4

        self.W_conv2 = self.weight_variable([4, 4, 32, 64])
        self.B_conv2 = self.bias_variable([64])
        self.stride2 = 2

        self.W_conv3 = self.weight_variable([3, 3, 64, 64])
        self.B_conv3 = self.bias_variable([64])
        self.stride3 = 1

        # Two fully connected layer
        self.W_fc4a = self.weight_variable([7*7*64, 512])
        self.B_fc4a = self.bias_variable([512])
```

```
        self.W_fc4b = self.weight_variable([7*7*64, 512])
        self.B_fc4b = self.bias_variable([512])

        # Value stream
        self.W_fc5a = self.weight_variable([512, 1])
        self.B_fc5a = self.bias_variable([1])

        # Advantage stream
        self.W_fc5b = self.weight_variable([512, self.output_size])
        self.B_fc5b = self.bias_variable([self.output_size])
```

We define the __call__ method and perform the convolutional operation:

```
    def __call__(self, input_tensor):
        if type(input_tensor) == list:
            input_tensor = tf.concat(1, input_tensor)

        with tf.variable_scope(self.name):
            # Perform convolutional on three layers

            self.h_conv1 = tf.nn.relu( tf.nn.conv2d(input_tensor,
self.W_conv1, strides=[1, self.stride1, self.stride1, 1], padding='VALID')
+ self.B_conv1 )

            self.h_conv2 = tf.nn.relu( tf.nn.conv2d(self.h_conv1,
self.W_conv2, strides=[1, self.stride2, self.stride2, 1], padding='VALID')
+ self.B_conv2 )

            self.h_conv3 = tf.nn.relu( tf.nn.conv2d(self.h_conv2,
self.W_conv3, strides=[1, self.stride3, self.stride3, 1], padding='VALID')
+ self.B_conv3 )


            # Flatten the convolutional output
            self.h_conv3_flat = tf.reshape(self.h_conv3, [-1, 7*7*64])
            # Fully connected layer
            self.h_fc4a = tf.nn.relu(tf.matmul(self.h_conv3_flat,
self.W_fc4a) + self.B_fc4a)

            self.h_fc4b = tf.nn.relu(tf.matmul(self.h_conv3_flat,
self.W_fc4b) + self.B_fc4b)


            # Compute value stream and advantage stream
            self.h_fc5a_value = tf.identity(tf.matmul(self.h_fc4a,
self.W_fc5a) + self.B_fc5a)
```

```
            self.h_fc5b_advantage = tf.identity(tf.matmul(self.h_fc4b,
    self.W_fc5b) + self.B_fc5b)


            # Club both the value and advantage stream
            self.h_fc6 = self.h_fc5a_value + ( self.h_fc5b_advantage -
    tf.reduce_mean(self.h_fc5b_advantage, reduction_indices=[1,],
    keep_dims=True) )


            return self.h_fc6
```

Replay memory

Now, we build the experience replay buffer, which is used for storing all the agent's experience. We sample a minibatch of experience from the replay buffer for training the network:

```
    class ReplayMemoryFast:
```

First, we define the __init__ method and initiate the buffer size:

```
        def __init__(self, memory_size, minibatch_size):

            # max number of samples to store
            self.memory_size = memory_size

            # minibatch size
            self.minibatch_size = minibatch_size
            self.experience = [None]*self.memory_size
            self.current_index = 0
            self.size = 0
```

Next, we define the store function for storing the experiences:

```
        def store(self, observation, action, reward, newobservation, is_terminal):
```

Store the experience as a tuple (current state, action, reward, next state, is it a terminal state):

```
            self.experience[self.current_index] = (observation, action, reward,
    newobservation, is_terminal)
            self.current_index += 1
            self.size = min(self.size+1, self.memory_size)
```

If the index is greater than the memory, then we flush the index by subtracting it with memory size:

```
if self.current_index >= self.memory_size:
    self.current_index -= self.memory_size
```

Next, we define a `sample` function for sampling a minibatch of experience:

```
def sample(self):
    if self.size < self.minibatch_size:
        return []

    # First we randomly sample some indices
    samples_index =
np.floor(np.random.random((self.minibatch_size,))*self.size)

    # select the experience from the sampled indexed
    samples = [self.experience[int(i)] for i in samples_index]

    return samples
```

Training the network

Now, we will see how to train the network.

First, we define the DQN class and initialize all variables in the __init__ method:

```
class DQN(object):
    def __init__(self, state_size,
                       action_size,
                       session,
                       summary_writer = None,
                       exploration_period = 1000,
                       minibatch_size = 32,
                       discount_factor = 0.99,
                       experience_replay_buffer = 10000,
                       target_qnet_update_frequency = 10000,
                       initial_exploration_epsilon = 1.0,
                       final_exploration_epsilon = 0.05,
                       reward_clipping = -1,
                      ):
```

Initialize all variables:

```
self.state_size = state_size
self.action_size = action_size


self.session = session
self.exploration_period = float(exploration_period)
self.minibatch_size = minibatch_size
self.discount_factor = tf.constant(discount_factor)
self.experience_replay_buffer = experience_replay_buffer
self.summary_writer = summary_writer
self.reward_clipping = reward_clipping


self.target_qnet_update_frequency = target_qnet_update_frequency
self.initial_exploration_epsilon = initial_exploration_epsilon
self.final_exploration_epsilon = final_exploration_epsilon
self.num_training_steps = 0
```

Initialize the primary dueling DQN by creating an instance to our QNetworkDueling class:

```
self.qnet = QNetworkDueling(self.state_size, self.action_size,
    "qnet")
```

Similarly, initialize the target dueling DQN:

```
self.target_qnet = QNetworkDueling(self.state_size,
    self.action_size, "target_qnet")
```

Next, initialize the optimizer as an RMSPropOptimizer:

```
self.qnet_optimizer =
    tf.train.RMSPropOptimizer(learning_rate=0.00025, decay=0.99, epsilon=0.01)
```

Now, initialize experience_replay_buffer by creating the instance to our ReplayMemoryFast class:

```
self.experience_replay =
    ReplayMemoryFast(self.experience_replay_buffer, self.minibatch_size)
    # Setup the computational graph
    self.create_graph()
```

Next, we define the `copy_to_target_network` function for copying weights from the primary network to our target network:

```
def copy_to_target_network(source_network, target_network):
    target_network_update = []

    for v_source, v_target in zip(source_network.variables(),
target_network.variables()):

        # update target network
        update_op = v_target.assign(v_source)
        target_network_update.append(update_op)

    return tf.group(*target_network_update)
```

Now, we define the `create_graph` function and build our computational graph:

```
def create_graph(self):
```

We calculate the `q_values` and select the action that has the maximum q value:

```
with tf.name_scope("pick_action"):

        # placeholder for state
        self.state = tf.placeholder(tf.float32, (None,)+self.state_size
, name="state")

        # placeholder for q values
        self.q_values = tf.identity(self.qnet(self.state) ,
name="q_values")

        # placeholder for predicted actions
        self.predicted_actions = tf.argmax(self.q_values, dimension=1 ,
name="predicted_actions")

        # plot histogram to track max q values
        tf.histogram_summary("Q values",
tf.reduce_mean(tf.reduce_max(self.q_values, 1))) # save max q-values to
track learning
```

Next, we calculate the target future reward:

```
with tf.name_scope("estimating_future_rewards"):
        self.next_state = tf.placeholder(tf.float32,
(None,)+self.state_size , name="next_state")

        self.next_state_mask = tf.placeholder(tf.float32, (None,) ,
name="next_state_mask")
```

```
            self.rewards = tf.placeholder(tf.float32, (None,) ,
name="rewards")

            self.next_q_values_targetqnet =
tf.stop_gradient(self.target_qnet(self.next_state),
name="next_q_values_targetqnet")
            self.next_q_values_qnet =
tf.stop_gradient(self.qnet(self.next_state), name="next_q_values_qnet")

            self.next_selected_actions = tf.argmax(self.next_q_values_qnet,
dimension=1)

            self.next_selected_actions_onehot =
tf.one_hot(indices=self.next_selected_actions, depth=self.action_size)

            self.next_max_q_values = tf.stop_gradient( tf.reduce_sum(
tf.mul( self.next_q_values_targetqnet, self.next_selected_actions_onehot )
, reduction_indices=[1,] ) * self.next_state_mask )

            self.target_q_values = self.rewards +
self.discount_factor*self.next_max_q_values
```

Next, we perform the optimization using RMS prop optimizer:

```
        with tf.name_scope("optimization_step"):
            self.action_mask = tf.placeholder(tf.float32, (None,
self.action_size) , name="action_mask")

            self.y = tf.reduce_sum( self.q_values * self.action_mask ,
reduction_indices=[1,])

            ## ERROR CLIPPING
            self.error = tf.abs(self.y - self.target_q_values)

            quadratic_part = tf.clip_by_value(self.error, 0.0, 1.0)
            linear_part = self.error - quadratic_part

            self.loss = tf.reduce_mean( 0.5*tf.square(quadratic_part) +
linear_part )

            # optimize the gradients

            qnet_gradients =
self.qnet_optimizer.compute_gradients(self.loss, self.qnet.variables())

                for i, (grad, var) in enumerate(qnet_gradients):
                    if grad is not None:
```

```
                    qnet_gradients[i] = (tf.clip_by_norm(grad, 10), var)

            self.qnet_optimize =
    self.qnet_optimizer.apply_gradients(qnet_gradients)
```

Copy the primary network weights to the target network:

```
            with tf.name_scope("target_network_update"):
                self.hard_copy_to_target =
    DQN.copy_to_target_network(self.qnet, self.target_qnet)
```

We define the `store` function for storing all the experience in the `experience_replay_buffer`:

```
        def store(self, state, action, reward, next_state, is_terminal):
            # rewards clipping
            if self.reward_clipping > 0.0:
                reward = np.clip(reward, -self.reward_clipping,
    self.reward_clipping)

            self.experience_replay.store(state, action, reward, next_state,
    is_terminal)
```

We define an `action` function for selecting actions using a decaying epsilon-greedy policy:

```
        def action(self, state, training = False):
            if self.num_training_steps > self.exploration_period:
                epsilon = self.final_exploration_epsilon
            else:
                epsilon = self.initial_exploration_epsilon -
    float(self.num_training_steps) * (self.initial_exploration_epsilon -
    self.final_exploration_epsilon) / self.exploration_period

            if not training:
                epsilon = 0.05

            if random.random() <= epsilon:
                action = random.randint(0, self.action_size-1)
            else:
                action = self.session.run(self.predicted_actions,
    {self.state:[state] } )[0]

            return action
```

Now, we define a `train` function for training our network:

```
def train(self):
```

Copy the primary network weights to the target network:

```
if self.num_training_steps == 0:
    print "Training starts..."
    self.qnet.copy_to(self.target_qnet)
```

Sample experiences from the replay memory:

```
minibatch = self.experience_replay.sample()
```

Get the states, actions, rewards, and next states from the `minibatch`:

```
batch_states = np.asarray( [d[0] for d in minibatch] )
actions = [d[1] for d in minibatch]
batch_actions = np.zeros( (self.minibatch_size, self.action_size) )
for i in xrange(self.minibatch_size):
    batch_actions[i, actions[i]] = 1

batch_rewards = np.asarray( [d[2] for d in minibatch] )
batch_newstates = np.asarray( [d[3] for d in minibatch] )

batch_newstates_mask = np.asarray( [not d[4] for d in minibatch] )
```

Perform the training operation:

```
scores, _, = self.session.run([self.q_values, self.qnet_optimize],
                              { self.state: batch_states,
                                self.next_state: batch_newstates,
                                self.next_state_mask:
batch_newstates_mask,

                                self.rewards: batch_rewards,
                                self.action_mask: batch_actions} )
```

Update the target network weights:

```
if self.num_training_steps % self.target_qnet_update_frequency ==
0:

        self.session.run( self.hard_copy_to_target )

        print 'mean maxQ in minibatch: ',np.mean(np.max(scores,1))

        str_ = self.session.run(self.summarize, { self.state:
batch_states,
                                self.next_state: batch_newstates,
                                self.next_state_mask:
```

```
batch_newstates_mask,
                                        self.rewards: batch_rewards,
                                        self.action_mask: batch_actions})

        self.summary_writer.add_summary(str_, self.num_training_steps)

        self.num_training_steps += 1
```

Car racing

So far, we have seen how to build a dueling DQN. Now, we will see how to make use of our dueling DQN when playing the car racing game.

First, let's import our necessary libraries:

```
import gym
import time
import logging
import os
import sys
import tensorflow as tf
```

Initialize all of the necessary variables:

```
ENV_NAME = 'Seaquest-v0'
TOTAL_FRAMES = 20000000
MAX_TRAINING_STEPS = 20*60*60/3
TESTING_GAMES = 30
MAX_TESTING_STEPS = 5*60*60/3
TRAIN_AFTER_FRAMES = 50000
epoch_size = 50000
MAX_NOOP_START = 30
LOG_DIR = 'logs'
outdir = 'results'
logger = tf.train.SummaryWriter(LOG_DIR)
# Intialize tensorflow session
session = tf.InteractiveSession()
```

Build the agent:

```
agent = DQN(state_size=env.observation_space.shape,
  action_size=env.action_space.n,
  session=session,
  summary_writer = logger,
  exploration_period = 1000000,
  minibatch_size = 32,
  discount_factor = 0.99,
  experience_replay_buffer = 1000000,
  target_qnet_update_frequency = 20000,
  initial_exploration_epsilon = 1.0,
  final_exploration_epsilon = 0.1,
  reward_clipping = 1.0,
  )
session.run(tf.initialize_all_variables())
logger.add_graph(session.graph)
saver = tf.train.Saver(tf.all_variables())
```

Store the recording:

```
env.monitor.start(outdir+'/'+ENV_NAME,force = True,
video_callable=multiples_video_schedule)
num_frames = 0
num_games = 0
current_game_frames = 0
init_no_ops = np.random.randint(MAX_NOOP_START+1)
last_time = time.time()
last_frame_count = 0.0
state = env.reset()
```

Now, let's start the training:

```
while num_frames <= TOTAL_FRAMES+1:
    if test_mode:
        env.render()
    num_frames += 1
    current_game_frames += 1
```

Select the action, given the current state:

```
action = agent.action(state, training = True)
```

Perform the action on the environment, receive the `reward`, and move to the `next_state`:

```
next_state,reward,done,_ = env.step(action)
```

Store this transitional information in the `experience_replay_buffer`:

```
    if current_game_frames >= init_no_ops:
        agent.store(state,action,reward,next_state,done)
    state = next_state
```

Train the agent:

```
    if num_frames>=TRAIN_AFTER_FRAMES:
        agent.train()

    if done or current_game_frames > MAX_TRAINING_STEPS:
        state = env.reset()
        current_game_frames = 0
        num_games += 1
        init_no_ops = np.random.randint(MAX_NOOP_START+1)
```

Save the network's parameters after every epoch:

```
    if num_frames % epoch_size == 0 and num_frames > TRAIN_AFTER_FRAMES:
        saver.save(session,
 outdir+"/"+ENV_NAME+"/model_"+str(num_frames/1000)+"k.ckpt")
        print "epoch: frames=",num_frames," games=",num_games
```

We test the performance for every two epochs:

```
    if num_frames % (2*epoch_size) == 0 and num_frames > TRAIN_AFTER_FRAMES:
        total_reward = 0
        avg_steps = 0
        for i in xrange(TESTING_GAMES):
            state = env.reset()
            init_no_ops = np.random.randint(MAX_NOOP_START+1)
            frm = 0

            while frm < MAX_TESTING_STEPS:
                frm += 1
                env.render()
                action = agent.action(state, training = False)
                if current_game_frames < init_no_ops:
                    action = 0
                state,reward,done,_ = env.step(action)
                total_reward += reward

                if done:
                    break

            avg_steps += frm
        avg_reward = float(total_reward)/TESTING_GAMES
```

```
        str_ = session.run( tf.scalar_summary('test reward
('+str(epoch_size/1000)+'k)', avg_reward) )
        logger.add_summary(str_, num_frames)
        state = env.reset()


env.monitor.close()
```

We can see how the agent is learning to win the car racing game, as shown in the following screenshot:

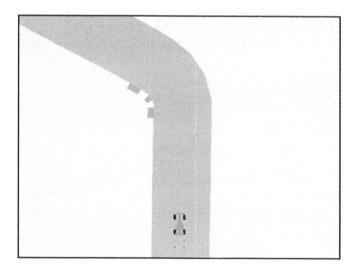

Summary

In this chapter, we have learned how to implement a dueling DQN in detail. We started off with the basic environment wrapper functions for preprocessing our game screens and then we defined the QNetworkDueling class. Here, we implemented a dueling Q Network, which splits the final fully connected layer of DQN into a value stream and an advantage stream and then combines these two streams to compute the q value. Following this, we saw how to create a replay buffer, which is used to store the experience and samples a minibatch of experience for training the network, and finally, we initialized our car racing environment using OpenAI's Gym and trained our agent. In our final chapter, Chapter 20, *Looking Ahead,* we will see some of the recent advancements in RL.

Questions

The question list is as follows:

1. What is the difference between a DQN and a dueling DQN?
2. Write the Python code for a replay buffer.
3. What is a target network?
4. Write the Python code for a prioritized experience replay buffer.
5. Create a Python function to decay an epsilon-greedy policy.
6. How does a dueling DQN differ from a double DQN?
7. Create a Python function for updating primary network weights to the target network.

Further reading

The following links will help expand your knowledge:

- **Flappy Bird using DQN**: `https://github.com/yenchenlin/DeepLearningFlappyBird`
- **Super Mario using DQN**: `https://github.com/JSDanielPark/tensorflow_dqn_supermario`

20
Looking Ahead

Over the past few hundred pages, we have faced numerous challenges, to which we applied reinforcement and deep learning algorithms. To conclude our **reinforcement learning** (**RL**) journey, this chapter will look at several aspects of the field that we have not covered yet. We will start by looking at several of the drawbacks of reinforcement learning, which any practitioner or researcher should be aware of. To end on a positive note, we will follow up by describing numerous exciting academic developments and achievements the field has seen in recent years.

The shortcomings of reinforcement learning

So far, we have only covered what reinforcement learning algorithms can do. To the reader, reinforcement learning may seem like the panacea for all kinds of problems. But why do we not see a ubiquitous application of reinforcement learning algorithms in real-life situations? The reality is that the field has a myriad of shortcomings that hinder commercial adoption.

Why is it necessary to talk about the field's flaws? We think this will help you build a more holistic, less biased view of reinforcement learning. Moreover, understanding the weaknesses of reinforcement learning and machine learning is an important quality of a good machine learning researcher or practitioner. In the following subsections, we will discuss a few of the most important limitations that reinforcement learning is currently facing.

Resource efficiency

Current deep reinforcement learning algorithms require vast amounts of time, training data, and computational resources in order to reach a desirable level of proficiency. For algorithms such as AlphaGo Zero, where our reinforcement learning algorithm learns to play Go with zero prior knowledge and experience, resource efficiency becomes a major bottleneck for taking such algorithms to commercial scales. Recall that when DeepMind implemented AlphaGo Zero, they needed to train the agent on tens of millions of games using hundreds of GPUs and thousands of CPUs. For AlphaGo Zero to reach a reasonable proficiency, it needs to play a number of games, equivalent to what hundreds of thousands of humans would play in their lifetimes.

Unless, in the future, the average consumer can readily leverage vast amounts of computational power that only the likes of Google and Nvidia can offer today, the ability to develop superhuman reinforcement learning algorithms will continue to be way beyond the public's reach. This means that powerful, resource-hungry reinforcement learning algorithms will be monopolized by a small consortium of institutions, which is probably not a great thing.

Thus, making reinforcement learning algorithms trainable under limited resources will continue to be an important issue that the community must address.

Reproducibility

In numerous fields of scientific research, a prevalent problem has been the inability to reproduce the experimental results claimed in academic papers and journals. In a 2016 survey conducted by Nature, the world's most renowned scientific journal, 70% of respondents claimed that they have failed to reproduce their own or another researcher's experimental results. Moreover, the attitude toward the inability to reproduce experimental results was a stark one, with 90% of researchers thinking that there is indeed a reproducibility crisis.

 The original work reported by nature can be found here: `https://www.nature.com/news/1-500-scientists-lift-the-lid-on-reproducibility-1.19970`.

While this survey targeted researchers across a number of disciplines, including biology and chemistry, reinforcement learning is also facing a similar problem. In the paper *Deep Reinforcement Learning Matters* (reference at the end of this chapter; you can view it at `https://arxiv.org/pdf/1709.06560.pdf` for the online version), Peter Henderson et al. study the effects of different configurations of a deep reinforcement learning algorithm on experimental outcomes. These configurations include hyperparameters, seeds for the random number generator, and network architecture.

In extreme cases, they found that, when training the same model on two sets of five different random seed configurations, the resulting average return for the two sets of models diverged significantly. Moreover, changing other settings, such as the architecture of the CNN, activation functions, and learning rates, have profound effects on the outcome.

What are the implications of inconsistent, unreproducible results? As the adoption and popularity of reinforcement learning and machine learning continues to grow at near exponential rates, the number of implementations of reinforcement learning algorithms freely available on the internet also increases. If those implementations cannot reproduce the results they claim to be able to achieve, this would cause major issues and potential danger in real-life applications. Certainly, no one would want their self-driving car to be implemented so that it cannot produce consistent decisions!

Explainability/accountability

We have seen how an agent's policy can return either a single action or a probability distribution over a set of possible actions and how its value function can return how desirable a certain state is. But how can a model explain how it arrived at such predictions? As reinforcement learning becomes more popular and potentially more prevalent in real-life applications, there will be an ever-increasing need to be able to explain the output of reinforcement learning algorithms.

Today, most advanced reinforcement learning algorithms incorporate deep neural networks, which, as of now, can only be represented as a set of weights and a sequence of non-linear functions. Moreover, due to its high dimensional nature, neural networks are not able to provide any meaningful, intuitive relationships between input and their corresponding output that can be understood easily by humans. Hence, deep learning algorithms are often referred to as black boxes, for it is difficult for us to understand what is really going on inside a neural network.

Why is it important for a reinforcement learning algorithm to be explainable? Suppose an autonomous car is involved in a car accident (let's assume it was just an innocuous bump between two cars and the drivers are not hurt). Human drivers would be able to explain what led to the crash; they can give reasons for why they performed a particular maneuver and what exactly happened when the accident occurred. This would help law enforcement ascertain the cause of the accident and potentially determine who or what was accountable. However, even if we create an agent that can drive cars sufficiently well using algorithms available today, this is simply not possible.

Without the ability to explain predictions, it will be difficult for users and the general public to trust software that uses any kind of machine learning, especially in use cases where the algorithms are accountable for making important decisions. This is a serious impediment to the adoption of reinforcement learning algorithms in practical applications.

Susceptibility to attacks

Deep learning algorithms have shown incredible results across numerous tasks, including computer vision, natural language processing, and speech recognition. In several tasks, deep learning has already surpassed human capabilities. However, recent work has shown that these algorithms are incredibly vulnerable to attacks. By attacks, we mean attempts to make imperceptible modifications to the input which causes the model to behave differently. Take the following example:

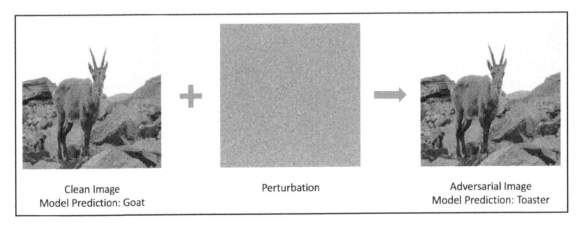

An illustration of adversarial attacks. By adding imperceptible perturbations to an image. an attacker can easily fool deep learning image classifiers.

The rightmost image is the result of adding the left image, which is the original image, and the middle image, which represents the perturbations added to the original image. Even the most accurate, well-performing deep neural network image classifier fails to identify the right image as a goat and instead predicts it to be a toaster.

These examples have shocked many in the research community, for people did not expect that deep learning algorithms can be incredibly brittle and susceptible to such attacks. This field is now called **adversarial machine learning** and has been rapidly increasing in prominence and importance as more researchers around the world are investigating the robustness and vulnerabilities of deep learning algorithms.

Reinforcement learning algorithms are also no stranger to these results and attacks. According to the paper titled *Robust Deep Reinforcement Learning with Adversarial Attacks* (https://arxiv.org/abs/1712.03632) by Anay Pattanaik et. al., adversarial attacks to reinforcement learning algorithms can be defined as any possible perturbation that leads the agent into an increased probability of taking the worst possible action in that state. For example, we can add noise to the screen of an Atari game with the intention of tricking the RL agent playing the game to make a poor decision, which leads to a lower score.

More serious applications include adding noise to street signs to trick a self-driving car into thinking that a STOP sign is a speed sign, making an ATM recognize a $100 check as a $1,000,000 one, or even fooling a facial-recognition system to identify an attacker's face as that of another user.

Needless to say, these vulnerabilities further add to the risks of adopting deep learning algorithms in practical, safety-critical use cases. While there are numerous ongoing efforts to countervail adversarial attacks, there is still a long way to go for deep learning algorithms to become robust enough for such use cases.

Upcoming developments in reinforcement learning

The past few sections may have painted a stark outlook for deep learning and reinforcement learning. However, there is no need to feel entirely discouraged; this is, in fact, an exciting time for DL and RL, where many significant advances in research are continuing to shape the field and cause it to evolve at a rapid pace. With increasing availability of computational resources and data, the possibilities of expanding and improving deep learning and reinforcement learning algorithms continue to expand.

Addressing the limitations

For one, the issues raised in the preceding section are recognized and acknowledged by the research community. There are several efforts being made to address them. In the work by Pattanaik et. al., not only do the authors demonstrate that current deep reinforcement learning algorithms are susceptible to adversarial attacks, they also propose techniques that can make the same algorithms more robust toward such attacks. In particular, by training deep RL algorithms on examples that were adversarially perturbed, the model can improve its robustness against similar attacks. This technique is commonly referred to as adversarial training.

Moreover, the research community is actively taking actions to solve the reproducibility problem. ICLR and ICML, two of the biggest conferences in machine learning, have hosted challenges where participants are invited to reimplement and re-run experiments conducted by submitted papers to reproduce the reported results. Participants are then required to critique the original work by writing a reproducibility report that describes the problem statement, experimental methodology, implementation details, analyses, and the reproducibility of the original paper. Organized by Joelle Pineau and McGill University, this challenge aims to promote transparency in experiments and academic work as well as to ensure the reproducibility and integrity of results.

More information on the ICLR 2018 reproducibility challenge can be found here: `https://www.cs.mcgill.ca/~jpineau/ICLR2018-ReproducibilityChallenge.html`. Similarly, the original ICML workshop on reproducibility can be found here: `https://sites.google.com/view/icml-reproducibility-workshop/home`.

Transfer learning

Another important topic that is increasing in importance and attention is transfer learning. Transfer learning is a paradigm in machine learning, where a model trained on one task is fine-tuned to accomplish another.

For example, we can train a model to recognize images of cars and use the weights of that model to initialize an identical model that learns to recognize trucks. The main intuition is that certain abstract concepts and features learned by training on one task are transferable to other similar tasks. This idea is applicable to many reinforcement learning problems as well. An agent that learns to play a particular Atari game should be able to play other Atari games proficiently without training entirely from scratch, much like how a human can.

Demis Hassabis, the founder of DeepMind and a pioneer in deep reinforcement learning, said in a recent talk that transfer learning is the key to general intelligence. And I think the key to doing transfer learning will be the acquisition of conceptual knowledge that is abstracted away from perceptual details of where you learned it from.

The Demis Hassabis quote and the talk in which this was mentioned can be found here: https://www.youtube.com/watch?v=YofMOh6_WKo

There have already been several advances in computer vision and natural language processing, where models initialized with knowledge and priors from one domain are used to learn about data from another domain.

This is especially useful when the second domain lacks data. Called **few-shot** or **one-shot** learning, these techniques allow models to learn to perform tasks well, even when the dataset is small, as illustrated in the following diagram:

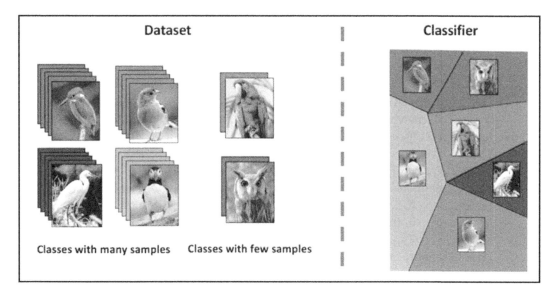

An illustration of a few-shot learning classifier learning good decision boundaries for classes with small volumes of data

Few-shot learning for reinforcement learning would involve having the agent learn to achieve high proficiency on a given task without a high dependence on time, data, and computational resources. Imagine a generalized game-playing agent that can easily be fine-tuned to perform well on any other video game using readily-available computational resources; this would make training RL algorithms a lot more efficient and thus more accessible to a wider audience.

Multi-agent reinforcement learning

Another promising area making significant strides is multi-agent reinforcement learning. Contrary to the problems we've seen where only one agent makes decisions, this topic involves having multiple agents make decisions simultaneously and cooperatively in order to achieve a common objective. One of the most significant works related to this has been OpenAI's Dota2-playing system, called **OpenAI Five**. Dota2 is one of the world's most popular **Massively Multiplayer Online Role Playing Game** (**MMORPGs**). Compared to traditional RL games such as Go and Atari, Dota2 is more complex for the following reasons:

- **Multiple agents**: Dota2 games involve two teams of five players, each fighting to destroy the other team's base. Hence there are multiple agents, not just one, making decisions simultaneously.
- **Observability**: The screen only shows the proximity of the agent's character instead of the whole map. This means that the whole game state, including the locations of opponents and what they are doing, is not observable. In reinforcement learning, we call this a *partially-observable* state.
- **High dimensionality**: A Dota2 agent's observations can include 20,000 points, each depicting what a human player may observe on the screen, including health, the location of the controlling character, the location of enemies, and any attacks. Go, on the other hand, requires fewer data points to construct an observation (19 x 19 board, past moves). Hence, observations have high dimensionality and complexity. This also goes for decisions, where a Dota2 AI's action space consists of 170,000 possibilities, which includes decisions on movement, casting spells, and using items.

For more information on OpenAI's Dota2 AI, check out their blogs on the project at https://blog.openai.com/openai-five/.

Moreover, by using novel upgrades on traditional reinforcement learning algorithms, each agent in OpenAI Five was able to learn to cooperate with one another in order to reach the common objective of destroying the enemy's base. They were even able to learn several team strategies that experienced human players employ. The following is a screenshot from a game being played between a team of Dota players and OpenAI Five:

OpenAI versus human players (source: https://www.youtube.com/watch?v=eaBYhLttETw)

Despite the extreme levels of resource requirements (240 GPUs, 120,000 CPU cores, ~200 human years of gameplay in a single day), this project demonstrates that current AI algorithms are indeed able to cooperate with one another to reach a common objective in a vastly complex environment. This work symbolizes another significant advancement in AI and RL research and demonstrates what the current technology is capable of.

Summary

This concludes our introductory journey into reinforcement learning. Over the course of this book, we learned how to implement agents that can play Atari games, navigate Minecraft, predict stock market prices, play the complex board game of Go, and even generate other neural networks to train on `CIFAR-10` data. In doing so, you acquired and became accustomed to some of the fundamental and state-of-the-art deep learning and reinforcement learning algorithms. In short, you have achieved a lot!

But the journey does not and should not end here. We hope that, with your newfound skills and knowledge, you will continue to utilize deep learning and reinforcement learning algorithms to tackle problems that you face outside of this book. More importantly, we hope that this guide motivates you to explore other fields of machine learning and further develop your knowledge and experience.

There are many obstacles for the reinforcement learning community to overcome. However, there is much to look forward to. With the increasing popularity and development of the field, we can't wait to see what new developments and milestones the field will achieve. We hope the reader, upon completing this guide, will feel more equipped and ready to build reinforcement learning algorithms and make significant contributions to the field.

References

Open Science Collaboration. (2015). *Estimating the reproducibility of psychological science*. Science, 349(6251), aac4716.

Henderson, P., Islam, R., Bachman, P., Pineau, J., Precup, D., and Meger, D. (2017). *Deep reinforcement learning that matters*. arXiv preprint arXiv:1709.06560.

Pattanaik, A., Tang, Z., Liu, S., Bommannan, G., and Chowdhary, G. (2018, July). *Robust deep reinforcement learning with adversarial attacks*. In Proceedings of the 17th International Conference on Autonomous Agents and MultiAgent Systems (pp. 2040-2042). International Foundation for Autonomous Agents and Multiagent Systems.

Assessments

Chapter 1: Introduction to Reinforcement Learning

1. **Reinforcement learning** (RL) is a branch of machine learning where the learning occurs via interacting with an environment.
2. RL works by train and error method, unlike other ML paradigms.
3. Agents are the software programs that make intelligent decisions and they are basically learners in RL.
4. Policy function specifies what action to take in each state and value function specifies the value of each state.
5. In model-based agent use the previous experience whereas in model-free learning there won't be any previous experience.
6. Deterministic, stochastic, fully observable, partially observable, discrete continuous, episodic and non-episodic.
7. OpenAI Universe provides rich environments for training RL agents.
8. Refer section *Applications of RL*.

Chapter 2: Getting Started with OpenAI and TensorFlow

1. ```
   conda create --name universe python=3.6 anaconda
   ```
2. With Docker, we can pack our application with its dependencies, which is called container, and we can simply run our applications on the server without using any external dependency with our packed Docker container.
3. ```
   gym.make(env_name)
   ```
4. ```
   from gym import envs
   print(envs.registry.all())
   ```
5. OpenAI Universe is an extension of OpenAI Gym and it also provides various rich environments.
   ```

6. Placeholder is used for feeding external data whereas variable is used for holding values.
7. Everything in TensorFlow will be represented as a computational graph that consists of nodes and edges, where nodes are the mathematical operations, say addition, multiplication and so on, and edges are the tensors.
8. Computation graphs will only be defined; in order to execute the computation graph, we use TensorFlow sessions.

Chapter 3: The Markov Decision Process and Dynamic Programming

1. The Markov property states that the future depends only on the present and not on the past.
2. MDP is an extension of the Markov chain. It provides a mathematical framework for modeling decision-making situations. Almost all RL problems can be modeled as MDP.
3. Refer section *Discount factor*.
4. The discount factor decides how much importance we give to the future rewards and immediate rewards.
5. We use Bellman function for solving the MDP.
6. Refer section *Deriving the Bellman equation for value and Q functions*.
7. Value function specifies goodness of a state and Q function specifies goodness of an action in that state.
8. Refer section *Value iteration* and *Policy iteration*.

Chapter 4: Gaming with Monte Carlo Methods

1. The Monte Carlo algorithm is used in RL when the model of the environment is not known.
2. Refer section *Estimating the value of pi using Monte Carlo*.
3. In Monte Carlo prediction, we approximate the value function by taking the mean return instead of the expected return.

4. In every visit Monte Carlo, we average the return every time the state is visited in an episode. But in the first visit MC method, we average the return only the first time the state is visited in an episode.
5. Refer section *Monte Carlo control*.
6. Refer section *On-policy Monte Carlo control* and *Off-policy Monte Carlo control*
7. Refer section *Let's play Blackjack with Monte Carlo*.

Chapter 5: Temporal Difference Learning

1. Monte Carlo methods are applied only for episodic tasks whereas TD learning can be applied to both episodic and nonepisodic tasks
2. The difference between the actual value and the predicted value is called TD error
3. Refer section *TD prediction* and *TD control*
4. Refer section *Solving taxi problem using Q learning*
5. In Q learning, we take action using an epsilon-greedy policy and, while updating the Q value, we simply pick up the maximum action. In SARSA, we take the action using the epsilon-greedy policy and also, while updating the Q value, we pick up the action using the epsilon-greedy policy.

Chapter 6: Multi-Armed Bandit Problem

1. An MAB is actually a slot machine, a gambling game played in a casino where you pull the arm (lever) and get a payout (reward) based on a randomly generated probability distribution. A single slot machine is called a one-armed bandit and, when there are multiple slot machines it is called multi-armed bandits or k-armed bandits.
2. An explore-exploit dilemma arises when the agent is not sure whether to explore new actions or exploit the best action using the previous experience.
3. The epsilon is used to for deciding whether the agent should explore or exploit actions with 1-epsilon we choose best action and with epsilon we explore new action.
4. We can solve explore-exploit dilemma using a various algorithm such epsilon-greedy policy, softmax exploration, UCB, Thompson sampling.

5. The UCB algorithm helps us in selecting the best arm based on a confidence interval.
6. In Thomson sampling, we estimate using prior distribution and in UCB we estimate using a confidence interval.

Chapter 8: Atari Games with Deep Q Network

1. **Deep Q Network (DQN)** is a neural network used for approximating the Q function.
2. Experience replay is used to remove the correlations between the agent's experience.
3. When we use the same network for predicting target value and predicted value there will lot of divergence so we use separate target network.
4. Because of the max operator DQN overestimates Q value.
5. By having two separate Q functions each learning independently double DQN avoids overestimating Q values.
6. Experiences are priorities based on TD error in prioritized experience replay.
7. Dueling DQN estimating the Q value precisely by breaking the Q function computation into value function and advantage function.

Chapter 9: Playing Doom with a Deep Recurrent Q Network

1. DRQN makes use of **recurrent neural network (RNN)** where DQN makes use of vanilla neural network.
2. DQN is not used applied when the MDP is partially observable.
3. Refer section *Doom with DRQN*.
4. DARQN makes use of attention mechanism unlike DRQN.
5. DARQN is used to understand and focus on particular area of game screen which is more important.
6. Soft and hard attention.
7. We set living reward to 0 which the agent does for each move, even though the move is not useful.

Chapter 10: The Asynchronous Advantage Actor Critic Network

1. A3C is the Asynchronous Advantage Actor Critic network which uses several agents to learn parallel.
2. Three A's are Asynchronous, Advantage, Actor Critic.
3. A3C requires less computation power and training time than DQN.
4. All agents (workers) works in copies of the environment and then global network aggregate their experience.
5. Entropy is used to ensure enough exploration.
6. Refer section *How A3C works*.

Chapter 11: Policy Gradients and Optimization

1. The policy gradient is one of the amazing algorithms in RL where we directly optimize the policy parameterized by some parameter.
2. Policy gradients are effective as we don't need to compute Q function to find the optimal policy.
3. The role of the Actor network is to determine the best actions in the state by tuning the parameter, and the role of the Critic is to evaluate the action produced by the Actor.
4. Refer section *Trust region policy optimization*
5. We iteratively improve the policy and we impose a constraint that **Kullback–Leibler (KL)** divergence between old policy and a new policy is to be less than some constant. This constraint is called the trust region constraint.
6. PPO modifies the objective function of TRPO by changing the constraint to a penalty a term so that we don't want to perform conjugate gradient.

Chapter 19: Capstone Project – Car Racing Using DQN

1. DQN computes the Q value directly whereas Dueling DQN breaks down the Q value computation into value function and advantage function.

2. Refer section *Replay memory*.

3. When we use the same network for predicting target value and predicted value there will lot of divergence so we use separate target network.

4. Refer section *Replay memory*.

5. Refer section *Dueling network.*

6. Dueling DQN breaks down the Q value computation into value function and advantage function whereas double DQN uses two Q function to avoid overestimation.

7. Refer section Dueling *network.*

Other Books You May Enjoy

If you enjoyed this book, you may be interested in these other books by Packt:

Artificial Intelligence with Python
Prateek Joshi

ISBN: 978-1-78646-439-2

- Realize different classification and regression techniques
- Understand the concept of clustering and how to use it to automatically segment data
- See how to build an intelligent recommender system
- Understand logic programming and how to use it
- Build automatic speech recognition systems
- Understand the basics of heuristic search and genetic programming
- Develop games using Artificial Intelligence
- Learn how reinforcement learning works
- Discover how to build intelligent applications centered on images, text, and time series data
- See how to use deep learning algorithms and build applications based on it

Statistics for Machine Learning
Pratap Dangeti

ISBN: 978-1-78829-575-8

- Understand the Statistical and Machine Learning fundamentals necessary to build models
- Understand the major differences and parallels between the statistical way and the Machine Learning way to solve problems
- Learn how to prepare data and feed models by using the appropriate Machine Learning algorithms from the more-than-adequate R and Python packages
- Analyze the results and tune the model appropriately to your own predictive goals
- Understand the concepts of required statistics for Machine Learning
- Introduce yourself to necessary fundamentals required for building supervised & unsupervised deep learning models
- Learn reinforcement learning and its application in the field of artificial intelligence domain

Leave a review - let other readers know what you think

Please share your thoughts on this book with others by leaving a review on the site that you bought it from. If you purchased the book from Amazon, please leave us an honest review on this book's Amazon page. This is vital so that other potential readers can see and use your unbiased opinion to make purchasing decisions, we can understand what our customers think about our products, and our authors can see your feedback on the title that they have worked with Packt to create. It will only take a few minutes of your time, but is valuable to other potential customers, our authors, and Packt. Thank you!

Index

OpenAI Universe
  about 15, 29
  video game bot, building 29, 31
OpenAI
  about 249
  Gym 249
  reference 41
optimal value 49

P

partially observable environment 14
partially observable Markov Decision Process
    (POMDP) 188
Pendulum
  specifications 266
pi value
  estimating, with Monte Carlo method 72, 75
placeholders 35
playout 324
policy function 11, 31, 47
policy gradient
  about 226
  URL 227
  using, for Lunar Lander 226
PolicyValueNetwork
  alphagozero_agent.py 348, 349, 351
  and MCTS, combining 347
prioritized experience replay 183, 184
Project Malmo 16
proportional prioritization 184
Proximal Policy Optimization (PPO) 245, 246

Q

Q learning, TD control
  about 97, 99
  and SARSA algorithm, differentiating 112
  used, for solving taxi problem 102, 104

R

rectifier nonlinearity (RELU) 149
recurrent deterministic policy gradient algorithm
    (RDPG) 273
recurrent neural network (RNN)
  about 187
REINFORCE method 392, 395

reinforcement learning (RL)
  about 7, 9, 167, 226
  algorithm 9
  comparing, with ML paradigms 10
  elements 10
reinforcement learning, developments
  about 459
  multi-agent reinforcement learning 462, 463
  transfer learning 460, 461, 462
reinforcement learning
  attacks, susceptibility to 458, 459
  basic elements 142
  explainability/accountability 457, 458
  limitations, addressing 460
  reproducibility 456, 457
  resource efficiency 456
  shortcomings 455
replay buffer
  building 443
RL environments
  continuous environment 14
  deterministic environment 13
  discrete environment 14
  episodic and non-episodic environment 14
  fully observable environment 13
  partially observable environment 14
  single and multi-agent environment 14
  stochastic environment 13
  types 13
RL platforms
  about 15
  DeepMind Lab 15
  OpenAI Gym 15
  OpenAI Universe 15
  Project Malmo 16
  RL-Glue 15
  ViZDoom 16
Robotics 255
rollout 324

S

SARSA algorithm, TD control
  about 105, 108
  and Q learning, differentiating 112
  used, for solving taxi problem 109